CLOCKWORK PLANET

VI

STORY BY YUU KAMIYA & TSUBAKI HIMANA
MANGA BY KURO
CHARACTER DESIGN BY SINO

ClockWork Planet
CONTENTS

VI

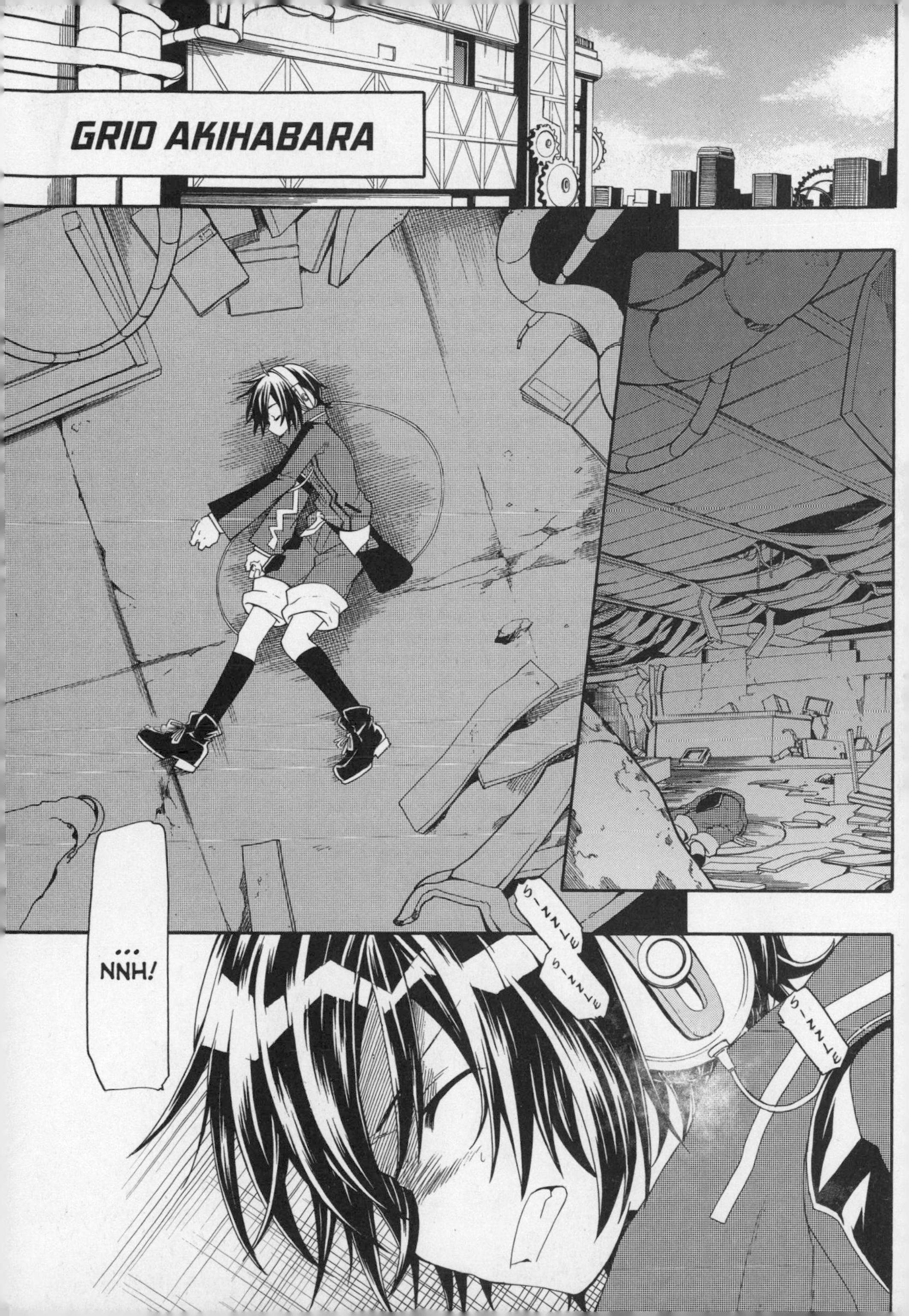
GRID AKIHABARA
...NNH!

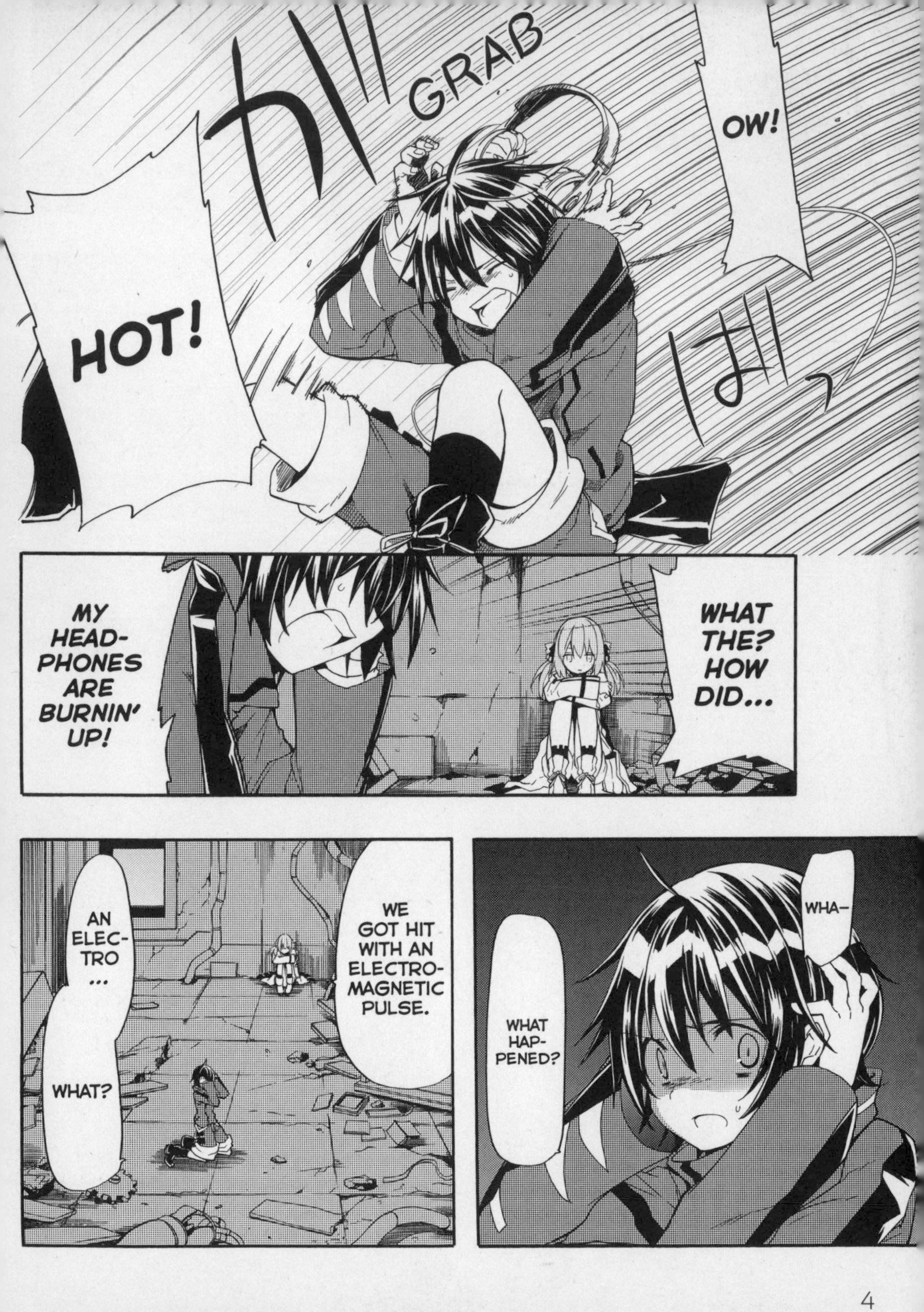
OW!
GRAB
HOT!
WHAT THE? HOW DID...
MY HEAD-PHONES ARE BURNIN' UP!
WHA-
WHAT HAP-PENED?
WE GOT HIT WITH AN ELECTRO-MAGNETIC PULSE.
AN ELEC-TRO...
WHAT?

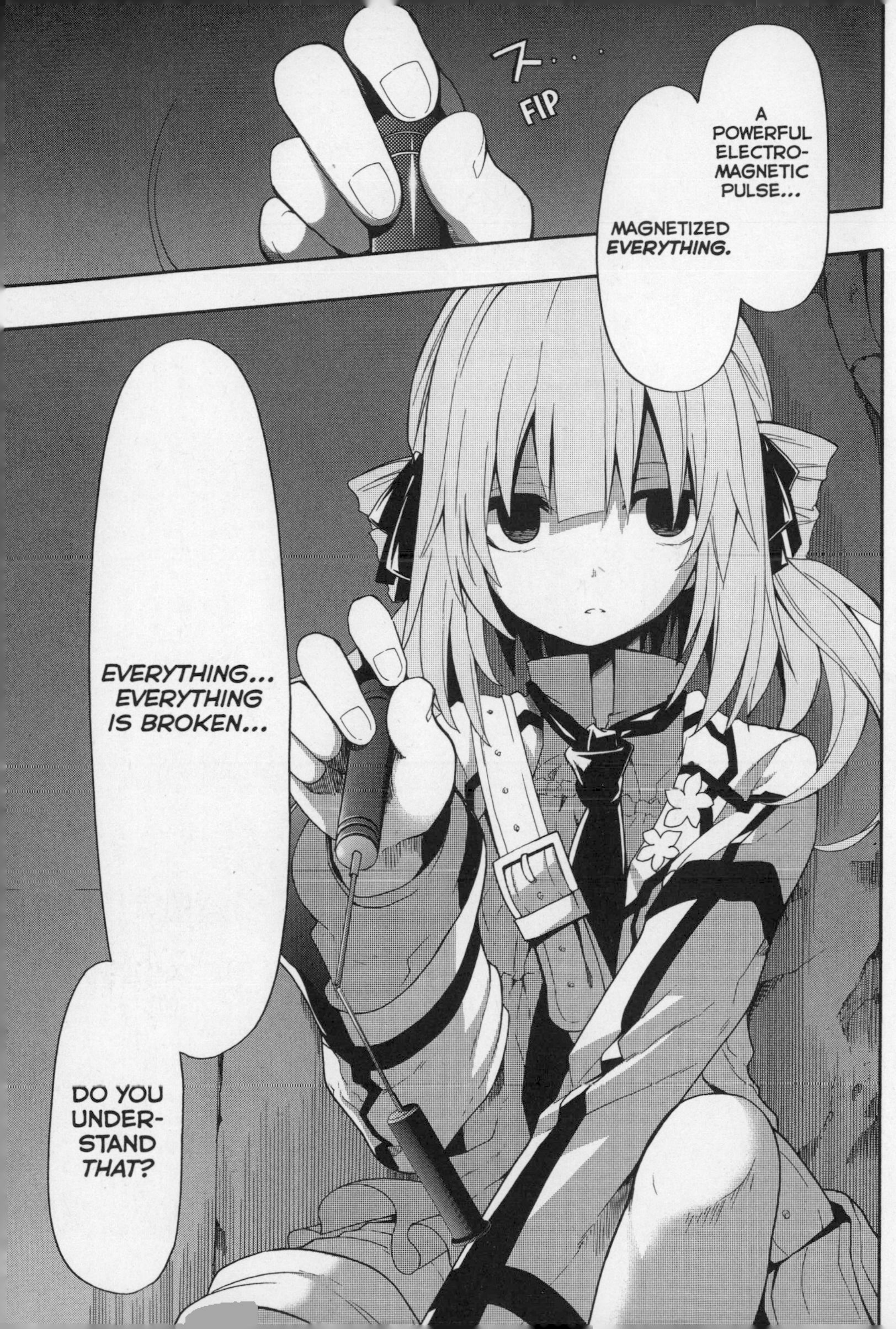
ス...
FIP
A POWERFUL ELECTRO-MAGNETIC PULSE...
MAGNETIZED EVERYTHING.
EVERYTHING... EVERYTHING IS BROKEN...
DO YOU UNDER-STAND THAT?

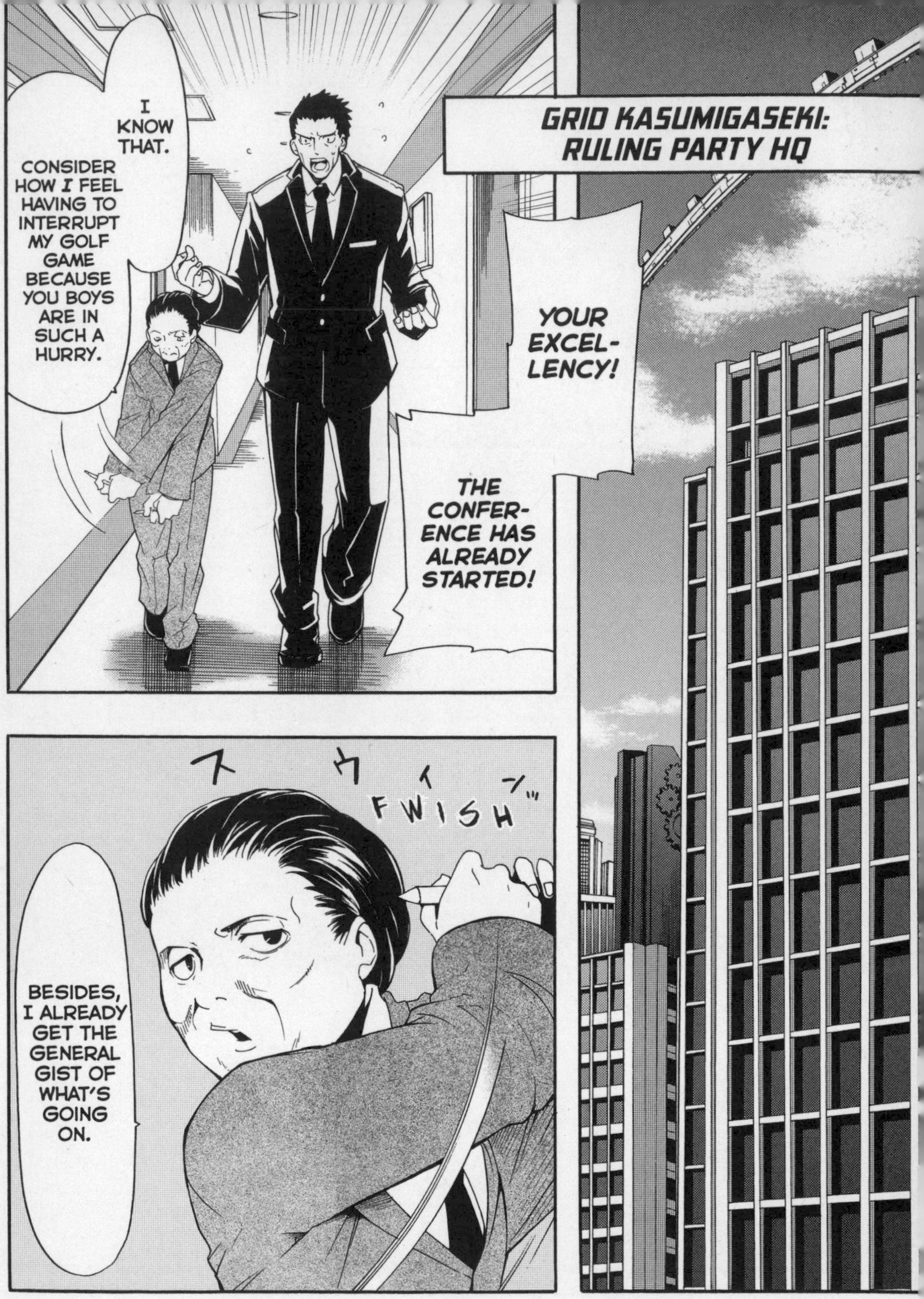
GRID KASUMIGASEKI: RULING PARTY HQ
YOUR EXCEL- LENCY!
THE CONFER- ENCE HAS ALREADY STARTED!
I KNOW THAT.
CONSIDER HOW I FEEL HAVING TO INTERRUPT MY GOLF GAME BECAUSE YOU BOYS ARE IN SUCH A HURRY.
FWISH
BESIDES, I ALREADY GET THE GENERAL GIST OF WHAT'S GOING ON.

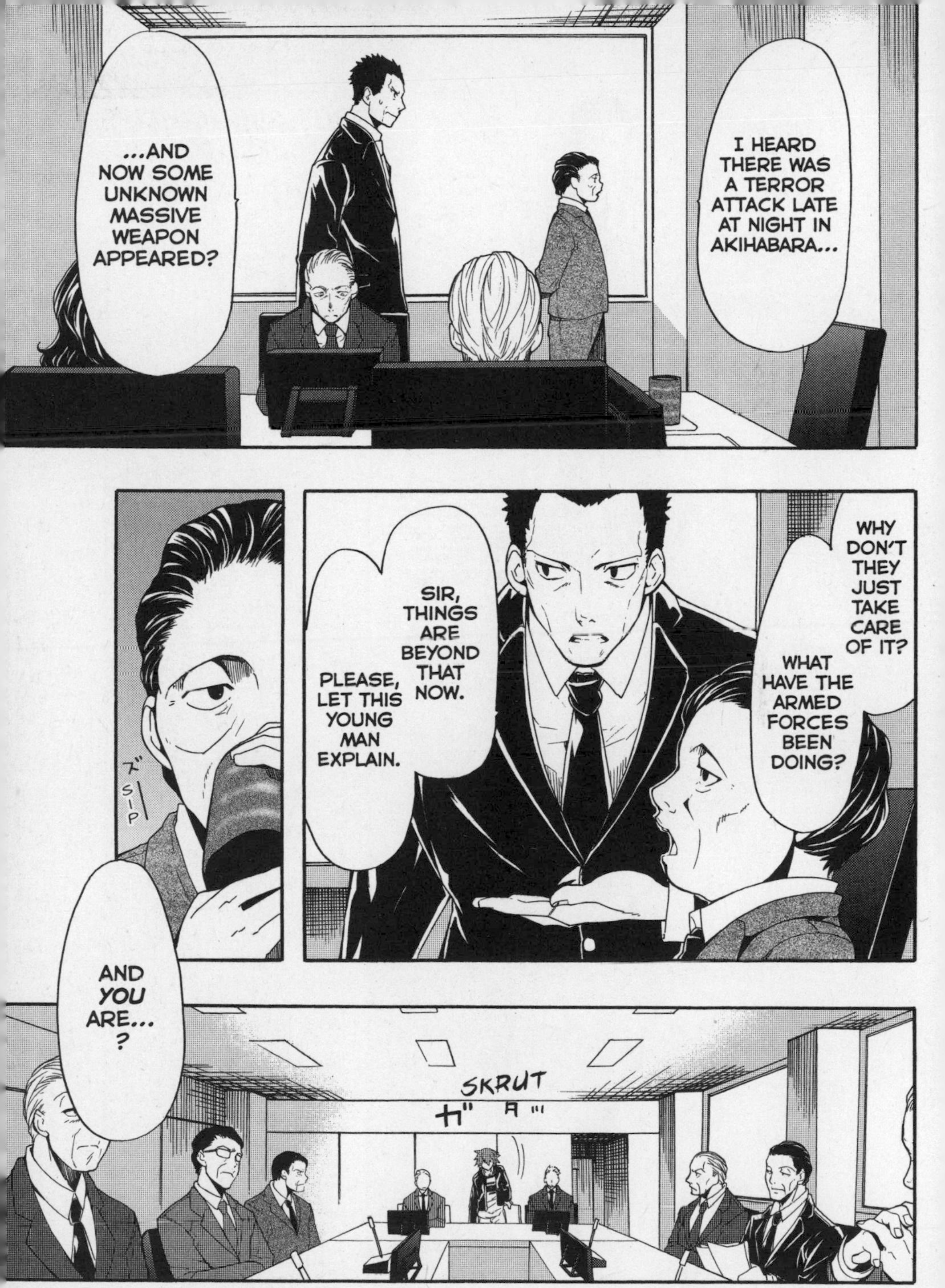
I HEARD THERE WAS A TERROR ATTACK LATE AT NIGHT IN AKIHABARA...
...AND NOW SOME UNKNOWN MASSIVE WEAPON APPEARED?
WHY DON'T THEY JUST TAKE CARE OF IT?
WHAT HAVE THE ARMED FORCES BEEN DOING?
SIR, THINGS ARE BEYOND THAT NOW.
PLEASE, LET THIS YOUNG MAN EXPLAIN.
ズ
SIP
AND *YOU* ARE...?
SKRUT
ガタッ

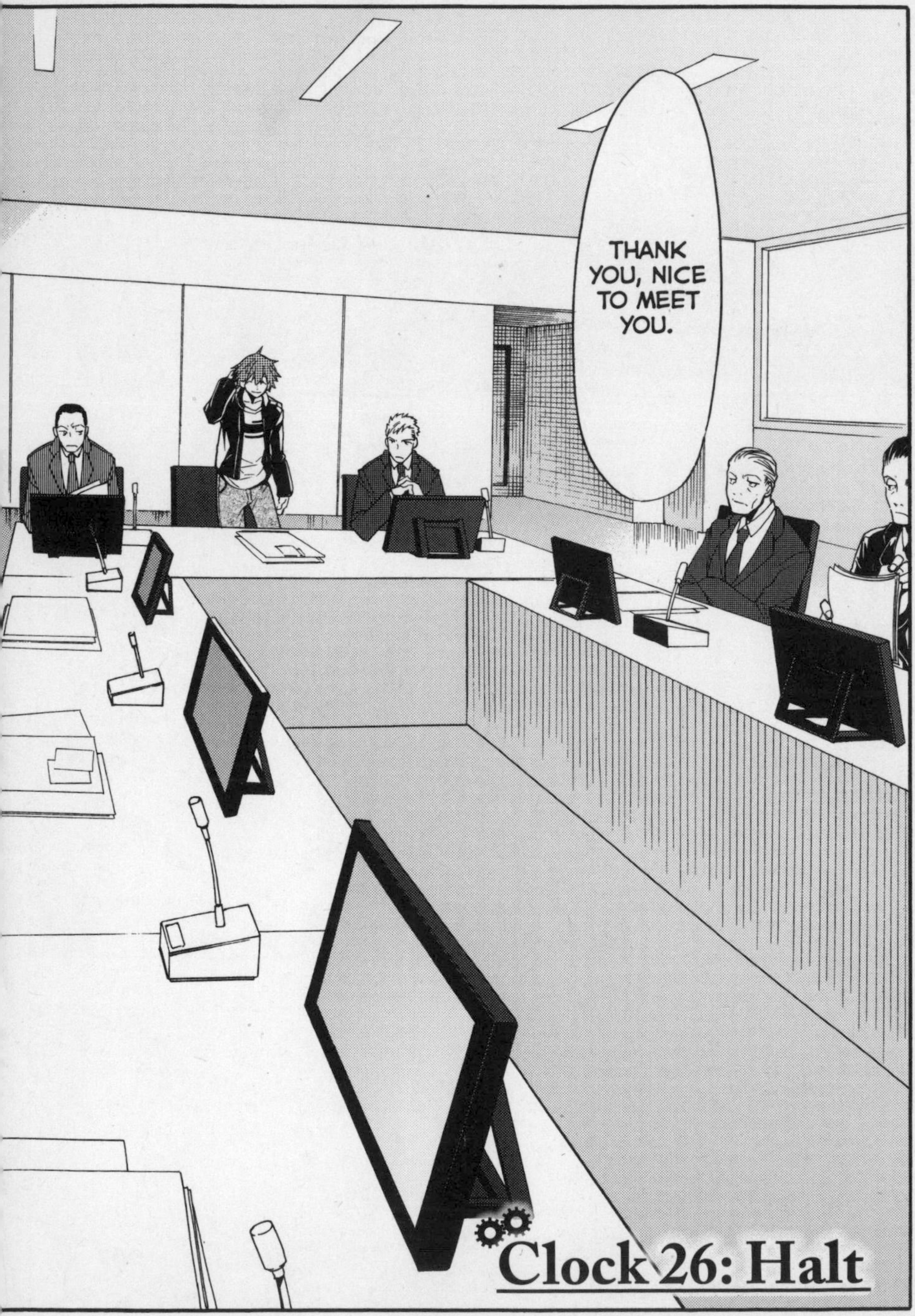
THANK YOU, NICE TO MEET YOU.
Clock 26: Halt

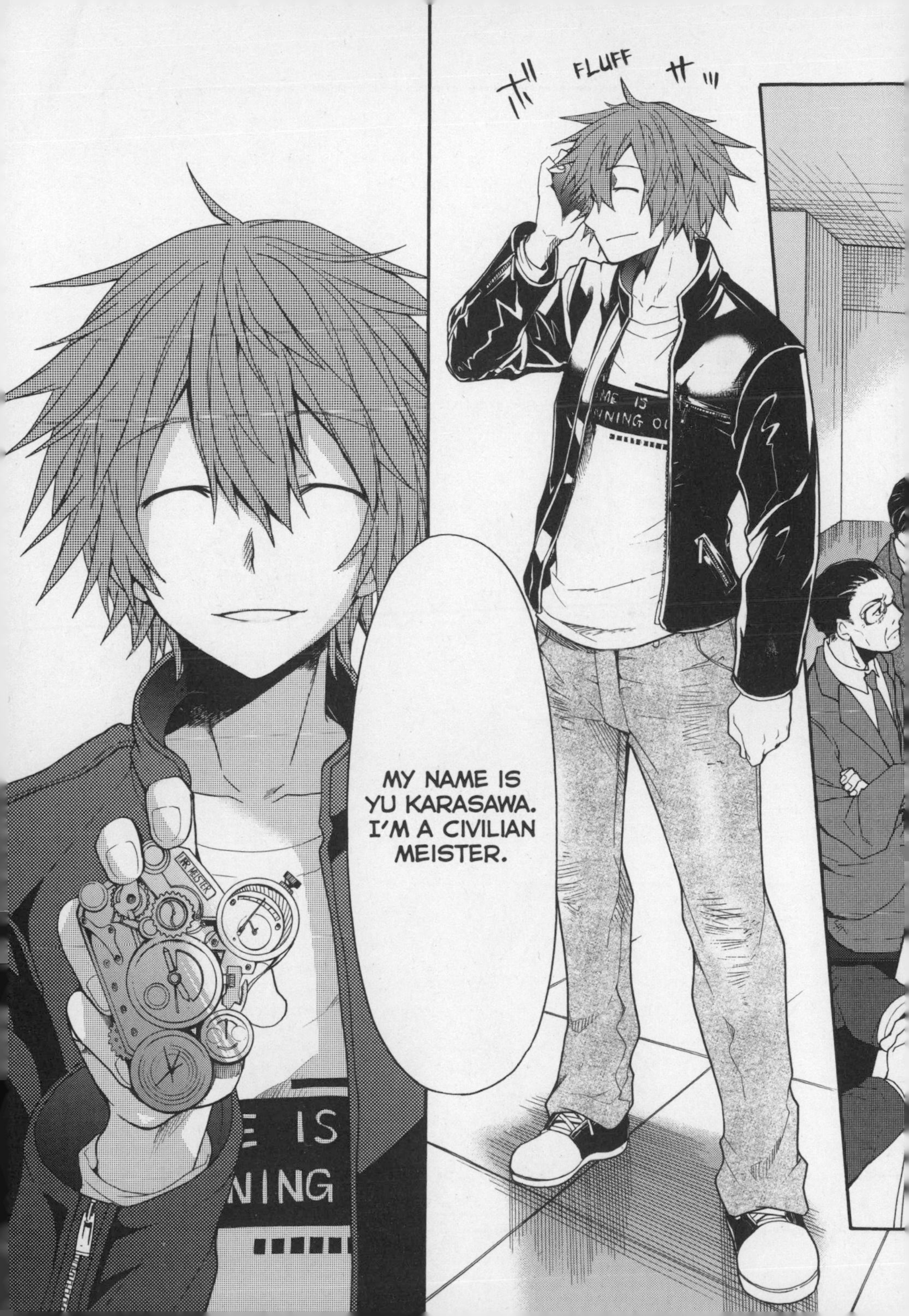
FLUFF
MY NAME IS YU KARASAWA. I'M A CIVILIAN MEISTER.

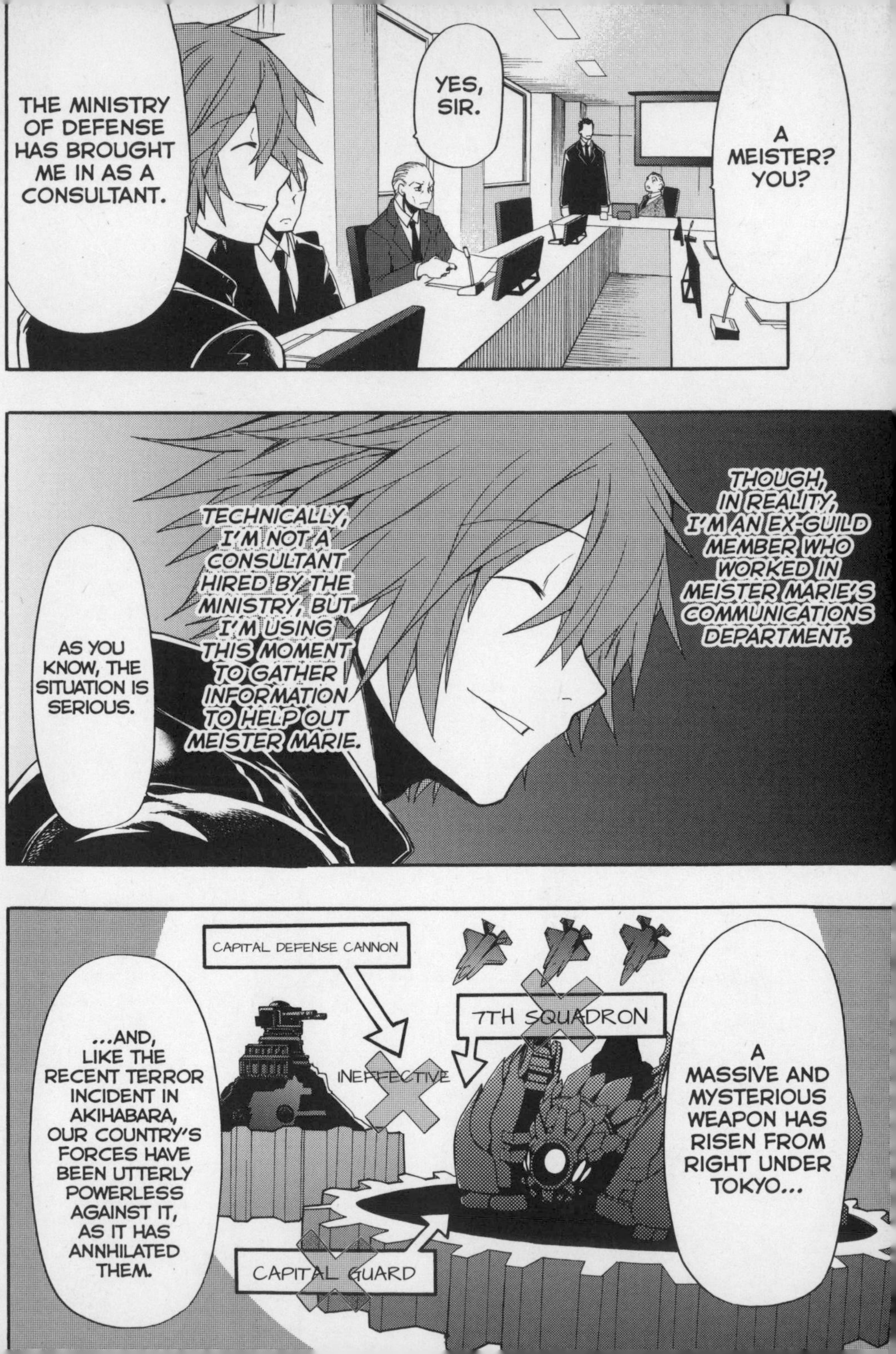
A MEISTER? YOU?
YES, SIR.
THE MINISTRY OF DEFENSE HAS BROUGHT ME IN AS A CONSULTANT.
THOUGH, IN REALITY, I'M AN EX-GUILD MEMBER WHO WORKED IN MEISTER MARIE'S COMMUNICATIONS DEPARTMENT.
TECHNICALLY, I'M NOT A CONSULTANT HIRED BY THE MINISTRY, BUT I'M USING THIS MOMENT TO GATHER INFORMATION TO HELP OUT MEISTER MARIE.
AS YOU KNOW, THE SITUATION IS SERIOUS.
A MASSIVE AND MYSTERIOUS WEAPON HAS RISEN FROM RIGHT UNDER TOKYO...
7TH SQUADRON
CAPITAL DEFENSE CANNON
INEFFECTIVE
CAPITAL GUARD
...AND, LIKE THE RECENT TERROR INCIDENT IN AKIHABARA, OUR COUNTRY'S FORCES HAVE BEEN UTTERLY POWERLESS AGAINST IT, AS IT HAS ANNHILATED THEM.

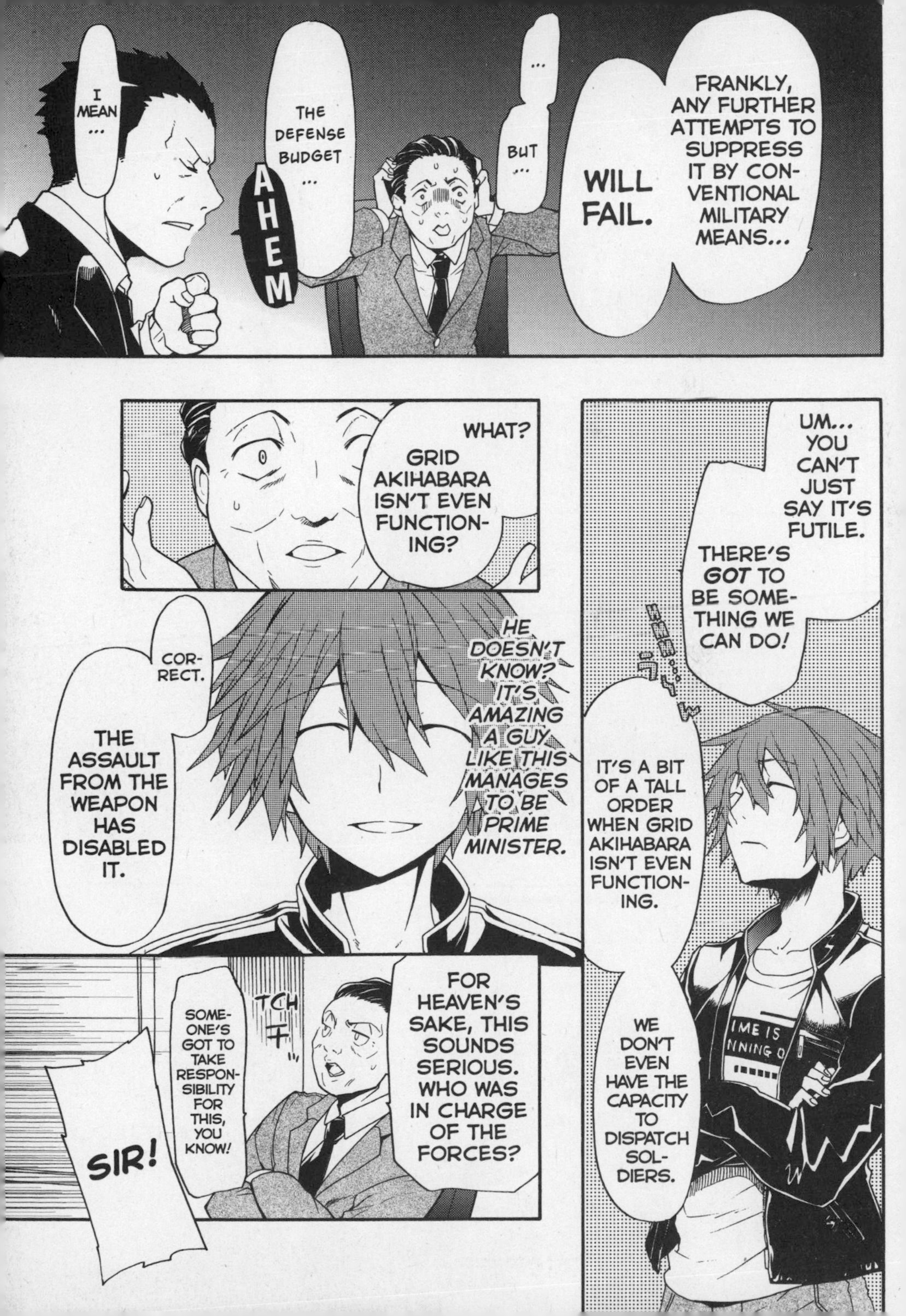
FRANKLY, ANY FURTHER ATTEMPTS TO SUPPRESS IT BY CONVENTIONAL MILITARY MEANS...
WILL FAIL.
...
BUT ...
THE DEFENSE BUDGET ...
AHEM
I MEAN ...
UM... YOU CAN'T JUST SAY IT'S FUTILE.
THERE'S *GOT* TO BE SOMETHING WE CAN DO!
IT'S A BIT OF A TALL ORDER WHEN GRID AKIHABARA ISN'T EVEN FUNCTIONING.
WE DON'T EVEN HAVE THE CAPACITY TO DISPATCH SOLDIERS.
IME IS
NNING O
WHAT?
GRID AKIHABARA ISN'T EVEN FUNCTIONING?
HE DOESN'T KNOW? IT'S AMAZING A GUY LIKE THIS MANAGES TO BE PRIME MINISTER.
CORRECT.
THE ASSAULT FROM THE WEAPON HAS DISABLED IT.
FOR HEAVEN'S SAKE, THIS SOUNDS SERIOUS. WHO WAS IN CHARGE OF THE FORCES?
TCH
SOMEONE'S GOT TO TAKE RESPONSIBILITY FOR THIS, YOU KNOW!
SIR!

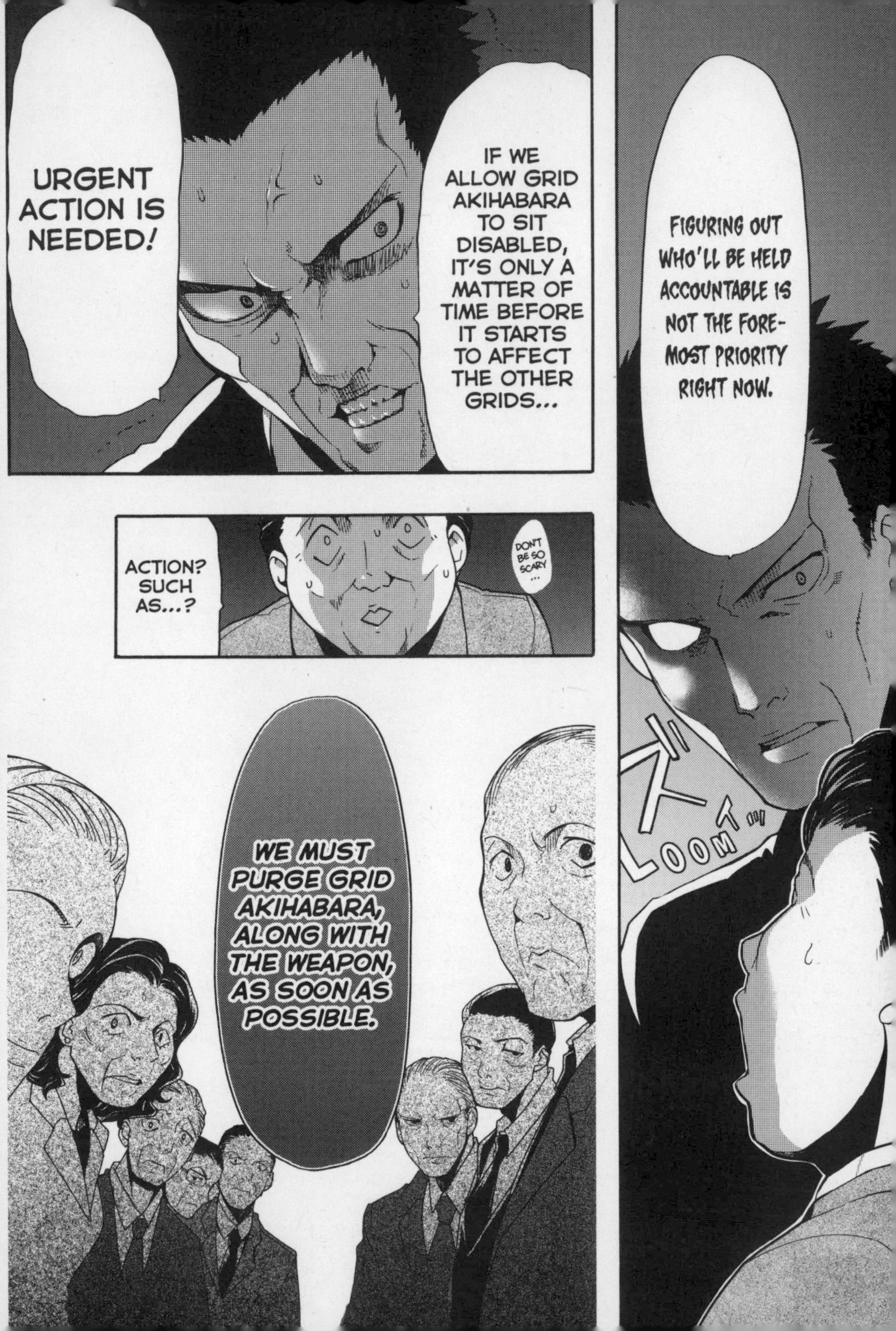
FIGURING OUT WHO'LL BE HELD ACCOUNTABLE IS NOT THE FORE-MOST PRIORITY RIGHT NOW.
LOOOM
IF WE ALLOW GRID AKIHABARA TO SIT DISABLED, IT'S ONLY A MATTER OF TIME BEFORE IT STARTS TO AFFECT THE OTHER GRIDS...
URGENT ACTION IS NEEDED!
DON'T BE SO SCARY...
ACTION? SUCH AS...?
WE MUST PURGE GRID AKIHABARA, ALONG WITH THE WEAPON, AS SOON AS POSSIBLE.

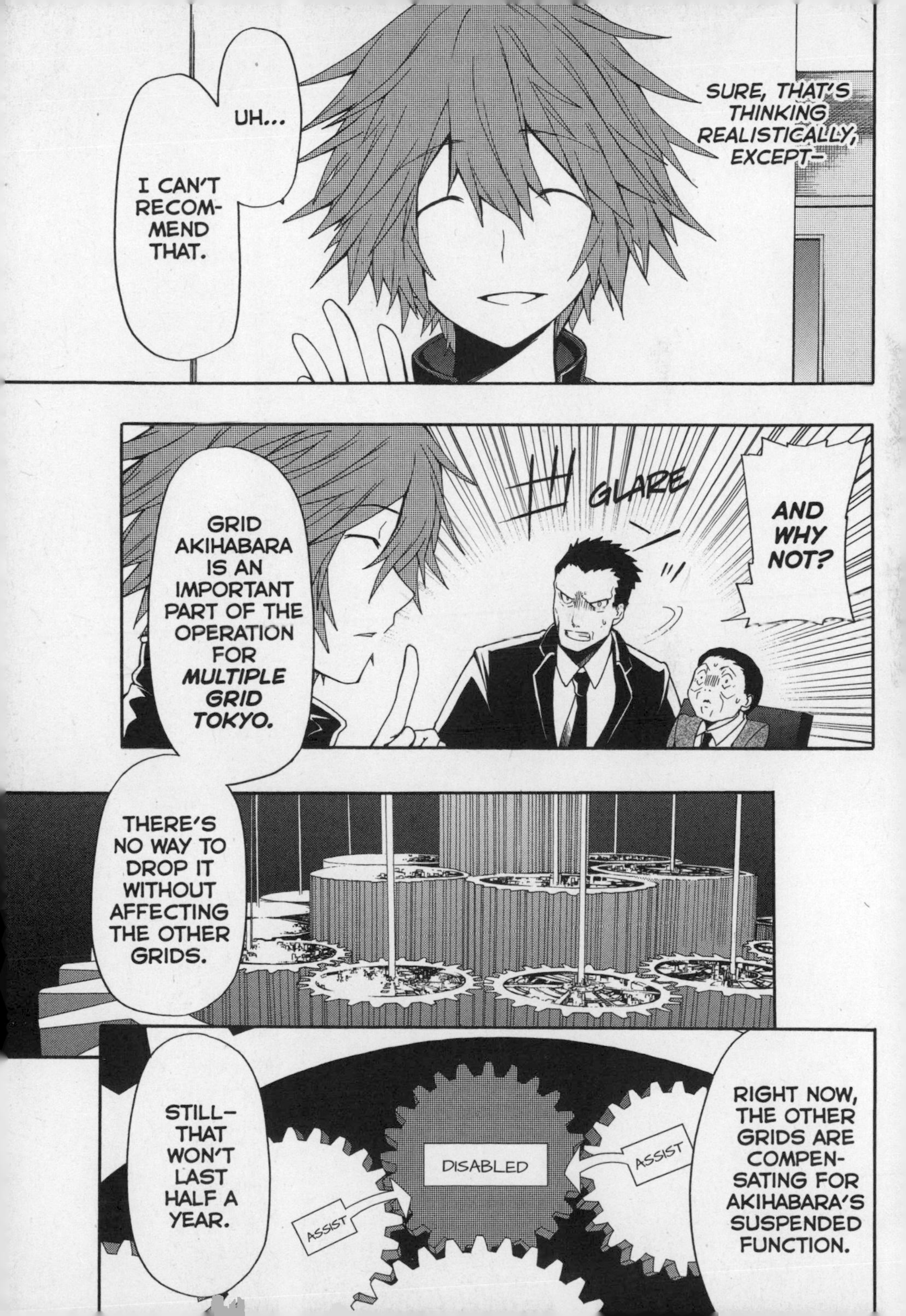
SURE, THAT'S THINKING REALISTICALLY, EXCEPT—
UH...
I CAN'T RECOMMEND THAT.
AND WHY NOT?
GLARE
GRID AKIHABARA IS AN IMPORTANT PART OF THE OPERATION FOR *MULTIPLE GRID TOKYO.*
THERE'S NO WAY TO DROP IT WITHOUT AFFECTING THE OTHER GRIDS.
RIGHT NOW, THE OTHER GRIDS ARE COMPENSATING FOR AKIHABARA'S SUSPENDED FUNCTION.
ASSIST
DISABLED
ASSIST
STILL— THAT WON'T LAST HALF A YEAR.

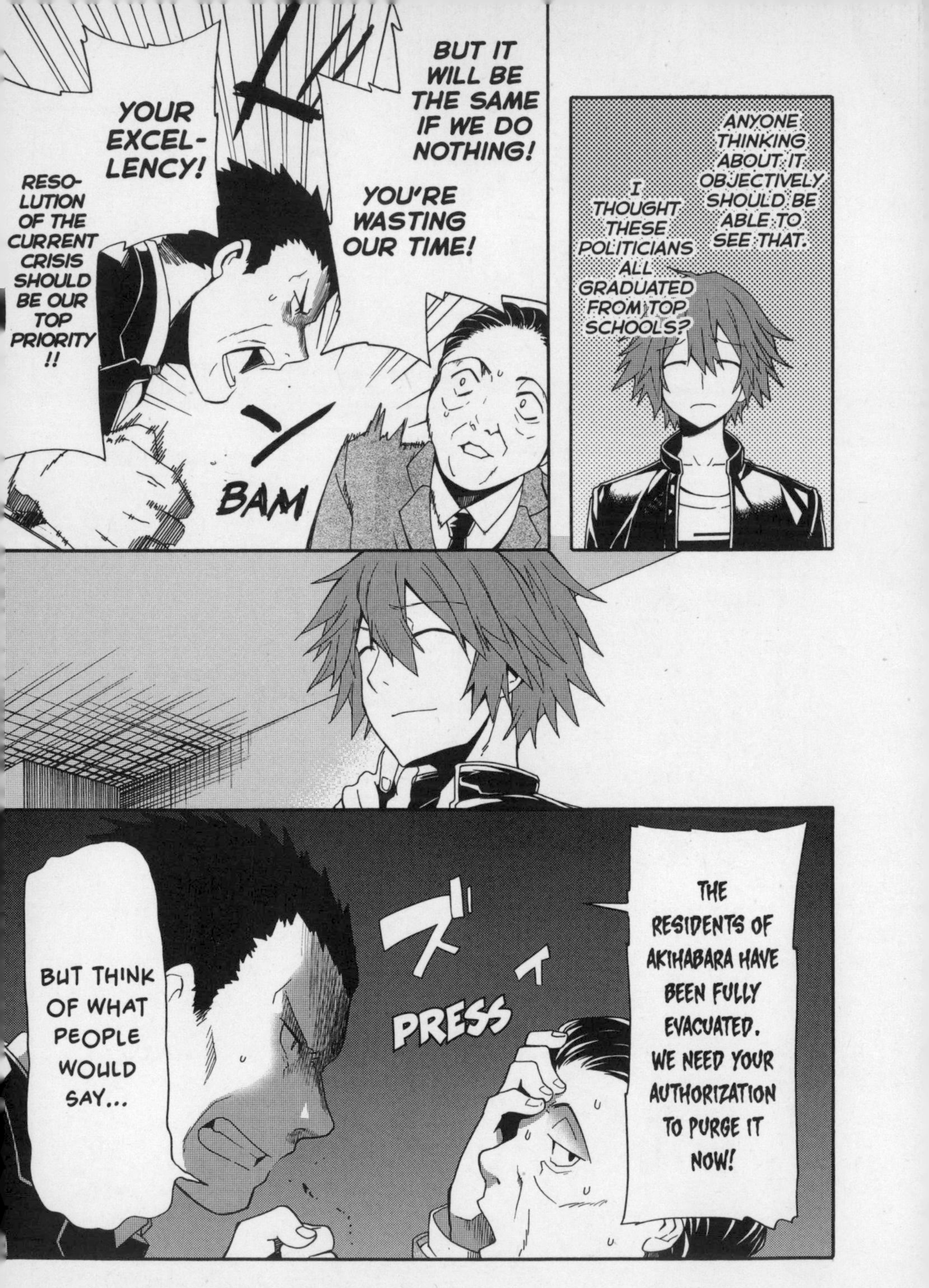
ANYONE THINKING ABOUT IT OBJECTIVELY SHOULD BE ABLE TO SEE THAT.
I THOUGHT THESE POLITICIANS ALL GRADUATED FROM TOP SCHOOLS?
BUT IT WILL BE THE SAME IF WE DO NOTHING!
YOUR EXCEL-LENCY!
YOU'RE WASTING OUR TIME!
RESO-LUTION OF THE CURRENT CRISIS SHOULD BE OUR TOP PRIORITY!!
BAM
THE RESIDENTS OF AKIHABARA HAVE BEEN FULLY EVACUATED. WE NEED YOUR AUTHORIZATION TO PURGE IT NOW!
ズイ
PRESS
BUT THINK OF WHAT PEOPLE WOULD SAY...

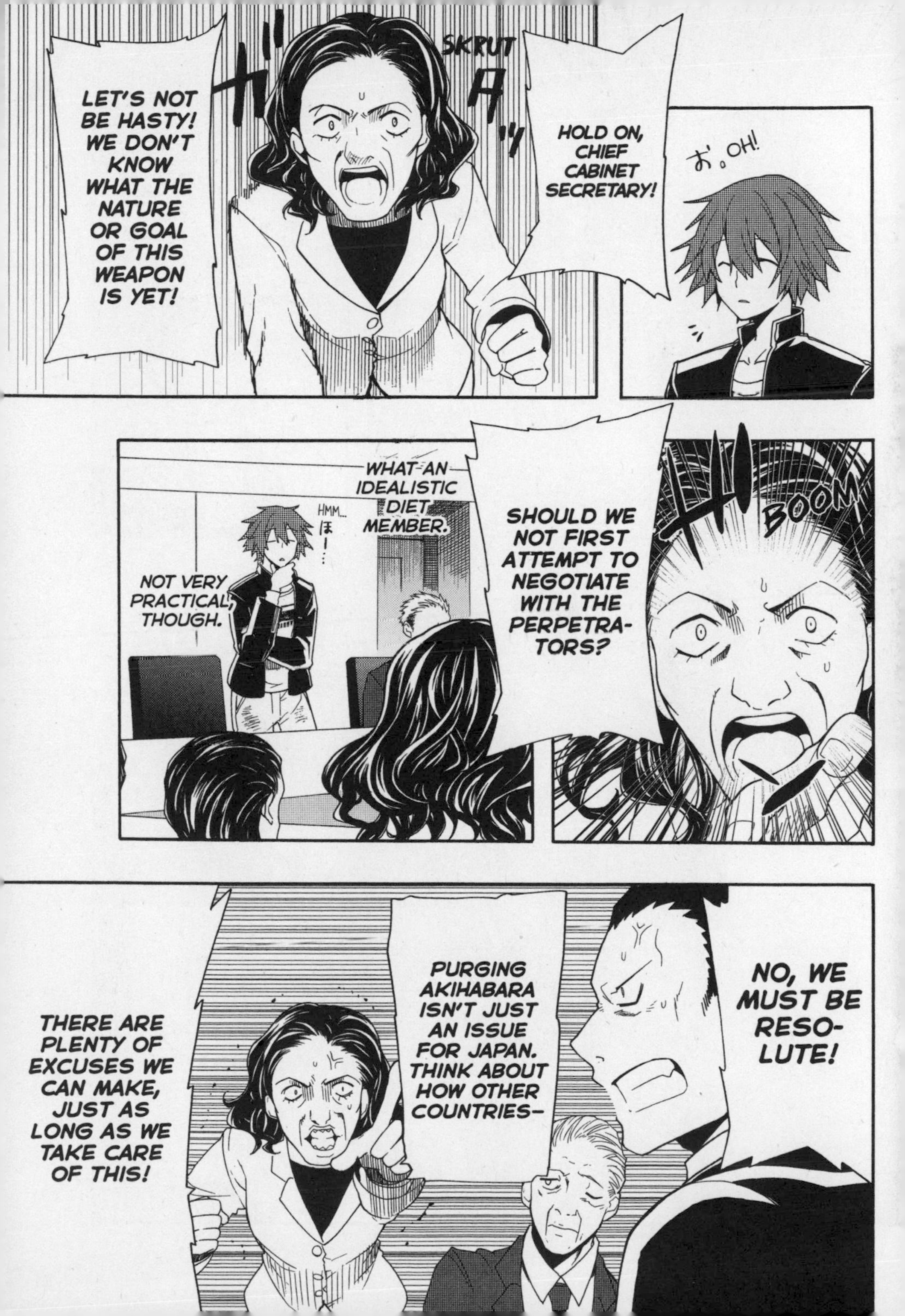
お。OH!
SKRUT
HOLD ON, CHIEF CABINET SECRETARY!
LET'S NOT BE HASTY! WE DON'T KNOW WHAT THE NATURE OR GOAL OF THIS WEAPON IS YET!
BOOM
SHOULD WE NOT FIRST ATTEMPT TO NEGOTIATE WITH THE PERPETRATORS?
WHAT AN IDEALISTIC DIET MEMBER.
HMM... ほー…
NOT VERY PRACTICAL, THOUGH.
NO, WE MUST BE RESOLUTE!
PURGING AKIHABARA ISN'T JUST AN ISSUE FOR JAPAN. THINK ABOUT HOW OTHER COUNTRIES–
THERE ARE PLENTY OF EXCUSES WE CAN MAKE, JUST AS LONG AS WE TAKE CARE OF THIS!

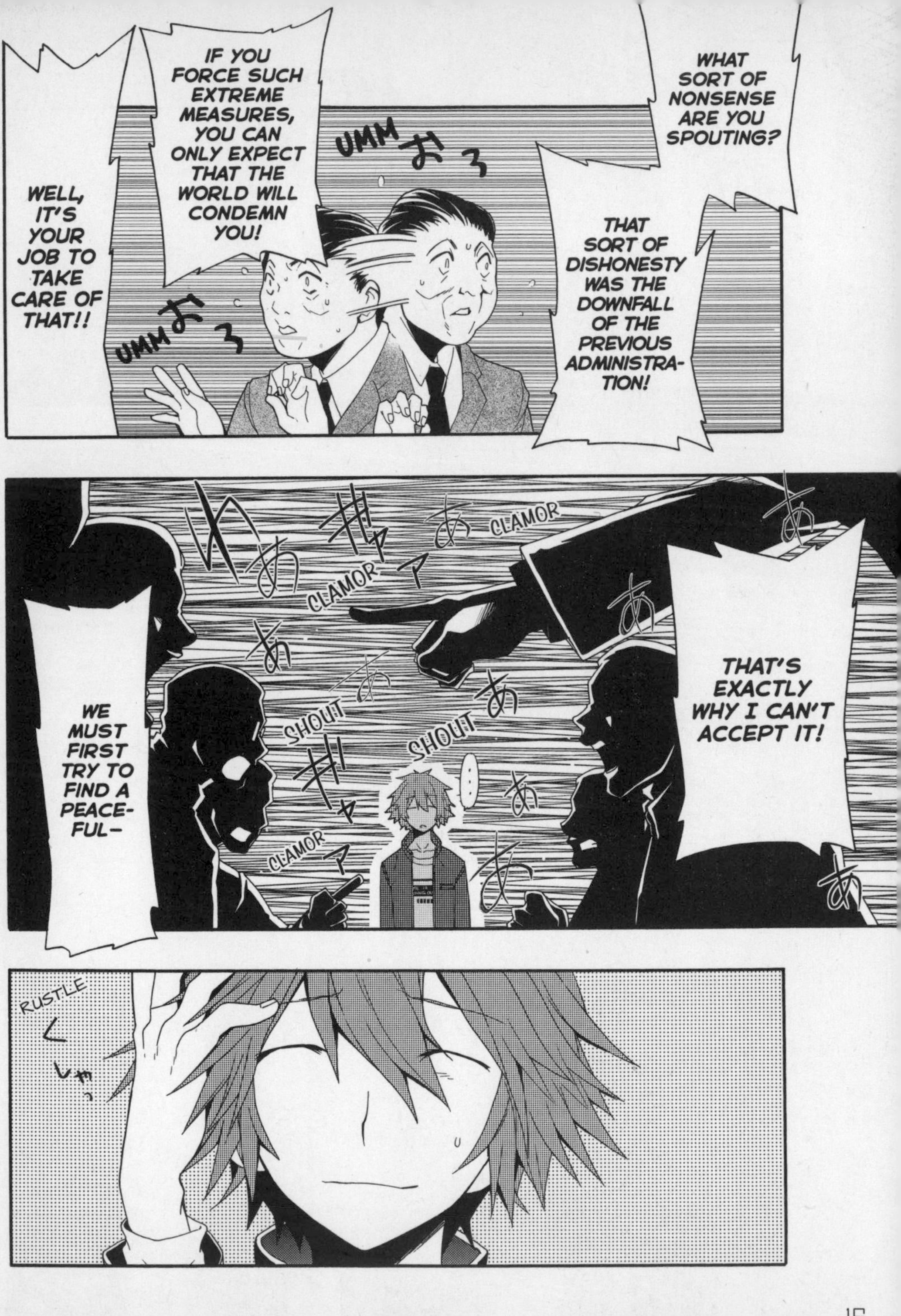
WHAT SORT OF NONSENSE ARE YOU SPOUTING?
THAT SORT OF DISHONESTY WAS THE DOWNFALL OF THE PREVIOUS ADMINISTRATION!
UMM おろ
IF YOU FORCE SUCH EXTREME MEASURES, YOU CAN ONLY EXPECT THAT THE WORLD WILL CONDEMN YOU!
WELL, IT'S YOUR JOB TO TAKE CARE OF THAT!!
UMM おろ
THAT'S EXACTLY WHY I CAN'T ACCEPT IT!
CLAMOR
CLAMOR
SHOUT
SHOUT
…
CLAMOR
WE MUST FIRST TRY TO FIND A PEACEFUL–
RUSTLE
くしゃっ

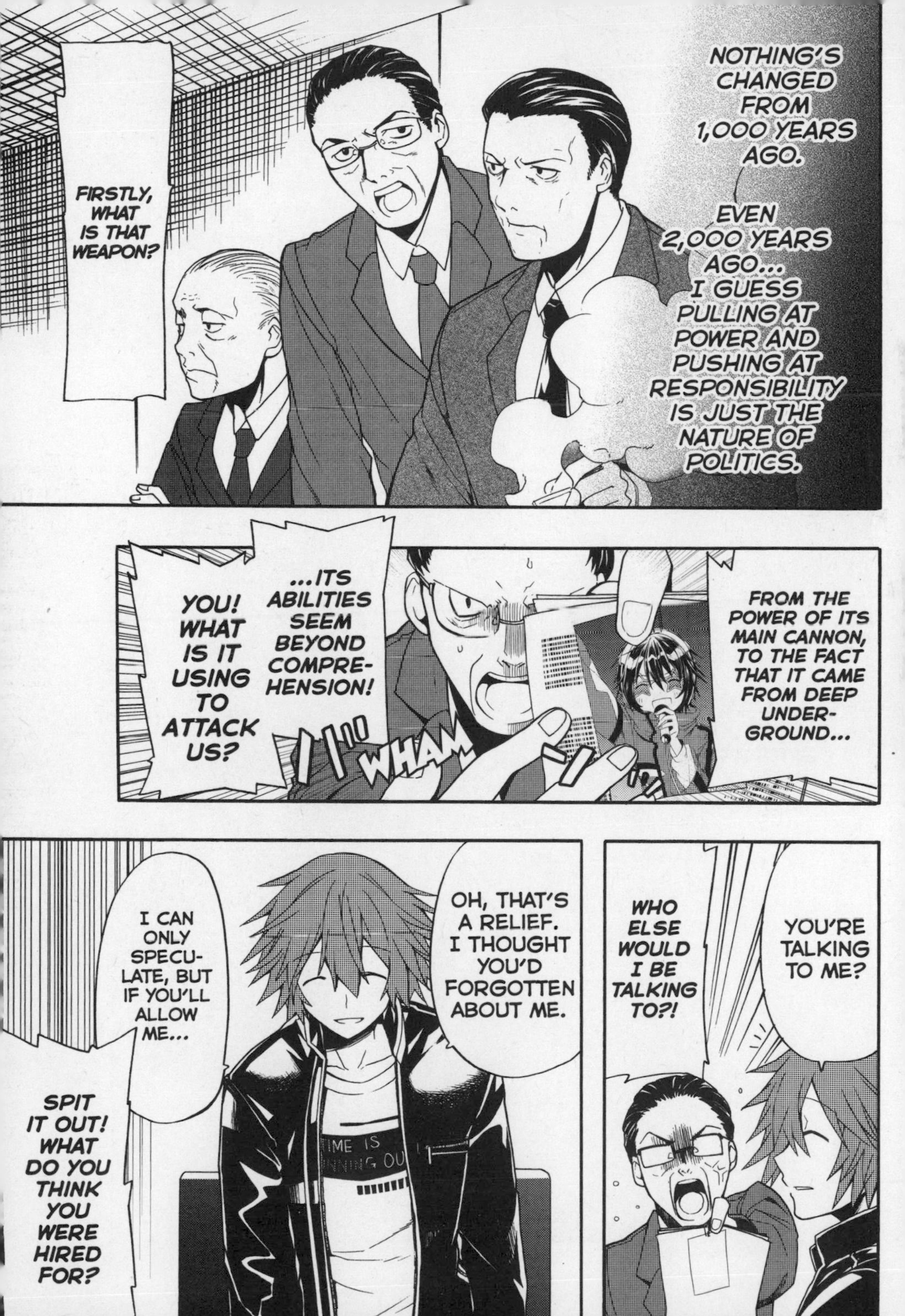
NOTHING'S CHANGED FROM 1,000 YEARS AGO.
EVEN 2,000 YEARS AGO... I GUESS PULLING AT POWER AND PUSHING AT RESPONSIBILITY IS JUST THE NATURE OF POLITICS.
FIRSTLY, WHAT IS THAT WEAPON?
FROM THE POWER OF ITS MAIN CANNON, TO THE FACT THAT IT CAME FROM DEEP UNDER-GROUND...
...ITS ABILITIES SEEM BEYOND COMPRE-HENSION!
YOU! WHAT IS IT USING TO ATTACK US?
WHAM
YOU'RE TALKING TO ME?
WHO ELSE WOULD I BE TALKING TO?!
OH, THAT'S A RELIEF. I THOUGHT YOU'D FORGOTTEN ABOUT ME.
I CAN ONLY SPECU-LATE, BUT IF YOU'LL ALLOW ME...
SPIT IT OUT! WHAT DO YOU THINK YOU WERE HIRED FOR?

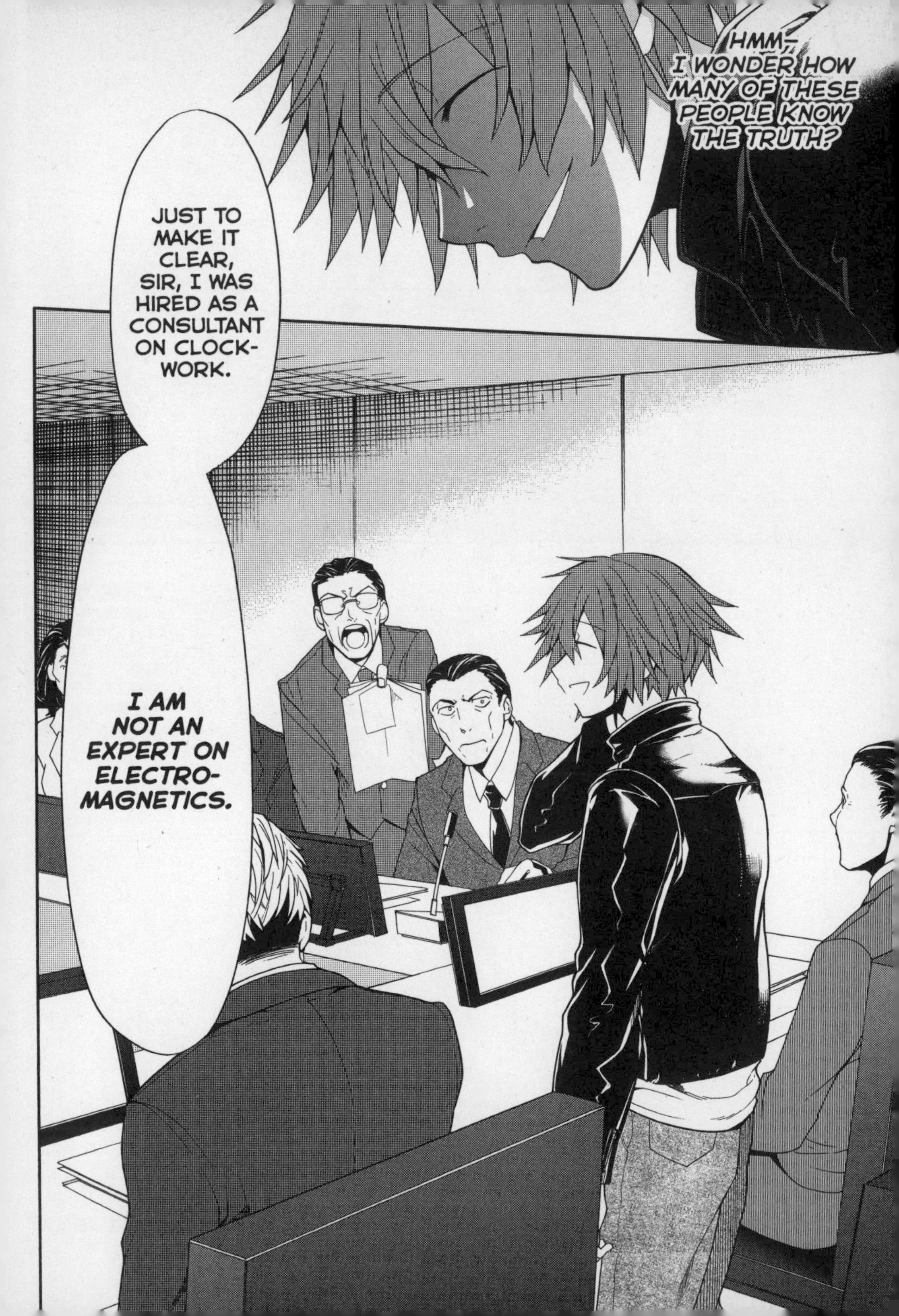
HMM, I WONDER HOW MANY OF THESE PEOPLE KNOW THE TRUTH?
JUST TO MAKE IT CLEAR, SIR, I WAS HIRED AS A CONSULTANT ON CLOCK-WORK.
I AM NOT AN EXPERT ON ELECTRO-MAGNETICS.

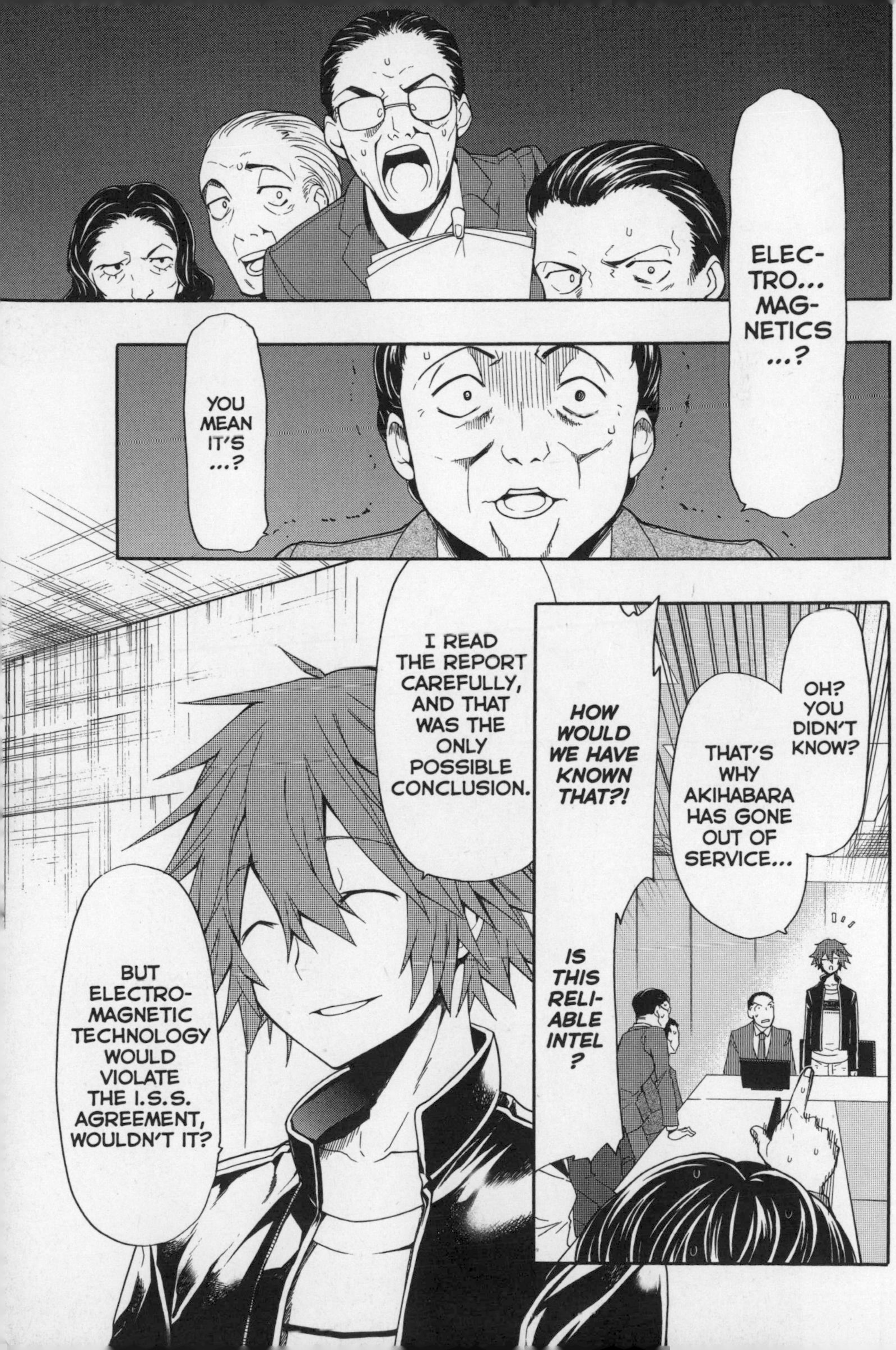
ELECTRO... MAGNETICS...?
YOU MEAN IT'S...?
OH? YOU DIDN'T KNOW?
THAT'S WHY AKIHABARA HAS GONE OUT OF SERVICE...
HOW WOULD WE HAVE KNOWN THAT?!
IS THIS RELIABLE INTEL?
I READ THE REPORT CAREFULLY, AND THAT WAS THE ONLY POSSIBLE CONCLUSION.
BUT ELECTROMAGNETIC TECHNOLOGY WOULD VIOLATE THE I.S.S. AGREEMENT, WOULDN'T IT?

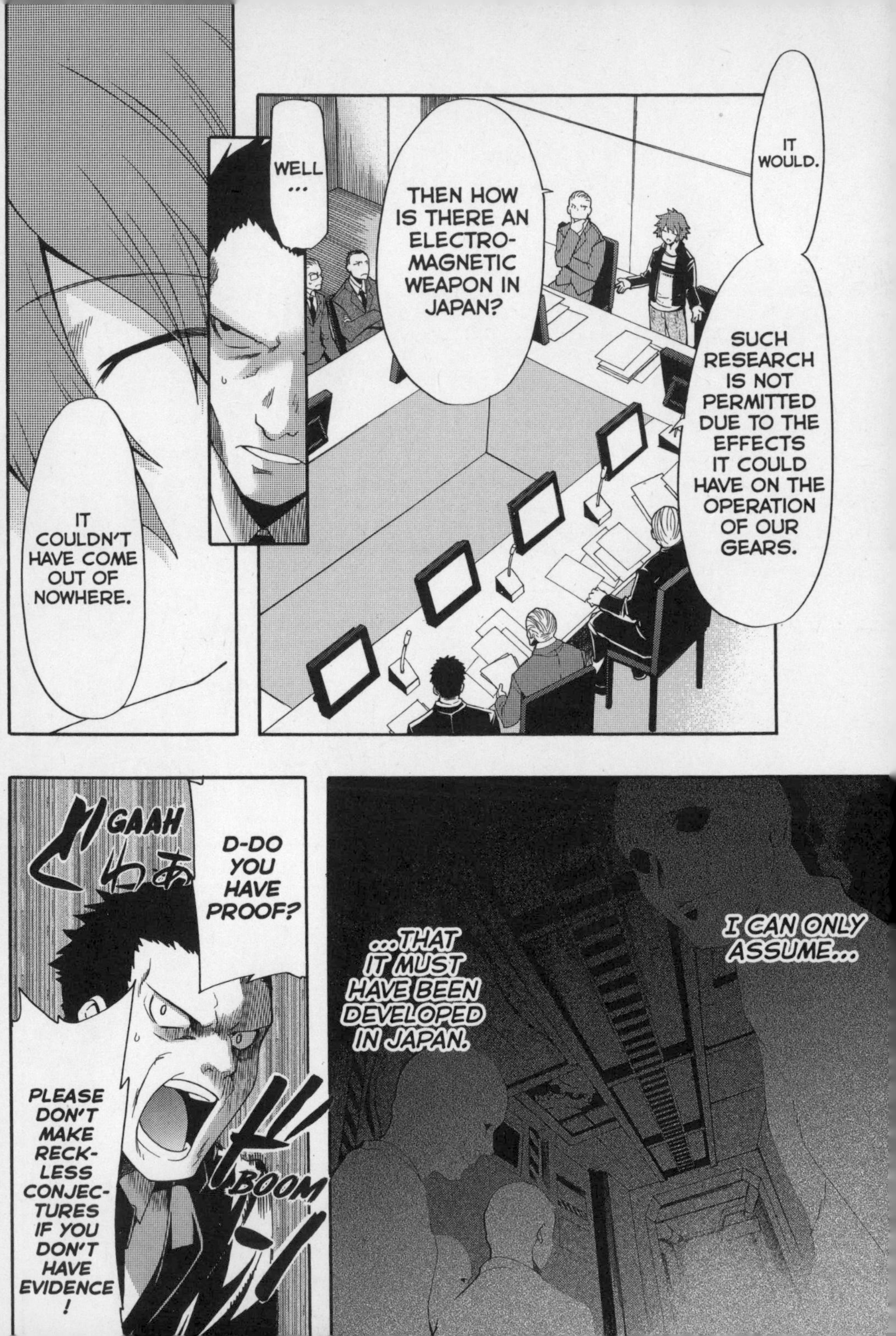
IT WOULD.
SUCH RESEARCH IS NOT PERMITTED DUE TO THE EFFECTS IT COULD HAVE ON THE OPERATION OF OUR GEARS.
THEN HOW IS THERE AN ELECTRO-MAGNETIC WEAPON IN JAPAN?
WELL ...
IT COULDN'T HAVE COME OUT OF NOWHERE.
I CAN ONLY ASSUME...
...THAT IT MUST HAVE BEEN DEVELOPED IN JAPAN.
くわぁ GAAH
D-DO YOU HAVE PROOF?
BOOM
PLEASE DON'T MAKE RECK-LESS CONJEC-TURES IF YOU DON'T HAVE EVIDENCE!

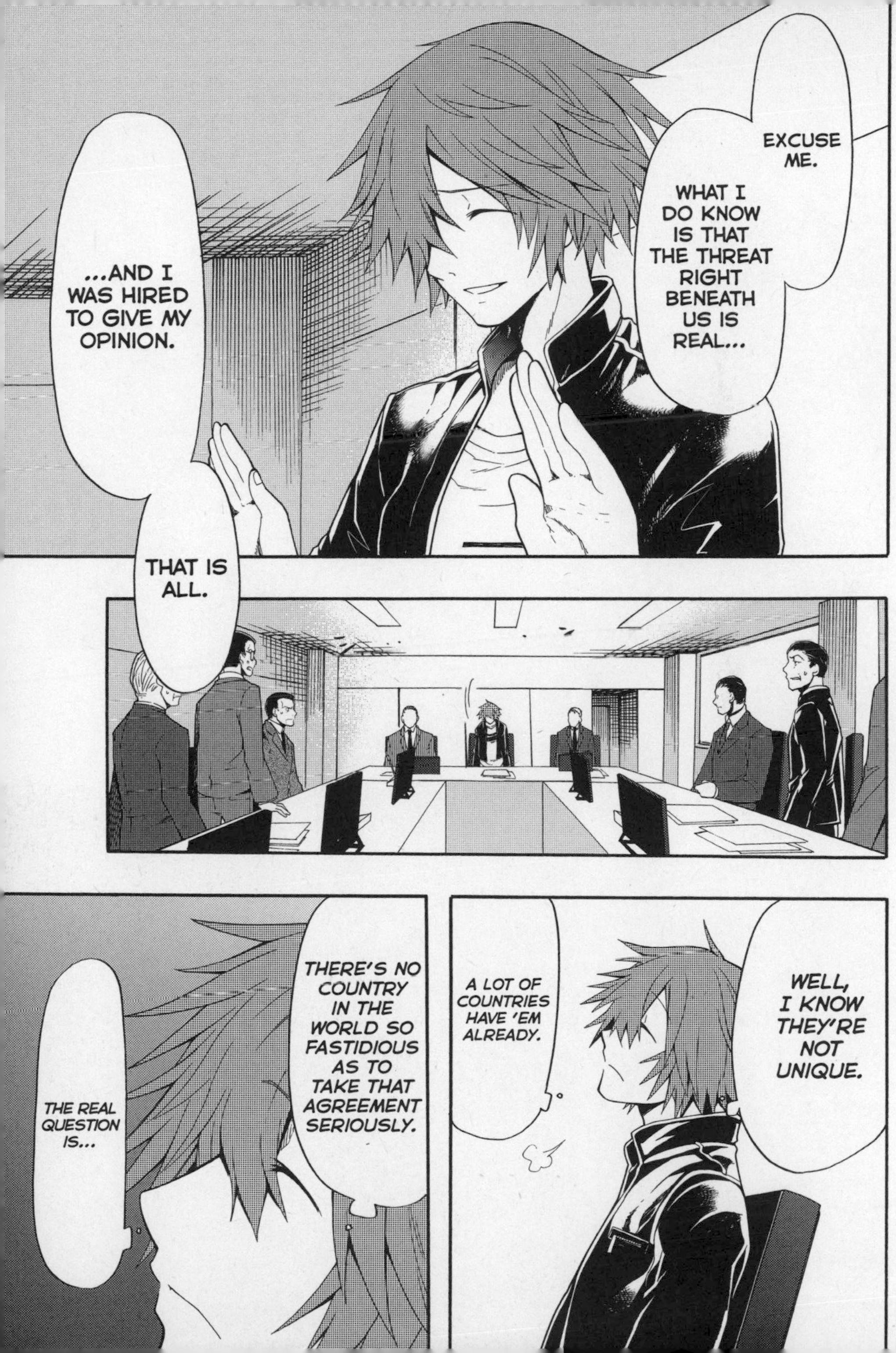
EXCUSE ME.
WHAT I DO KNOW IS THAT THE THREAT RIGHT BENEATH US IS REAL...
...AND I WAS HIRED TO GIVE MY OPINION.
THAT IS ALL.
WELL, I KNOW THEY'RE NOT UNIQUE.
A LOT OF COUNTRIES HAVE 'EM ALREADY.
THERE'S NO COUNTRY IN THE WORLD SO FASTIDIOUS AS TO TAKE THAT AGREEMENT SERIOUSLY.
THE REAL QUESTION IS...

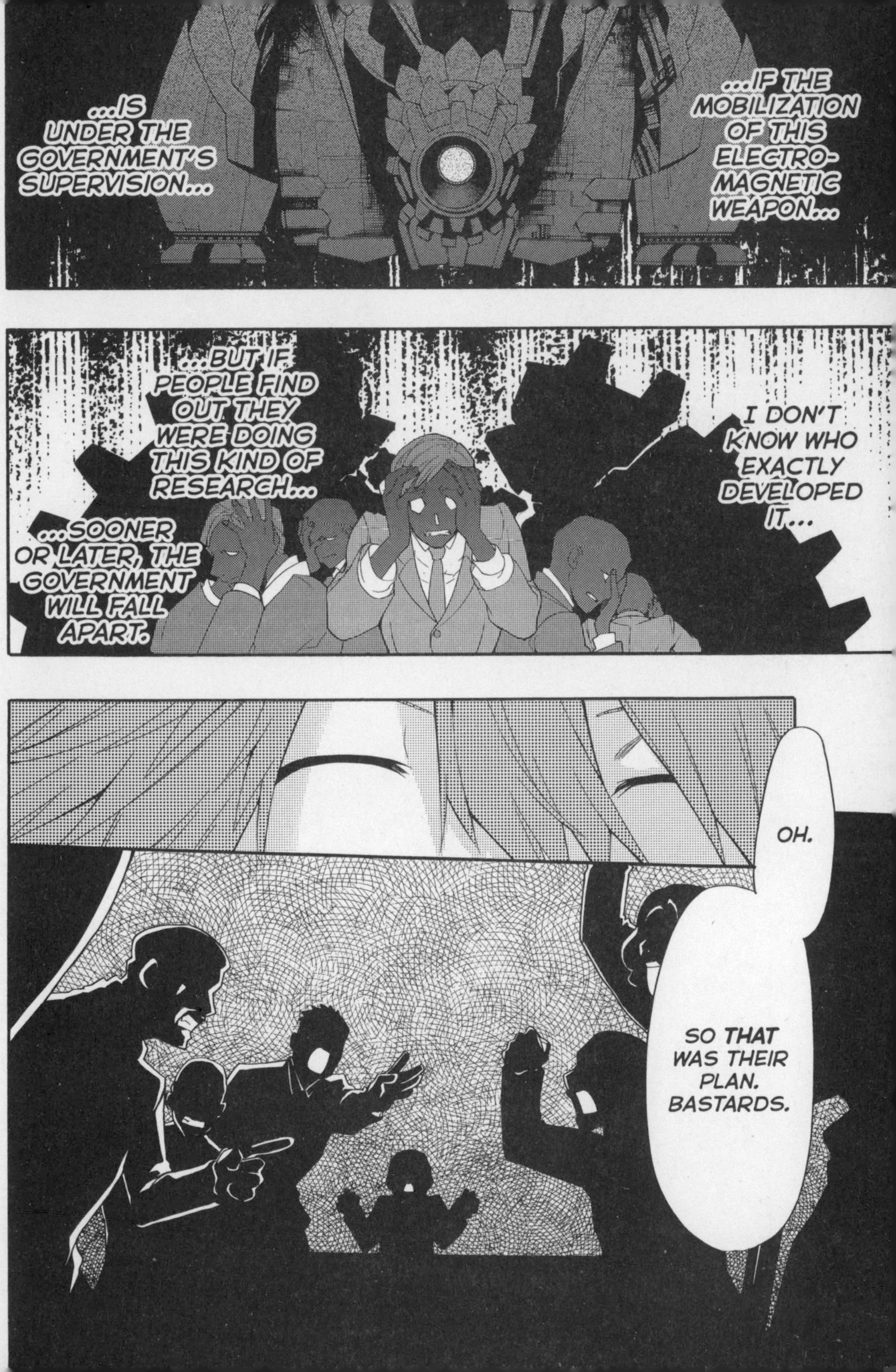
...IF THE MOBILIZATION OF THIS ELECTRO-MAGNETIC WEAPON...
...IS UNDER THE GOVERNMENT'S SUPERVISION...
I DON'T KNOW WHO EXACTLY DEVELOPED IT...
...BUT IF PEOPLE FIND OUT THEY WERE DOING THIS KIND OF RESEARCH...
...SOONER OR LATER, THE GOVERNMENT WILL FALL APART.
OH.
SO THAT WAS THEIR PLAN. BASTARDS.

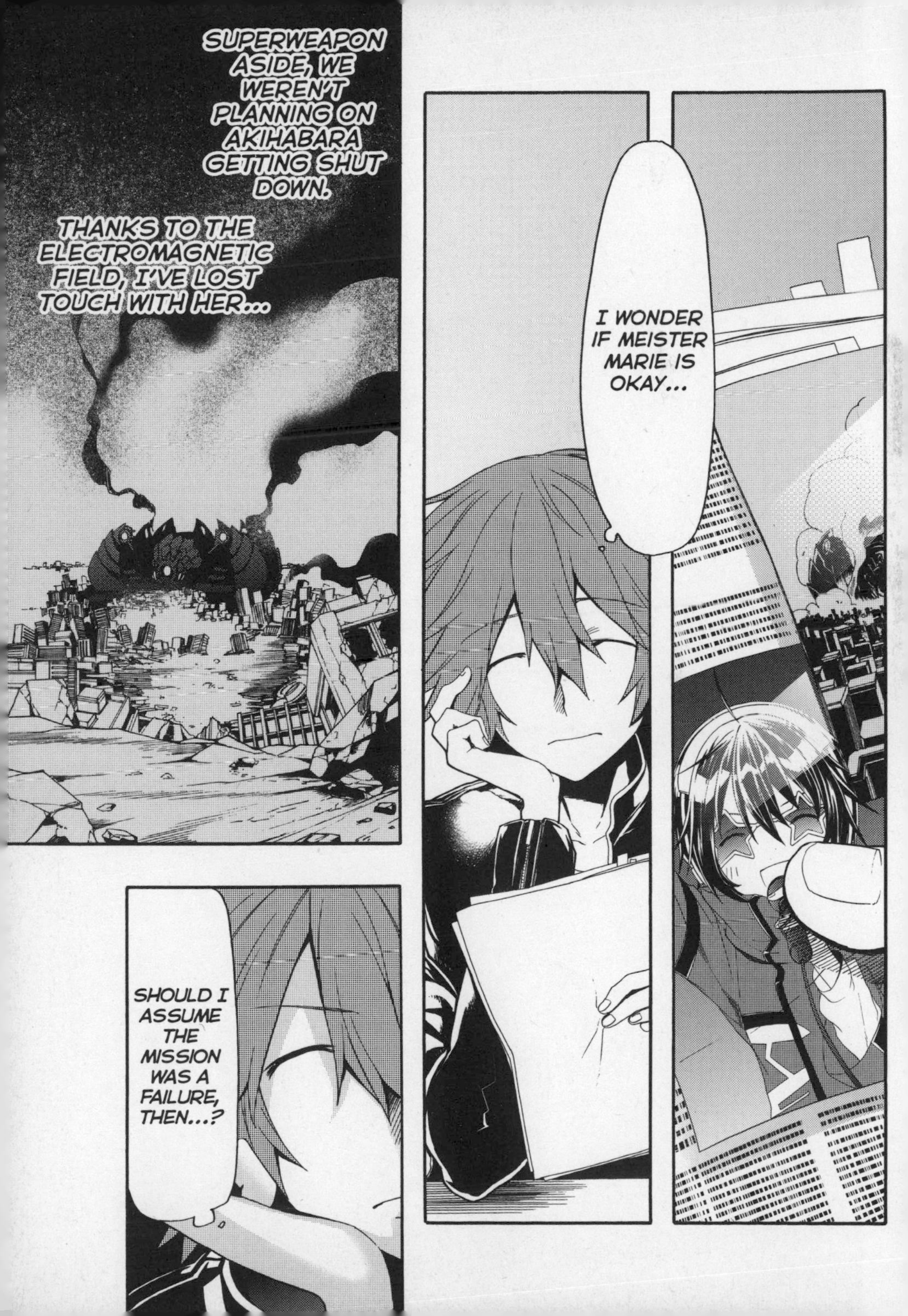
I WONDER IF MEISTER MARIE IS OKAY...
SUPERWEAPON ASIDE, WE WEREN'T PLANNING ON AKIHABARA GETTING SHUT DOWN.
THANKS TO THE ELECTROMAGNETIC FIELD, I'VE LOST TOUCH WITH HER...
SHOULD I ASSUME THE MISSION WAS A FAILURE, THEN...?

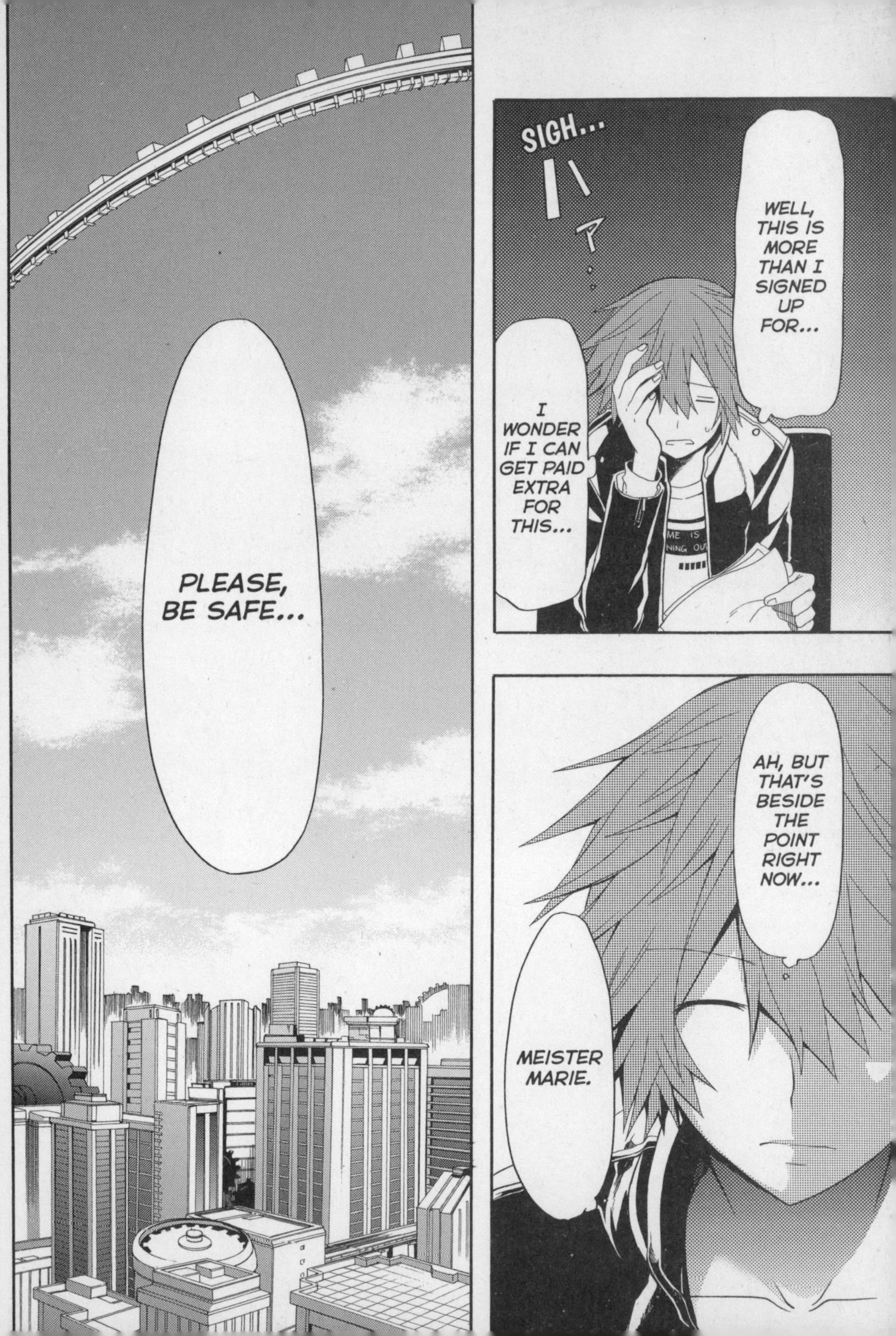
SIGH...
ハア…
WELL, THIS IS MORE THAN I SIGNED UP FOR...
I WONDER IF I CAN GET PAID EXTRA FOR THIS...
AH, BUT THAT'S BESIDE THE POINT RIGHT NOW...
MEISTER MARIE.
PLEASE, BE SAFE...

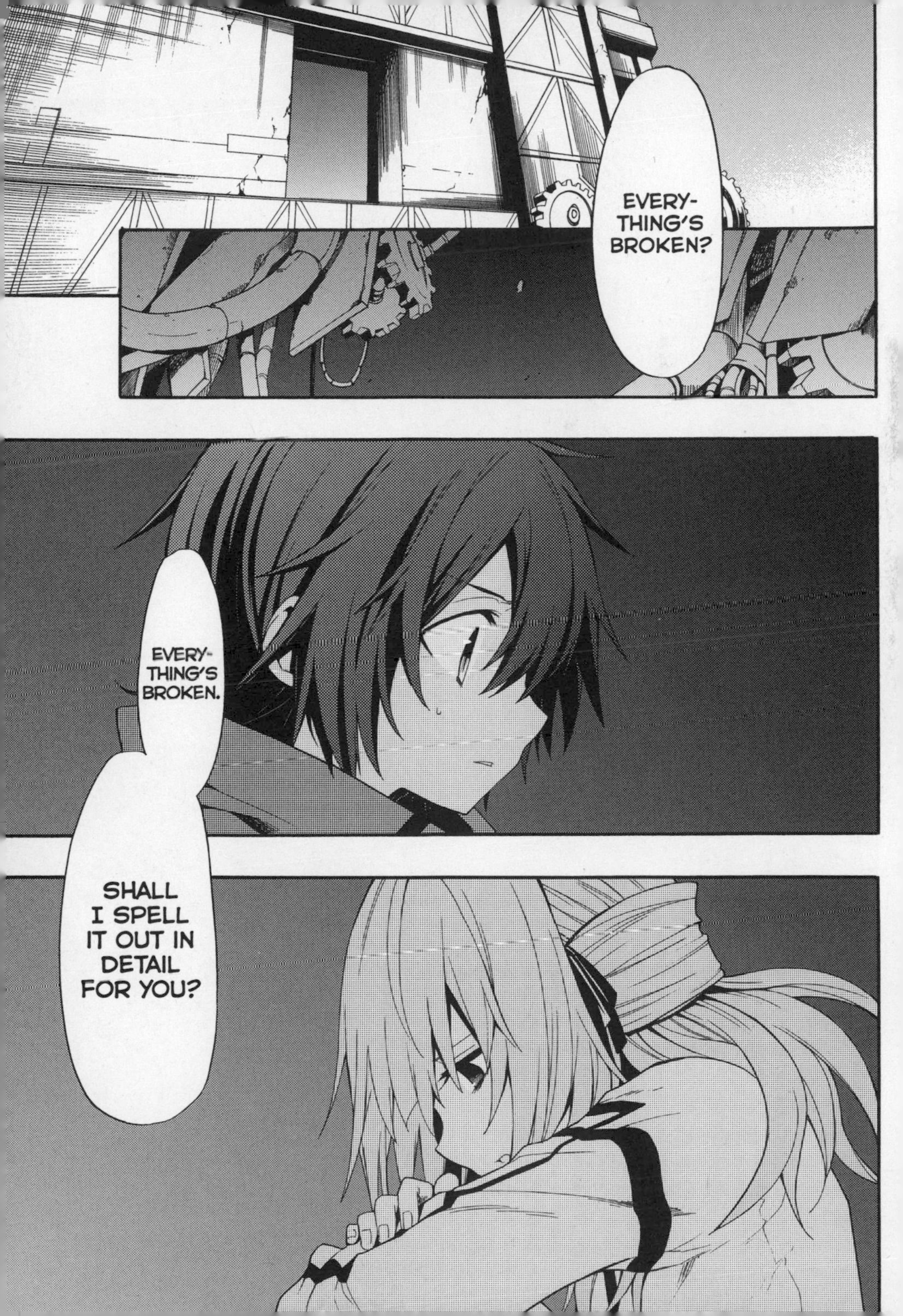
EVERY-THING'S BROKEN?
EVERY-THING'S BROKEN.
SHALL I SPELL IT OUT IN DETAIL FOR YOU?

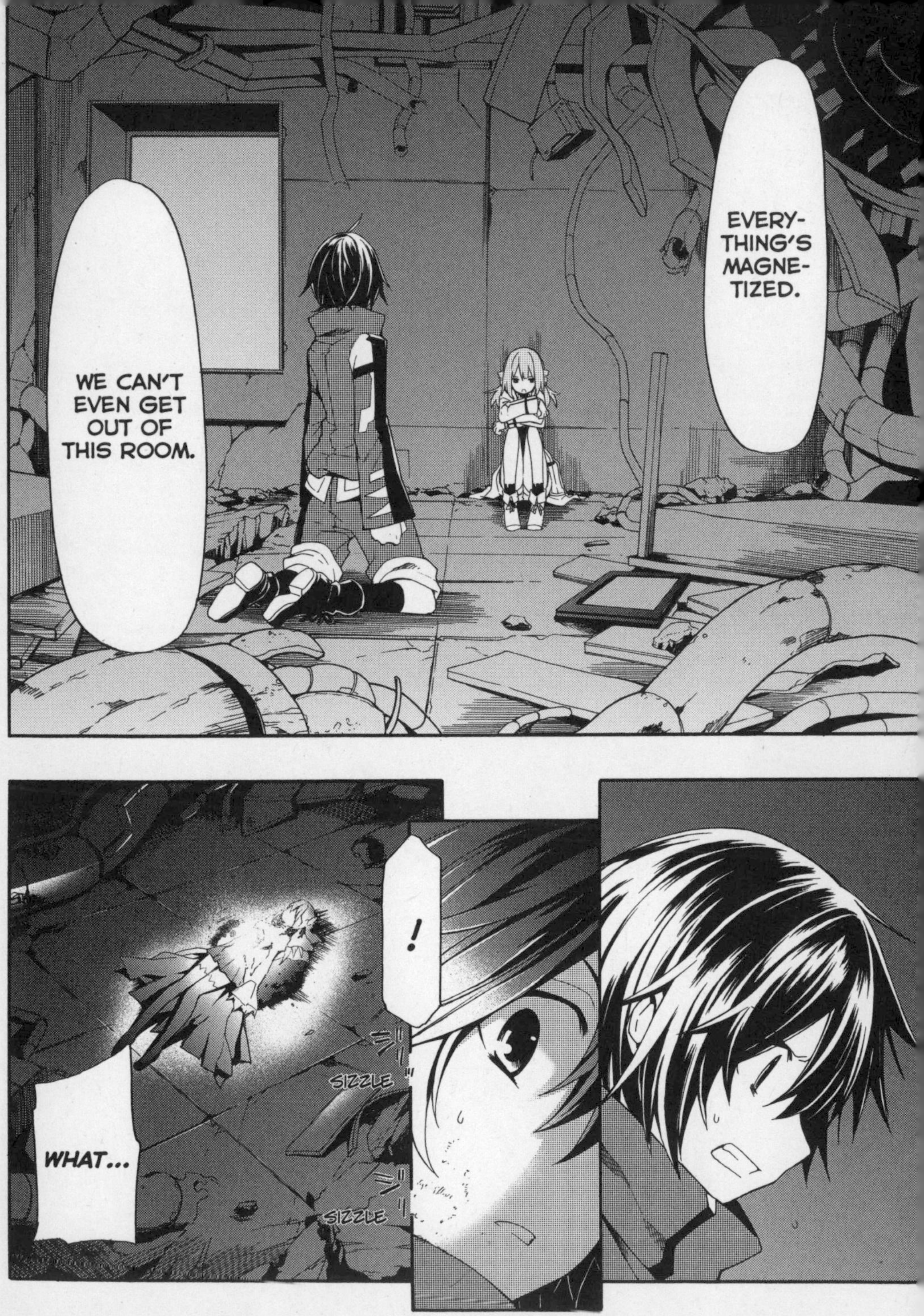
EVERY-
THING'S
MAGNE-
TIZED.
WE CAN'T EVEN GET OUT OF THIS ROOM.
!
SIZZLE
SIZZLE
WHAT...

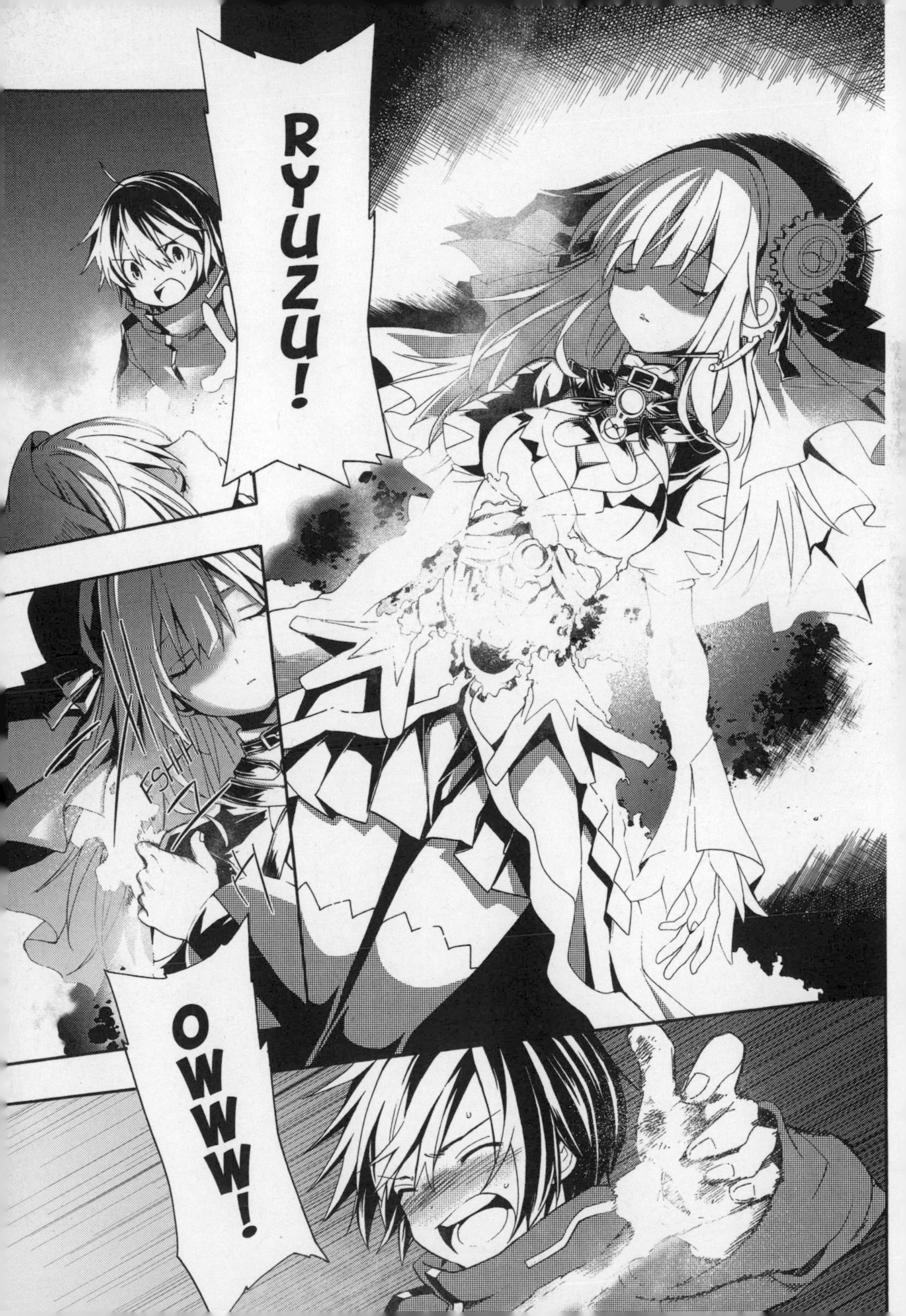
RYUZU!
FSHH
OWWW!

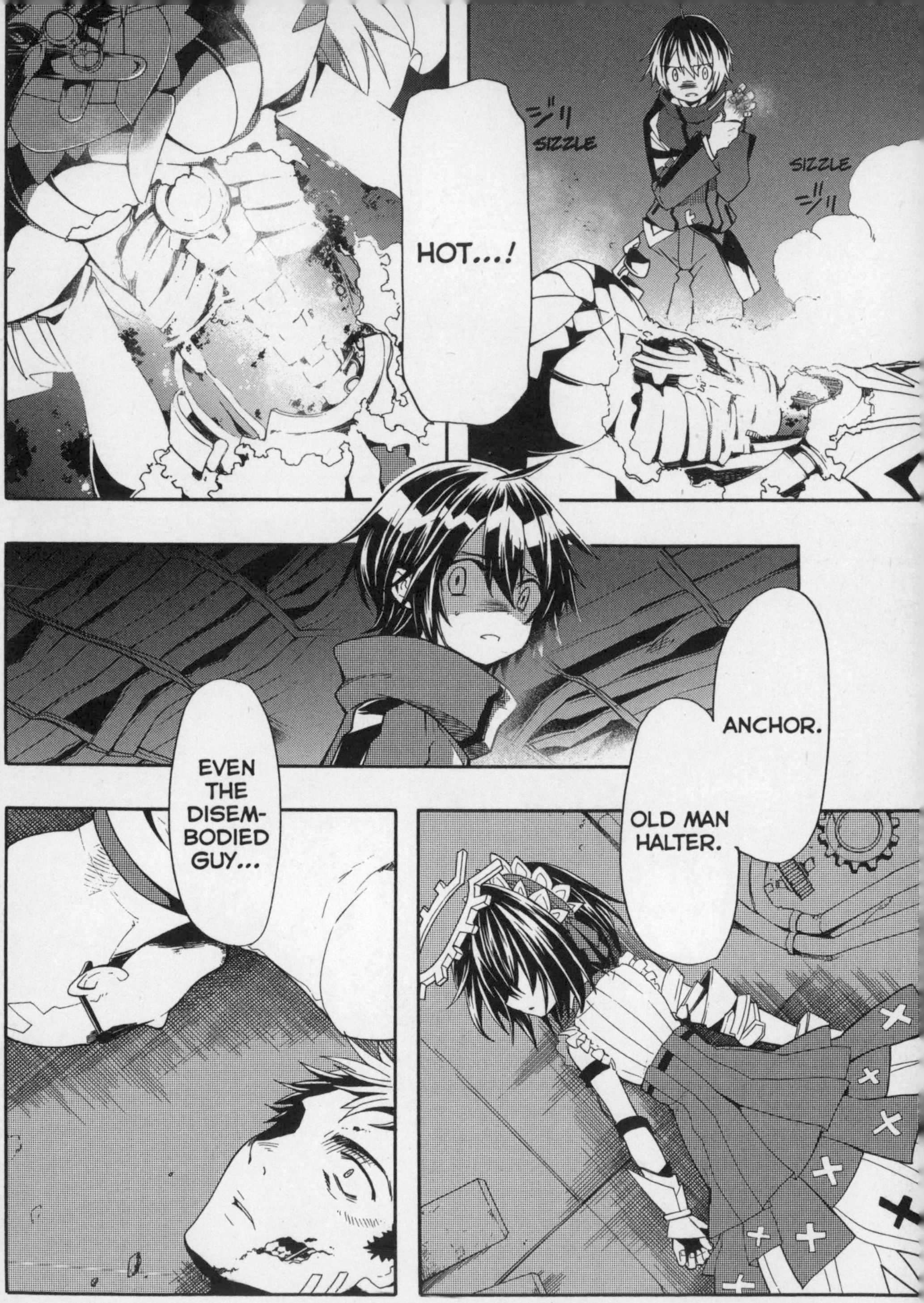
ジリ
SIZZLE
ジリ
SIZZLE
HOT...!
ANCHOR.
OLD MAN HALTER.
EVEN THE DISEM-BODIED GUY...

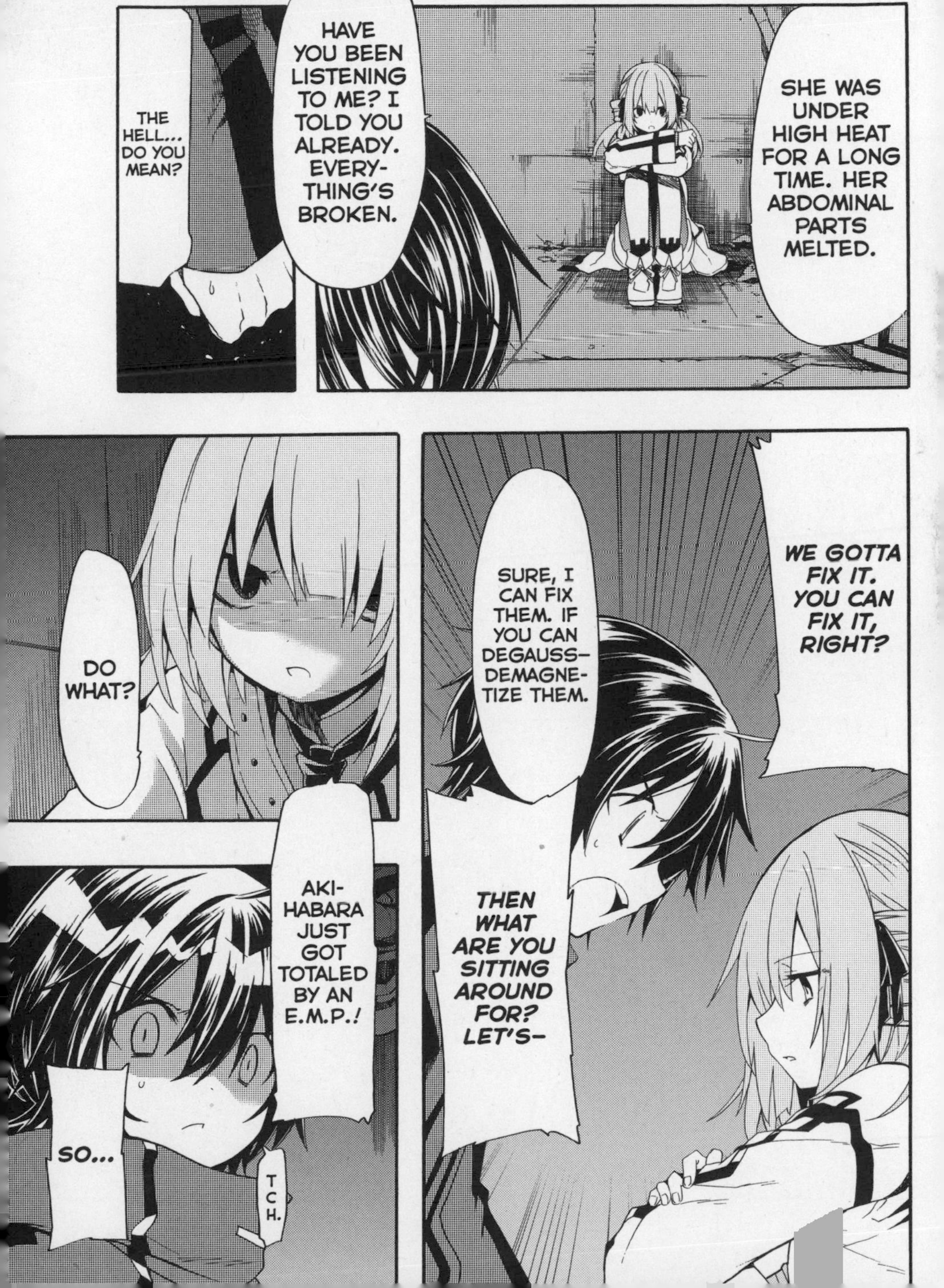
SHE WAS UNDER HIGH HEAT FOR A LONG TIME. HER ABDOMINAL PARTS MELTED.
HAVE YOU BEEN LISTENING TO ME? I TOLD YOU ALREADY. EVERY-THING'S BROKEN.
THE HELL... DO YOU MEAN?
WE GOTTA FIX IT. YOU CAN FIX IT, RIGHT?
SURE, I CAN FIX THEM. IF YOU CAN DEGAUSS-DEMAGNE-TIZE THEM.
THEN WHAT ARE YOU SITTING AROUND FOR? LET'S-
DO WHAT?
AKI-HABARA JUST GOT TOTALED BY AN E.M.P.!
SO...
TCH.

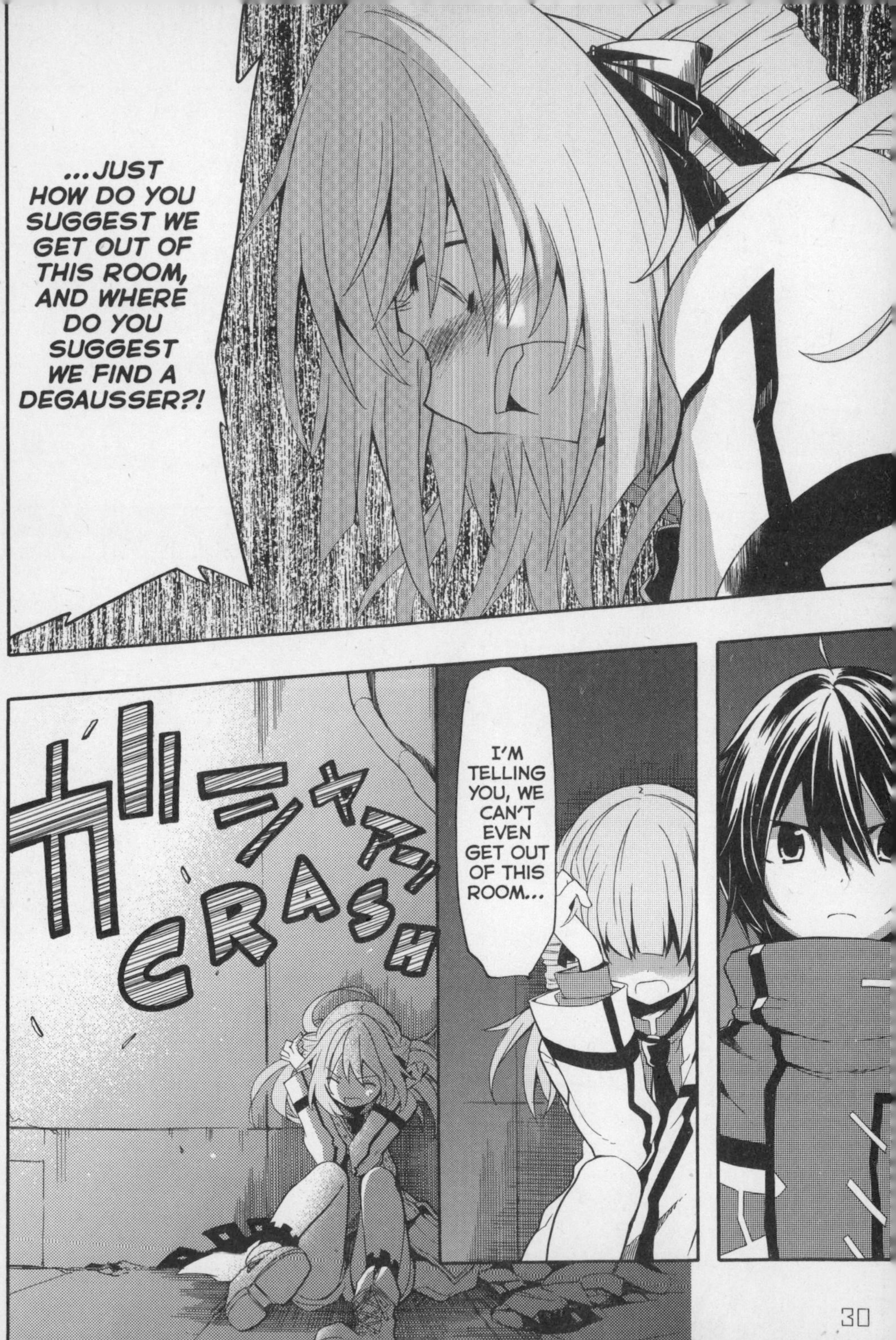
...JUST HOW DO YOU SUGGEST WE GET OUT OF THIS ROOM, AND WHERE DO YOU SUGGEST WE FIND A DEGAUSSER?!
I'M TELLING YOU, WE CAN'T EVEN GET OUT OF THIS ROOM...
ガシャアッ
CRASH

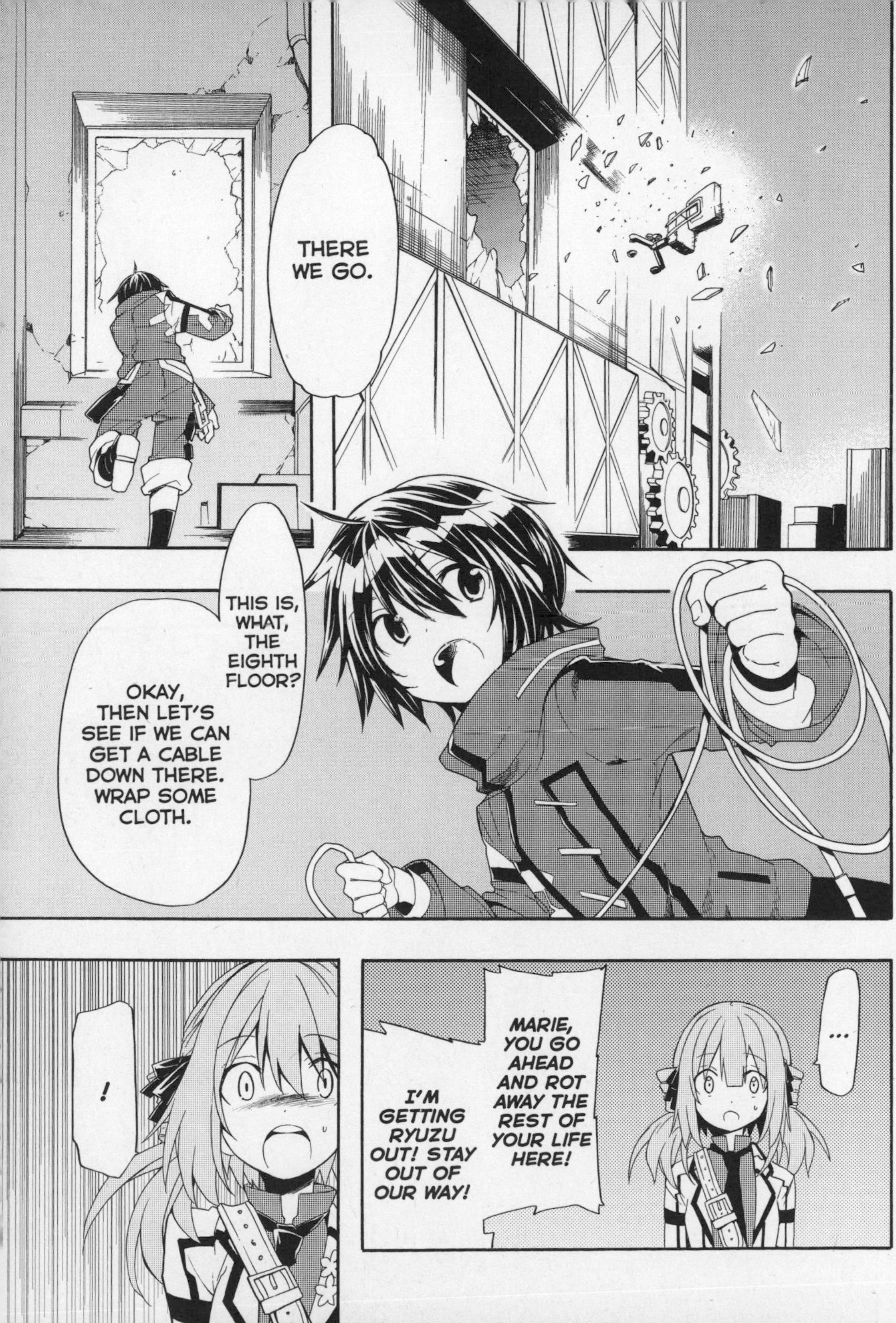
THERE WE GO.
THIS IS, WHAT, THE EIGHTH FLOOR?
OKAY, THEN LET'S SEE IF WE CAN GET A CABLE DOWN THERE. WRAP SOME CLOTH.
...
MARIE, YOU GO AHEAD AND ROT AWAY THE REST OF YOUR LIFE HERE!
I'M GETTING RYUZU OUT! STAY OUT OF OUR WAY!
!

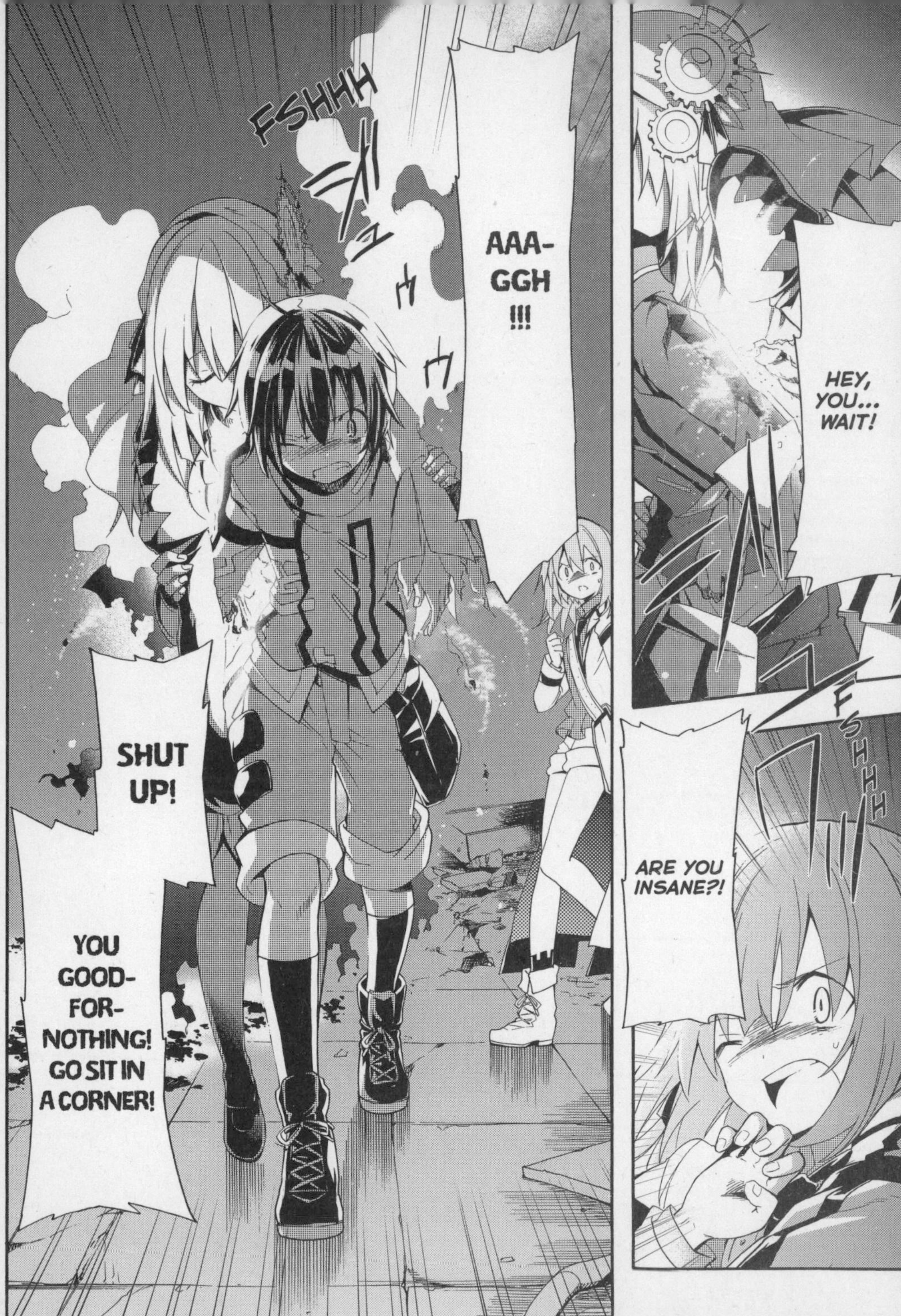
HEY, YOU... WAIT!
FSHHH
ARE YOU INSANE?!
FSHHH
AAA-GGH!!!
SHUT UP!
YOU GOOD-FOR-NOTHING! GO SIT IN A CORNER!

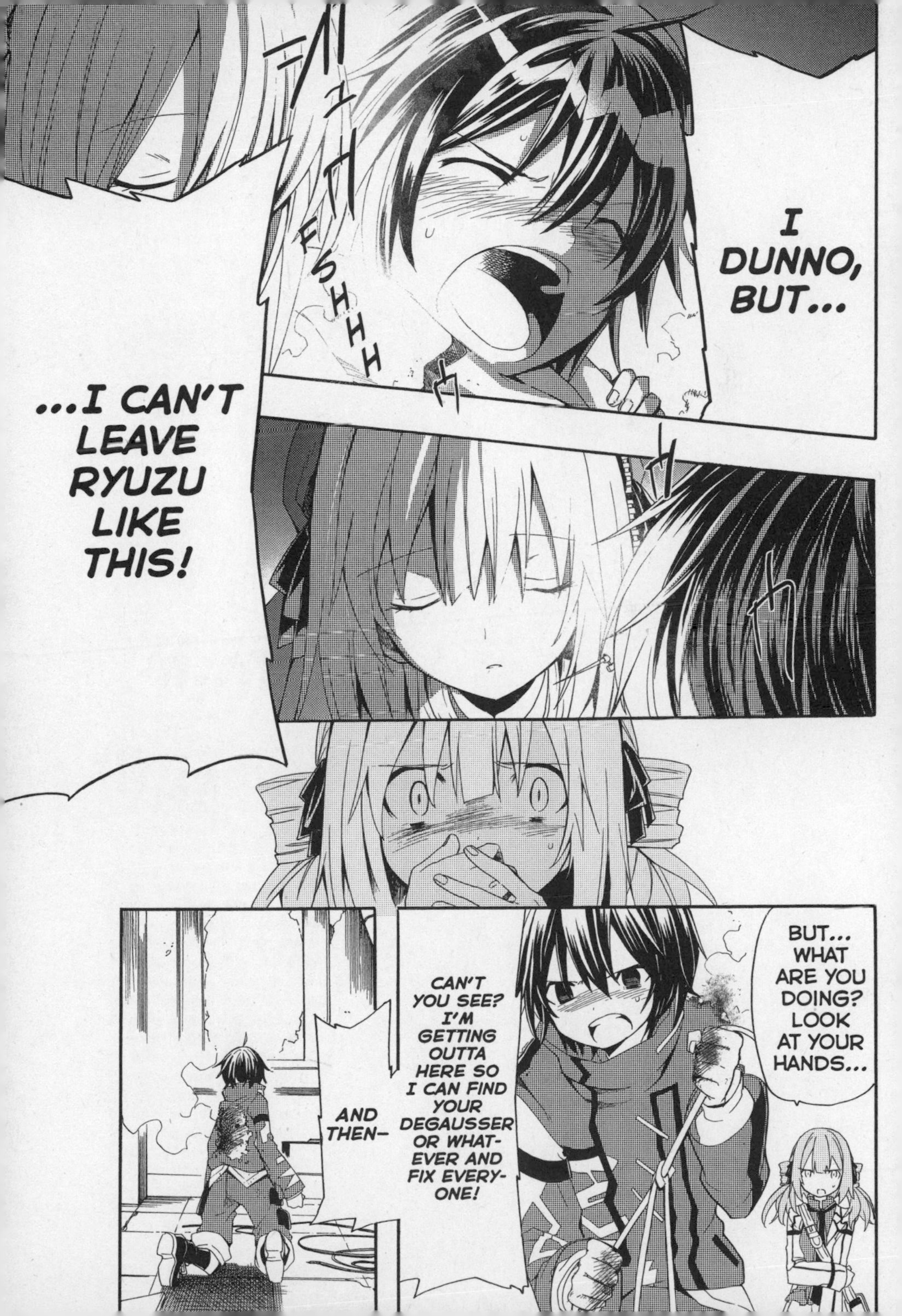
I DUNNO, BUT...
FSHHHH
...I CAN'T LEAVE RYUZU LIKE THIS!
BUT... WHAT ARE YOU DOING? LOOK AT YOUR HANDS...
CAN'T YOU SEE? I'M GETTING OUTTA HERE SO I CAN FIND YOUR DEGAUSSER OR WHAT-EVER AND FIX EVERY-ONE!
AND THEN—

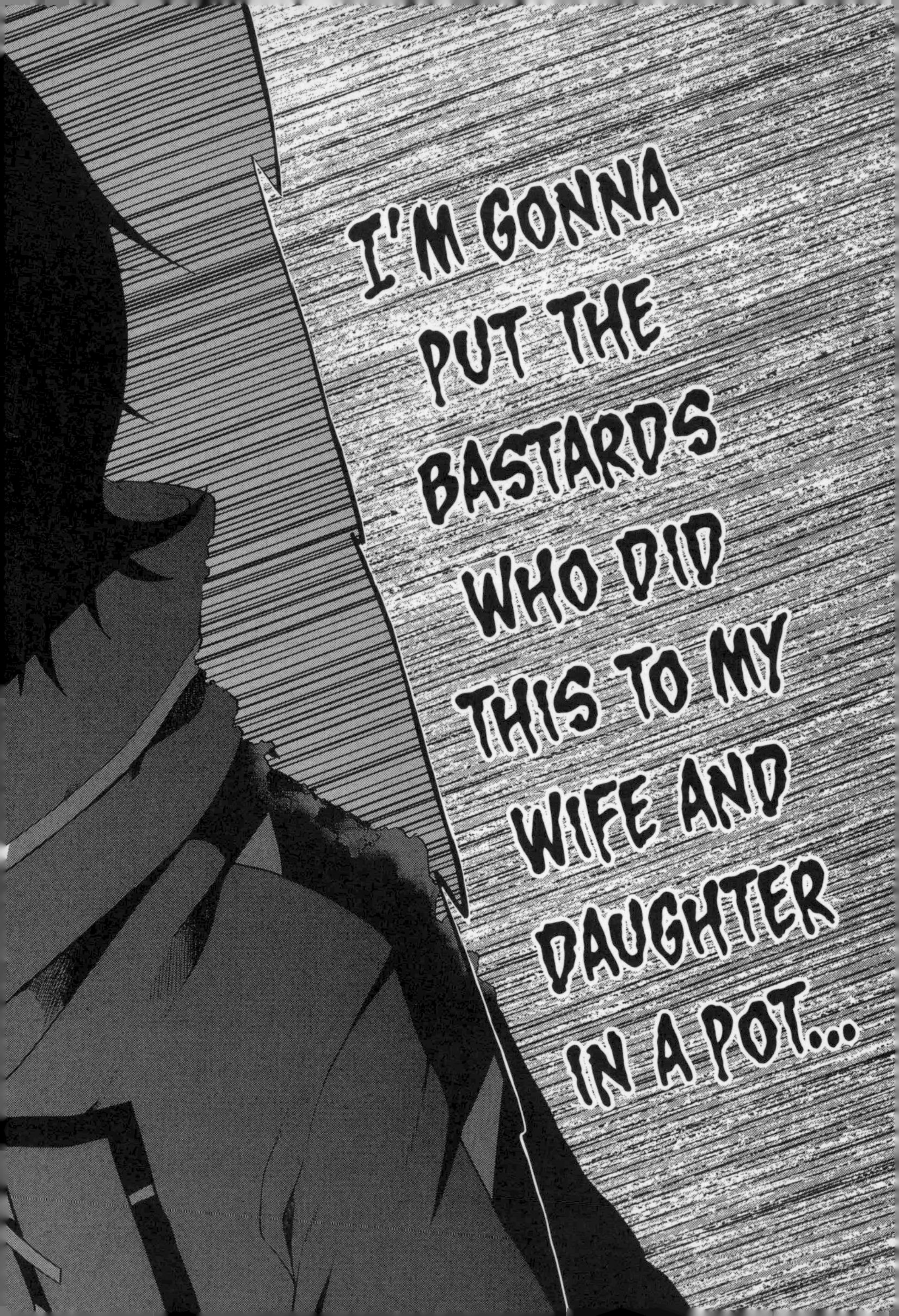
I'M GONNA PUT THE BASTARDS WHO DID THIS TO MY WIFE AND DAUGHTER IN A POT...

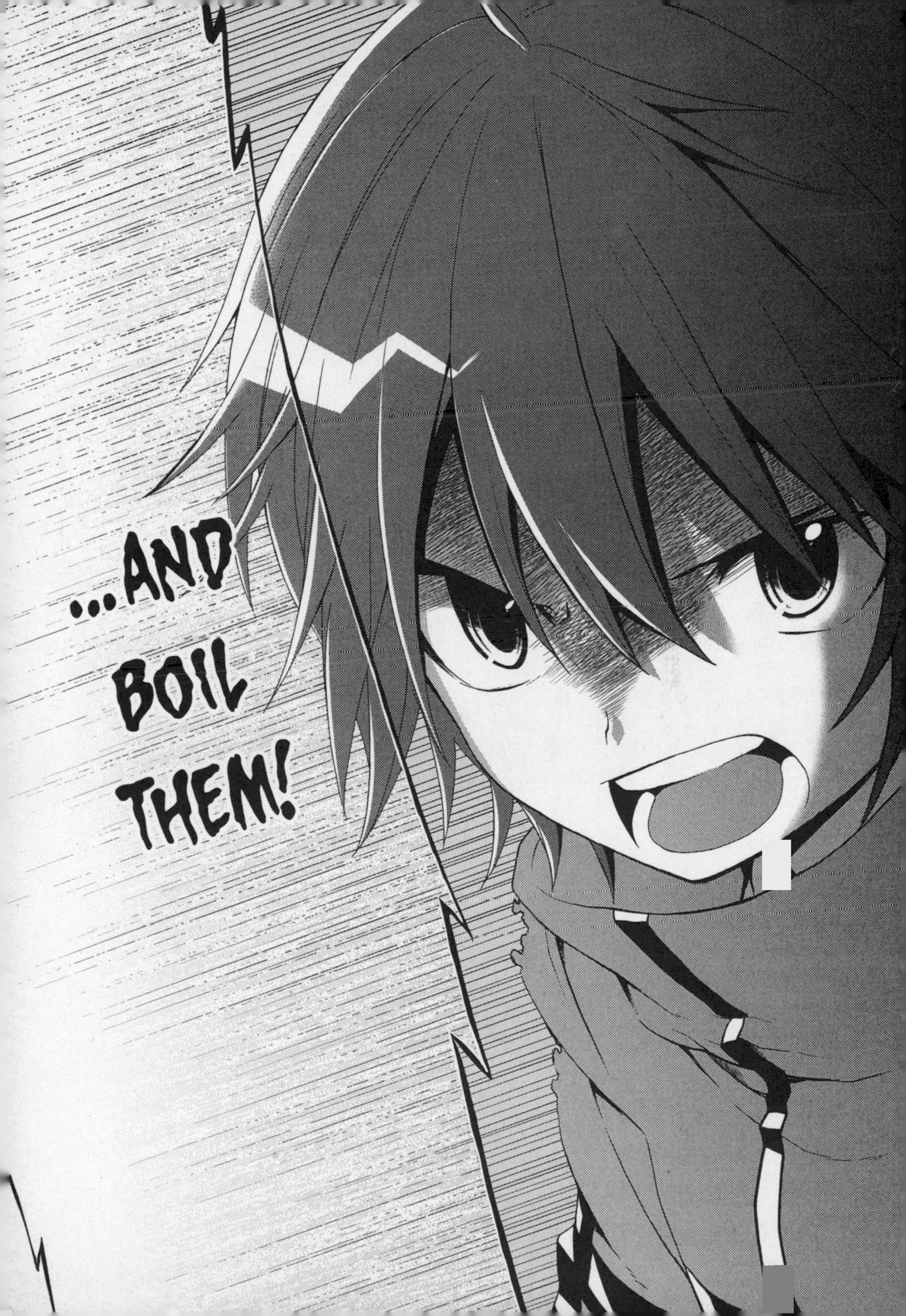
...AND BOIL THEM!

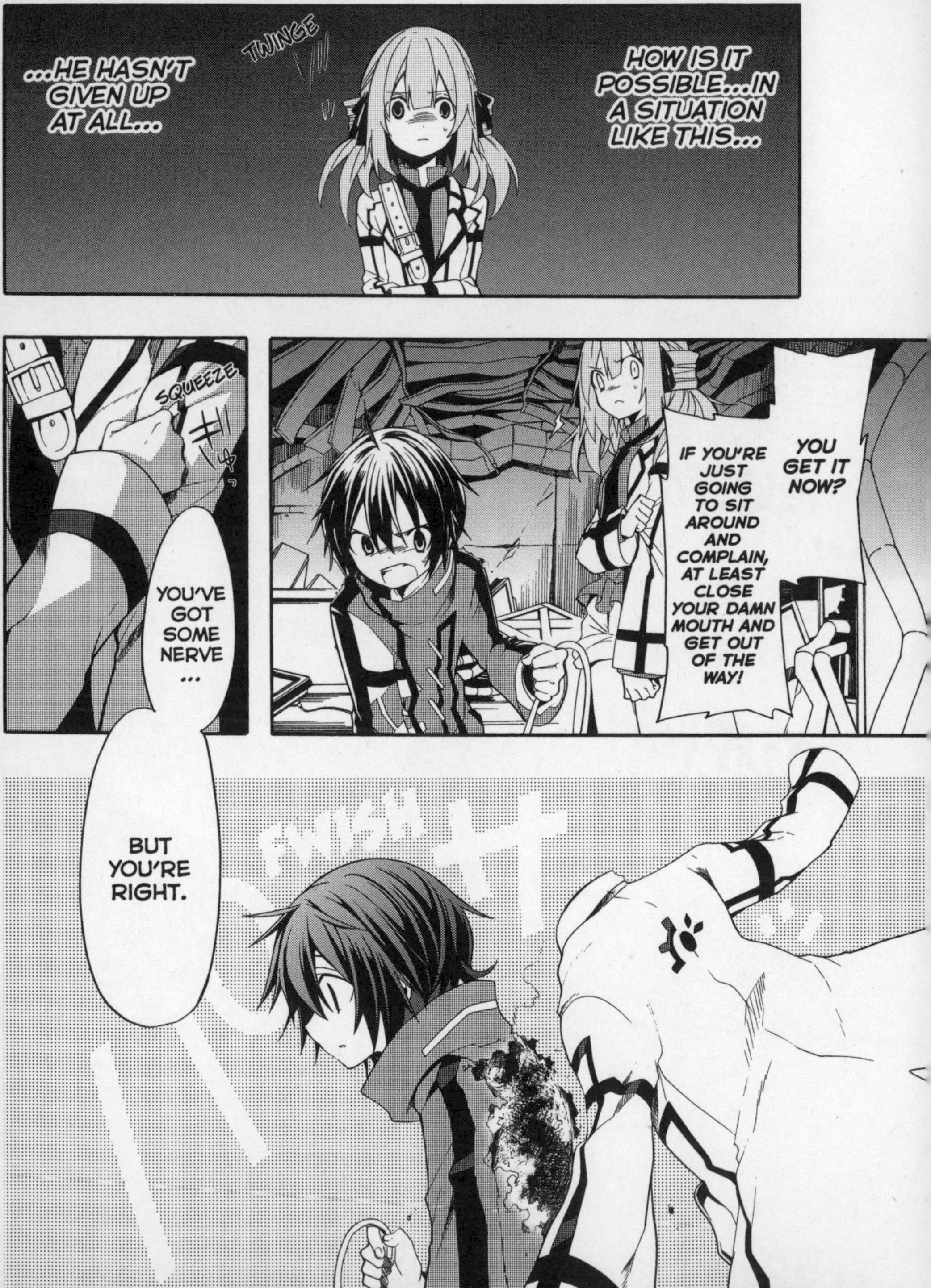
HOW IS IT POSSIBLE...IN A SITUATION LIKE THIS...
TWINGE
...HE HASN'T GIVEN UP AT ALL...
YOU GET IT NOW?
IF YOU'RE JUST GOING TO SIT AROUND AND COMPLAIN, AT LEAST CLOSE YOUR DAMN MOUTH AND GET OUT OF THE WAY!
SQUEEZE
YOU'VE GOT SOME NERVE ...
BUT YOU'RE RIGHT.

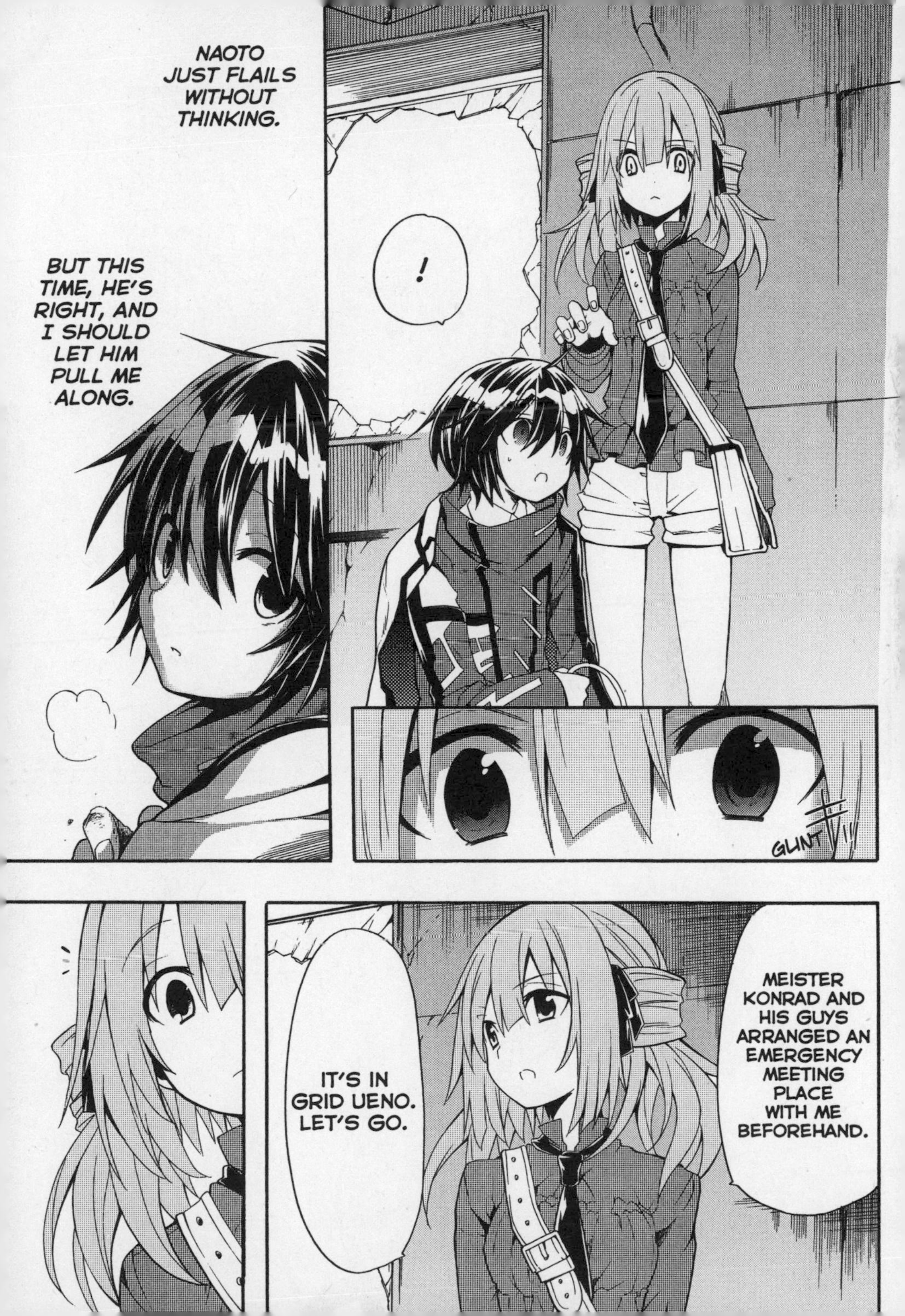
!
GLINT
NAOTO JUST FLAILS WITHOUT THINKING.
BUT THIS TIME, HE'S RIGHT, AND I SHOULD LET HIM PULL ME ALONG.
MEISTER KONRAD AND HIS GUYS ARRANGED AN EMERGENCY MEETING PLACE WITH ME BEFOREHAND.
IT'S IN GRID UENO. LET'S GO.

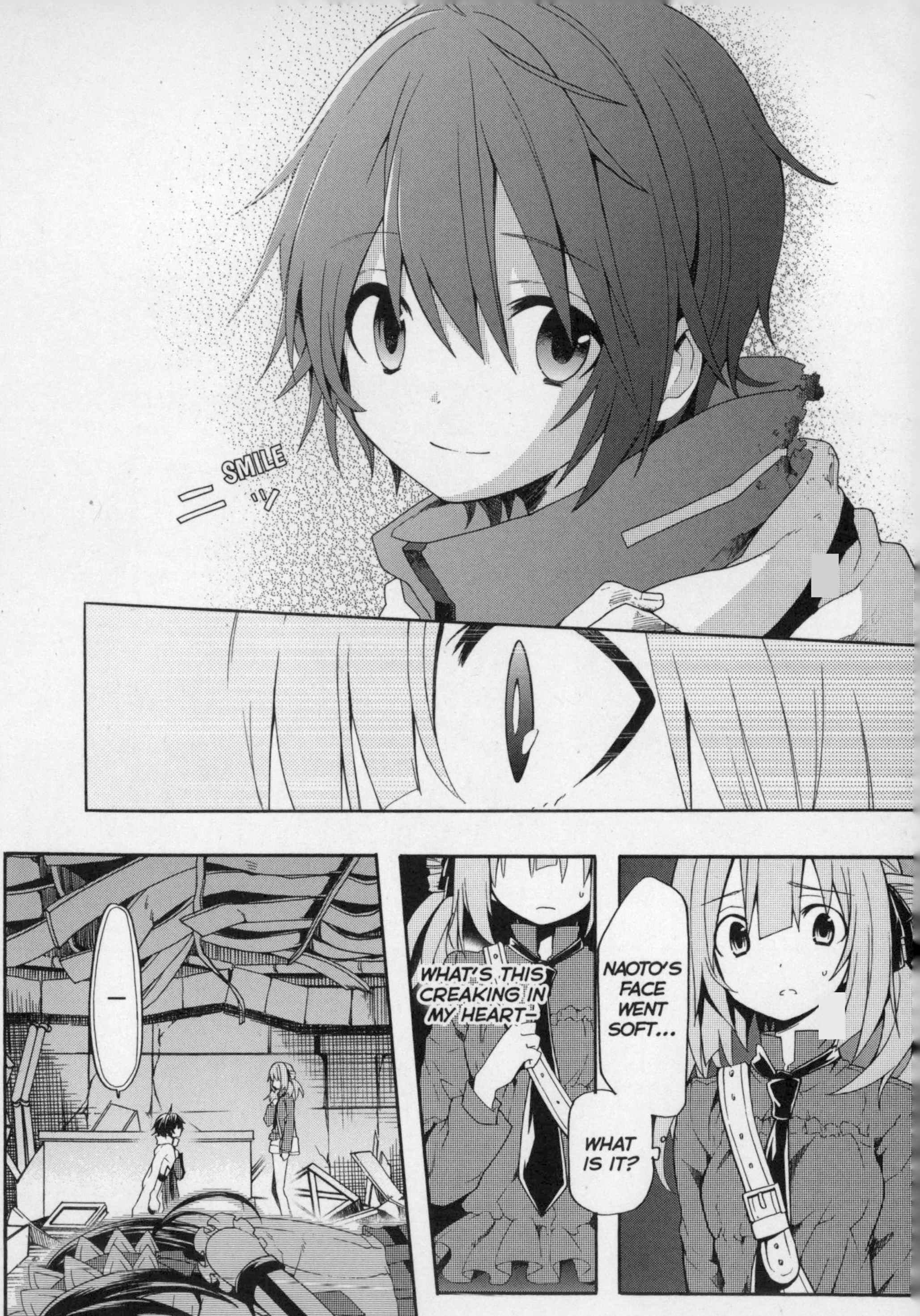
SMILE
ニッ
NAOTO'S FACE WENT SOFT...
WHAT IS IT?
WHAT'S THIS CREAKING IN MY HEART—
—

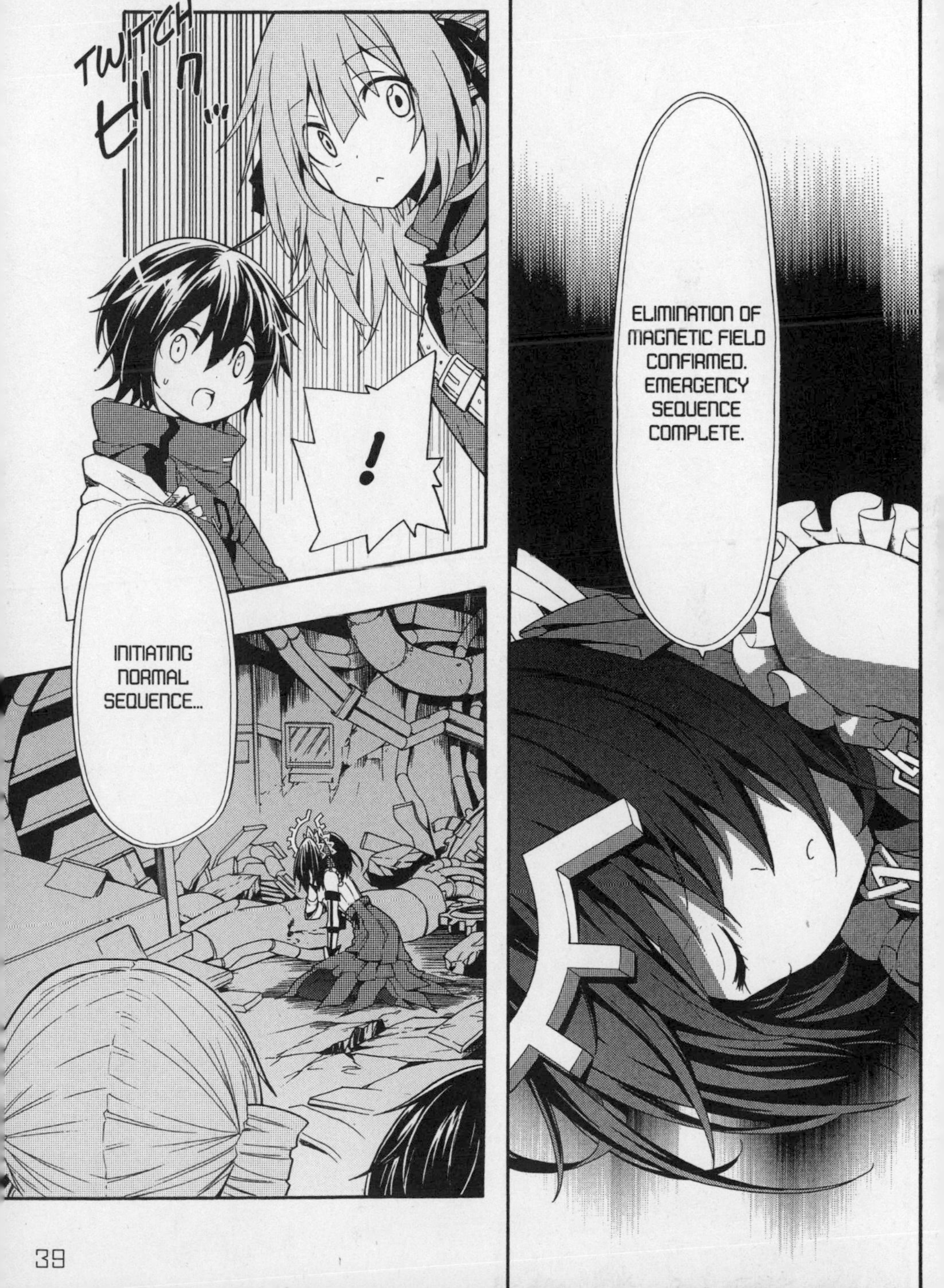
ELIMINATION OF MAGNETIC FIELD CONFIRMED. EMERGENCY SEQUENCE COMPLETE.
TWITCH
ビクッ
!
INITIATING NORMAL SEQUENCE...

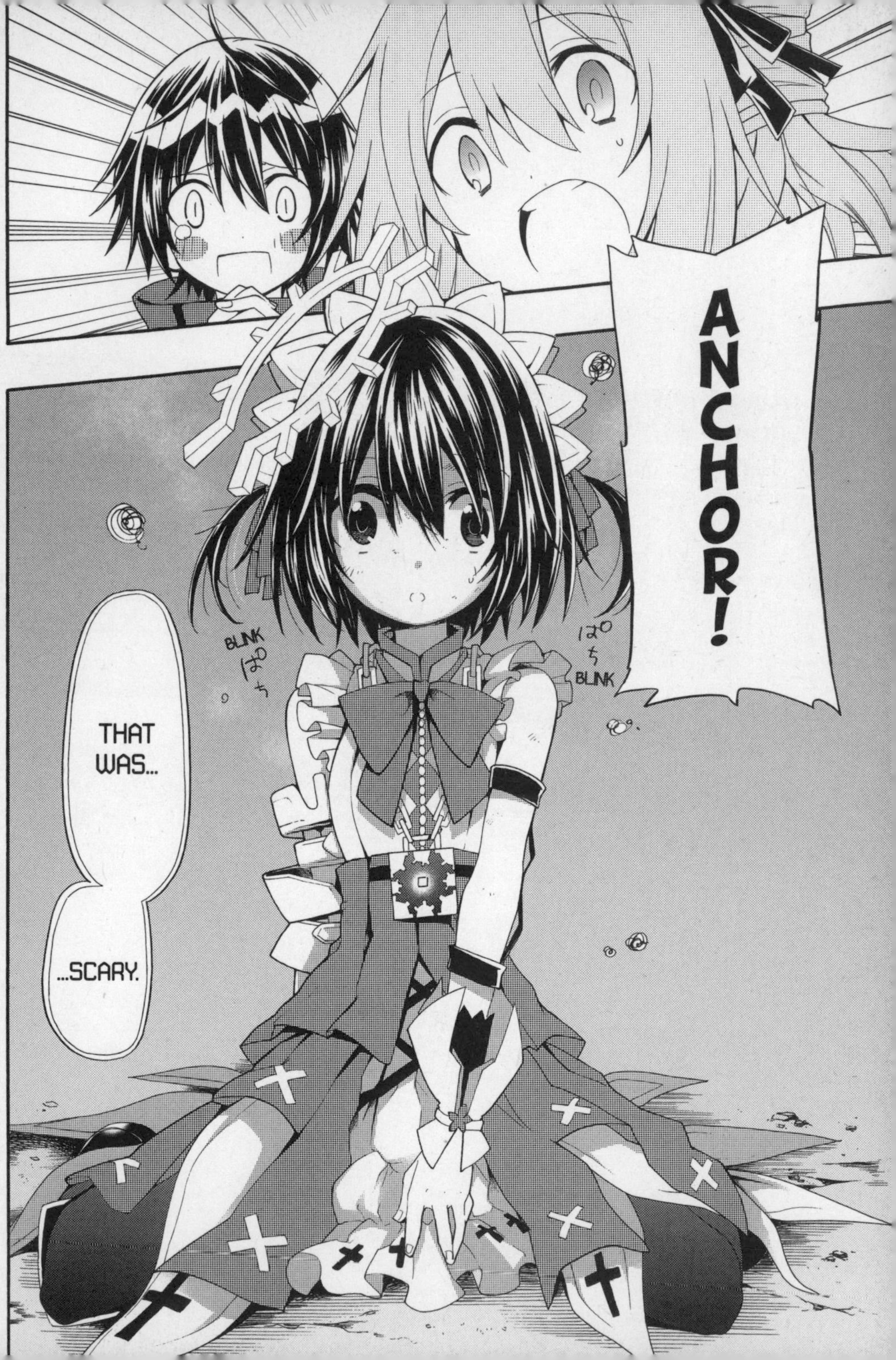
ANCHOR!
ぱち BLINK
BLINK ぱち
THAT WAS...
...SCARY.

CLOCKWORK PLANET

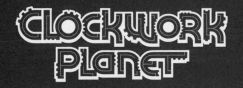

Clockwork Planet

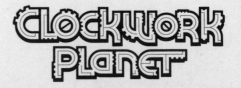

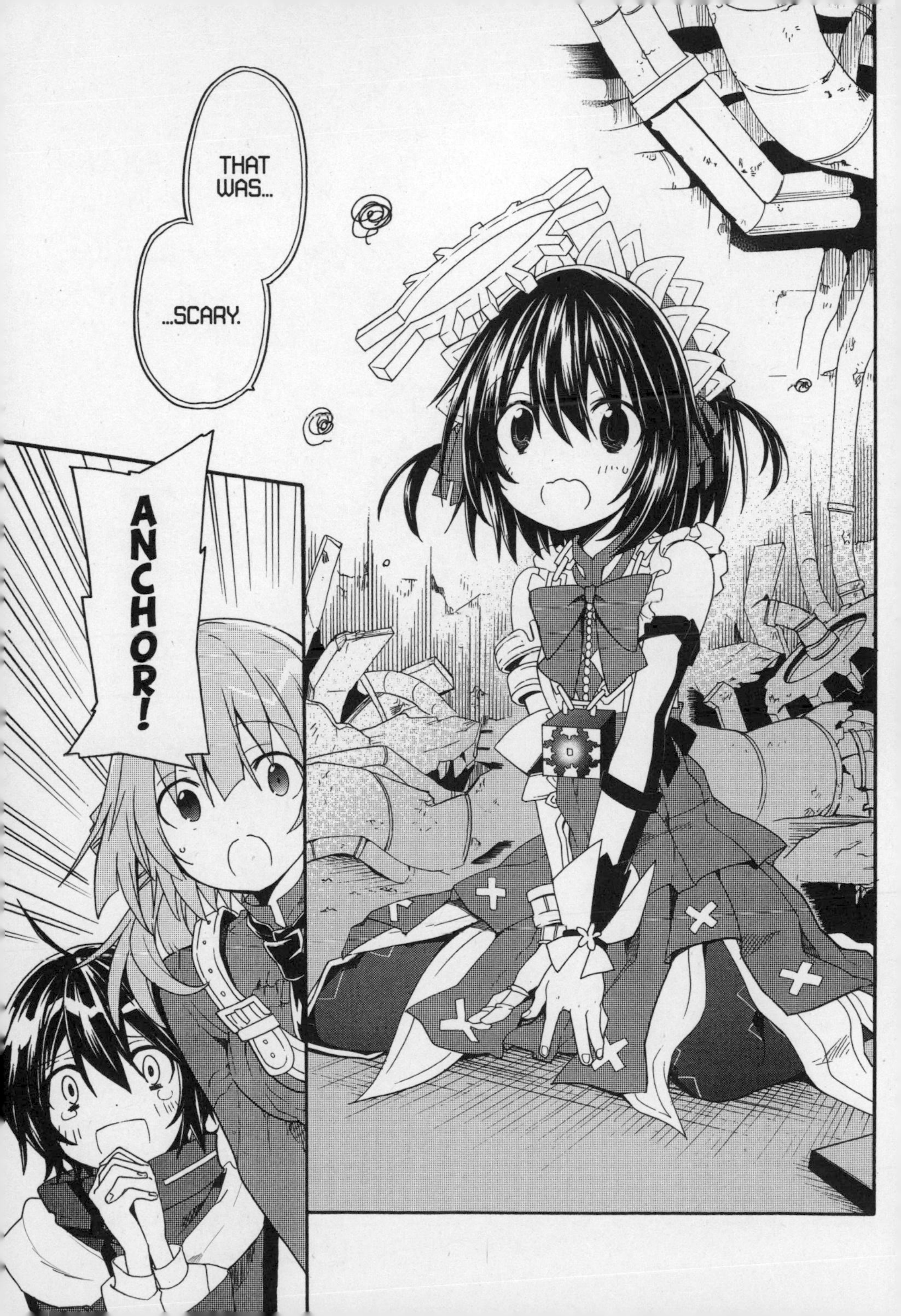
THAT WAS... ...SCARY.
ANCHOR!

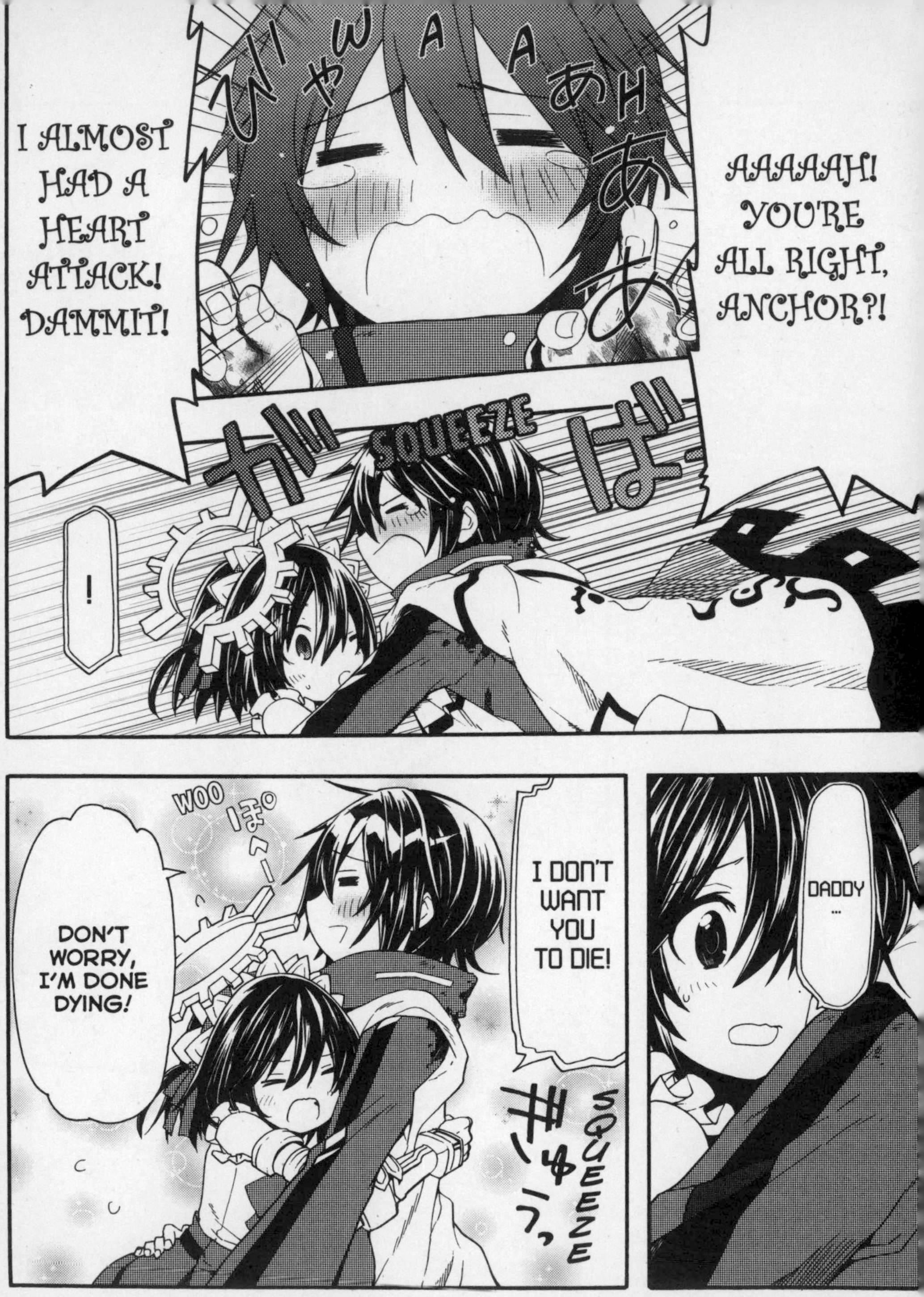
WAAH
AAAAAH! YOU'RE ALL RIGHT, ANCHOR?!
I ALMOST HAD A HEART ATTACK! DAMMIT!
SQUEEZE
!
DADDY ...
I DON'T WANT YOU TO DIE!
SQUEEZE
WOO
DON'T WORRY, I'M DONE DYING!

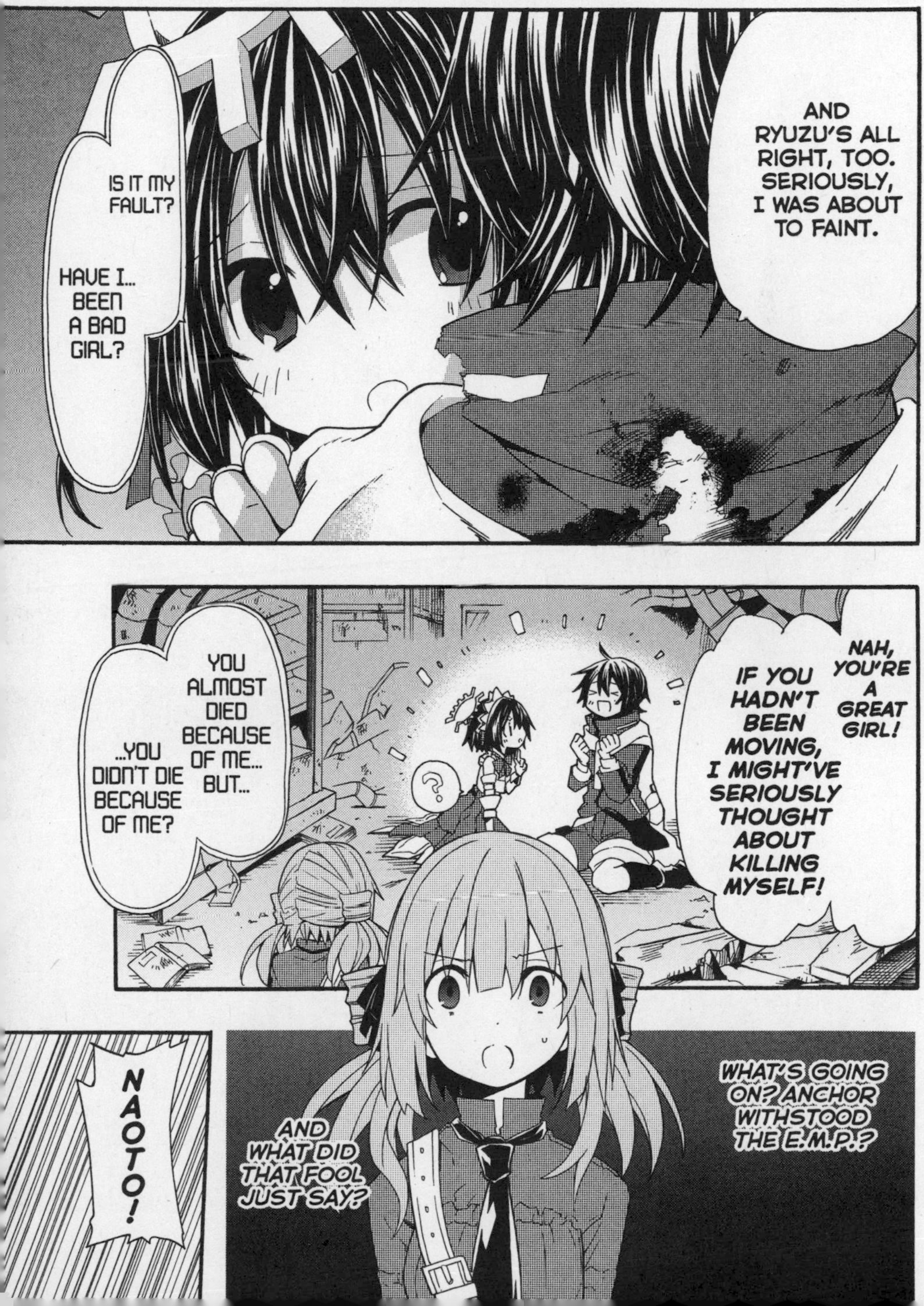
AND RYUZU'S ALL RIGHT, TOO. SERIOUSLY, I WAS ABOUT TO FAINT.
IS IT MY FAULT?
HAVE I... BEEN A BAD GIRL?
NAH, YOU'RE A GREAT GIRL!
IF YOU HADN'T BEEN MOVING, I MIGHT'VE SERIOUSLY THOUGHT ABOUT KILLING MYSELF!
?
YOU ALMOST DIED BECAUSE OF ME... BUT...
...YOU DIDN'T DIE BECAUSE OF ME?
WHAT'S GOING ON? ANCHOR WITHSTOOD THE E.M.P.?
AND WHAT DID THAT FOOL JUST SAY?
NAOTO!

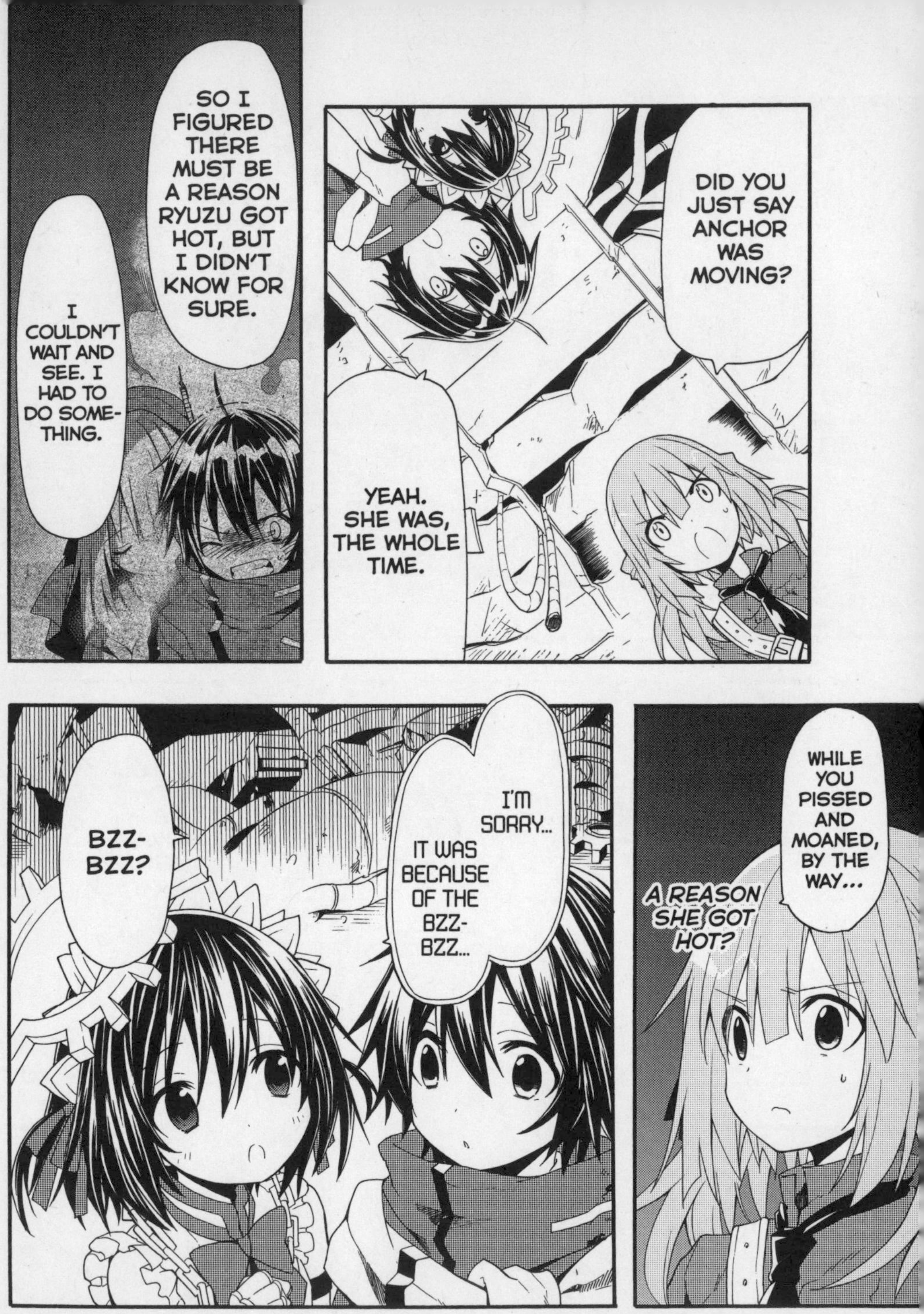
DID YOU JUST SAY ANCHOR WAS MOVING?
YEAH. SHE WAS, THE WHOLE TIME.
SO I FIGURED THERE MUST BE A REASON RYUZU GOT HOT, BUT I DIDN'T KNOW FOR SURE.
I COULDN'T WAIT AND SEE. I HAD TO DO SOME-THING.
WHILE YOU PISSED AND MOANED, BY THE WAY...
A REASON SHE GOT HOT?
I'M SORRY... IT WAS BECAUSE OF THE BZZ-BZZ...
BZZ-BZZ?

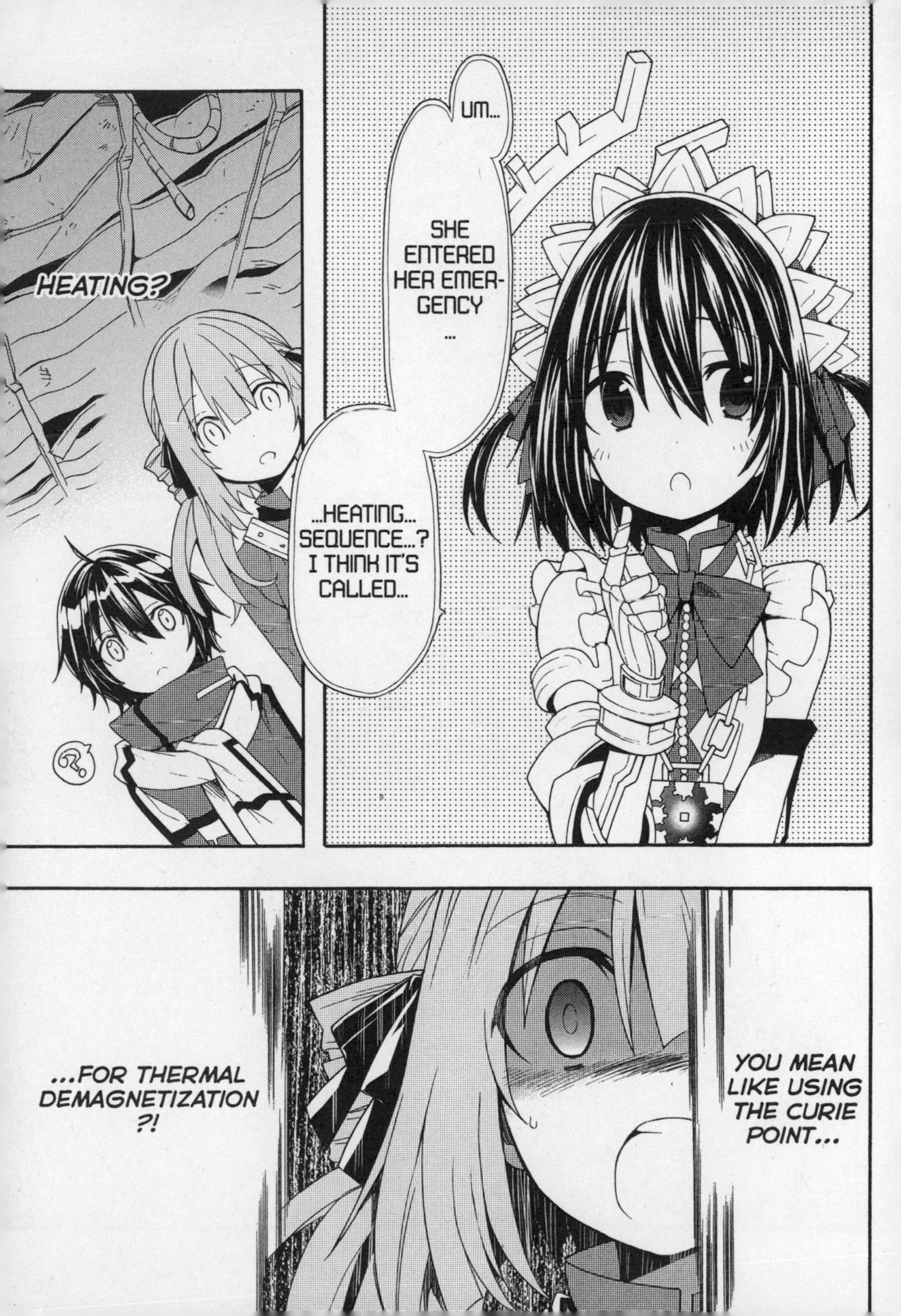
UM...
SHE ENTERED HER EMERGENCY ...
...HEATING... SEQUENCE...? I THINK IT'S CALLED...
HEATING?
YOU MEAN LIKE USING THE CURIE POINT...
...FOR THERMAL DEMAGNETIZATION ?!

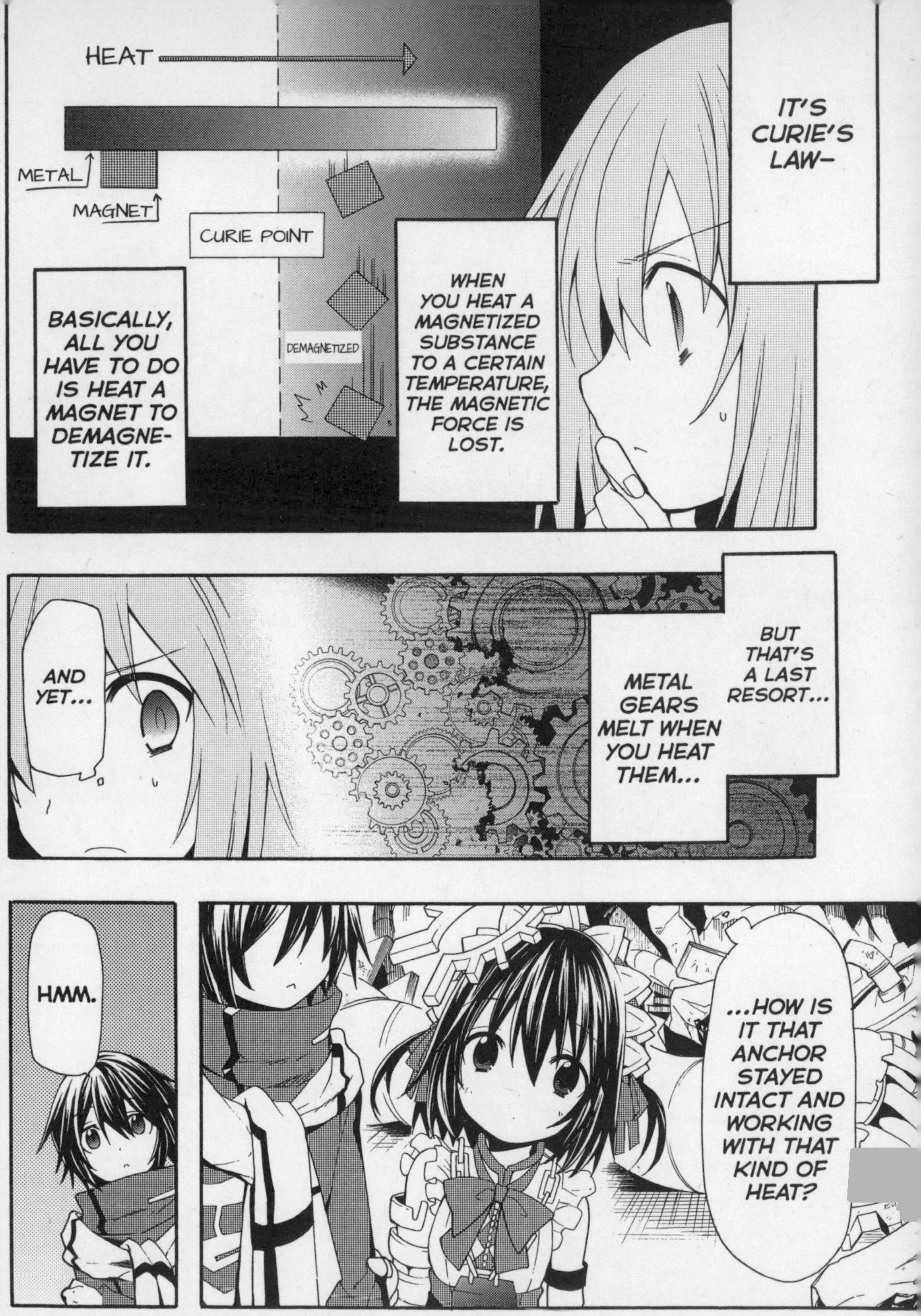

IT'S CURIE'S LAW—
WHEN YOU HEAT A MAGNETIZED SUBSTANCE TO A CERTAIN TEMPERATURE, THE MAGNETIC FORCE IS LOST.
HEAT
METAL
MAGNET
CURIE POINT
DEMAGNETIZED
BASICALLY, ALL YOU HAVE TO DO IS HEAT A MAGNET TO DEMAGNETIZE IT.
BUT THAT'S A LAST RESORT...
METAL GEARS MELT WHEN YOU HEAT THEM...
AND YET...
...HOW IS IT THAT ANCHOR STAYED INTACT AND WORKING WITH THAT KIND OF HEAT?
HMM.

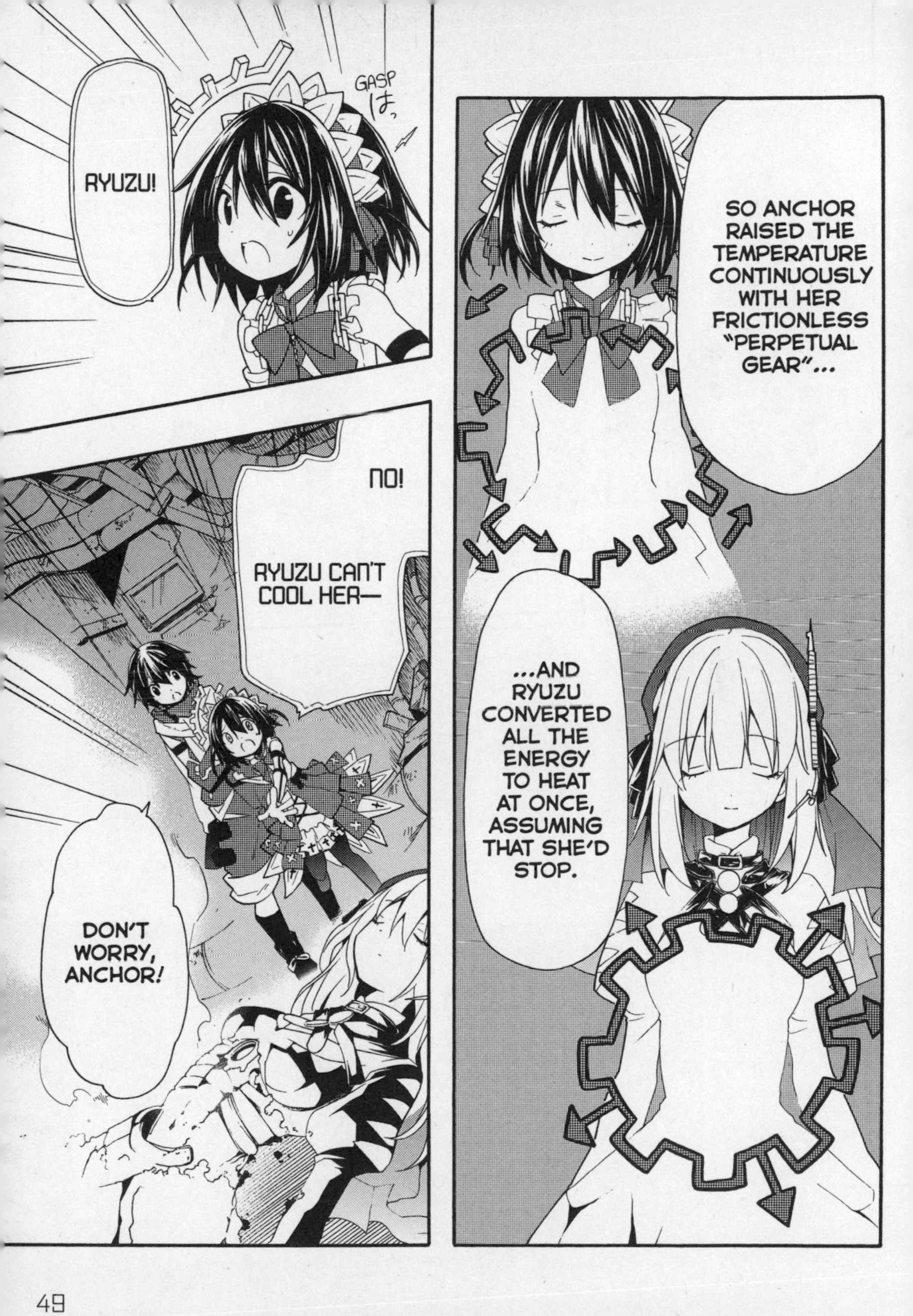
SO ANCHOR RAISED THE TEMPERATURE CONTINUOUSLY WITH HER FRICTIONLESS "PERPETUAL GEAR"...
...AND RYUZU CONVERTED ALL THE ENERGY TO HEAT AT ONCE, ASSUMING THAT SHE'D STOP.
GASP は っ
RYUZU!
NO!
RYUZU CAN'T COOL HER—
DON'T WORRY, ANCHOR!

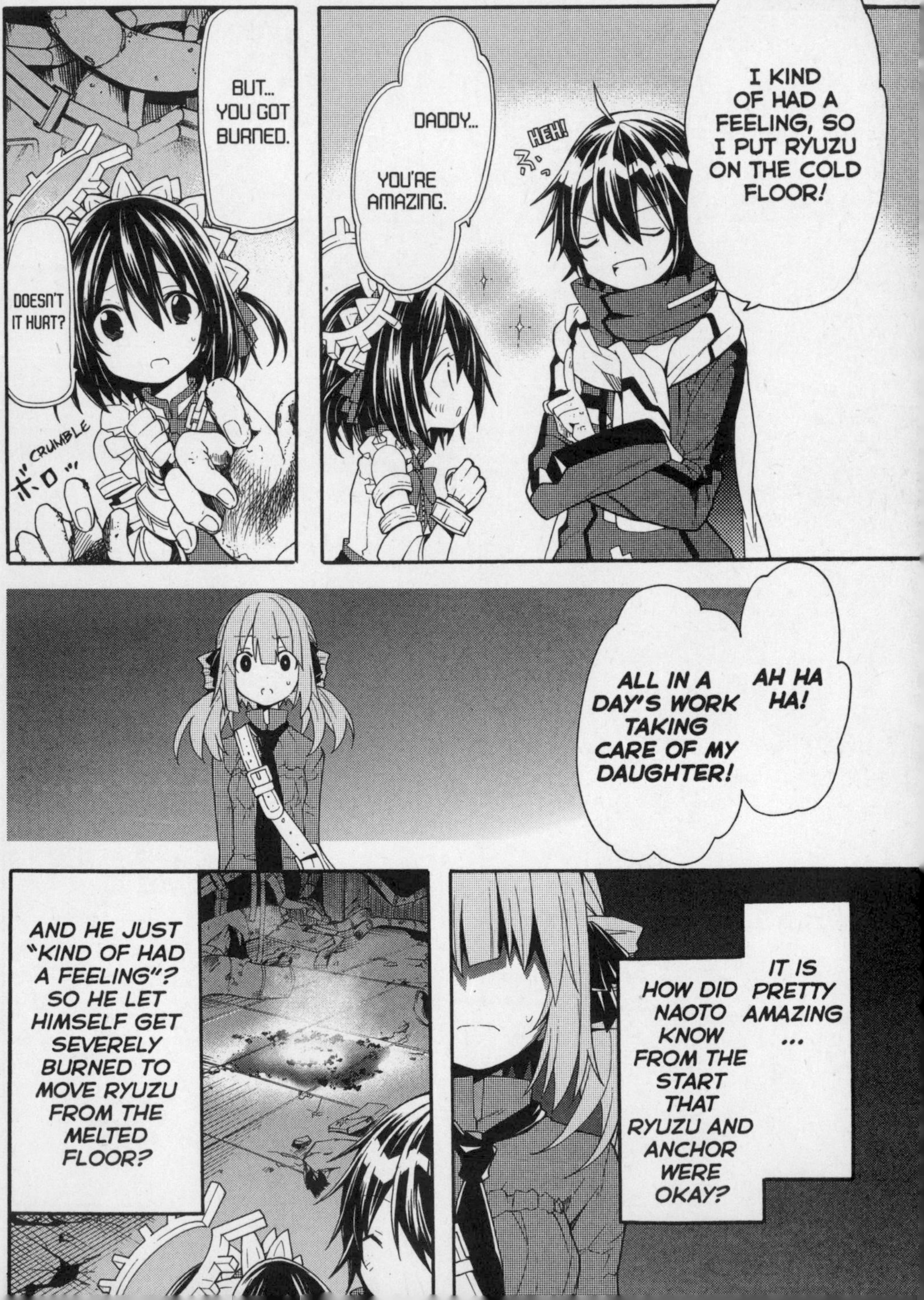
I KIND OF HAD A FEELING, SO I PUT RYUZU ON THE COLD FLOOR!
HEH!
DADDY...
YOU'RE AMAZING.
BUT... YOU GOT BURNED.
DOESN'T IT HURT?
CRUMBLE
AH HA HA!
ALL IN A DAY'S WORK TAKING CARE OF MY DAUGHTER!
IT IS PRETTY AMAZING...
HOW DID NAOTO KNOW FROM THE START THAT RYUZU AND ANCHOR WERE OKAY?
AND HE JUST "KIND OF HAD A FEELING"? SO HE LET HIMSELF GET SEVERELY BURNED TO MOVE RYUZU FROM THE MELTED FLOOR?

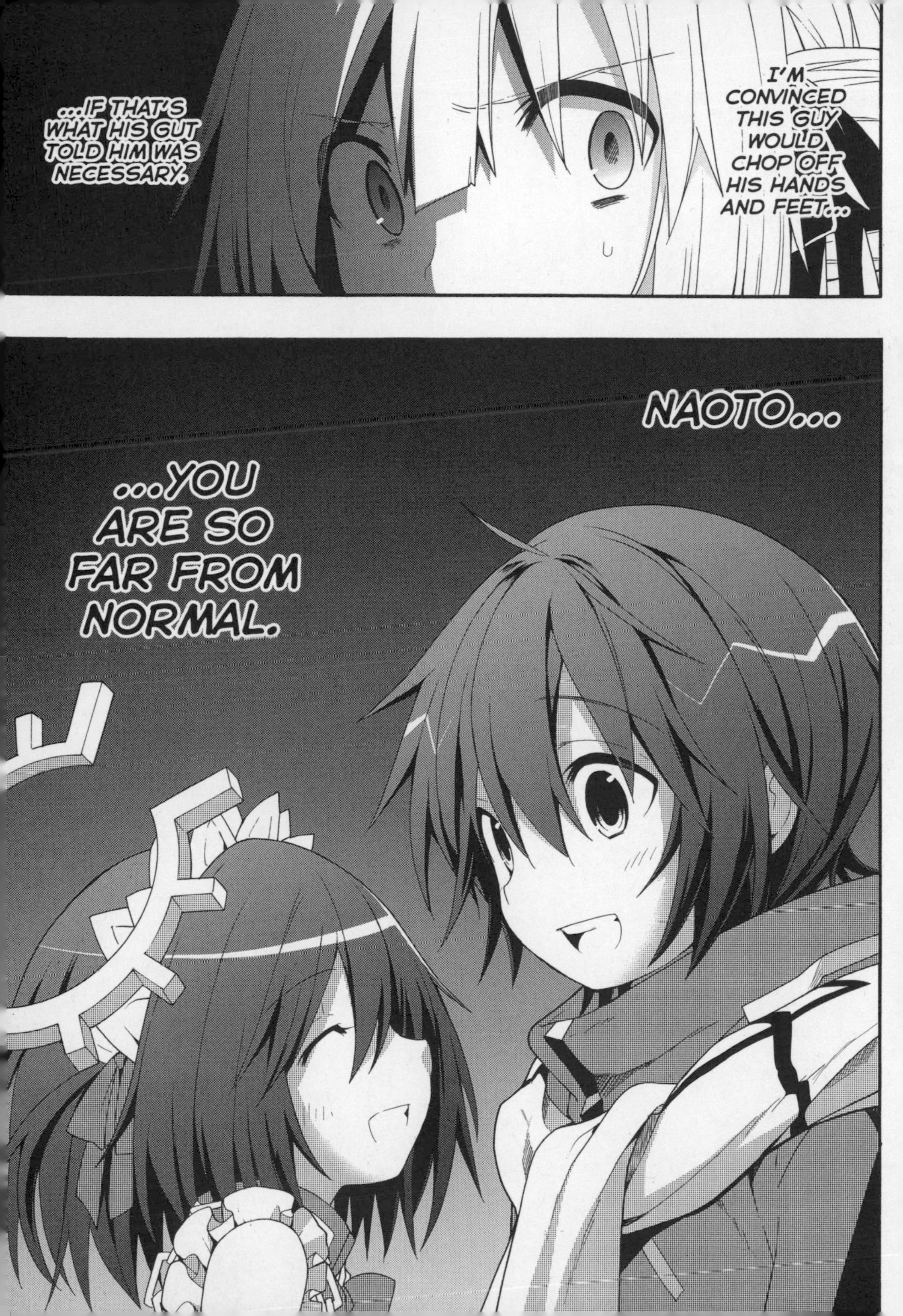
I'M CONVINCED THIS GUY WOULD CHOP OFF HIS HANDS AND FEET...
...IF THAT'S WHAT HIS GUT TOLD HIM WAS NECESSARY.
NAOTO...
...YOU ARE SO FAR FROM NORMAL.

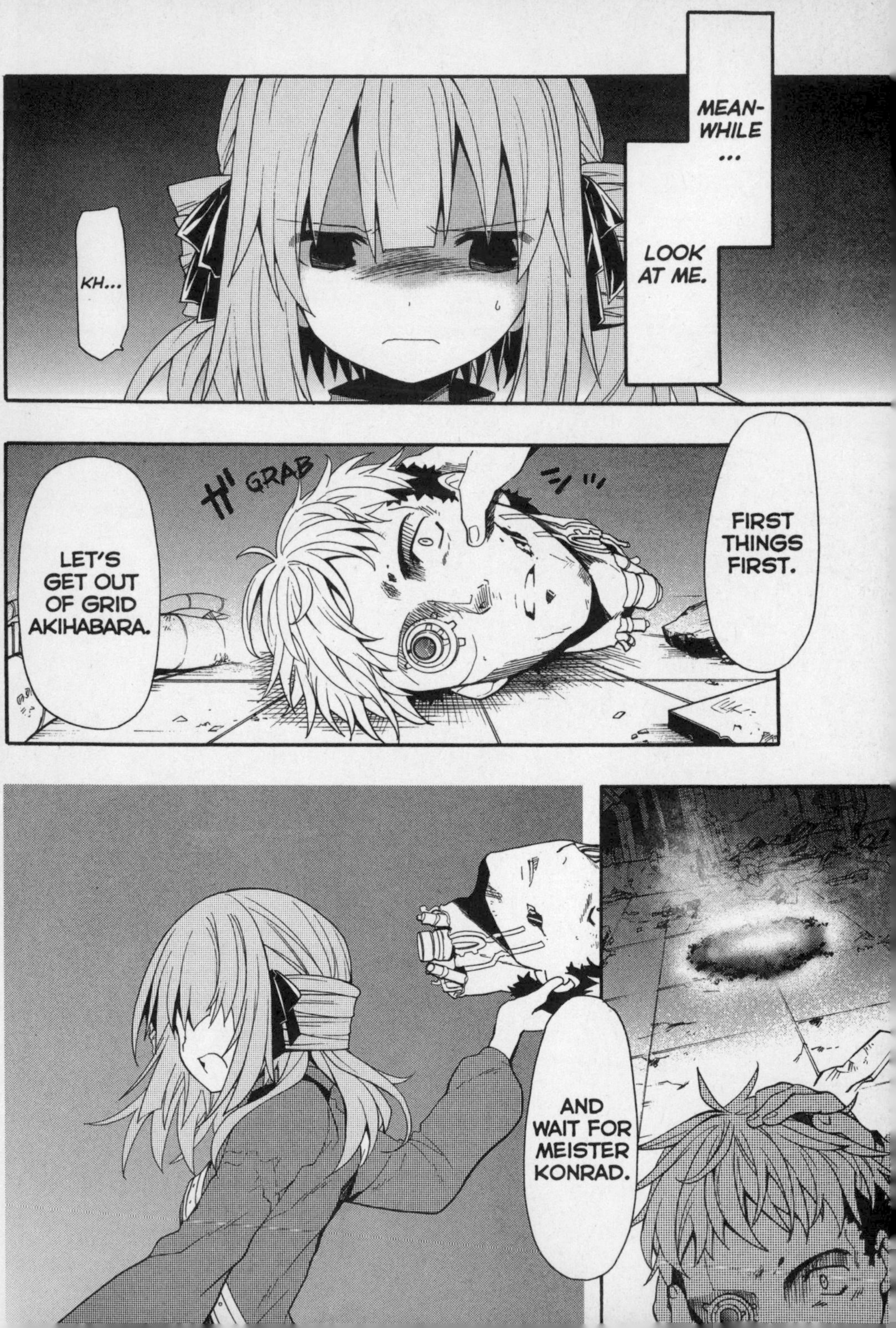
MEAN-WHILE...
LOOK AT ME.
KH...
FIRST THINGS FIRST.
GRAB
LET'S GET OUT OF GRID AKIHABARA.
AND WAIT FOR MEISTER KONRAD.

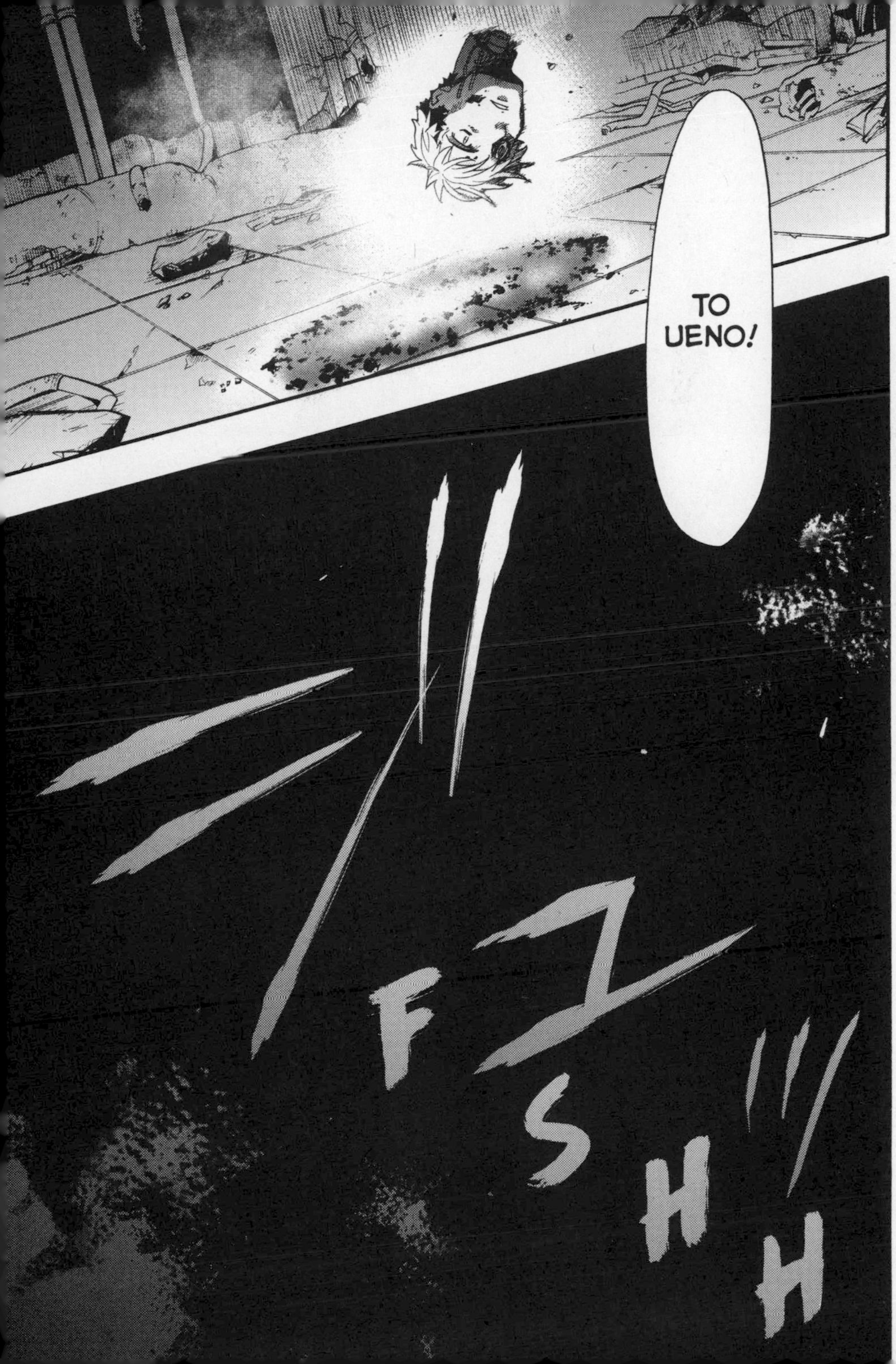
TO UENO!
FSHH

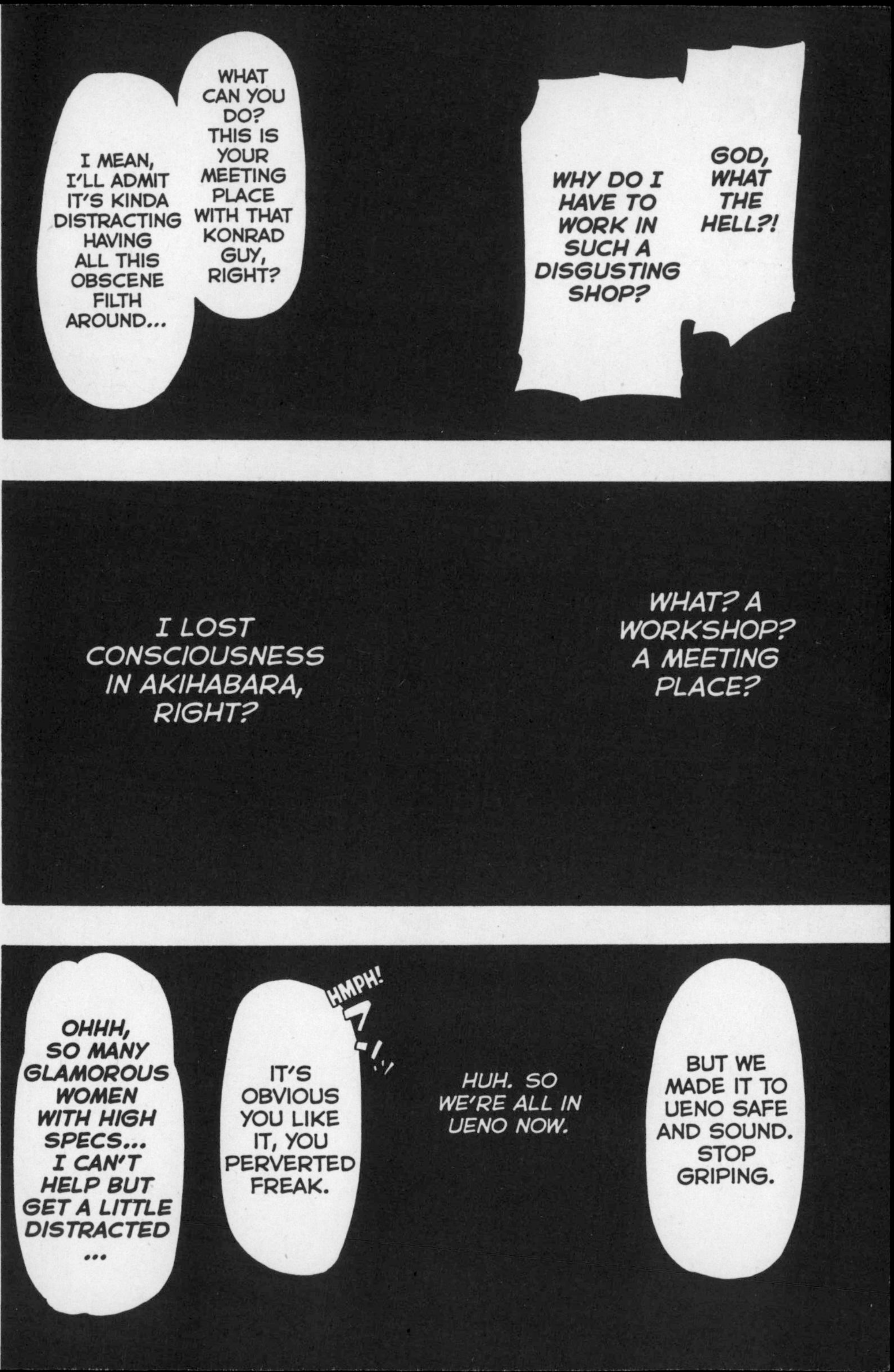
GOD, WHAT THE HELL?!
WHY DO I HAVE TO WORK IN SUCH A DISGUSTING SHOP?
WHAT CAN YOU DO? THIS IS YOUR MEETING PLACE WITH THAT KONRAD GUY, RIGHT?
I MEAN, I'LL ADMIT IT'S KINDA DISTRACTING HAVING ALL THIS OBSCENE FILTH AROUND...
WHAT? A WORKSHOP? A MEETING PLACE?
I LOST CONSCIOUSNESS IN AKIHABARA, RIGHT?
BUT WE MADE IT TO UENO SAFE AND SOUND. STOP GRIPING.
HUH. SO WE'RE ALL IN UENO NOW.
HMPH!
IT'S OBVIOUS YOU LIKE IT, YOU PERVERTED FREAK.
OHHH, SO MANY GLAMOROUS WOMEN WITH HIGH SPECS... I CAN'T HELP BUT GET A LITTLE DISTRACTED ...

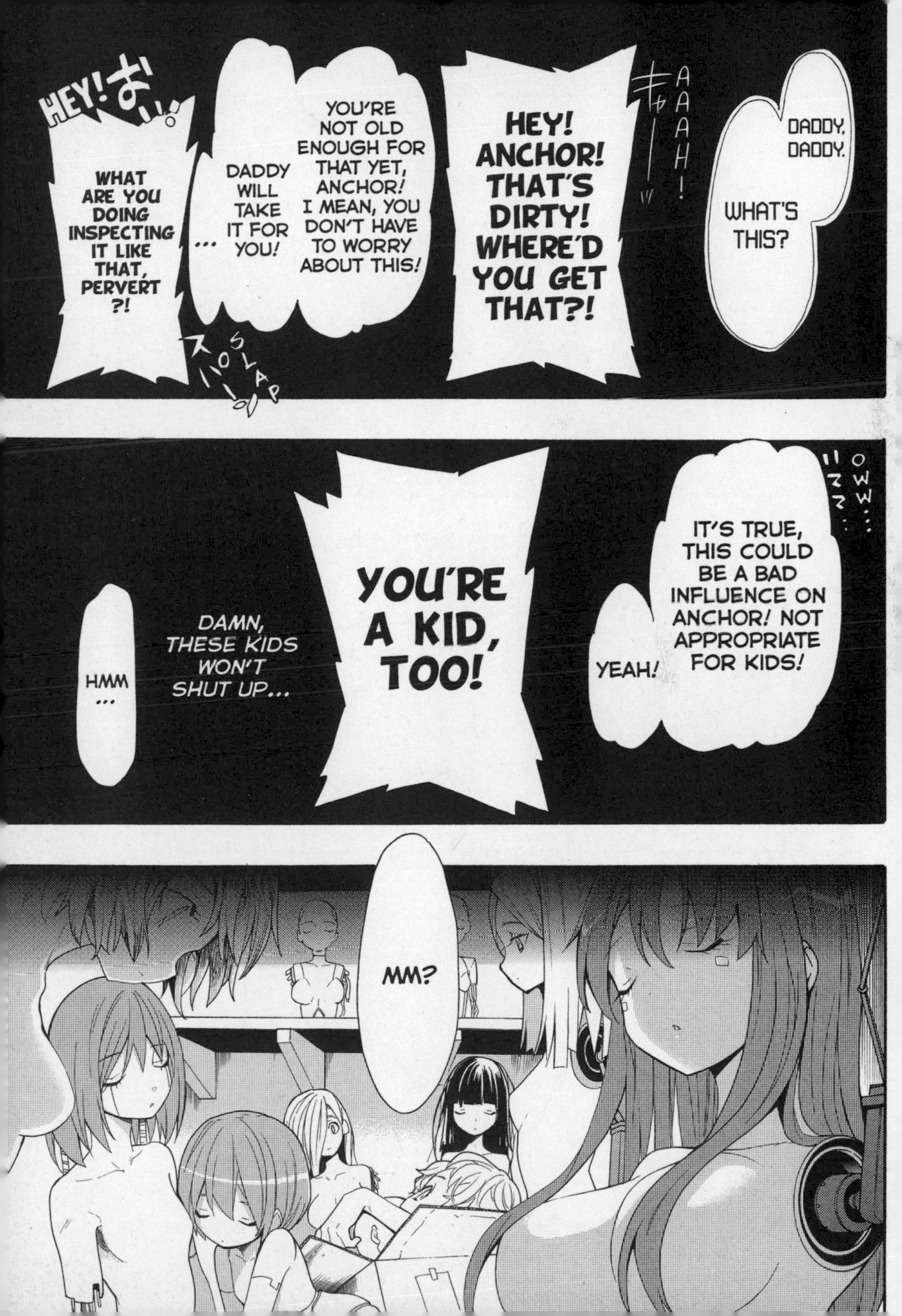
DADDY, DADDY.
WHAT'S THIS?
AAAAH!
HEY! ANCHOR! THAT'S DIRTY! WHERE'D YOU GET THAT?!
YOU'RE NOT OLD ENOUGH FOR THAT YET, ANCHOR! I MEAN, YOU DON'T HAVE TO WORRY ABOUT THIS!
DADDY WILL TAKE IT FOR YOU!
...
HEY!
WHAT ARE YOU DOING INSPECTING IT LIKE THAT, PERVERT?!
SLAP
OWW...
IT'S TRUE, THIS COULD BE A BAD INFLUENCE ON ANCHOR! NOT APPROPRIATE FOR KIDS!
YEAH!
YOU'RE A KID, TOO!
DAMN, THESE KIDS WON'T SHUT UP...
HMM...
MM?

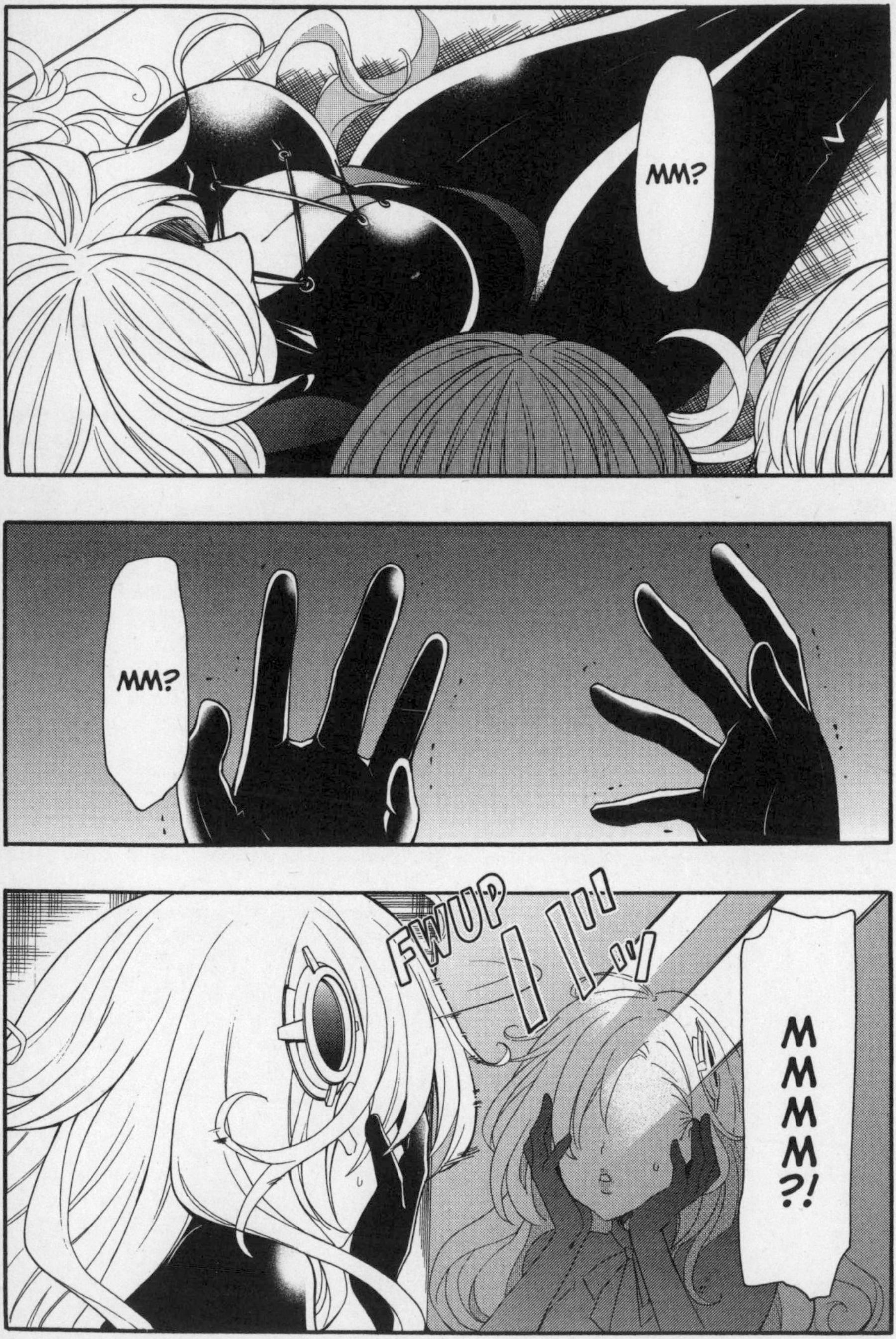
MM?
MM?
FWUP
MMMM?!

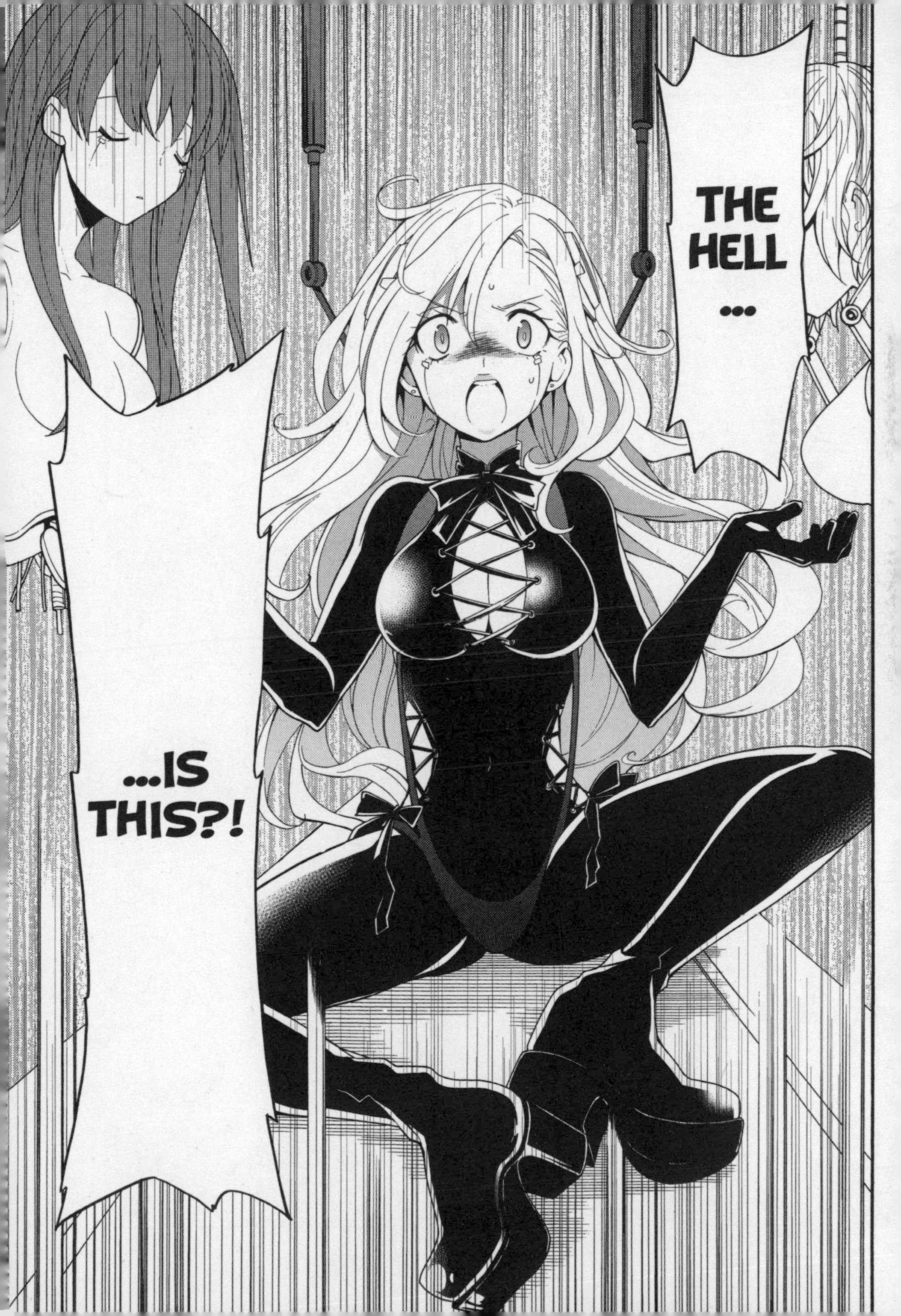
THE HELL ...
...IS THIS?!

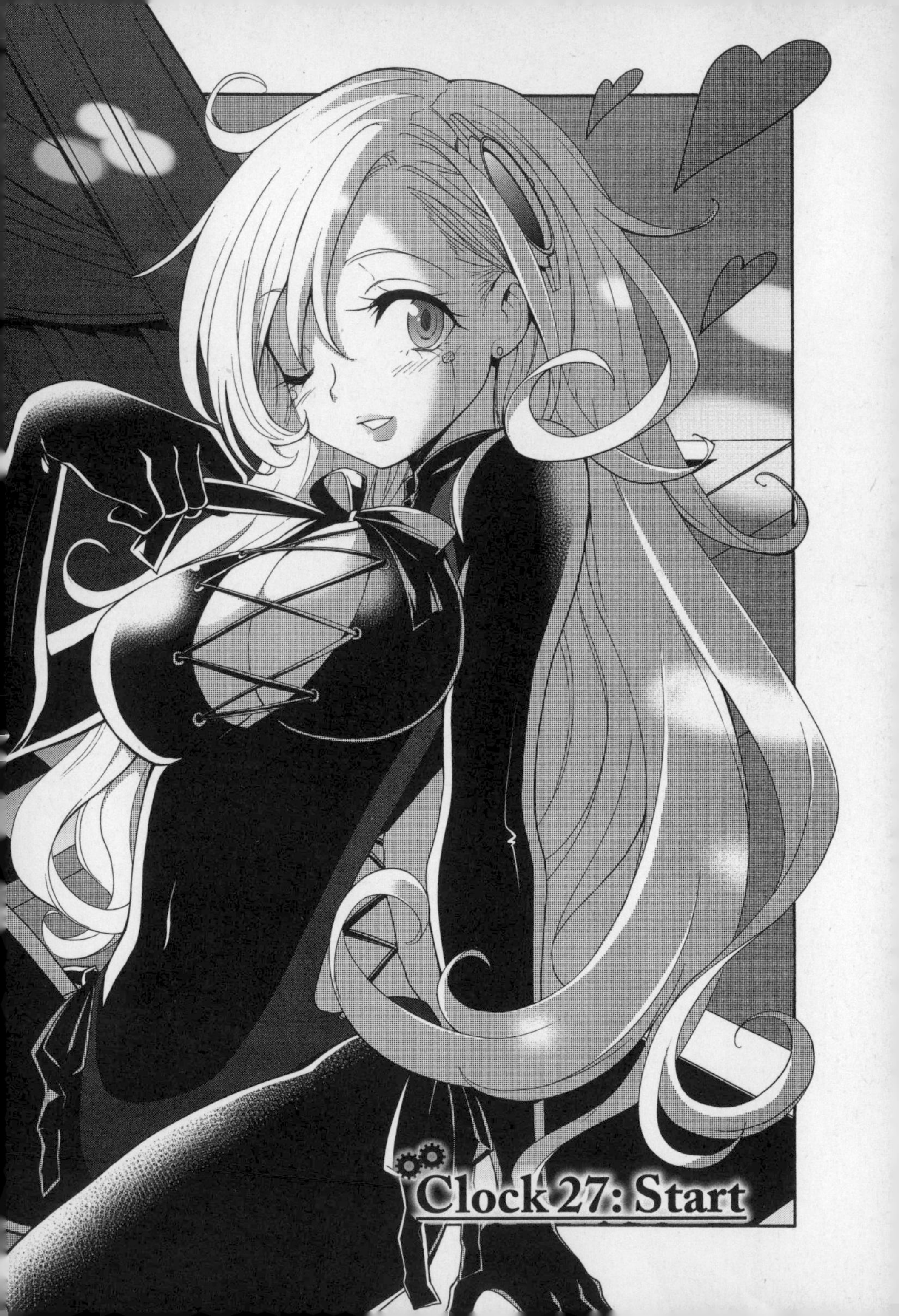
Clock 27: Start

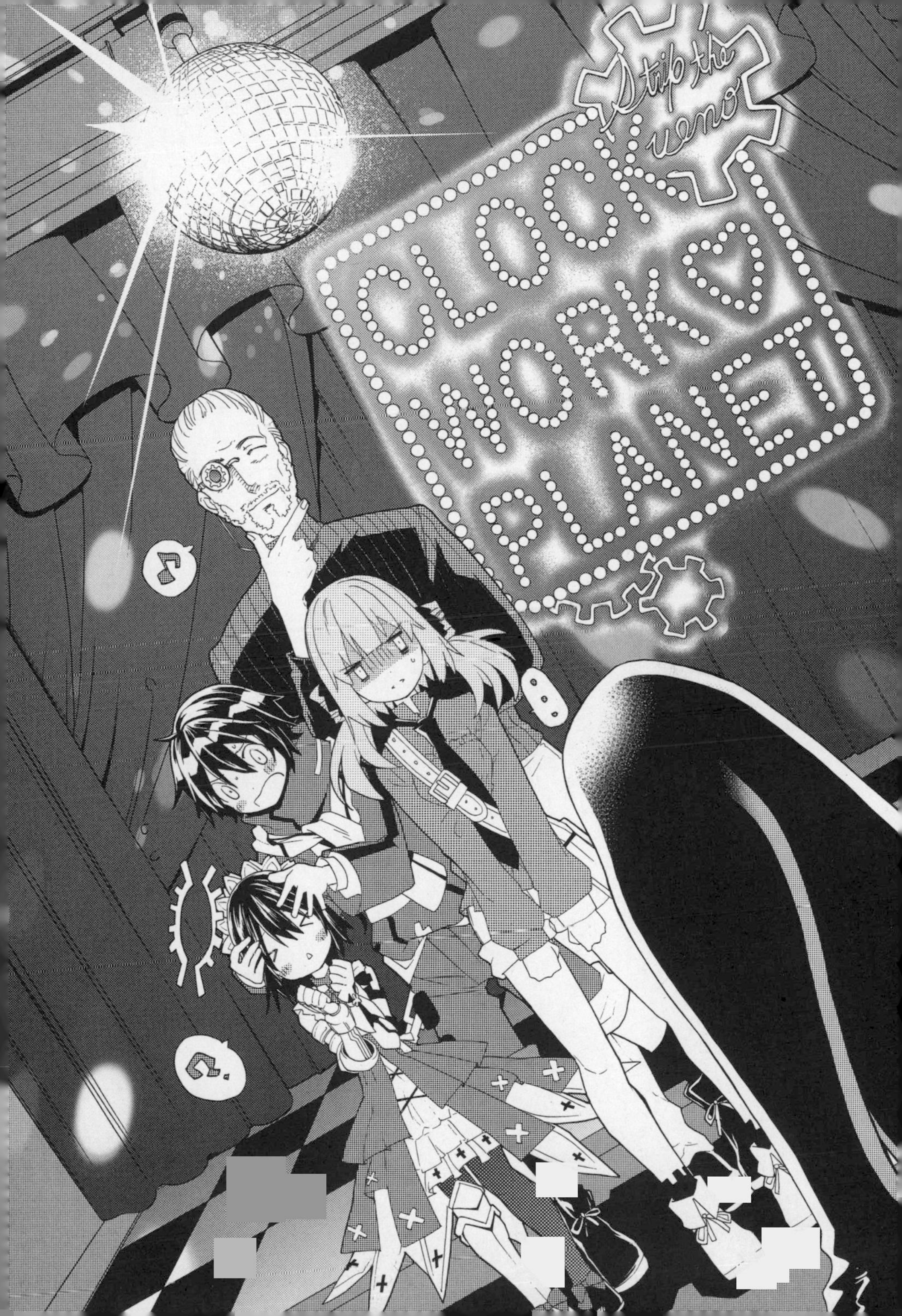
Strip the ueno
CLOCK
WORK
PLANET

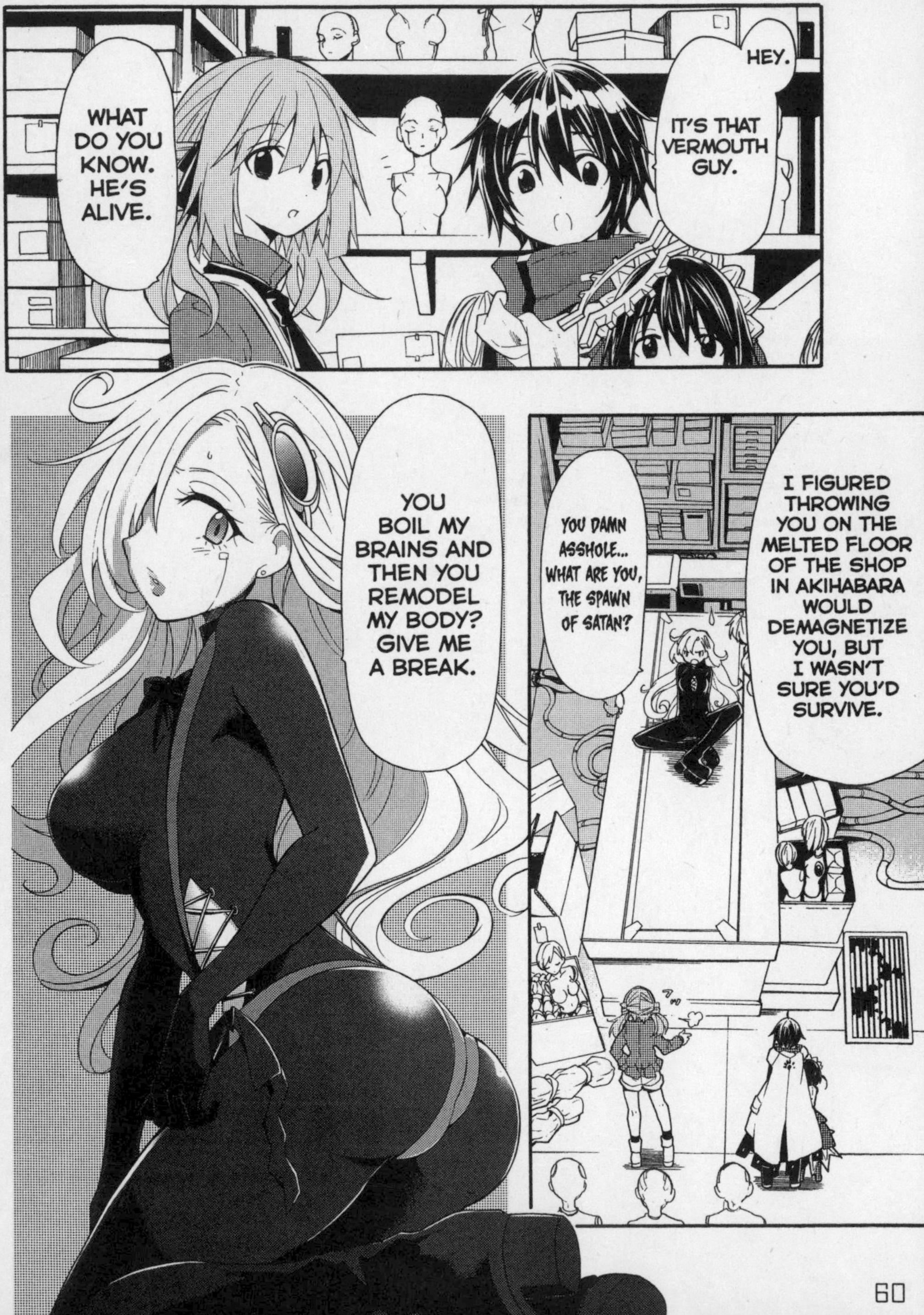
HEY.
IT'S THAT VERMOUTH GUY.
WHAT DO YOU KNOW. HE'S ALIVE.
I FIGURED THROWING YOU ON THE MELTED FLOOR OF THE SHOP IN AKIHABARA WOULD DEMAGNETIZE YOU, BUT I WASN'T SURE YOU'D SURVIVE.
YOU DAMN ASSHOLE... WHAT ARE YOU, THE SPAWN OF SATAN?
YOU BOIL MY BRAINS AND THEN YOU REMODEL MY BODY? GIVE ME A BREAK.

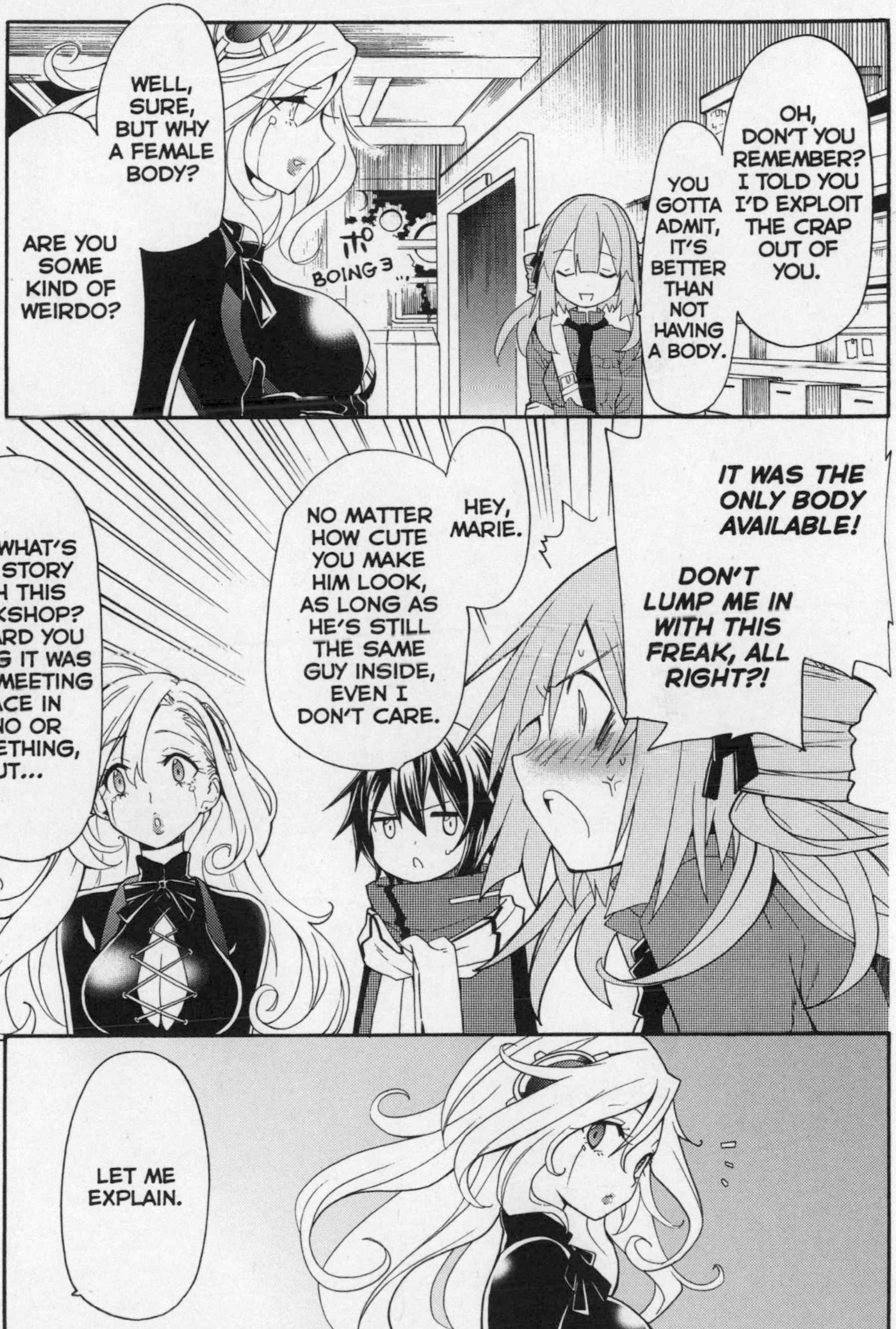
OH, DON'T YOU REMEMBER? I TOLD YOU I'D EXPLOIT THE CRAP OUT OF YOU.
YOU GOTTA ADMIT, IT'S BETTER THAN NOT HAVING A BODY.
BOING
WELL, SURE, BUT WHY A FEMALE BODY?
ARE YOU SOME KIND OF WEIRDO?
IT WAS THE ONLY BODY AVAILABLE!
DON'T LUMP ME IN WITH THIS FREAK, ALL RIGHT?!
HEY, MARIE.
NO MATTER HOW CUTE YOU MAKE HIM LOOK, AS LONG AS HE'S STILL THE SAME GUY INSIDE, EVEN I DON'T CARE.
BUT WHAT'S THE STORY WITH THIS WORKSHOP? I HEARD YOU SAYING IT WAS YOUR MEETING PLACE IN UENO OR SOMETHING, BUT...
LET ME EXPLAIN.

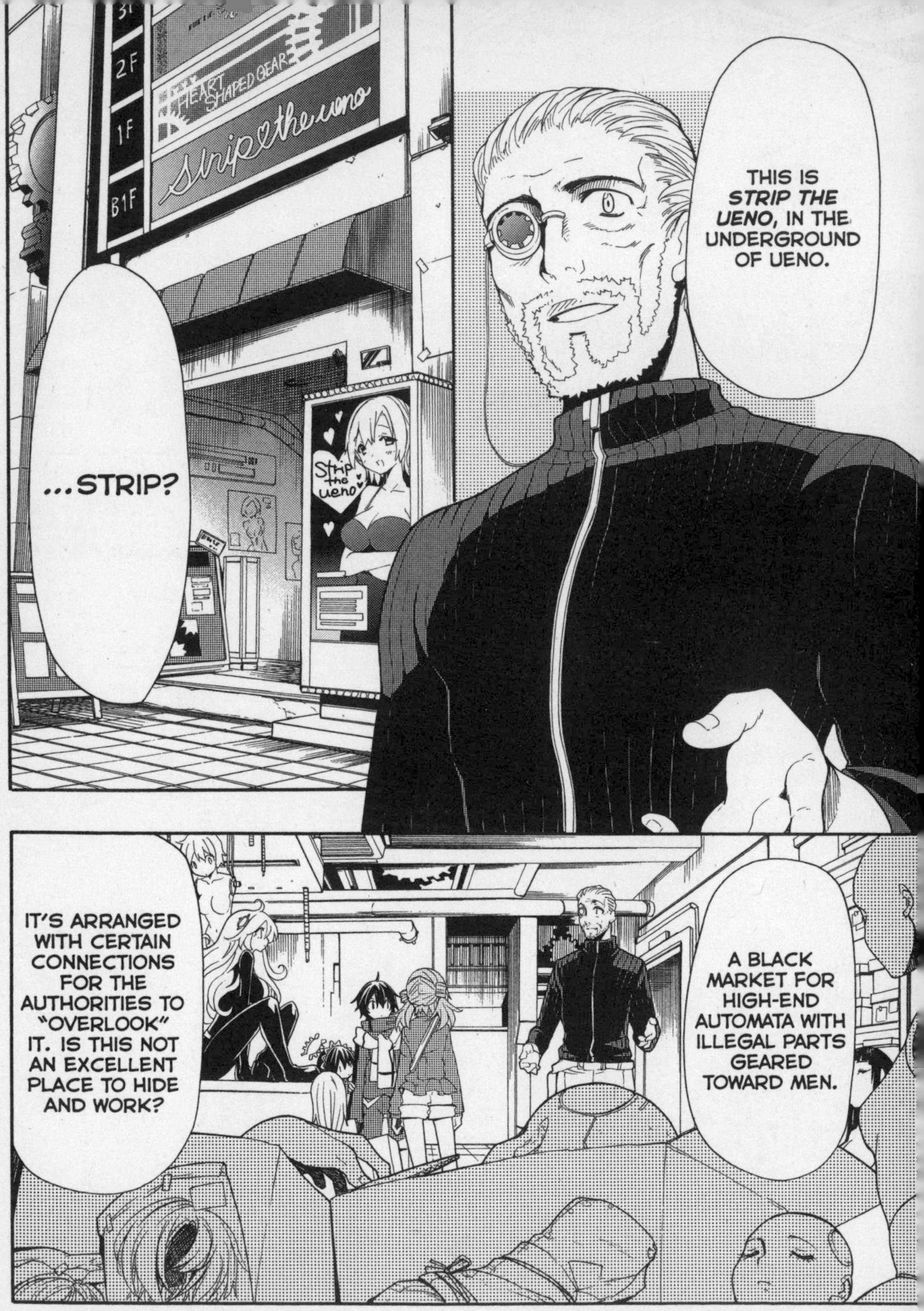
B1F
1F
2F
HEART SHAPED GEAR
strip the ueno
THIS IS *STRIP THE UENO*, IN THE UNDERGROUND OF UENO.
Strip the ueno
...STRIP?
A BLACK MARKET FOR HIGH-END AUTOMATA WITH ILLEGAL PARTS GEARED TOWARD MEN.
IT'S ARRANGED WITH CERTAIN CONNECTIONS FOR THE AUTHORITIES TO "OVERLOOK" IT. IS THIS NOT AN EXCELLENT PLACE TO HIDE AND WORK?

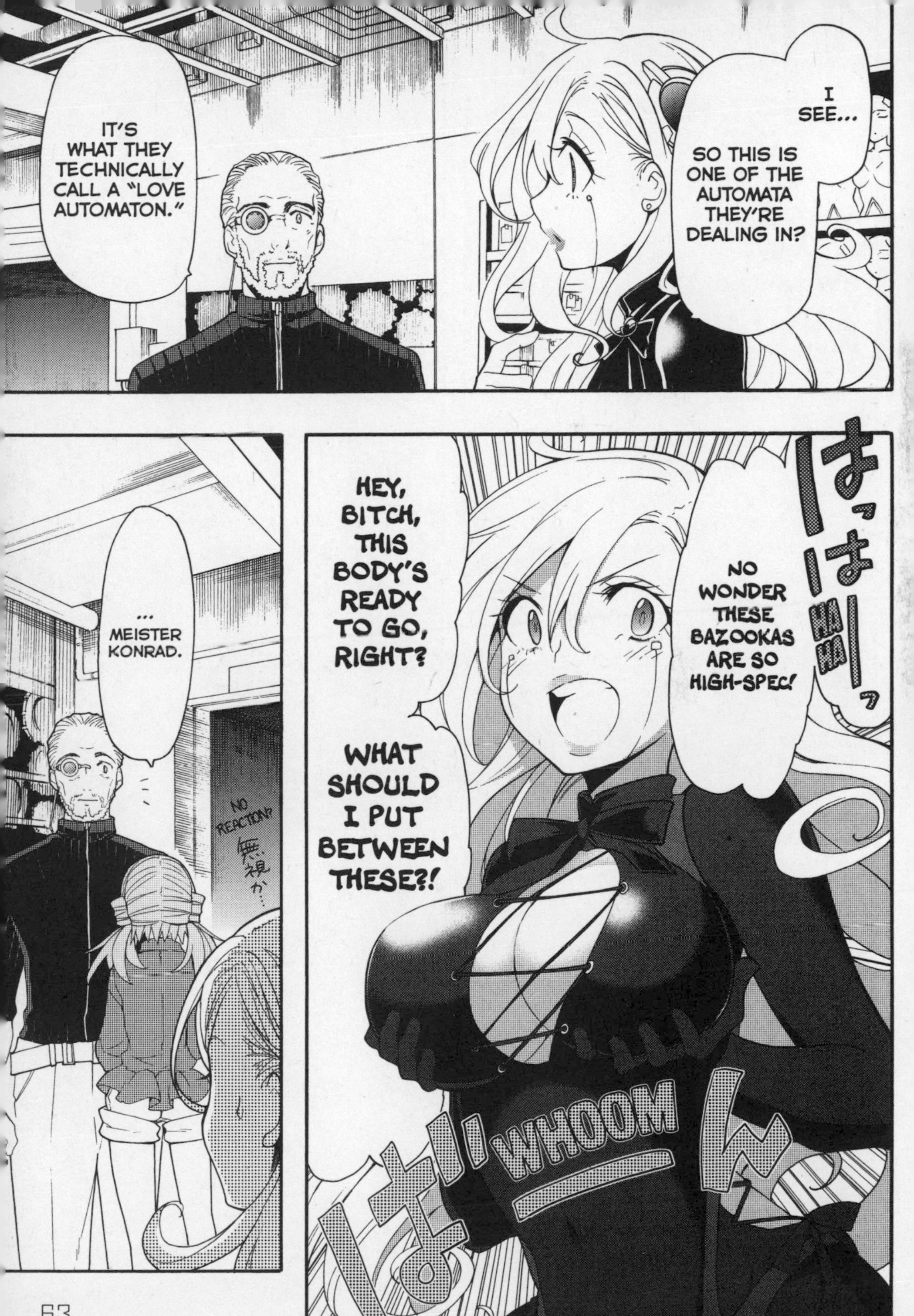
I SEE...
SO THIS IS ONE OF THE AUTOMATA THEY'RE DEALING IN?
IT'S WHAT THEY TECHNICALLY CALL A "LOVE AUTOMATON."
はっはーっ
HA HA
NO WONDER THESE BAZOOKAS ARE SO HIGH-SPEC!
HEY, BITCH, THIS BODY'S READY TO GO, RIGHT?
WHAT SHOULD I PUT BETWEEN THESE?!
ばいん
WHOOM
... MEISTER KONRAD.
NO REACTION?
無視か…

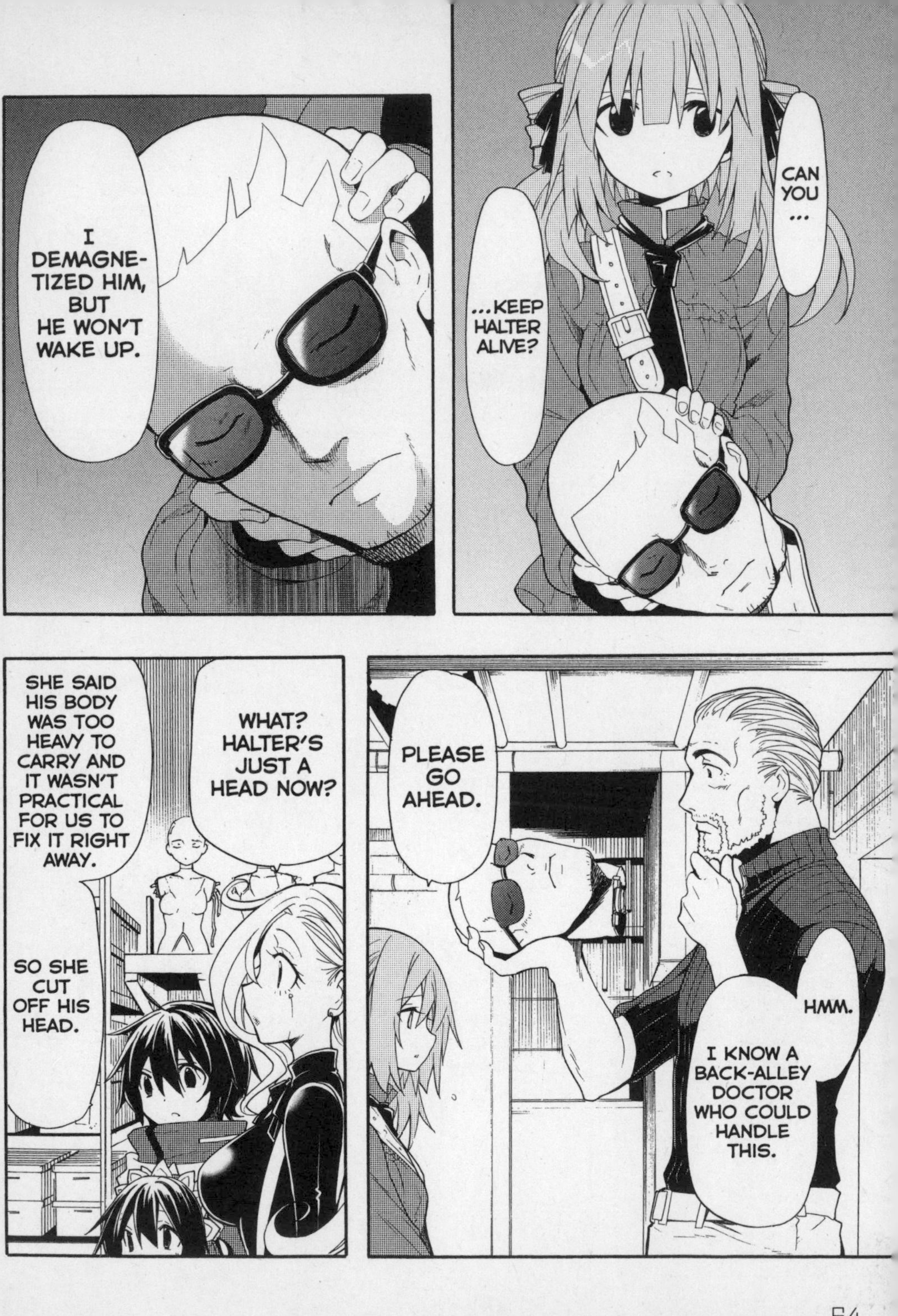
CAN YOU ...
...KEEP HALTER ALIVE?
I DEMAGNETIZED HIM, BUT HE WON'T WAKE UP.
PLEASE GO AHEAD.
HMM.
I KNOW A BACK-ALLEY DOCTOR WHO COULD HANDLE THIS.
WHAT? HALTER'S JUST A HEAD NOW?
SHE SAID HIS BODY WAS TOO HEAVY TO CARRY AND IT WASN'T PRACTICAL FOR US TO FIX IT RIGHT AWAY.
SO SHE CUT OFF HIS HEAD.

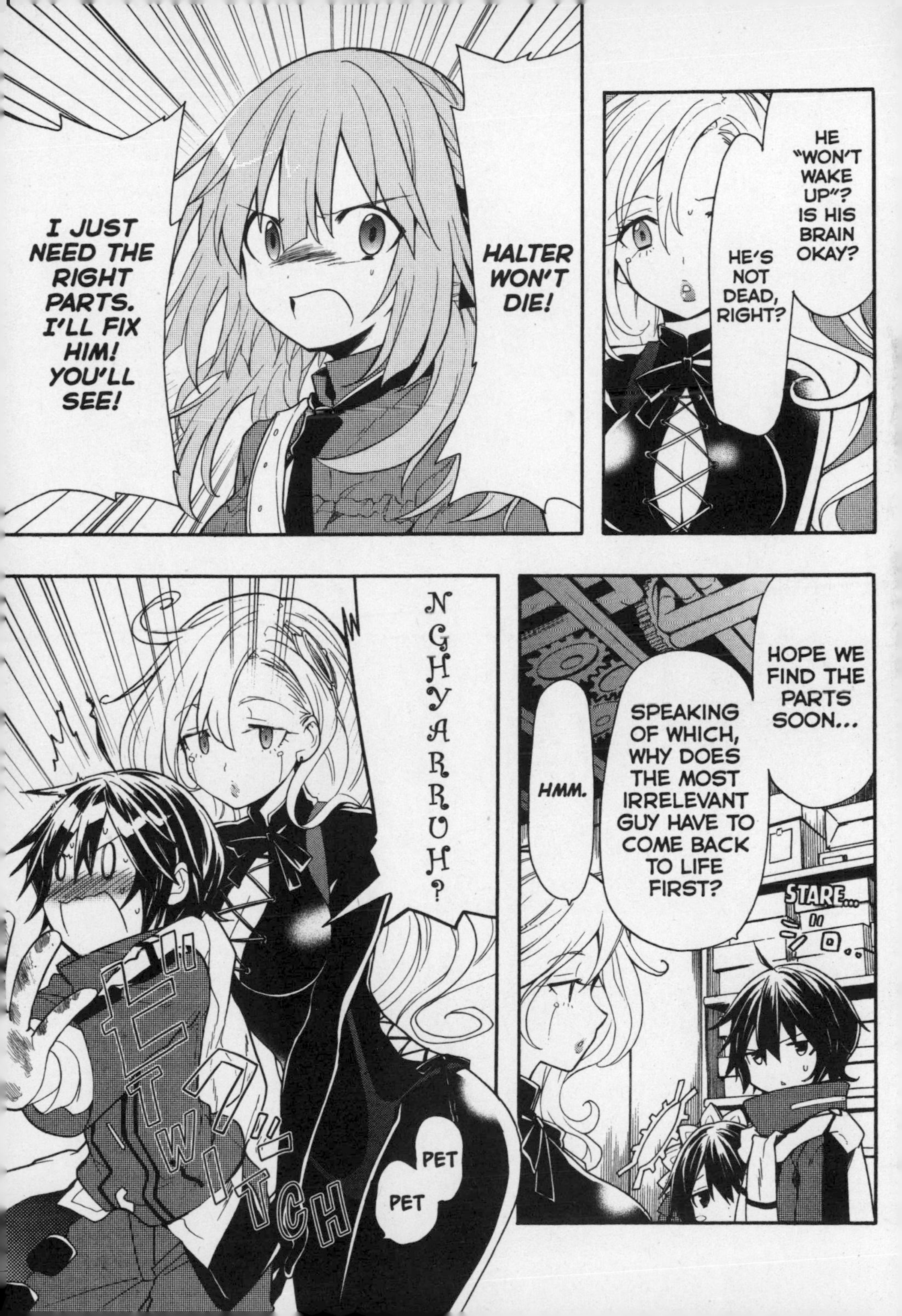
HE "WON'T WAKE UP"? IS HIS BRAIN OKAY?
HE'S NOT DEAD, RIGHT?
HALTER WON'T DIE!
I JUST NEED THE RIGHT PARTS. I'LL FIX HIM! YOU'LL SEE!
HOPE WE FIND THE PARTS SOON...
SPEAKING OF WHICH, WHY DOES THE MOST IRRELEVANT GUY HAVE TO COME BACK TO LIFE FIRST?
HMM.
STARE...
NGHYARRUH?
TWITCH
PET
PET

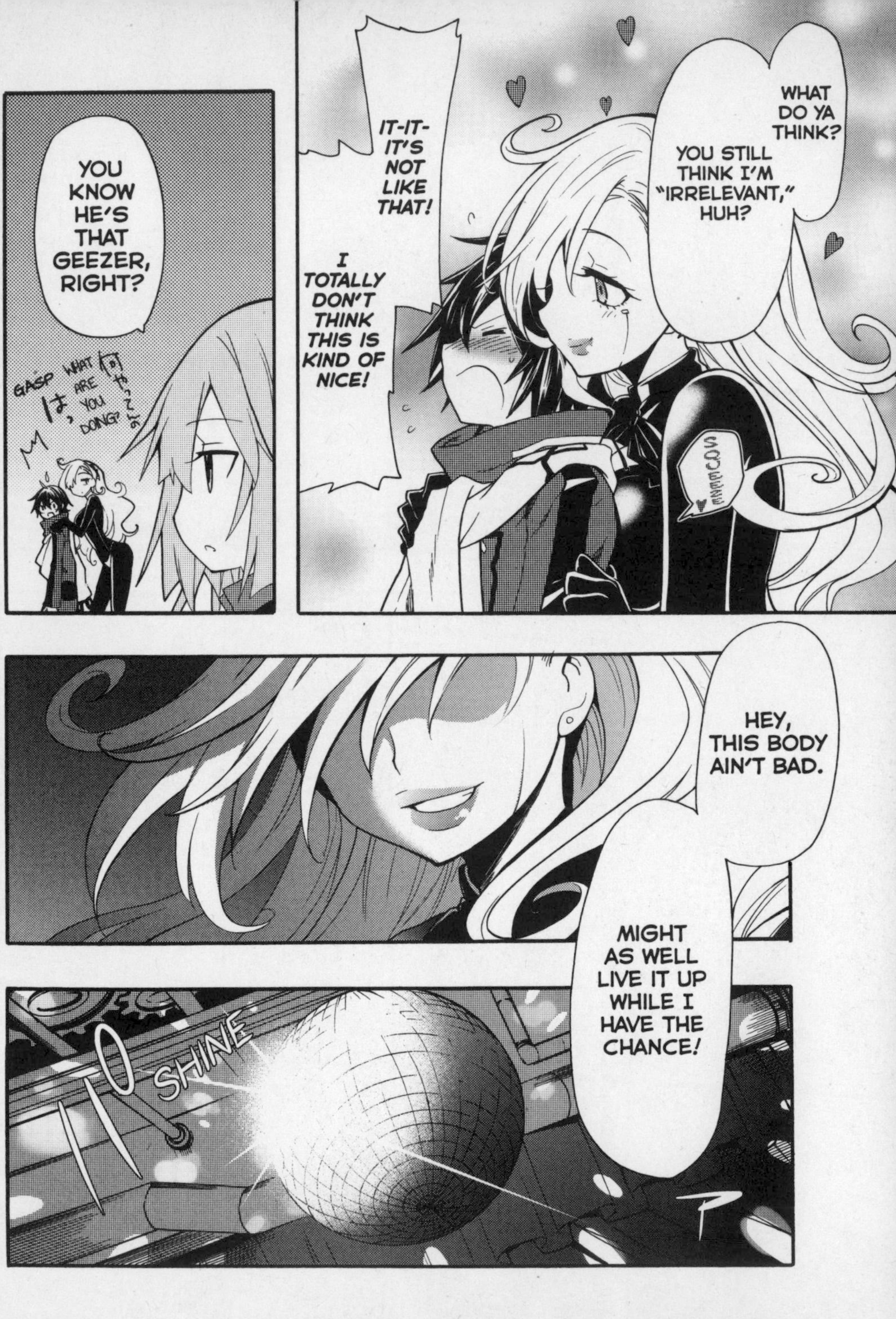
WHAT DO YA THINK?
YOU STILL THINK I'M "IRRELEVANT," HUH?
IT-IT-IT'S NOT LIKE THAT!
I TOTALLY DON'T THINK THIS IS KIND OF NICE!
SQUEEZE
YOU KNOW HE'S THAT GEEZER, RIGHT?
GASP
WHAT ARE YOU DOING?
HEY, THIS BODY AIN'T BAD.
MIGHT AS WELL LIVE IT UP WHILE I HAVE THE CHANCE!
SHINE

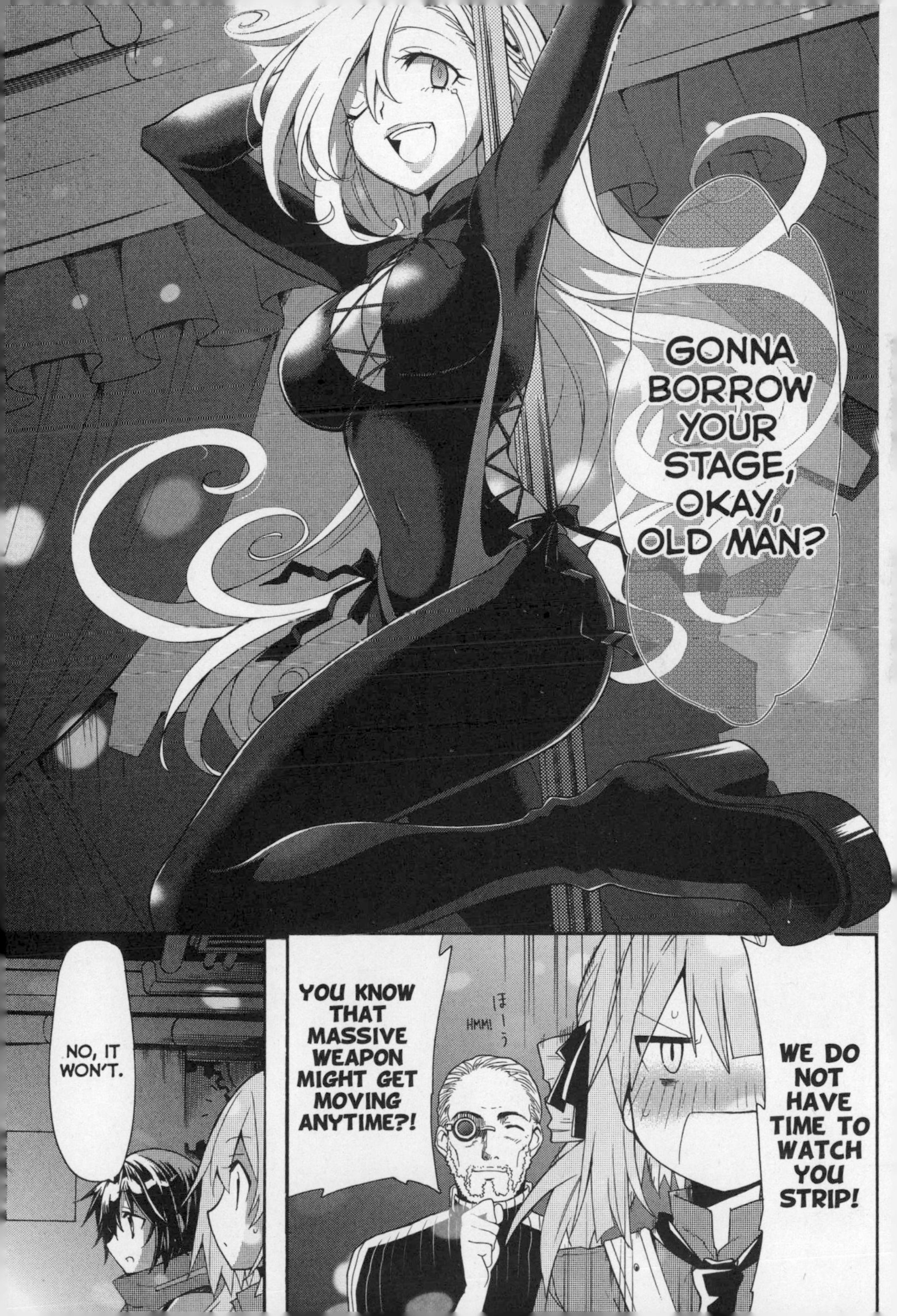
GONNA BORROW YOUR STAGE, OKAY, OLD MAN?
WE DO NOT HAVE TIME TO WATCH YOU STRIP!
YOU KNOW THAT MASSIVE WEAPON MIGHT GET MOVING ANYTIME?!
HMM!
NO, IT WON'T.

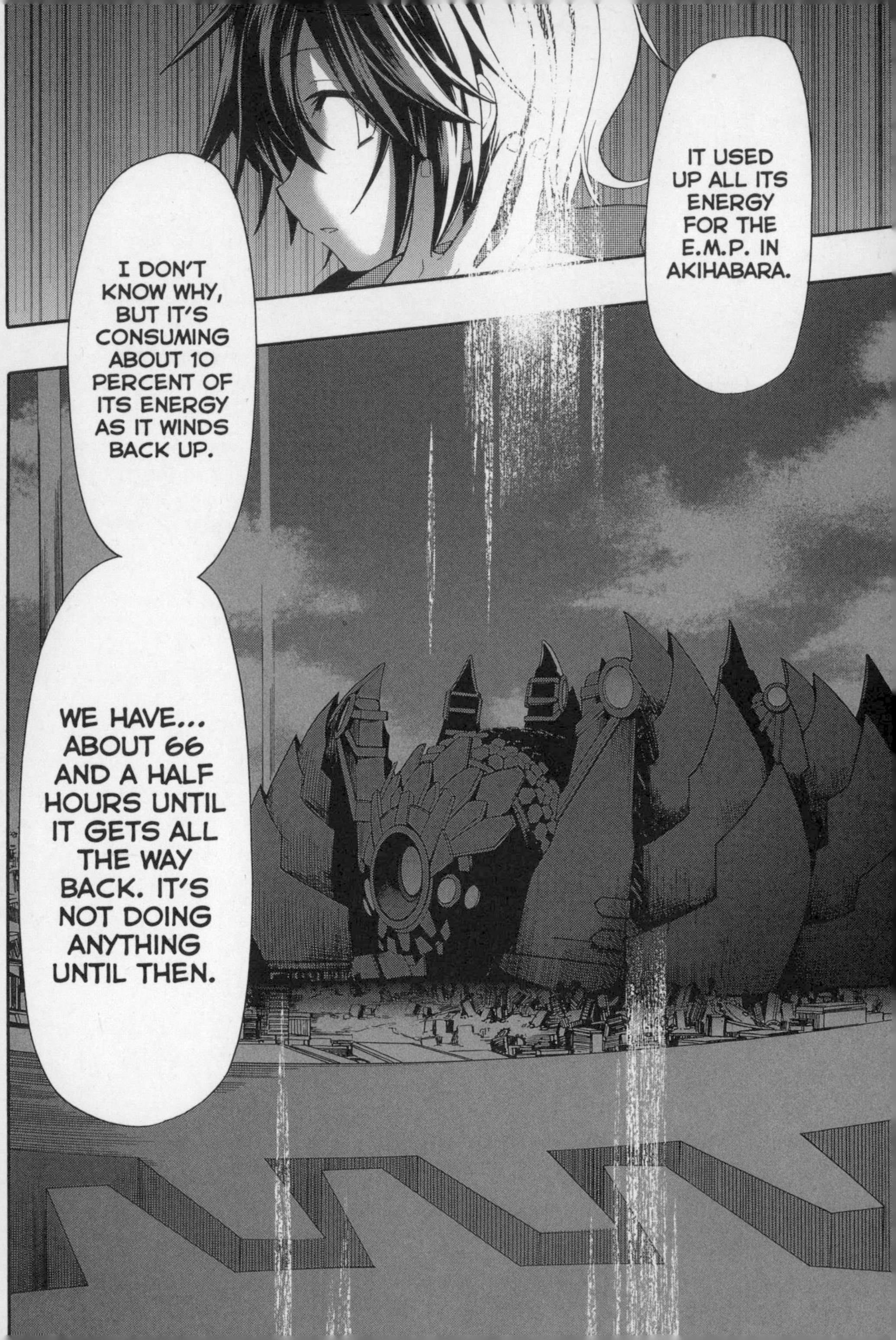
IT USED UP ALL ITS ENERGY FOR THE E.M.P. IN AKIHABARA.
I DON'T KNOW WHY, BUT IT'S CONSUMING ABOUT 10 PERCENT OF ITS ENERGY AS IT WINDS BACK UP.
WE HAVE... ABOUT 66 AND A HALF HOURS UNTIL IT GETS ALL THE WAY BACK. IT'S NOT DOING ANYTHING UNTIL THEN.

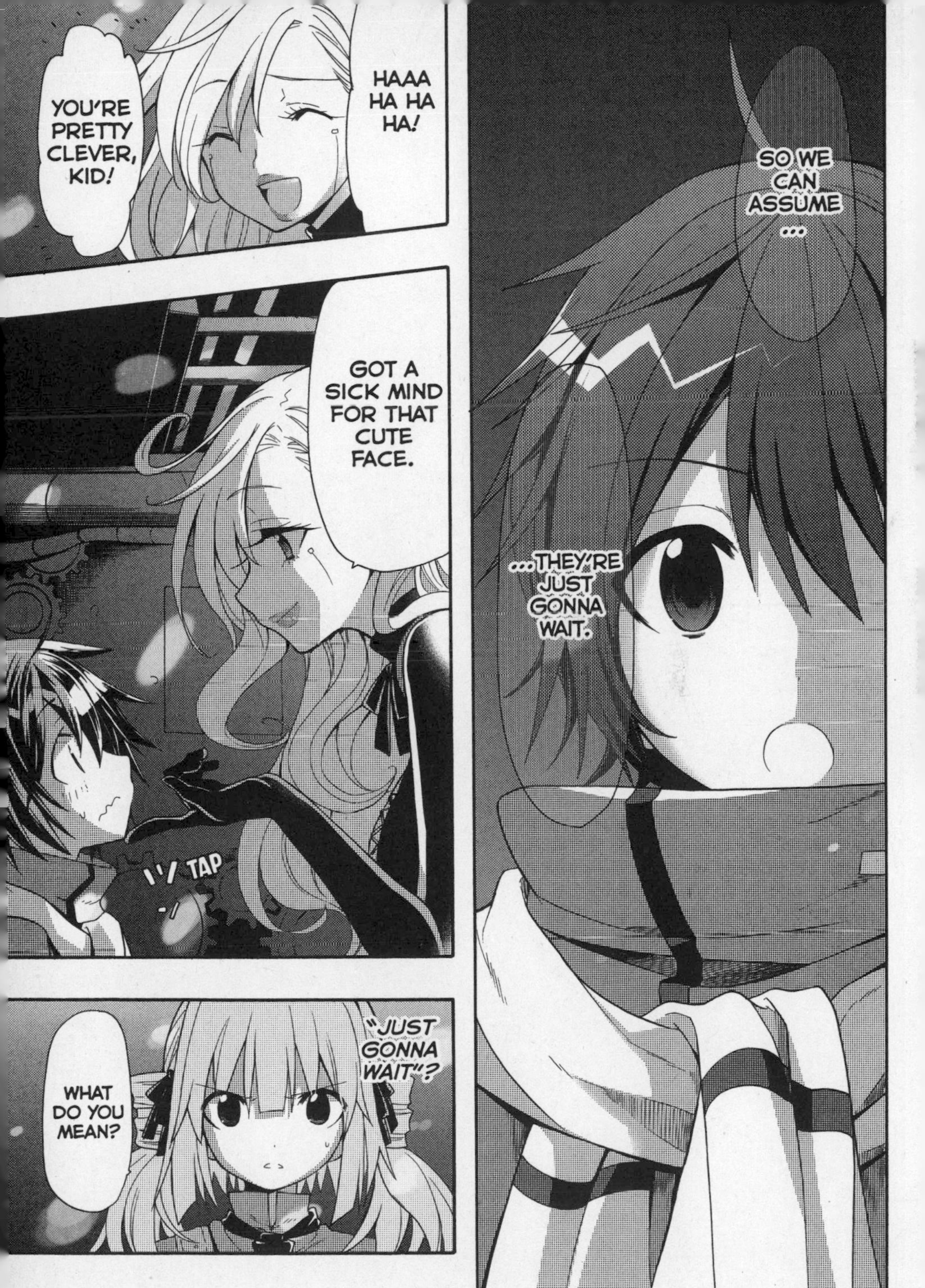
SO WE CAN ASSUME ...
...THEY'RE JUST GONNA WAIT.
HAAA HA HA HA!
YOU'RE PRETTY CLEVER, KID!
GOT A SICK MIND FOR THAT CUTE FACE.
TAP
"JUST GONNA WAIT"?
WHAT DO YOU MEAN?

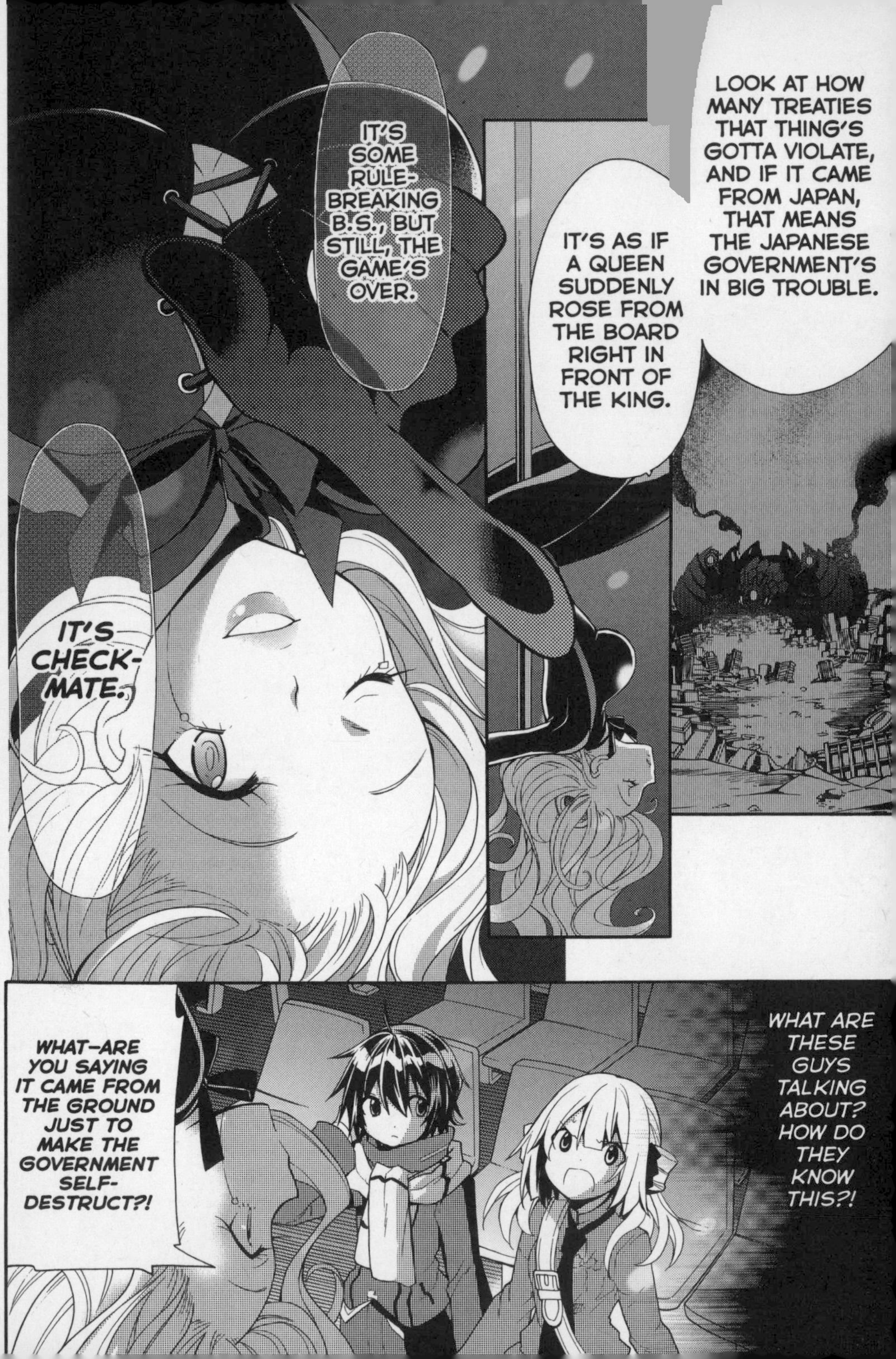
LOOK AT HOW MANY TREATIES THAT THING'S GOTTA VIOLATE, AND IF IT CAME FROM JAPAN, THAT MEANS THE JAPANESE GOVERNMENT'S IN BIG TROUBLE.
IT'S AS IF A QUEEN SUDDENLY ROSE FROM THE BOARD RIGHT IN FRONT OF THE KING.
IT'S SOME RULE-BREAKING B.S., BUT STILL, THE GAME'S OVER.
IT'S CHECK-MATE.
WHAT ARE THESE GUYS TALKING ABOUT? HOW DO THEY KNOW THIS?!
WHAT—ARE YOU SAYING IT CAME FROM THE GROUND JUST TO MAKE THE GOVERNMENT SELF-DESTRUCT?!

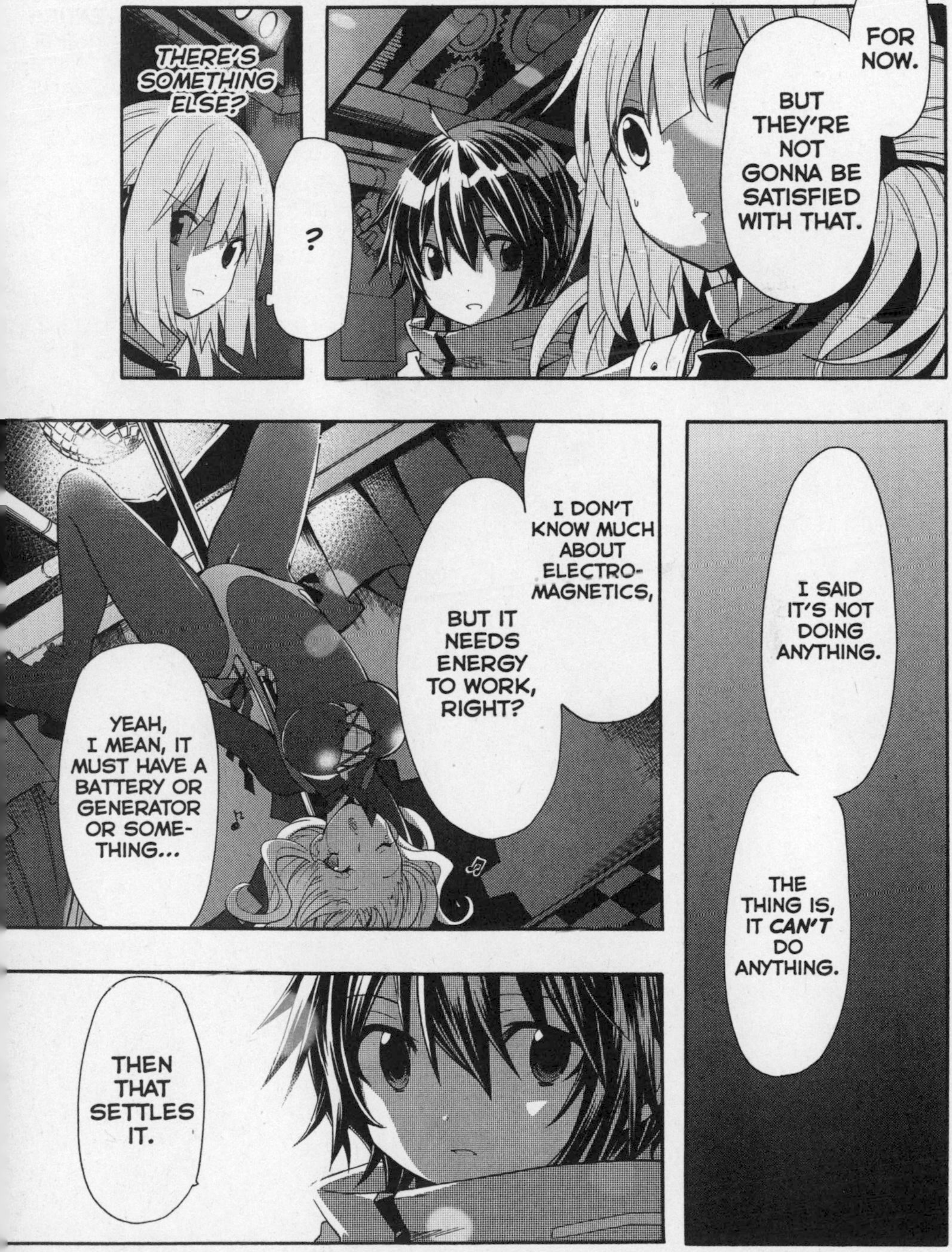
FOR NOW.
BUT THEY'RE NOT GONNA BE SATISFIED WITH THAT.
?
THERE'S SOMETHING ELSE?
I SAID IT'S NOT DOING ANYTHING.
THE THING IS, IT *CAN'T* DO ANYTHING.
I DON'T KNOW MUCH ABOUT ELECTRO-MAGNETICS,
BUT IT NEEDS ENERGY TO WORK, RIGHT?
YEAH, I MEAN, IT MUST HAVE A BATTERY OR GENERATOR OR SOME-THING...
THEN THAT SETTLES IT.

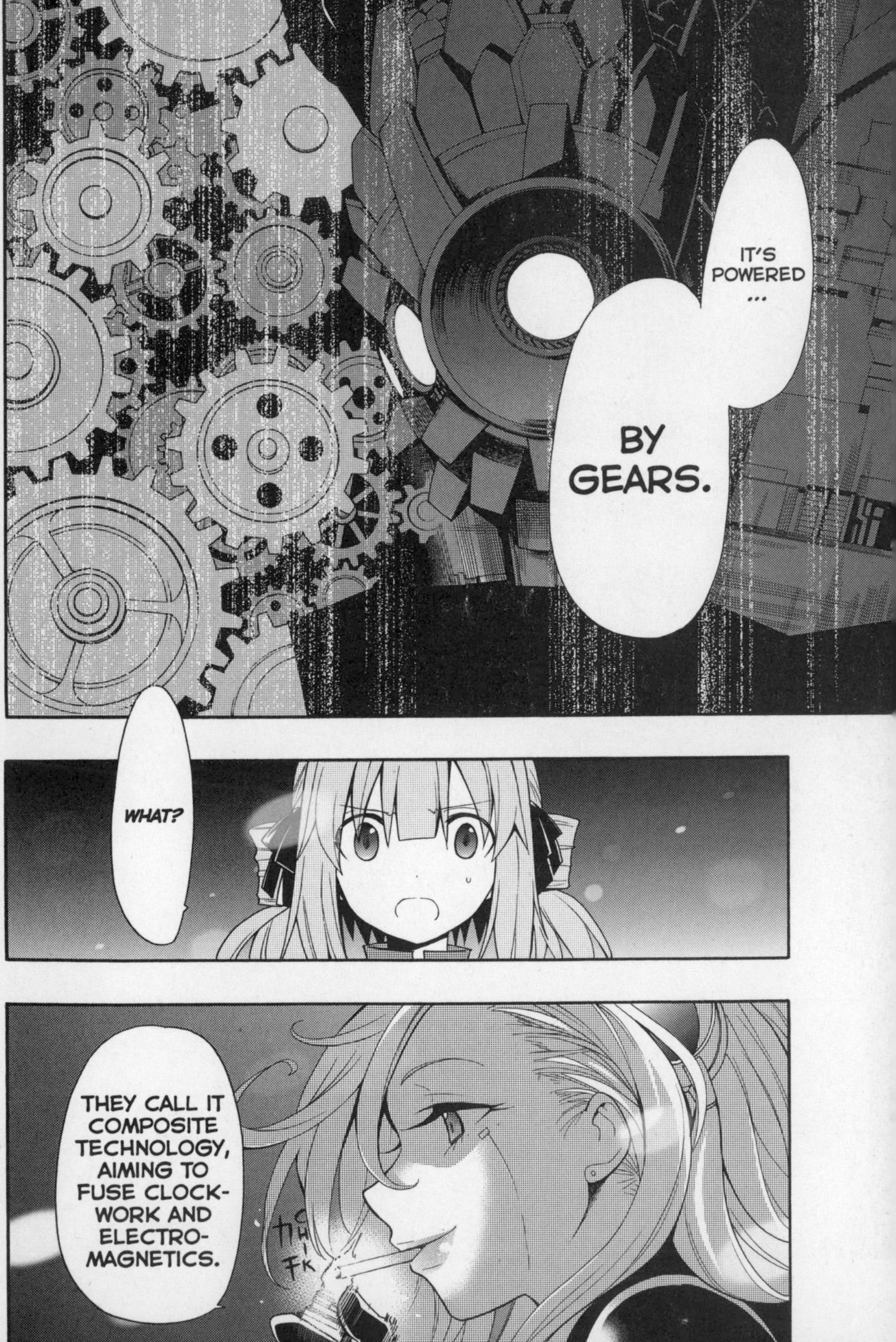
IT'S POWERED ...
BY GEARS.
WHAT?
THEY CALL IT COMPOSITE TECHNOLOGY, AIMING TO FUSE CLOCK-WORK AND ELECTRO-MAGNETICS.
CHIK

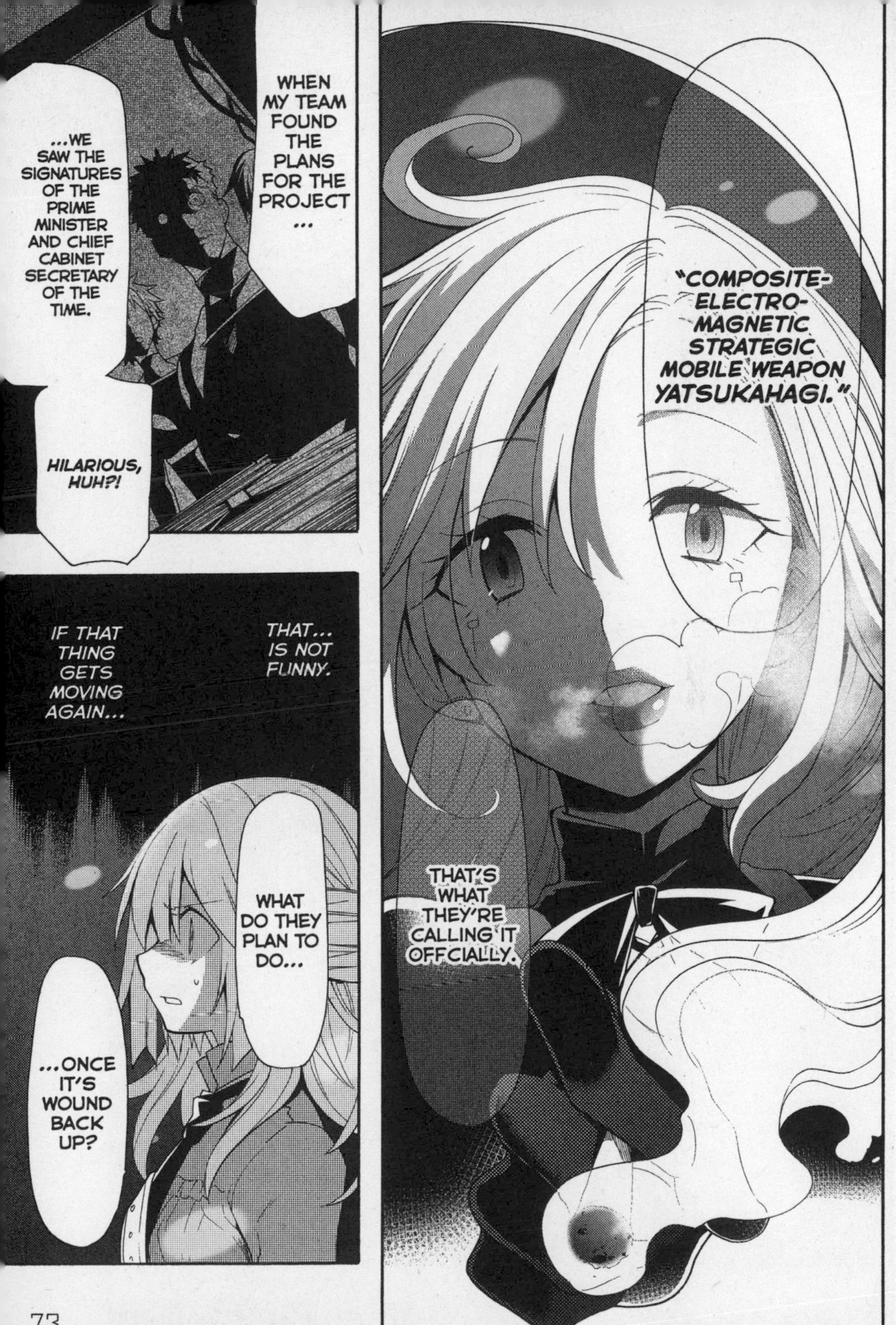
"COMPOSITE-ELECTRO-MAGNETIC STRATEGIC MOBILE WEAPON YATSUKAHAGI."
THAT'S WHAT THEY'RE CALLING IT OFFCIALLY.
WHEN MY TEAM FOUND THE PLANS FOR THE PROJECT...
...WE SAW THE SIGNATURES OF THE PRIME MINISTER AND CHIEF CABINET SECRETARY OF THE TIME.
HILARIOUS, HUH?!
THAT... IS NOT FUNNY.
IF THAT THING GETS MOVING AGAIN...
WHAT DO THEY PLAN TO DO...
...ONCE IT'S WOUND BACK UP?

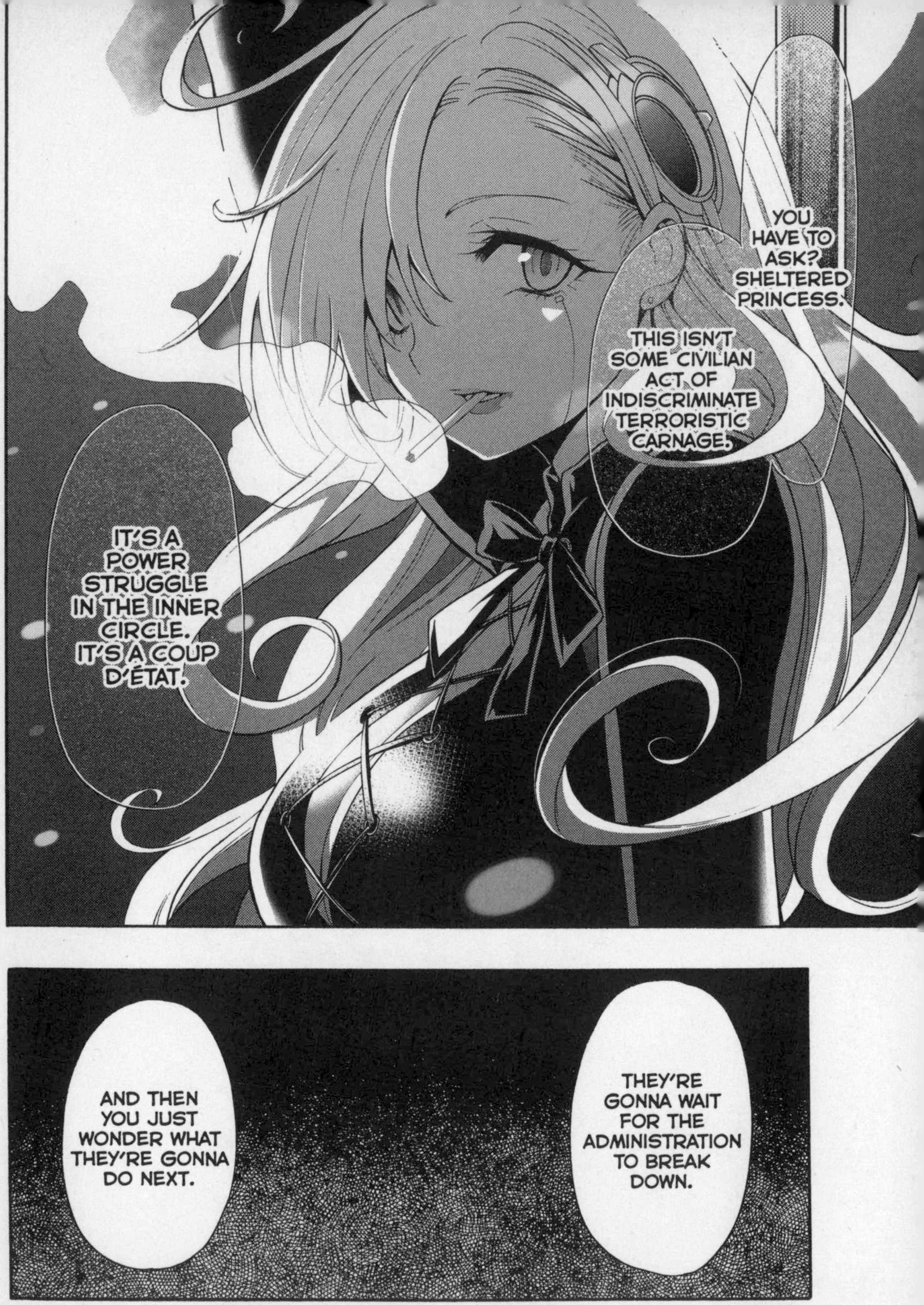
YOU HAVE TO ASK? SHELTERED PRINCESS.
THIS ISN'T SOME CIVILIAN ACT OF INDISCRIMINATE TERRORISTIC CARNAGE.
IT'S A POWER STRUGGLE IN THE INNER CIRCLE. IT'S A COUP D'ÉTAT.
THEY'RE GONNA WAIT FOR THE ADMINISTRATION TO BREAK DOWN.
AND THEN YOU JUST WONDER WHAT THEY'RE GONNA DO NEXT.

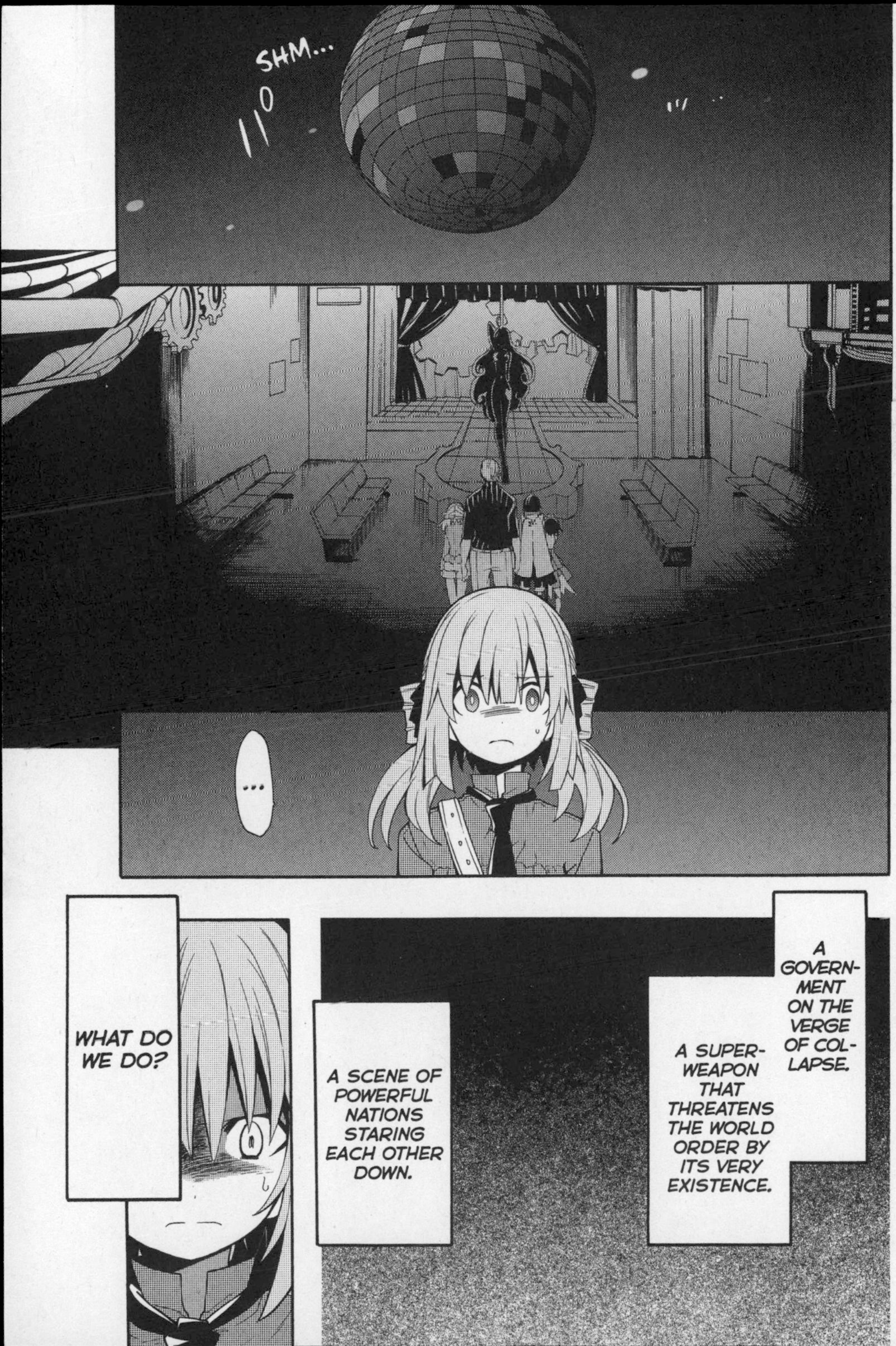
SHM...
...
A GOVERN-MENT ON THE VERGE OF COL-LAPSE.
A SUPER-WEAPON THAT THREATENS THE WORLD ORDER BY ITS VERY EXISTENCE.
A SCENE OF POWERFUL NATIONS STARING EACH OTHER DOWN.
WHAT DO WE DO?

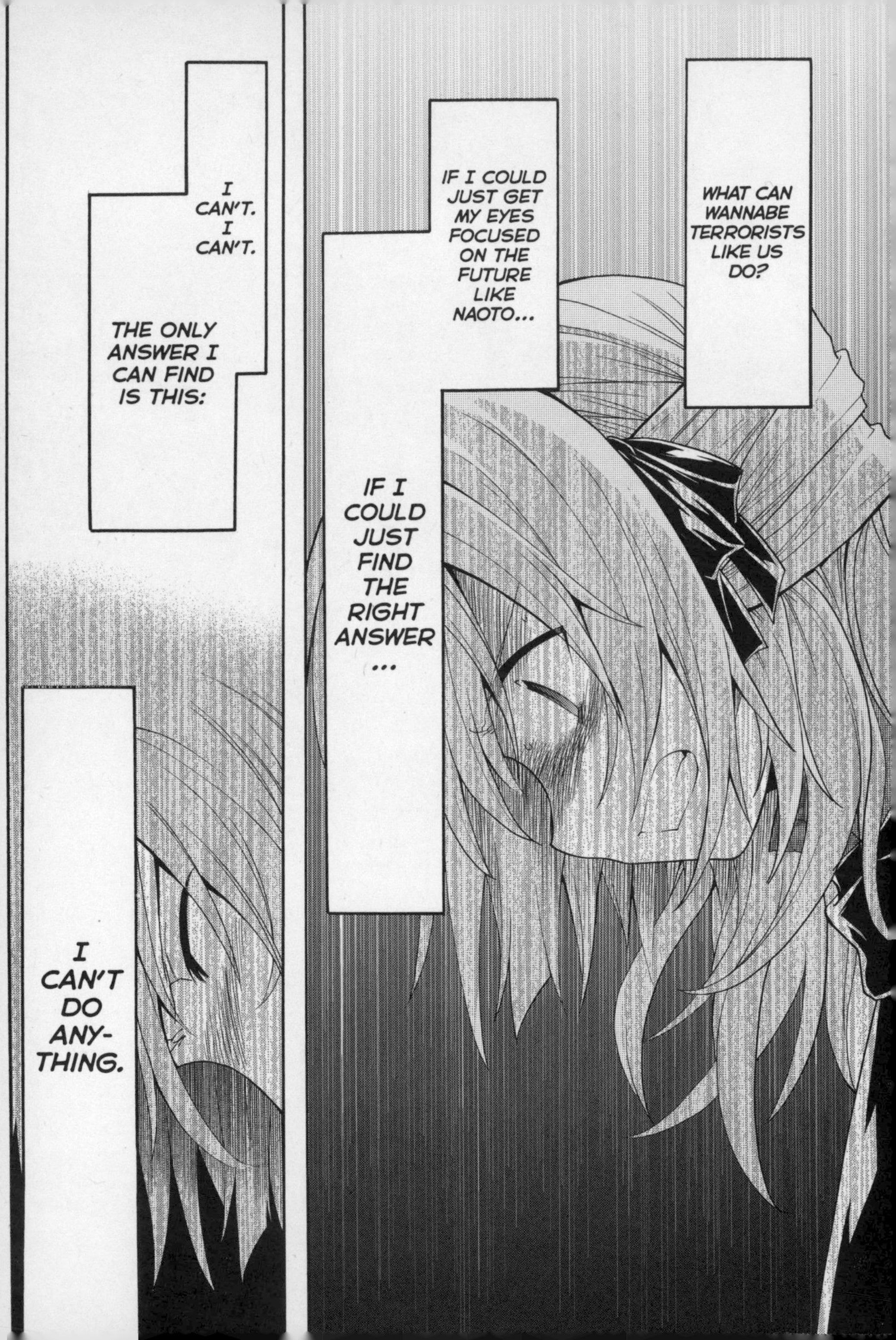
WHAT CAN WANNABE TERRORISTS LIKE US DO?
IF I COULD JUST GET MY EYES FOCUSED ON THE FUTURE LIKE NAOTO...
IF I COULD JUST FIND THE RIGHT ANSWER ...
I CAN'T. I CAN'T.
THE ONLY ANSWER I CAN FIND IS THIS:
I CAN'T DO ANYTHING.

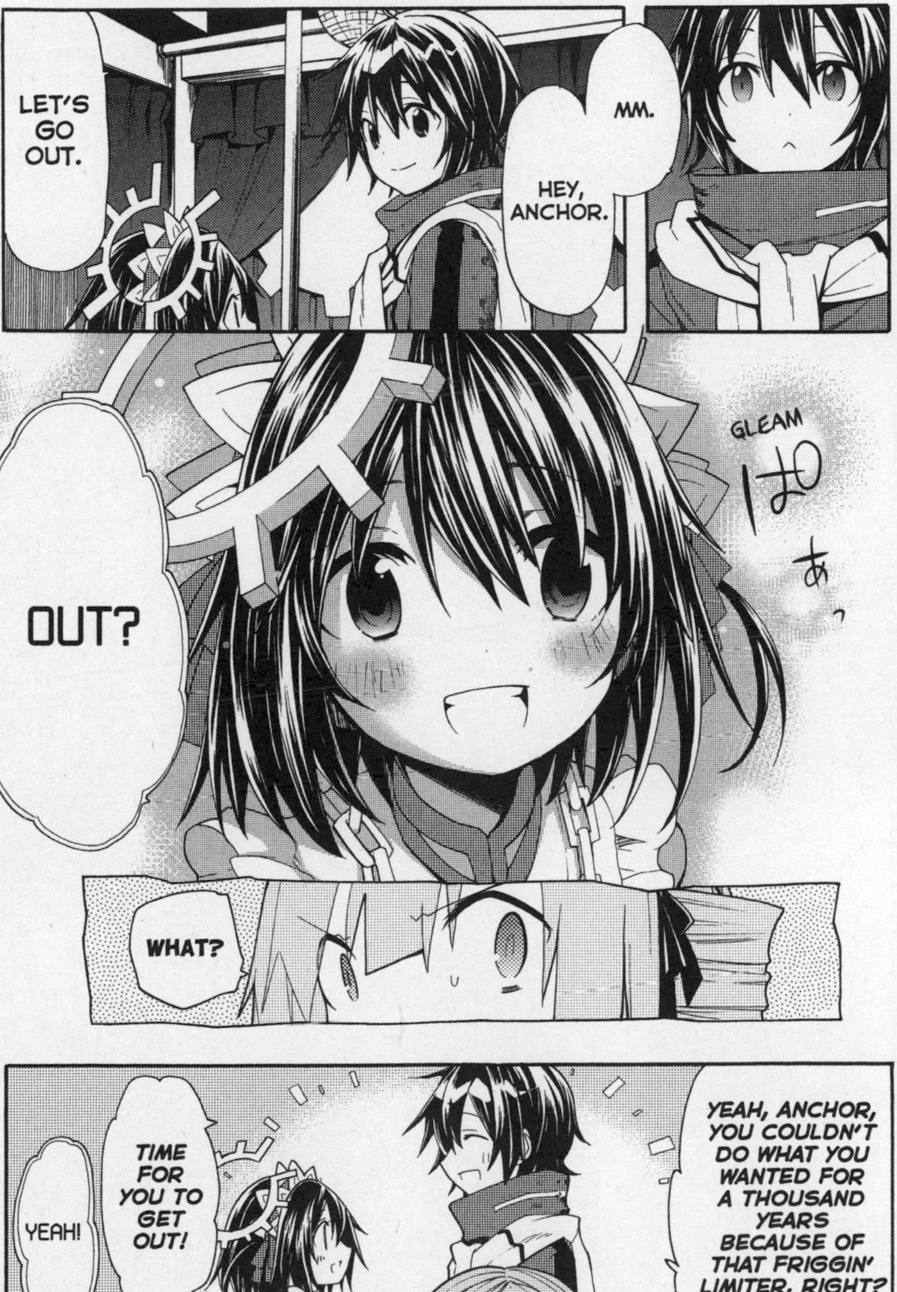
MM.
HEY, ANCHOR.
LET'S GO OUT.
GLEAM
OUT?
WHAT?
YEAH, ANCHOR, YOU COULDN'T DO WHAT YOU WANTED FOR A THOUSAND YEARS BECAUSE OF THAT FRIGGIN' LIMITER, RIGHT?
TIME FOR YOU TO GET OUT!
YEAH!

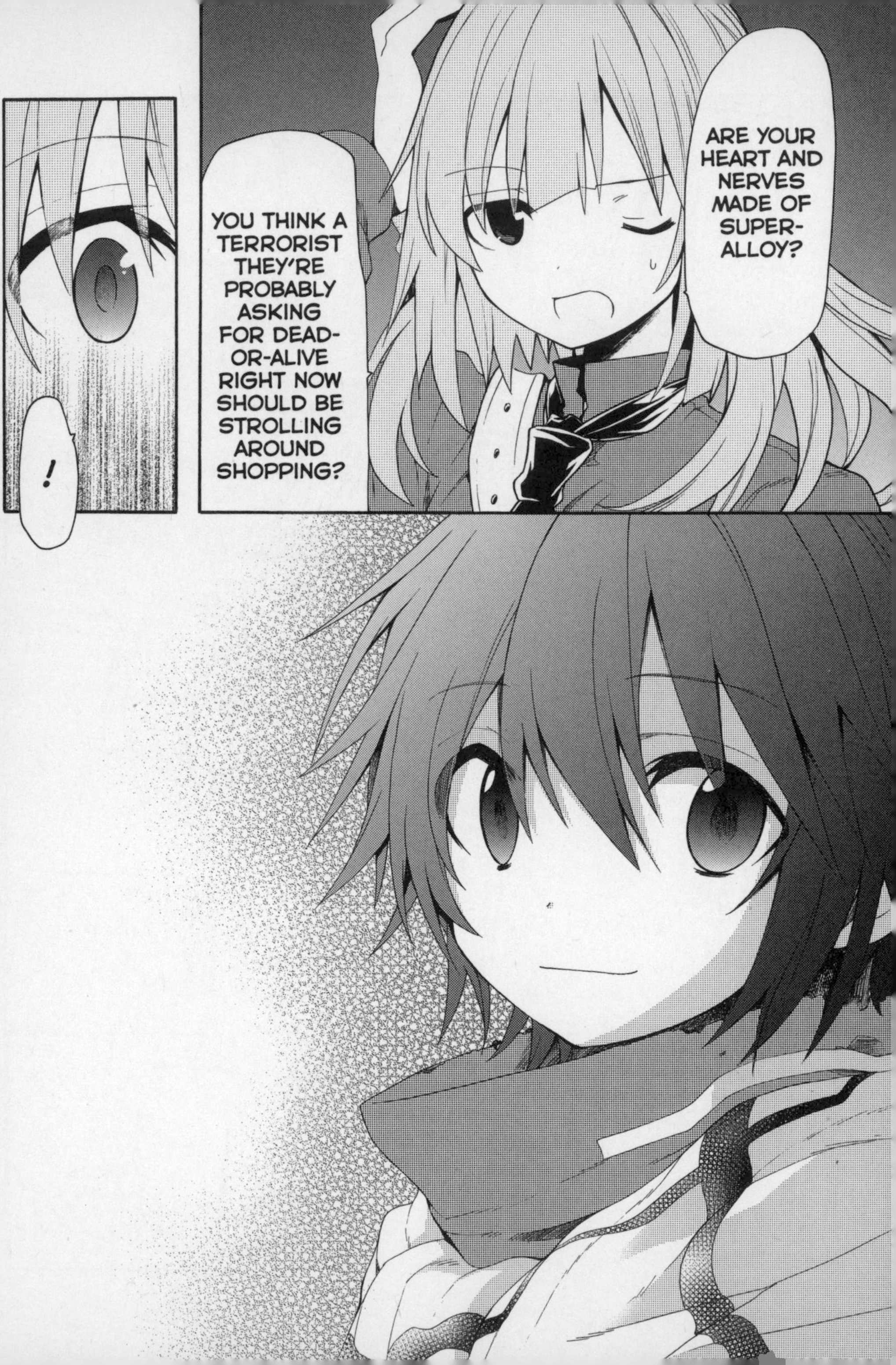
ARE YOUR HEART AND NERVES MADE OF SUPER-ALLOY?
YOU THINK A TERRORIST THEY'RE PROBABLY ASKING FOR DEAD-OR-ALIVE RIGHT NOW SHOULD BE STROLLING AROUND SHOPPING?
!

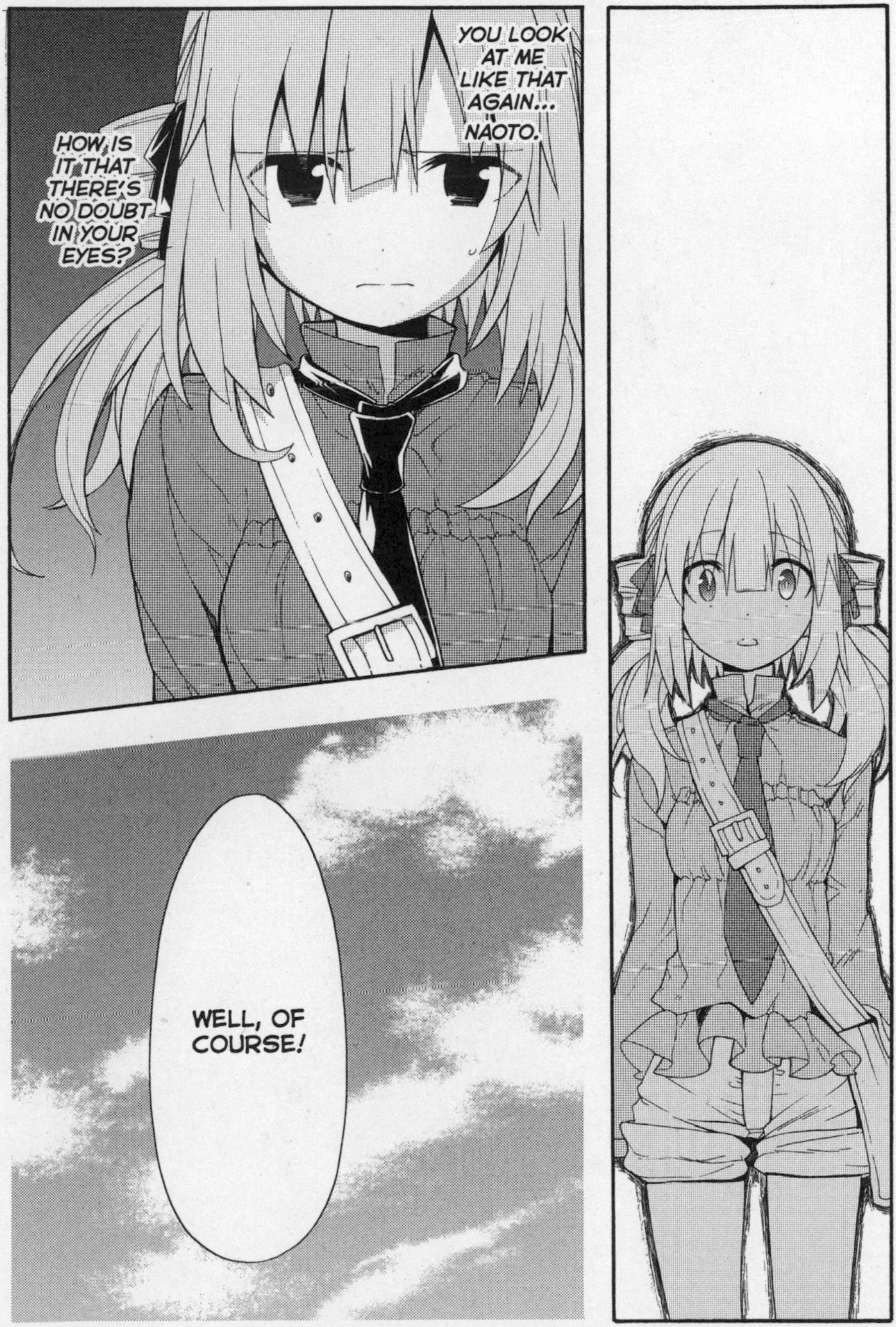
YOU LOOK AT ME LIKE THAT AGAIN... NAOTO.
HOW IS IT THAT THERE'S NO DOUBT IN YOUR EYES?
WELL, OF COURSE!

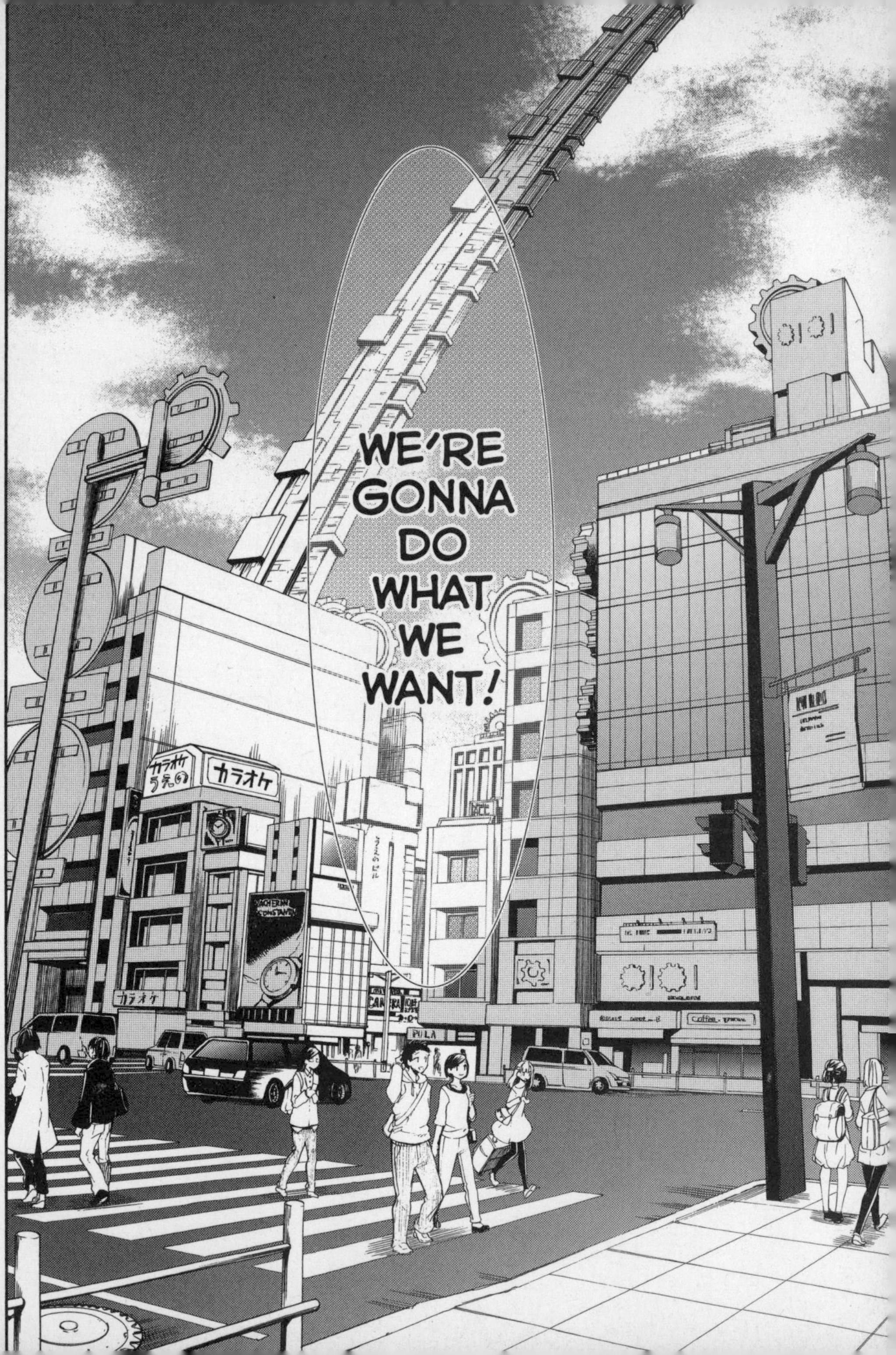
WE'RE GONNA DO WHAT WE WANT!
カラオケ
カラオケ
PULA

CLOCKWORK PLANET

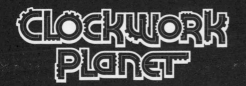

Clockwork Planet

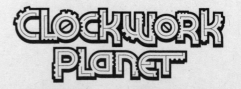

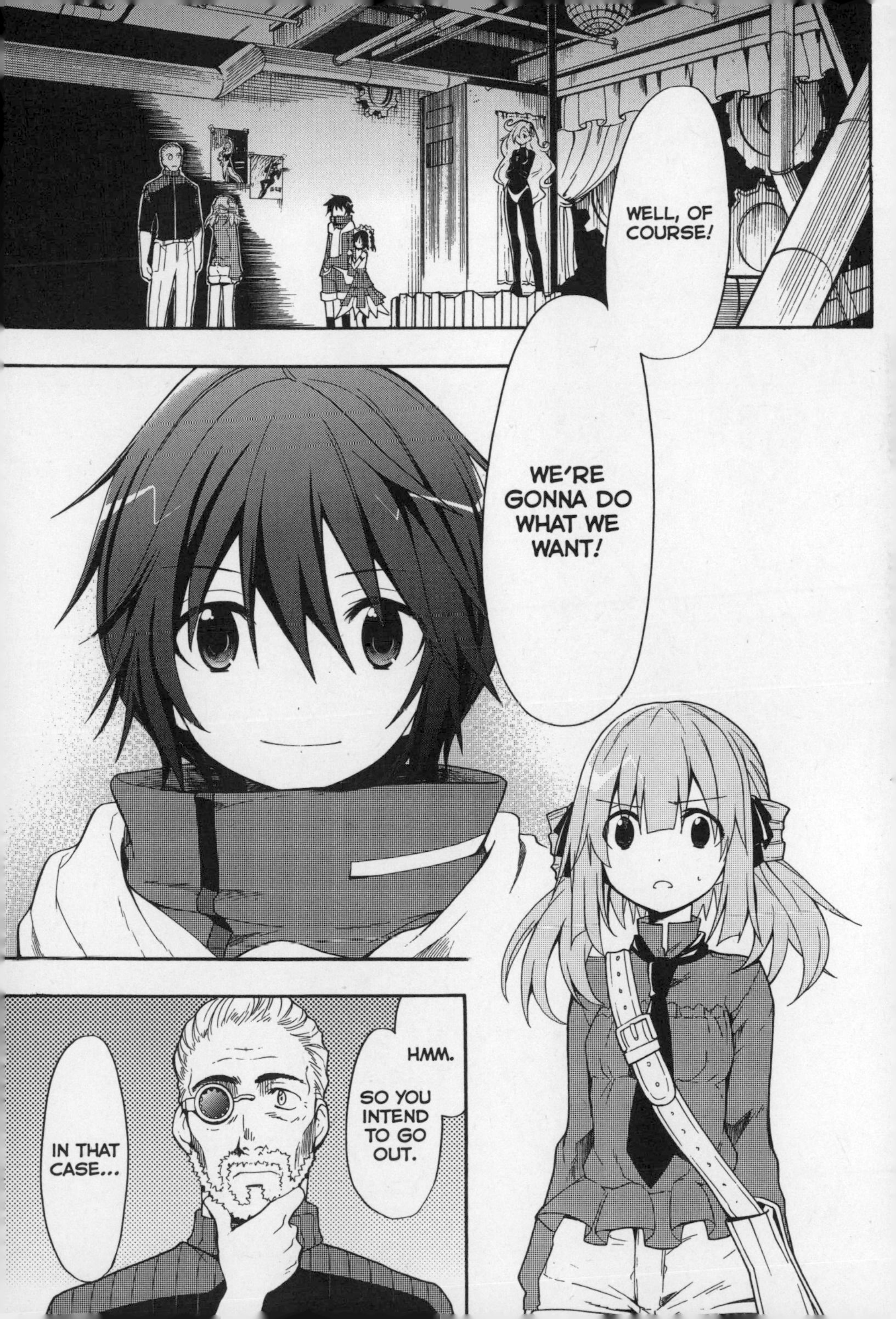
WELL, OF COURSE!
WE'RE GONNA DO WHAT WE WANT!
HMM.
SO YOU INTEND TO GO OUT.
IN THAT CASE...

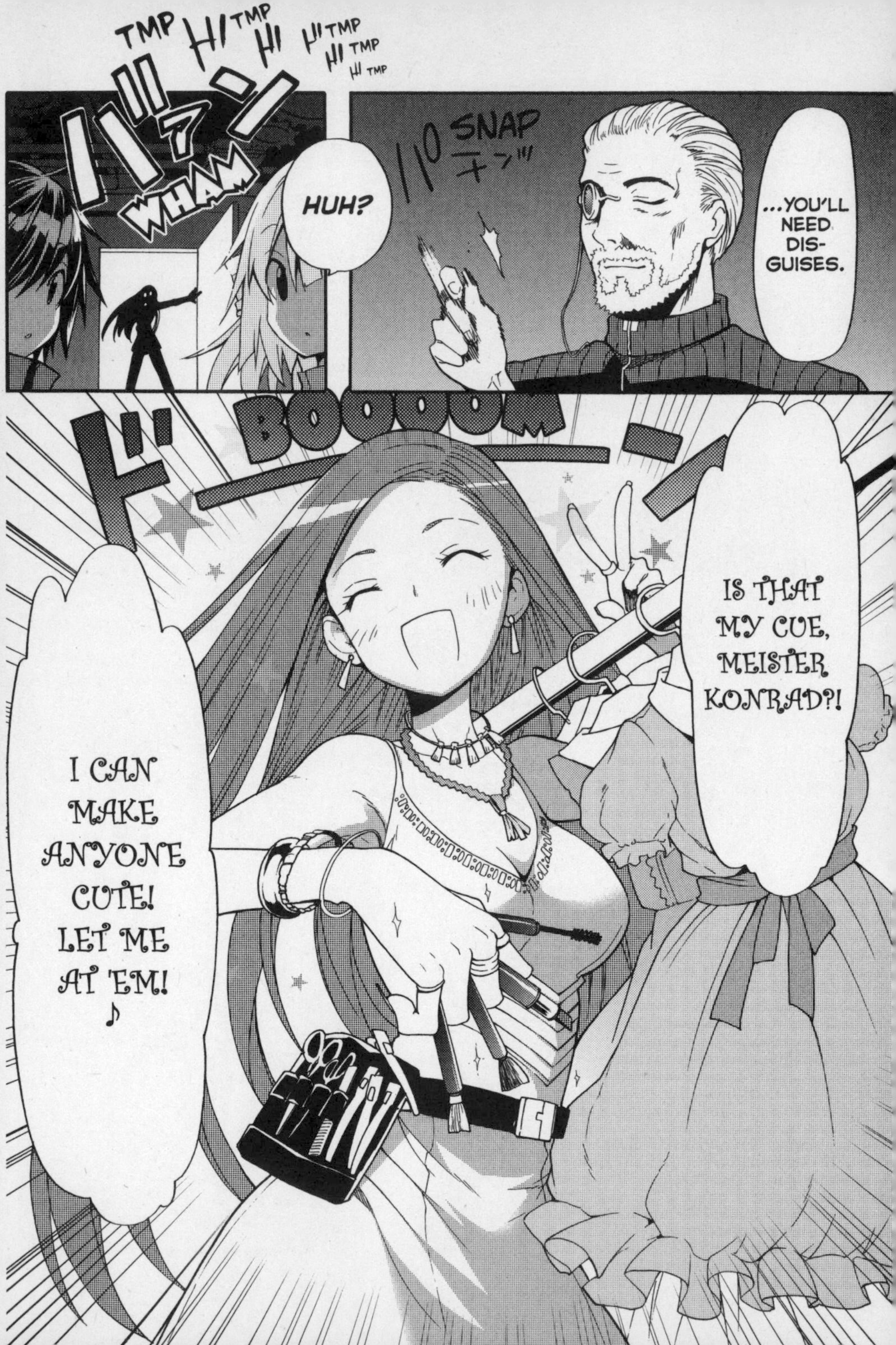
...YOU'LL NEED DIS-GUISES.
SNAP
HUH?
WHAM
TMP TMP TMP TMP TMP
BOOOOM
IS THAT MY CUE, MEISTER KONRAD?!
I CAN MAKE ANYONE CUTE! LET ME AT 'EM! ♪

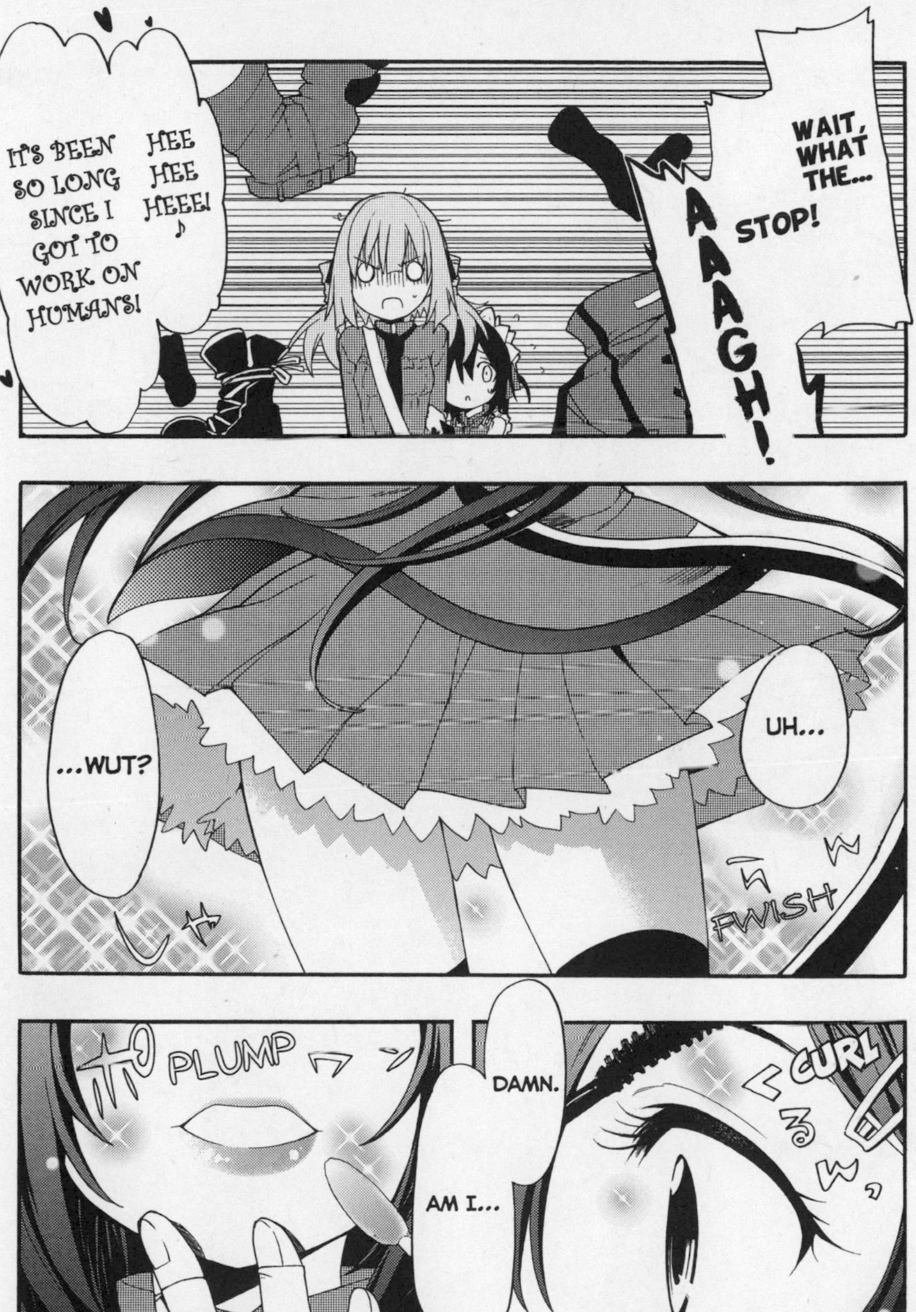
WAIT, WHAT THE... STOP!
AAAAGH!
IT'S BEEN SO LONG SINCE I GOT TO WORK ON HUMANS!
HEE HEE HEEE! ♪
UH...
...WUT?
FWISH
CURL
DAMN.
AM I...
PLUMP

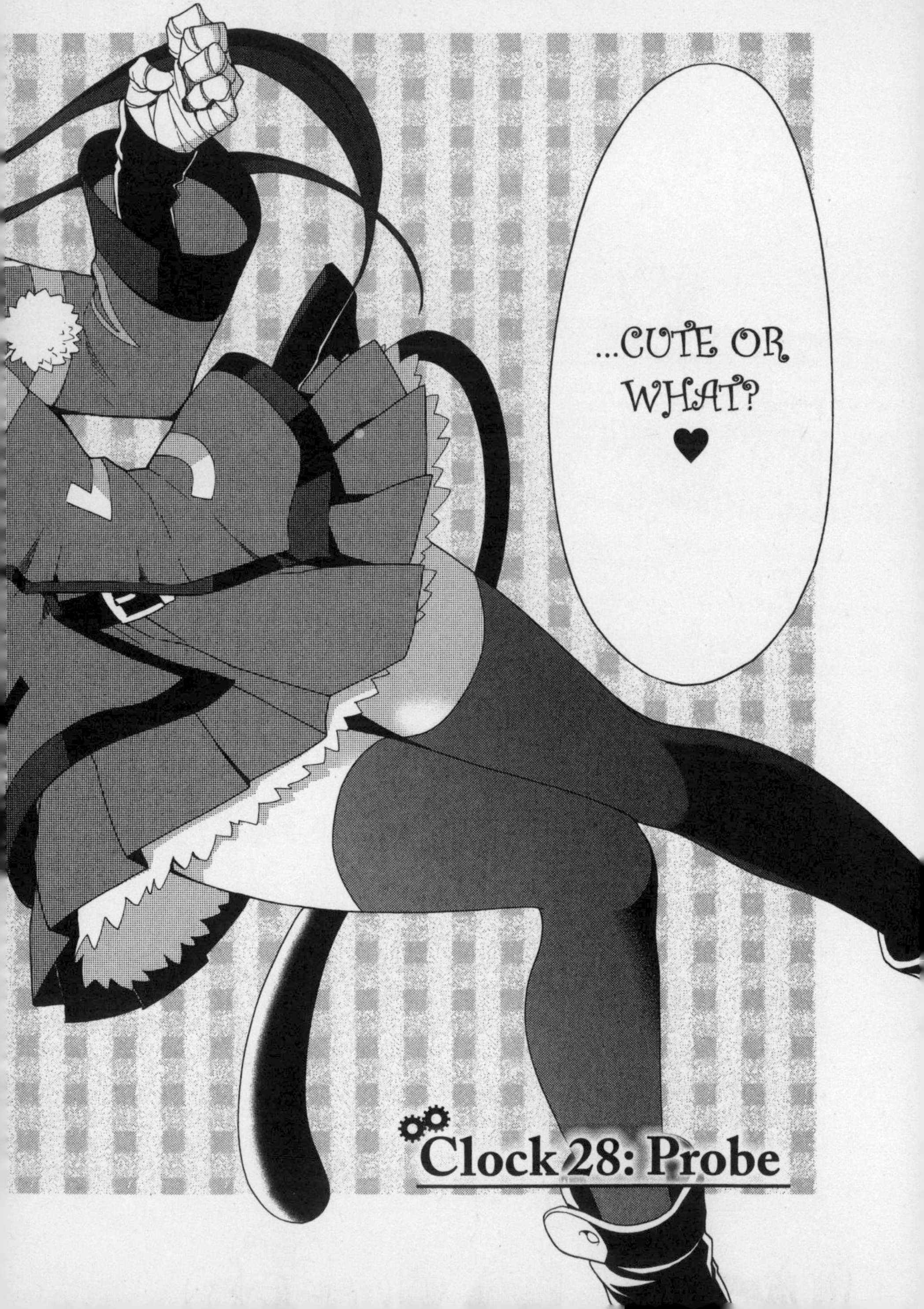
...CUTE OR WHAT? ♥

Clock 28: Probe

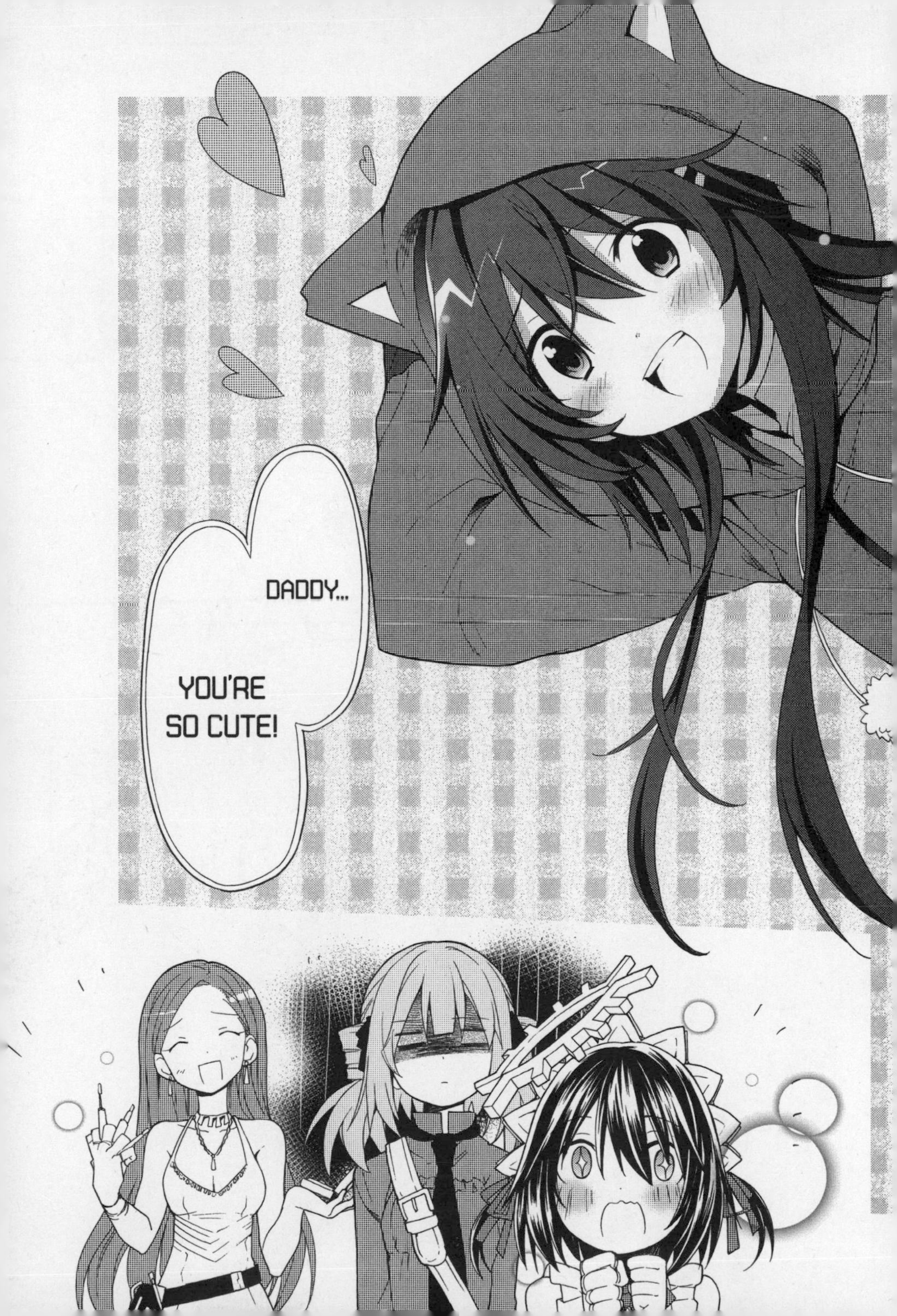
DADDY...
YOU'RE SO CUTE!

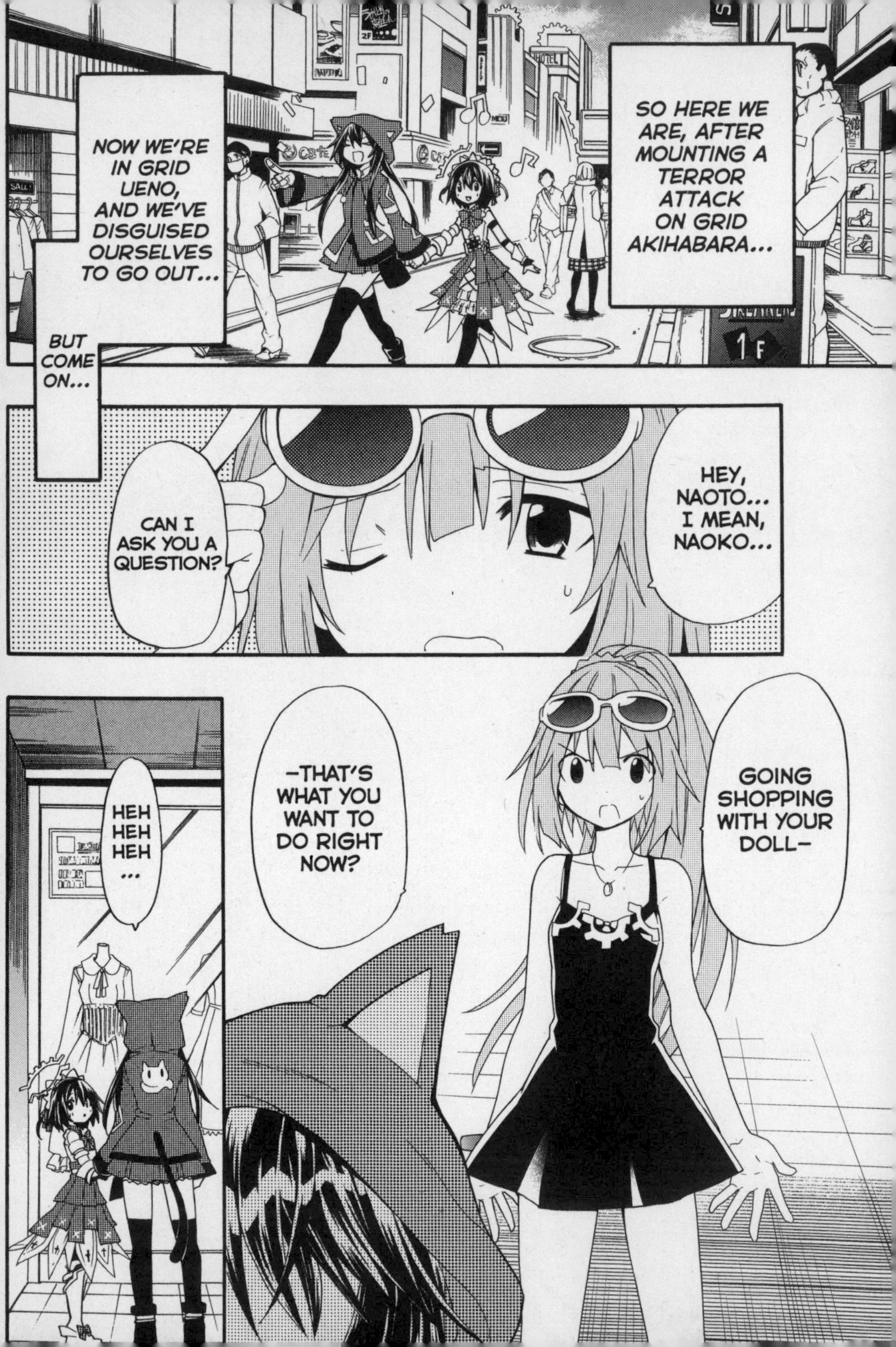
SO HERE WE ARE, AFTER MOUNTING A TERROR ATTACK ON GRID AKIHABARA...
NOW WE'RE IN GRID UENO, AND WE'VE DISGUISED OURSELVES TO GO OUT...
BUT COME ON...
HEY, NAOTO... I MEAN, NAOKO...
CAN I ASK YOU A QUESTION?
GOING SHOPPING WITH YOUR DOLL–
–THAT'S WHAT YOU WANT TO DO RIGHT NOW?
HEH HEH HEH ...

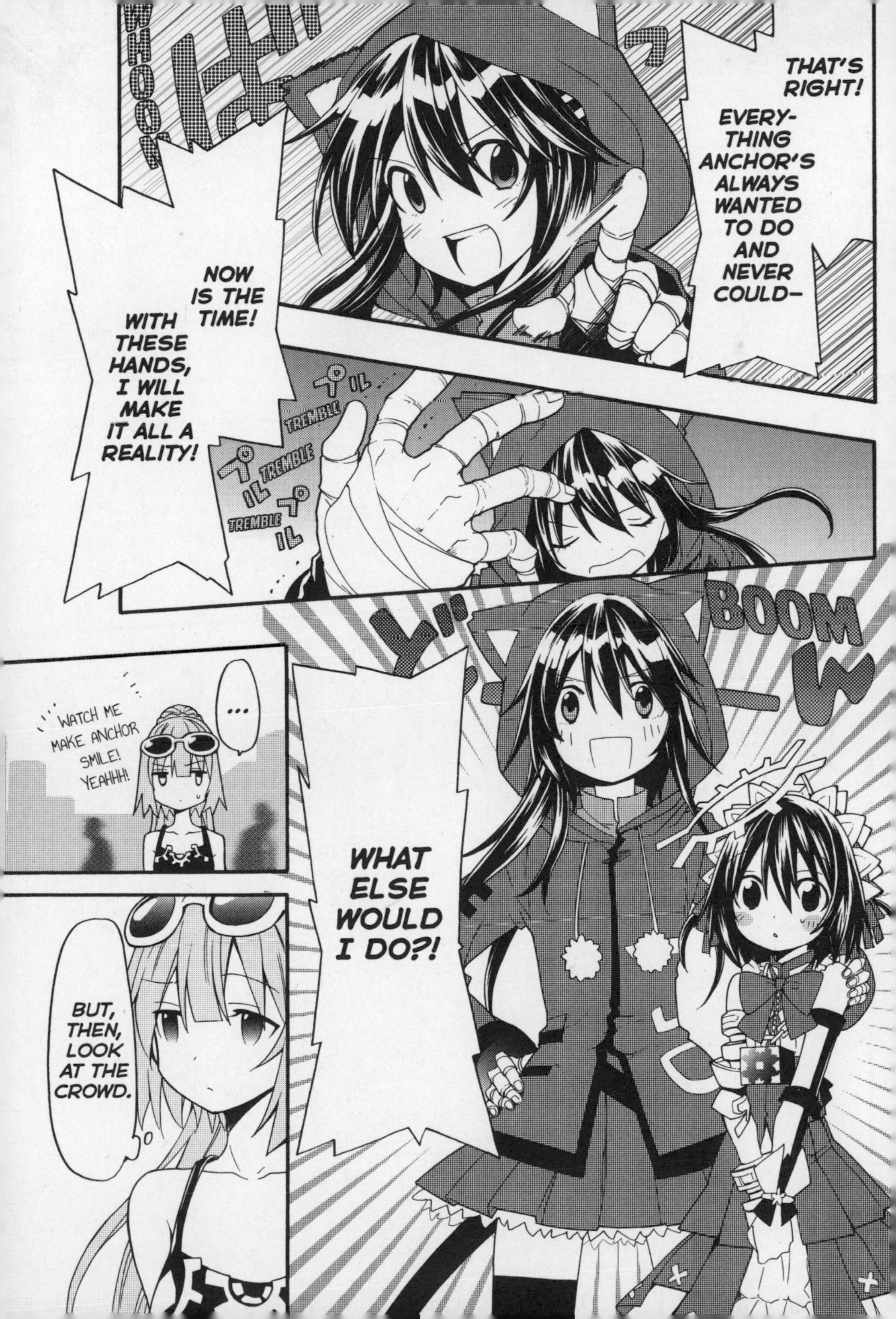
WHOO
THAT'S RIGHT! EVERY-THING ANCHOR'S ALWAYS WANTED TO DO AND NEVER COULD—
NOW IS THE TIME! WITH THESE HANDS, I WILL MAKE IT ALL A REALITY!
TREMBLE
TREMBLE
TREMBLE
BOOM
WHAT ELSE WOULD I DO?!
...
WATCH ME MAKE ANCHOR SMILE! YEAHHH!
BUT, THEN, LOOK AT THE CROWD.

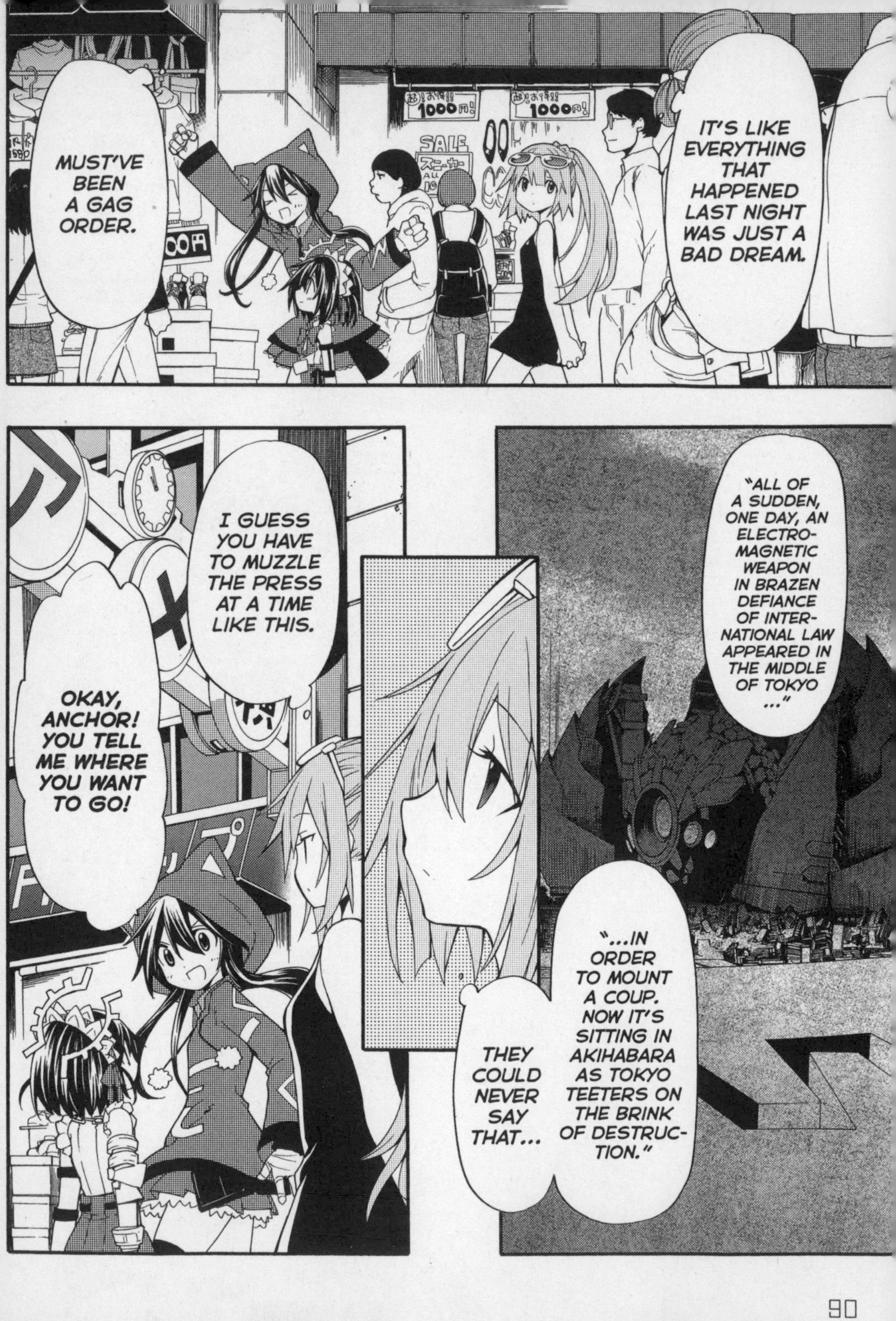
IT'S LIKE EVERYTHING THAT HAPPENED LAST NIGHT WAS JUST A BAD DREAM.
MUST'VE BEEN A GAG ORDER.
1000円!
1000円!
SALE
"ALL OF A SUDDEN, ONE DAY, AN ELECTRO-MAGNETIC WEAPON IN BRAZEN DEFIANCE OF INTER-NATIONAL LAW APPEARED IN THE MIDDLE OF TOKYO ..."
"...IN ORDER TO MOUNT A COUP. NOW IT'S SITTING IN AKIHABARA AS TOKYO TEETERS ON THE BRINK OF DESTRUC-TION."
THEY COULD NEVER SAY THAT...
I GUESS YOU HAVE TO MUZZLE THE PRESS AT A TIME LIKE THIS.
OKAY, ANCHOR! YOU TELL ME WHERE YOU WANT TO GO!

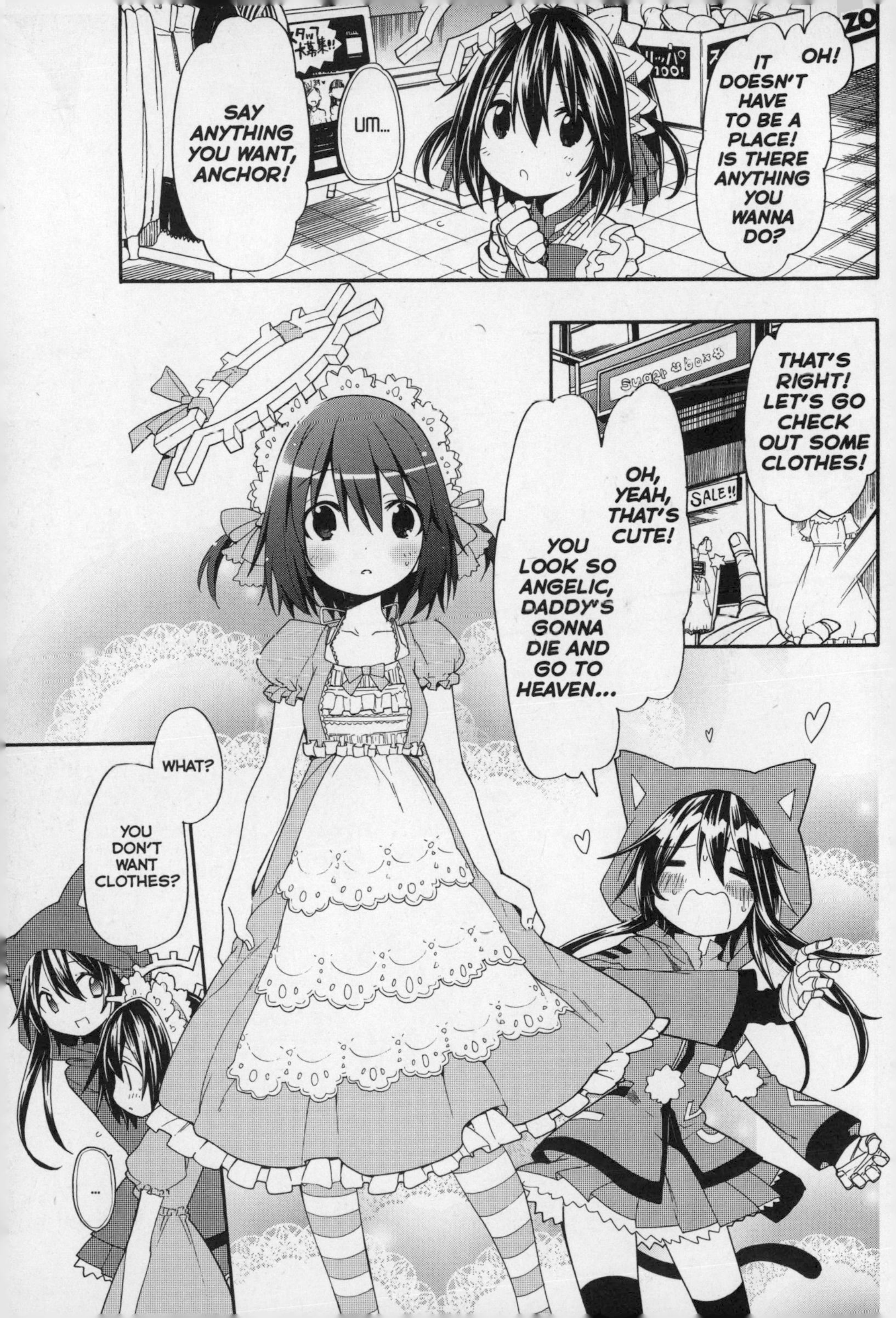
OH!
IT DOESN'T HAVE TO BE A PLACE! IS THERE ANYTHING YOU WANNA DO?
UM...
SAY ANYTHING YOU WANT, ANCHOR!
THAT'S RIGHT! LET'S GO CHECK OUT SOME CLOTHES!
SALE!!
OH, YEAH, THAT'S CUTE!
YOU LOOK SO ANGELIC, DADDY'S GONNA DIE AND GO TO HEAVEN...
WHAT?
YOU DON'T WANT CLOTHES?
...

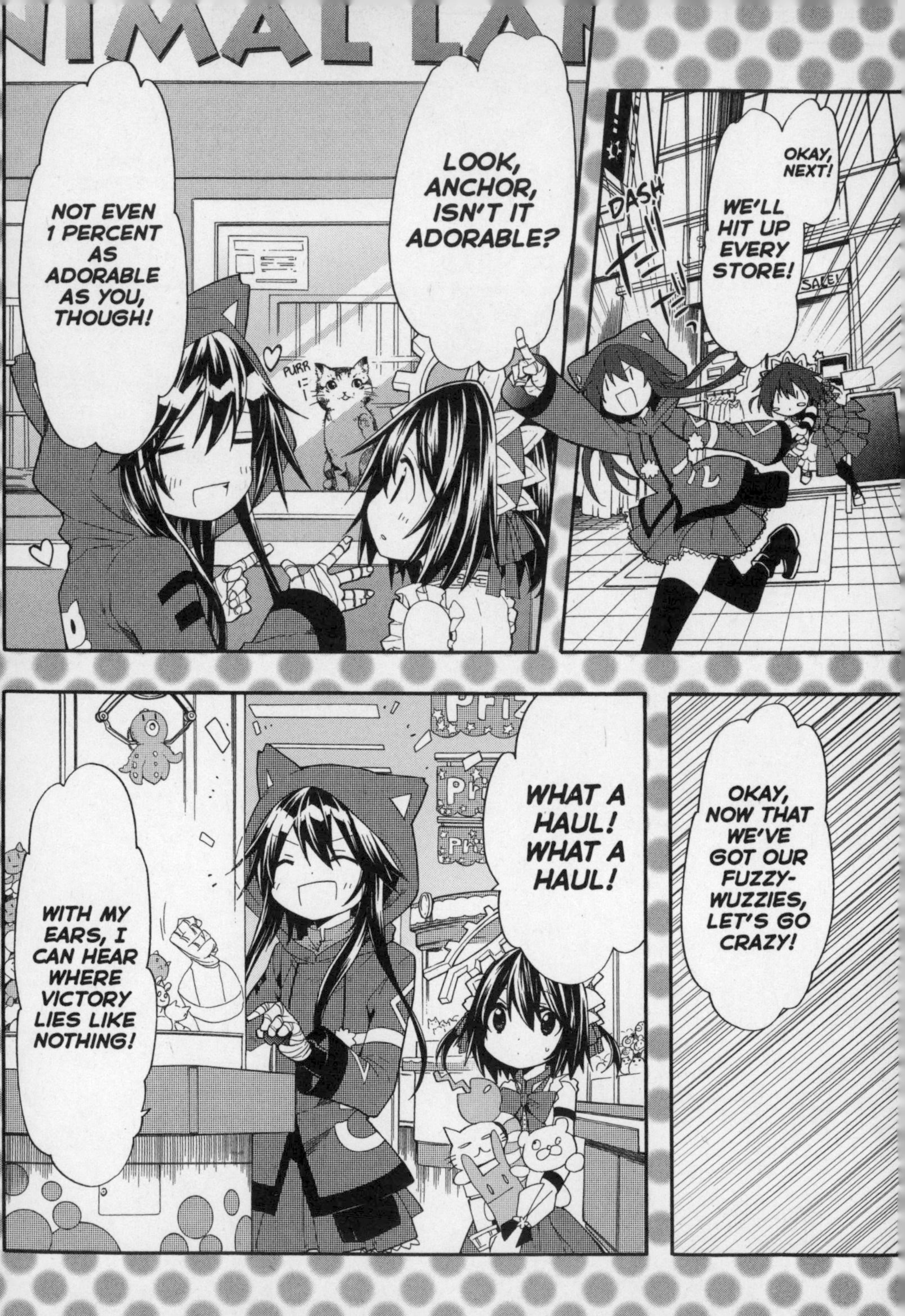
OKAY, NEXT!
WE'LL HIT UP EVERY STORE!
DASH
SALE!
NIMAL LA
LOOK, ANCHOR, ISN'T IT ADORABLE?
NOT EVEN 1 PERCENT AS ADORABLE AS YOU, THOUGH!
PURR
OKAY, NOW THAT WE'VE GOT OUR FUZZY-WUZZIES, LET'S GO CRAZY!
WHAT A HAUL! WHAT A HAUL!
WITH MY EARS, I CAN HEAR WHERE VICTORY LIES LIKE NOTHING!

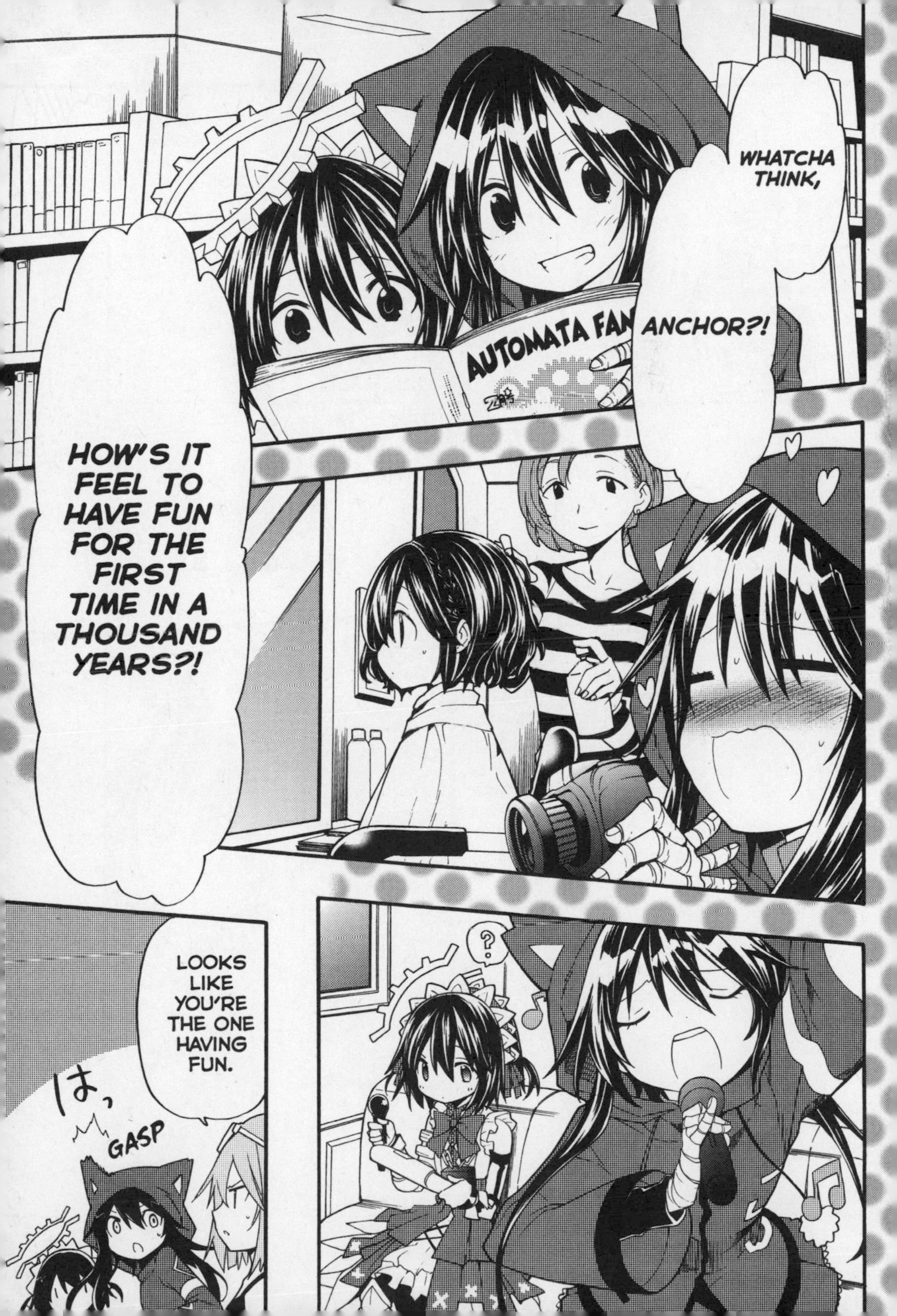
WHATCHA THINK, ANCHOR?!
AUTOMATA FAN
HOW'S IT FEEL TO HAVE FUN FOR THE FIRST TIME IN A THOUSAND YEARS?!
?
LOOKS LIKE YOU'RE THE ONE HAVING FUN.
は、
GASP

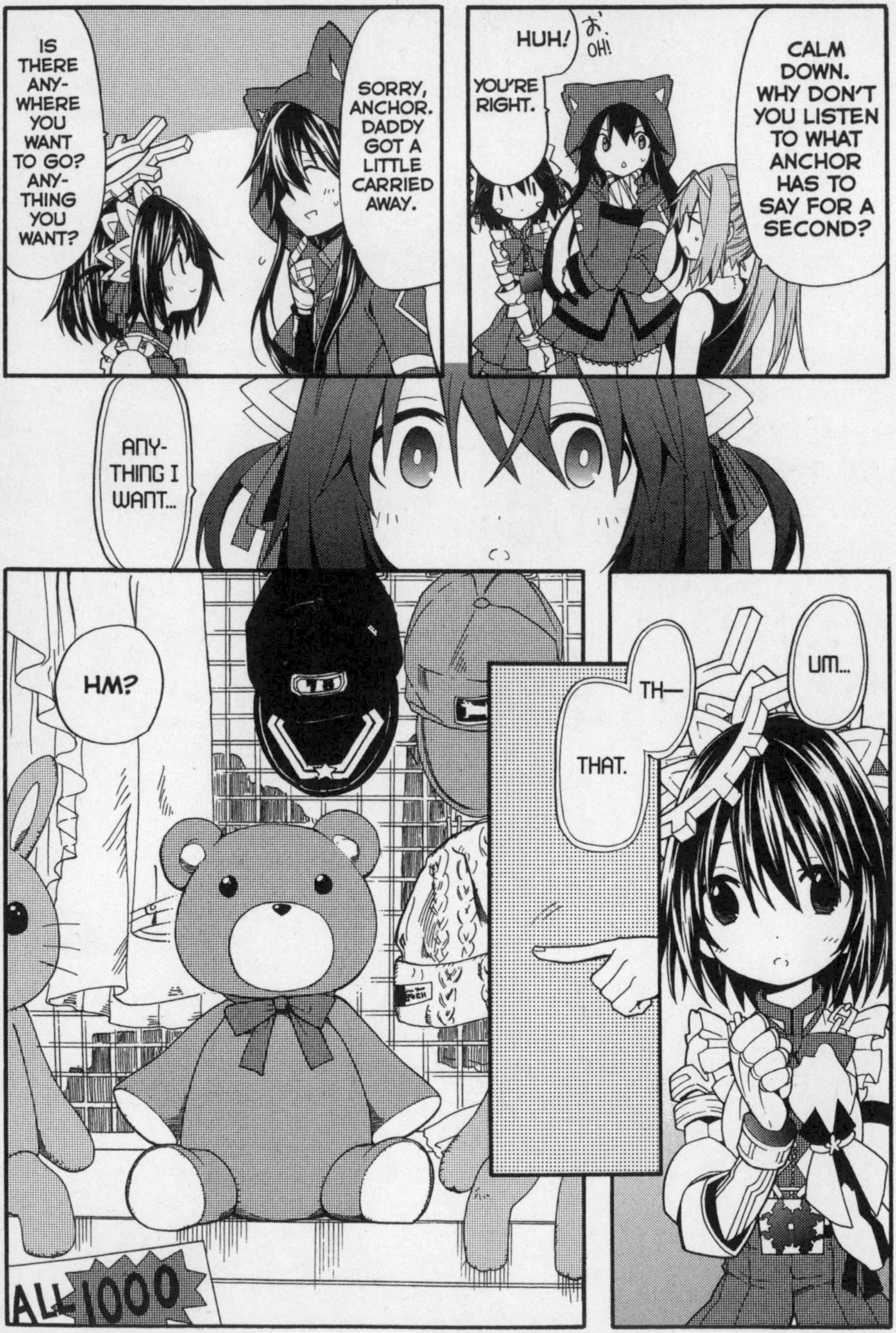
CALM DOWN. WHY DON'T YOU LISTEN TO WHAT ANCHOR HAS TO SAY FOR A SECOND?
HUH!
お OH!
YOU'RE RIGHT.
SORRY, ANCHOR. DADDY GOT A LITTLE CARRIED AWAY.
IS THERE ANYWHERE YOU WANT TO GO? ANYTHING YOU WANT?
ANYTHING I WANT...
UM...
TH— THAT.
HM?
ALL 1000

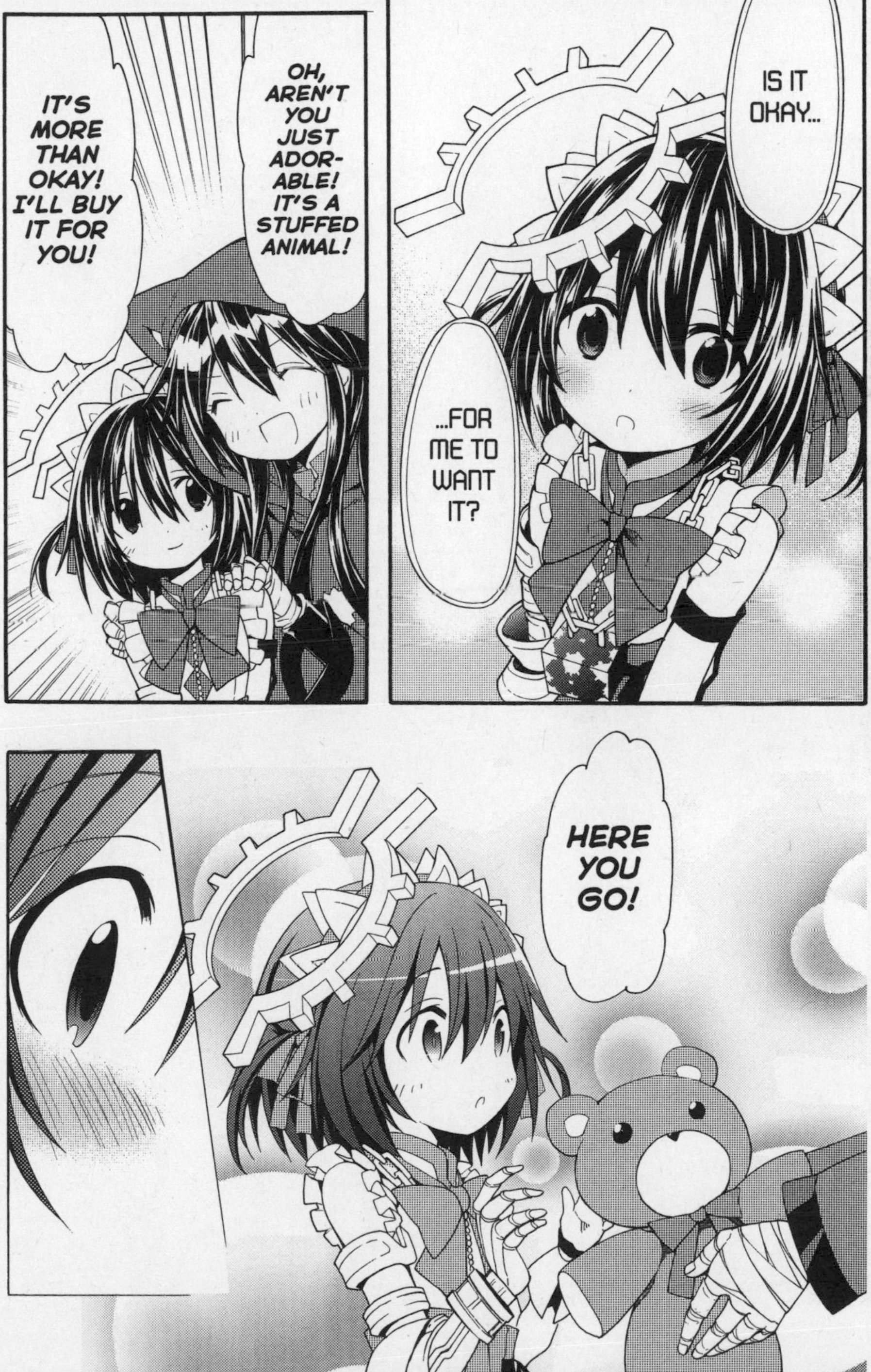
IS IT OKAY...
...FOR ME TO WANT IT?
OH, AREN'T YOU JUST ADORABLE! IT'S A STUFFED ANIMAL!
IT'S MORE THAN OKAY! I'LL BUY IT FOR YOU!
HERE YOU GO!

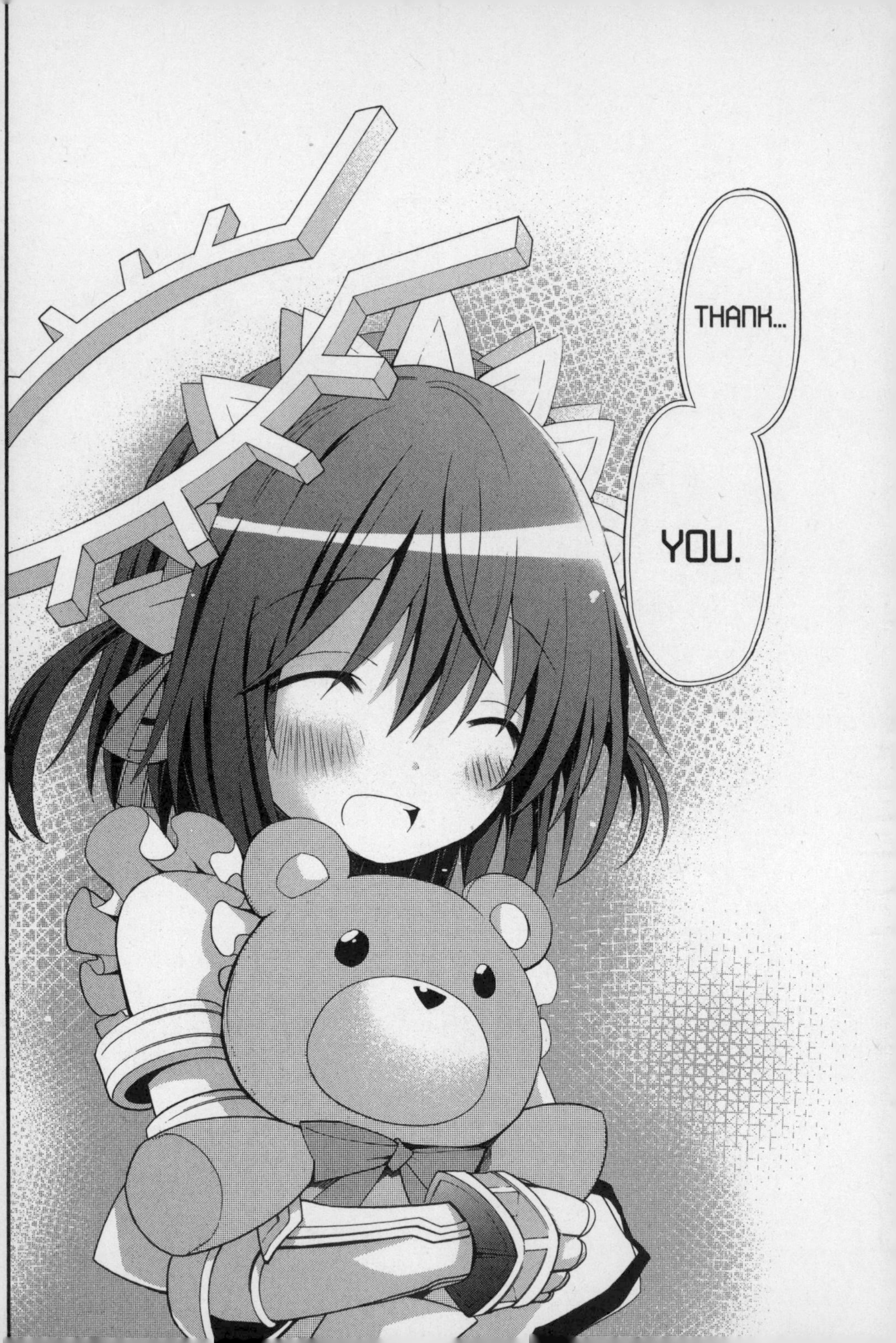
THANK...
YOU.

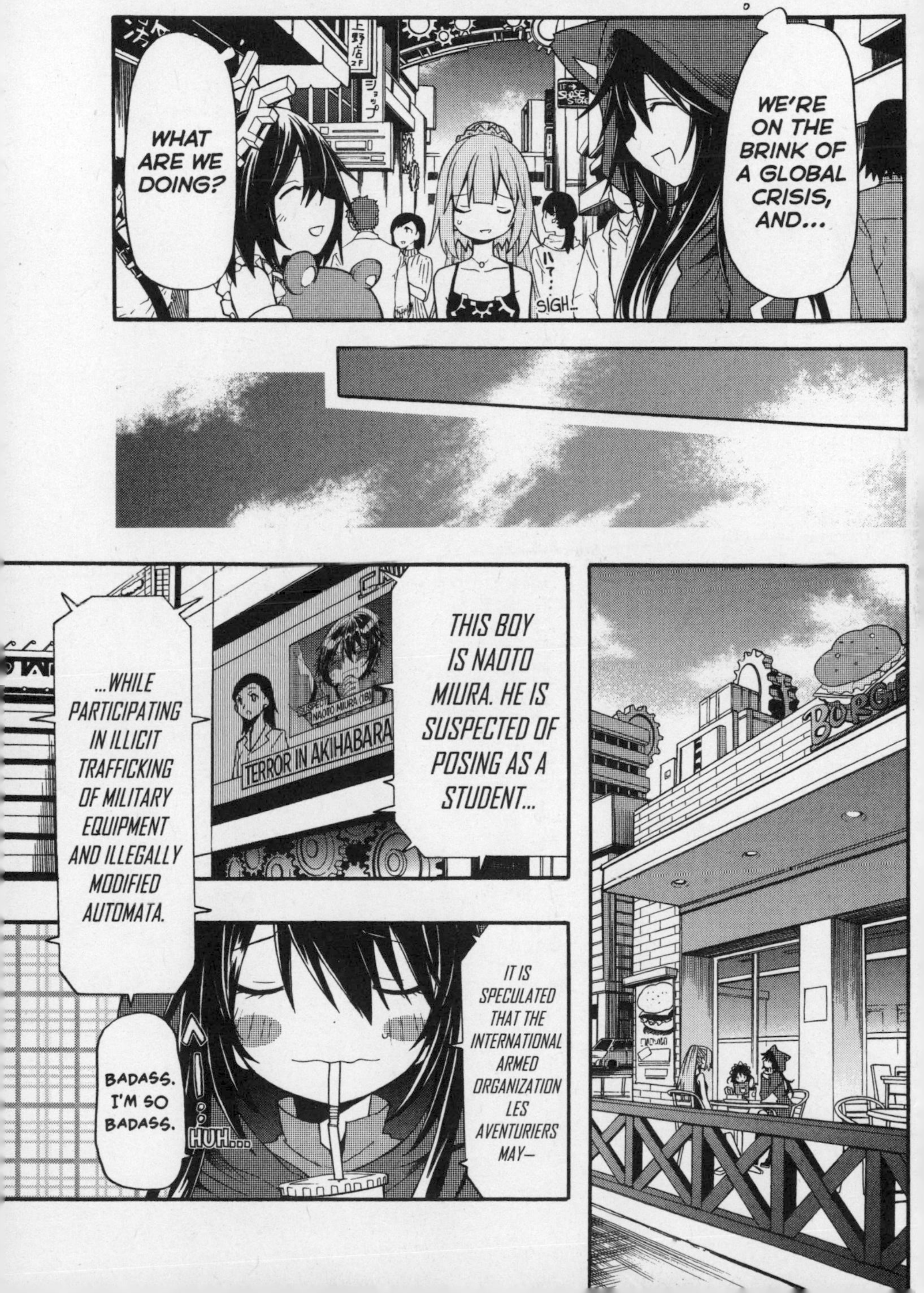
WE'RE ON THE BRINK OF A GLOBAL CRISIS, AND...
WHAT ARE WE DOING?
SIGH...
TERROR IN AKIHABARA
SUSPECT NAOTO MIURA (16)
THIS BOY IS NAOTO MIURA. HE IS SUSPECTED OF POSING AS A STUDENT...
...WHILE PARTICIPATING IN ILLICIT TRAFFICKING OF MILITARY EQUIPMENT AND ILLEGALLY MODIFIED AUTOMATA.
IT IS SPECULATED THAT THE INTERNATIONAL ARMED ORGANIZATION LES AVENTURIERS MAY—
HUH...
BADASS. I'M SO BADASS.

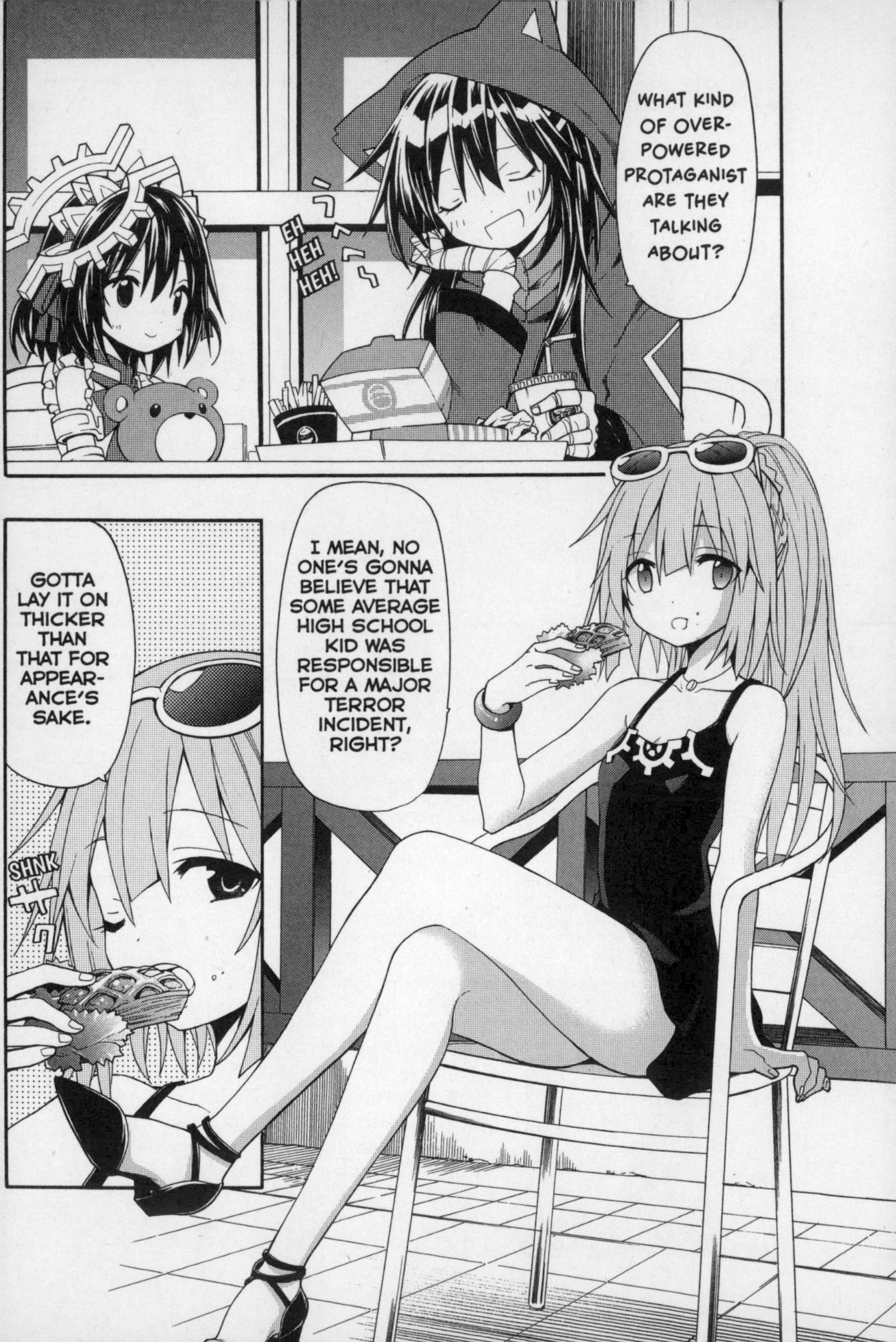
WHAT KIND OF OVER-POWERED PROTAGANIST ARE THEY TALKING ABOUT?
EH HEH HEH!
I MEAN, NO ONE'S GONNA BELIEVE THAT SOME AVERAGE HIGH SCHOOL KID WAS RESPONSIBLE FOR A MAJOR TERROR INCIDENT, RIGHT?
GOTTA LAY IT ON THICKER THAN THAT FOR APPEARANCE'S SAKE.
SHNK

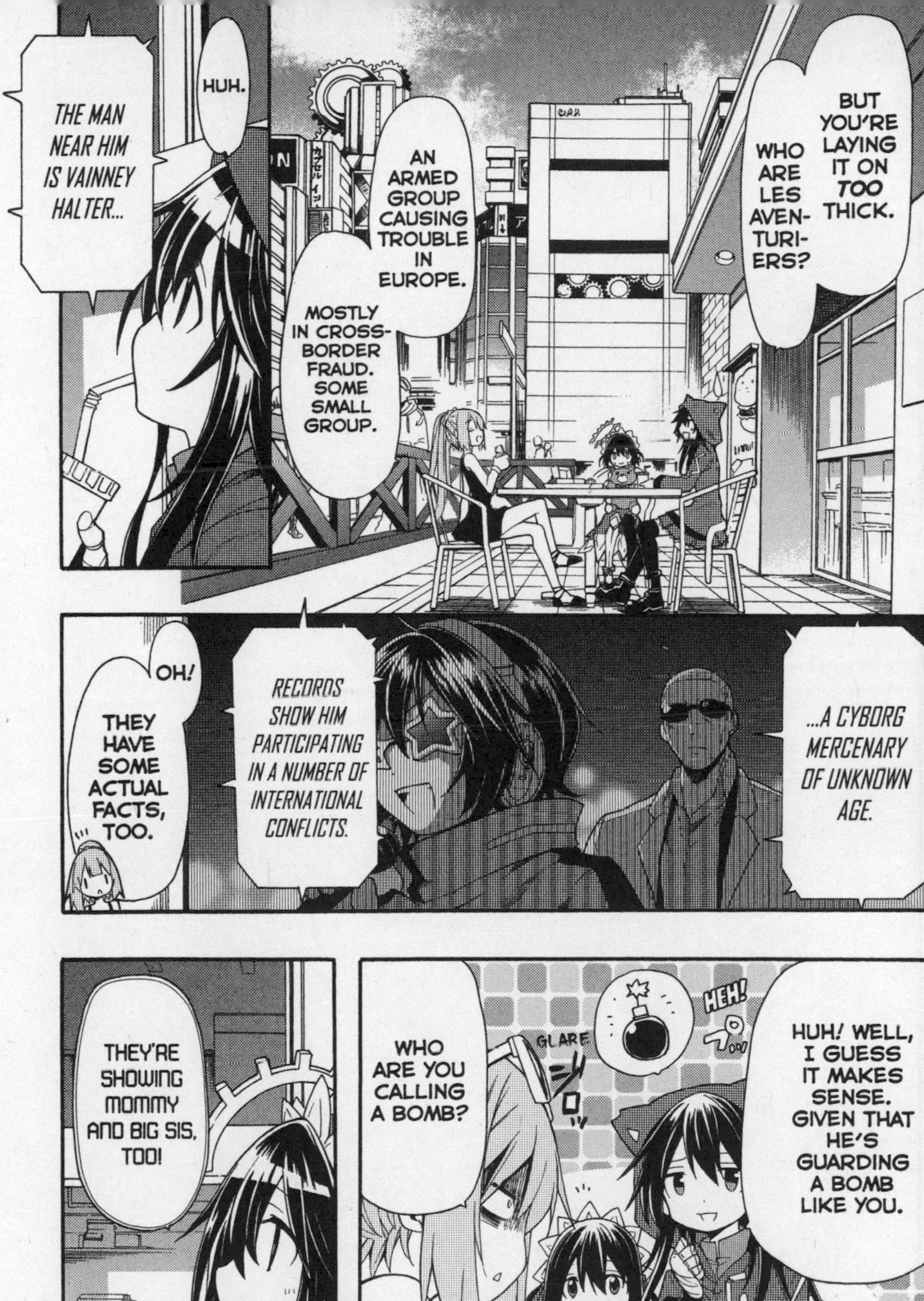
BUT YOU'RE LAYING IT ON *TOO* THICK.
WHO ARE LES AVENTURIERS?
AN ARMED GROUP CAUSING TROUBLE IN EUROPE.
MOSTLY IN CROSS-BORDER FRAUD. SOME SMALL GROUP.
HUH.
THE MAN NEAR HIM IS VAINNEY HALTER...
...A CYBORG MERCENARY OF UNKNOWN AGE.
RECORDS SHOW HIM PARTICIPATING IN A NUMBER OF INTERNATIONAL CONFLICTS.
OH!
THEY HAVE SOME ACTUAL FACTS, TOO.
HUH! WELL, I GUESS IT MAKES SENSE. GIVEN THAT HE'S GUARDING A BOMB LIKE YOU.
HEH!
GLARE
WHO ARE YOU CALLING A BOMB?
THEY'RE SHOWING MOMMY AND BIG SIS, TOO!

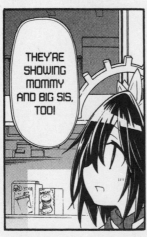

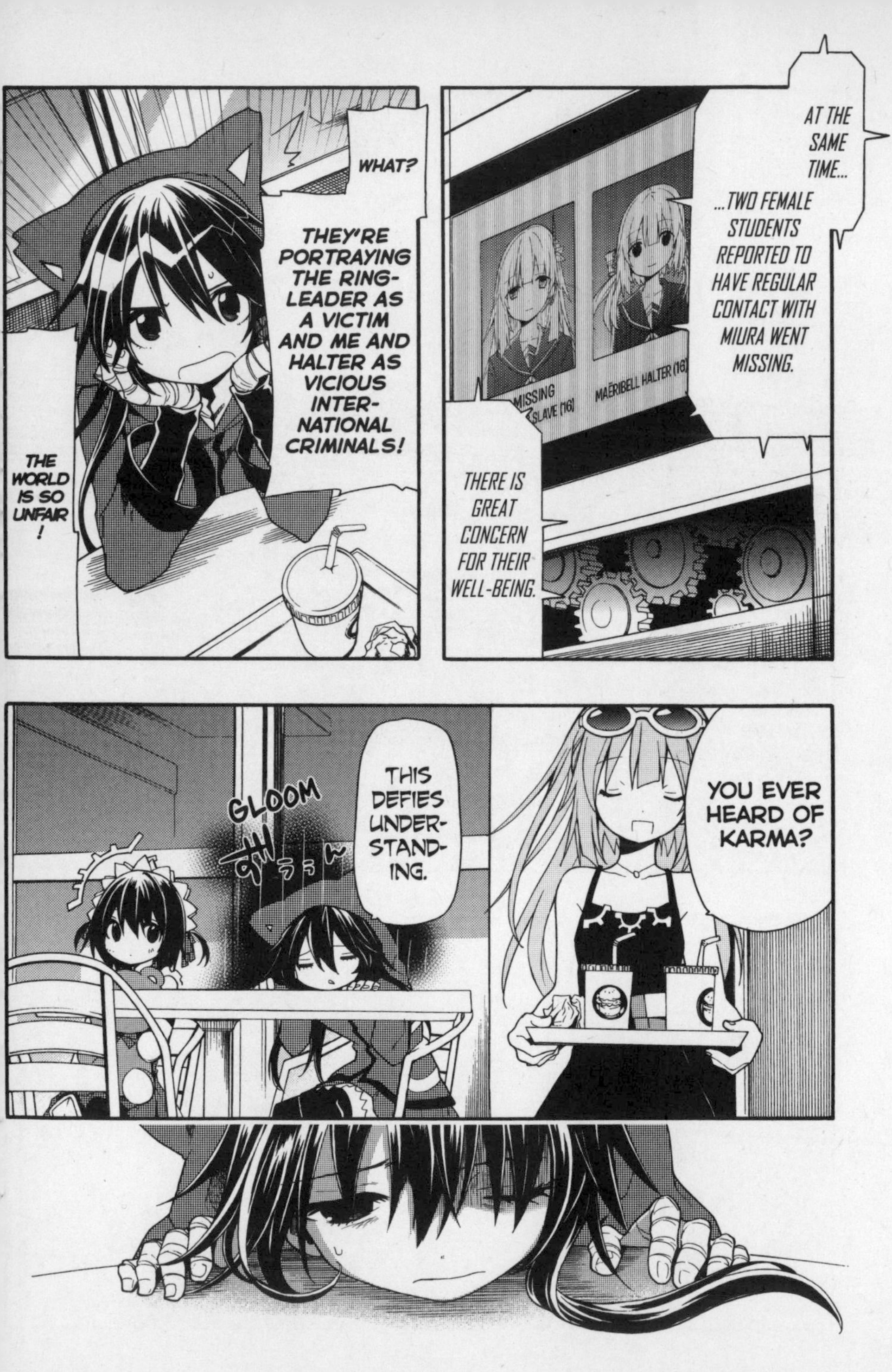
AT THE SAME TIME...
...TWO FEMALE STUDENTS REPORTED TO HAVE REGULAR CONTACT WITH MIURA WENT MISSING.
MISSING
SLAVE (16)
MAERIBELL HALTER (16)
THERE IS GREAT CONCERN FOR THEIR WELL-BEING.
WHAT?
THEY'RE PORTRAYING THE RING-LEADER AS A VICTIM AND ME AND HALTER AS VICIOUS INTER-NATIONAL CRIMINALS!
THE WORLD IS SO UNFAIR!
YOU EVER HEARD OF KARMA?
THIS DEFIES UNDER-STAND-ING.
GLOOM

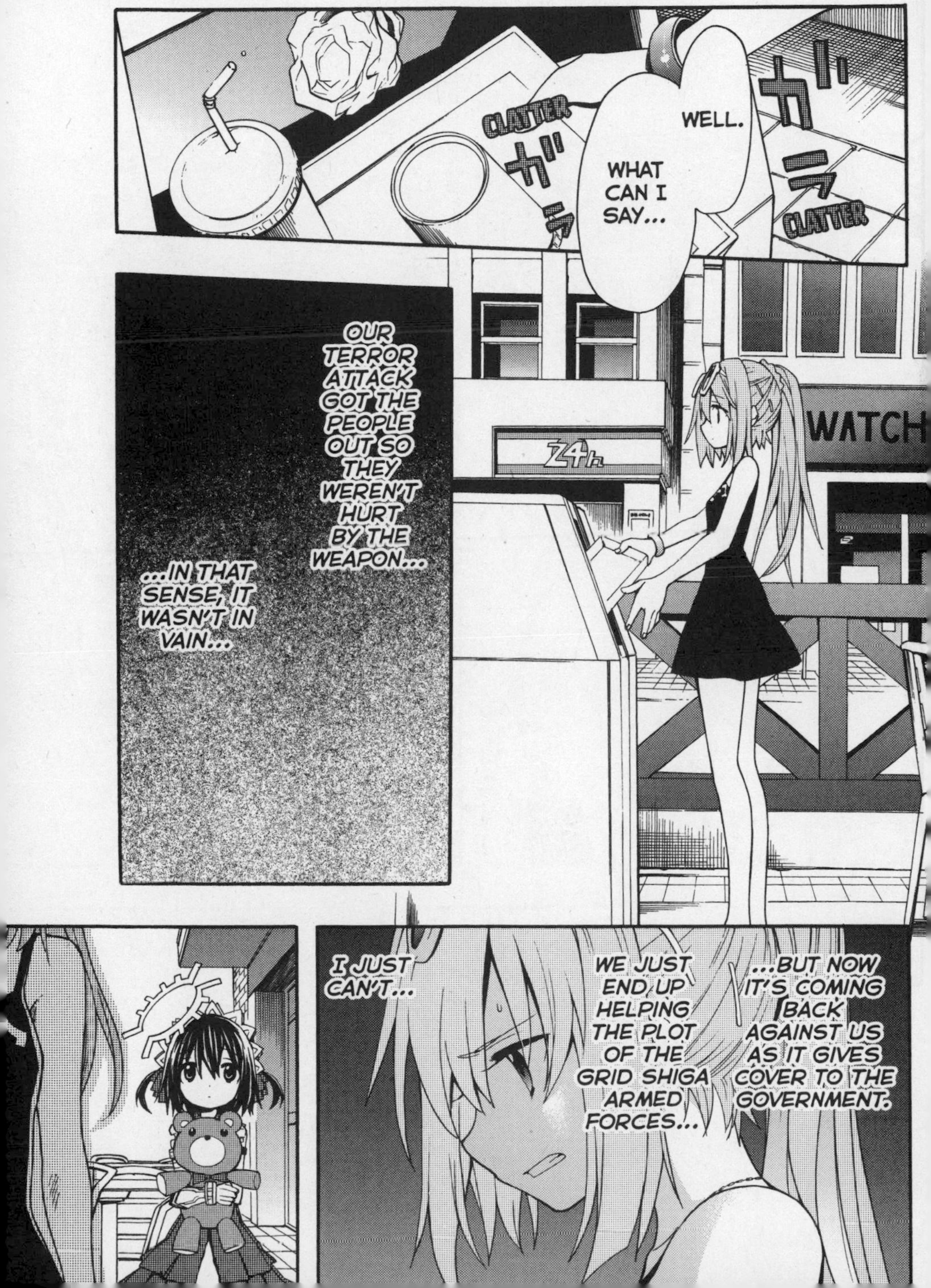
CLATTER
WELL.
WHAT CAN I SAY...
CLATTER
24h
WATCH
OUR TERROR ATTACK GOT THE PEOPLE OUT SO THEY WEREN'T HURT BY THE WEAPON...
...IN THAT SENSE, IT WASN'T IN VAIN...
...BUT NOW IT'S COMING BACK AGAINST US AS IT GIVES COVER TO THE GOVERNMENT.
WE JUST END UP HELPING THE PLOT OF THE GRID SHIGA ARMED FORCES...
I JUST CAN'T...

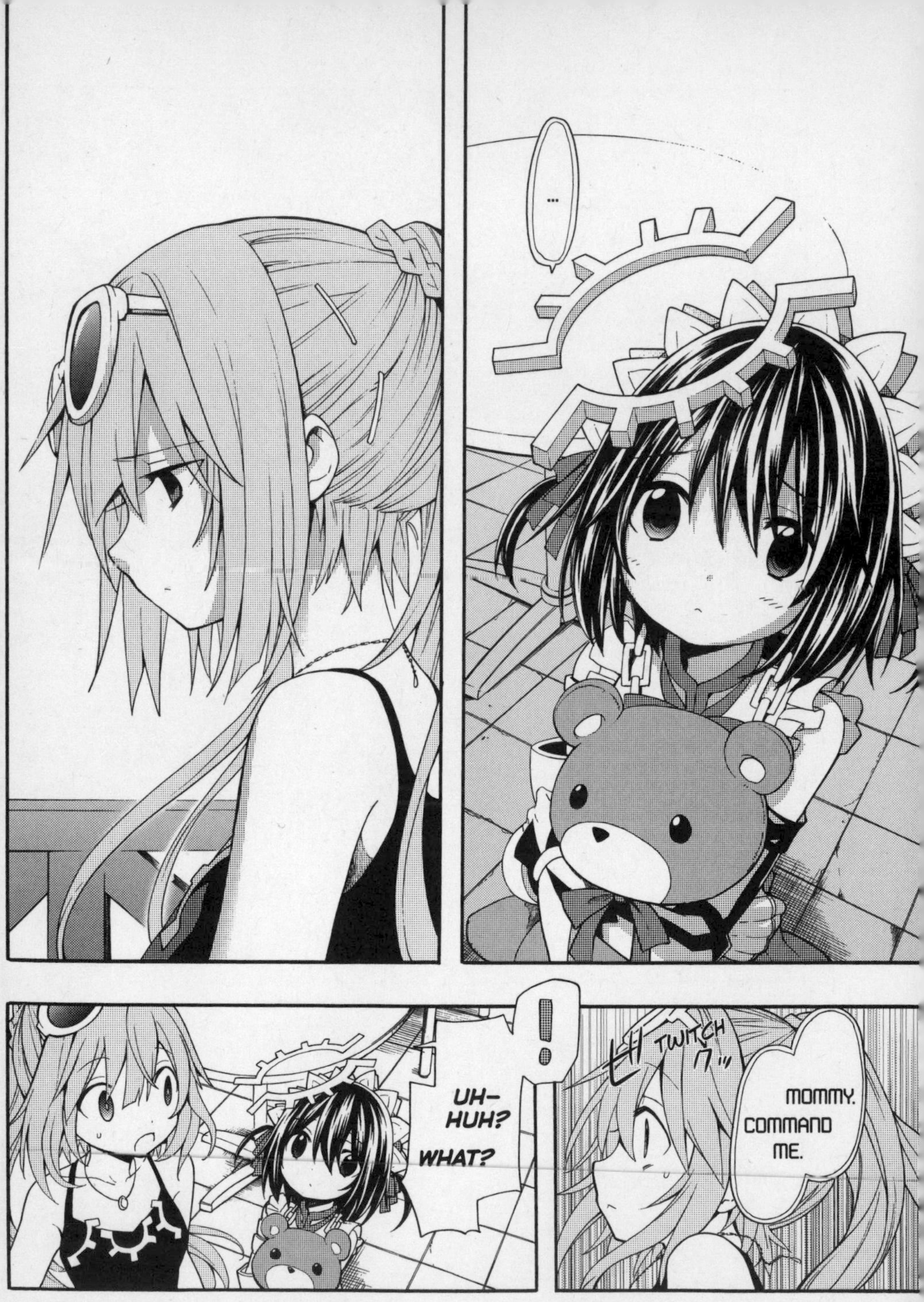
...
TWITCH
MOMMY. COMMAND ME.
!
UH-HUH?
WHAT?

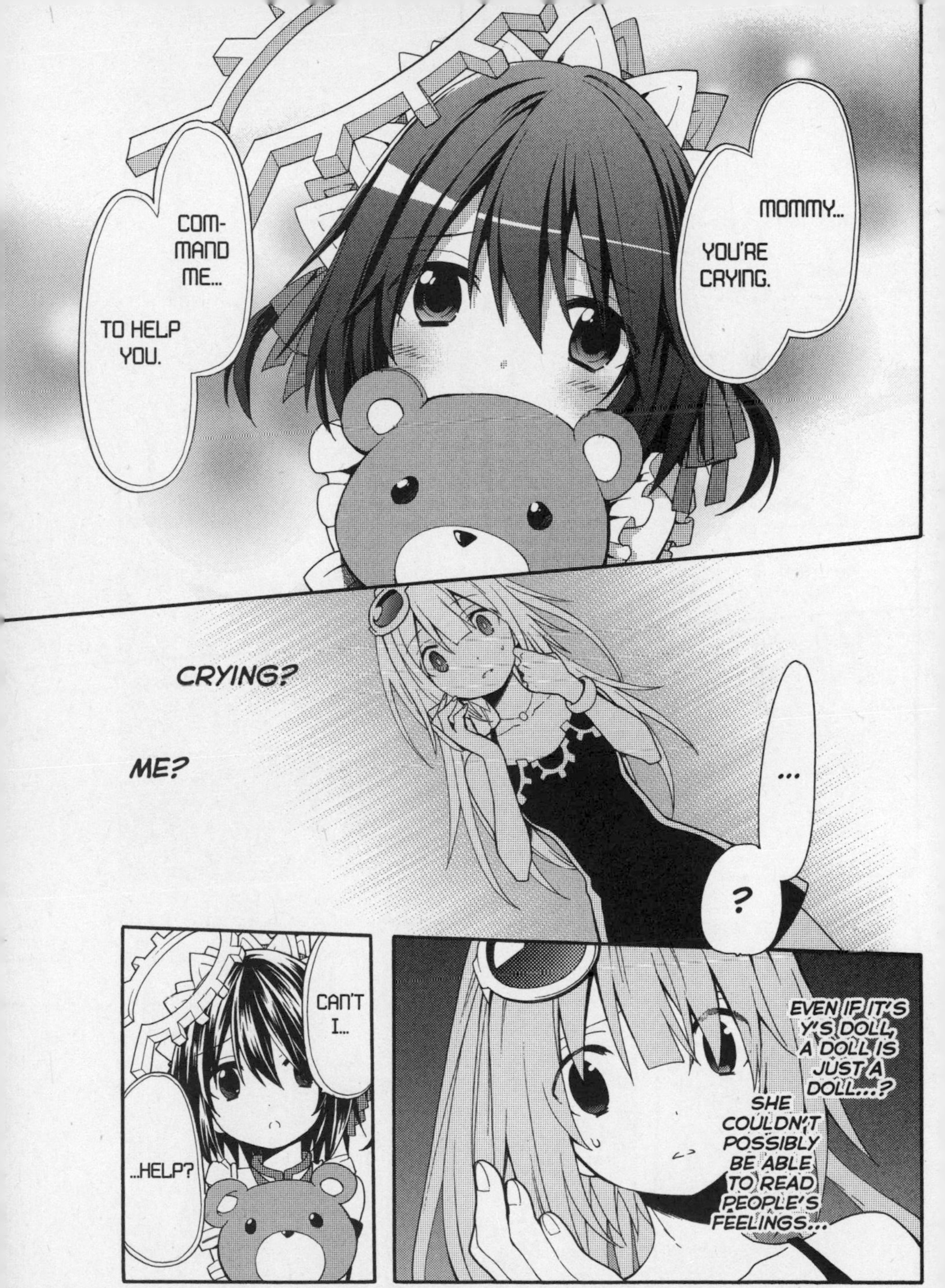
MOMMY... YOU'RE CRYING.
COM-MAND ME... TO HELP YOU.
CRYING?
ME?
...
?
EVEN IF IT'S Y'S DOLL, A DOLL IS JUST A DOLL...?
SHE COULDN'T POSSIBLY BE ABLE TO READ PEOPLE'S FEELINGS...
CAN'T I...
...HELP?

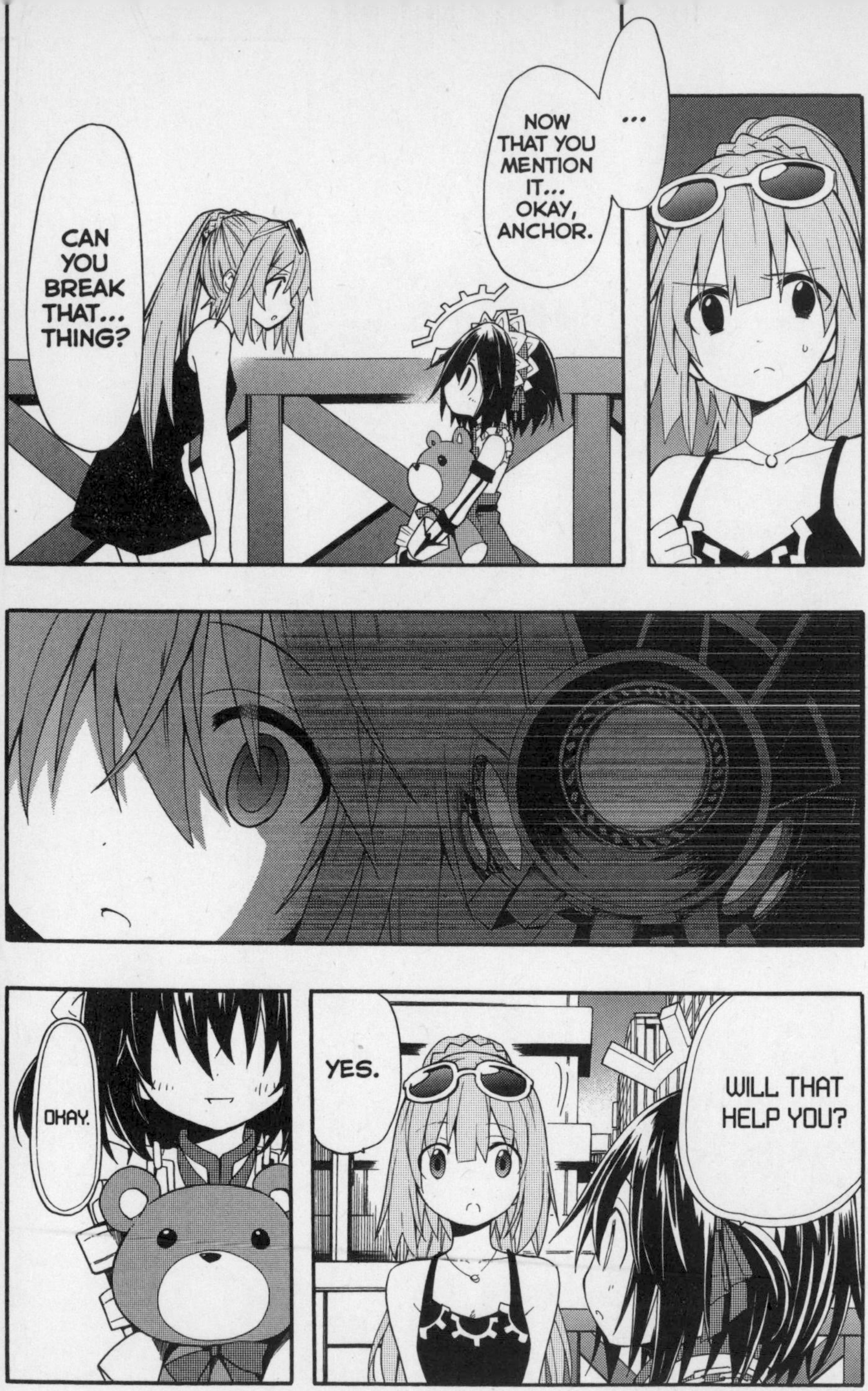
...
NOW THAT YOU MENTION IT... OKAY, ANCHOR.
CAN YOU BREAK THAT... THING?
WILL THAT HELP YOU?
YES.
OKAY.

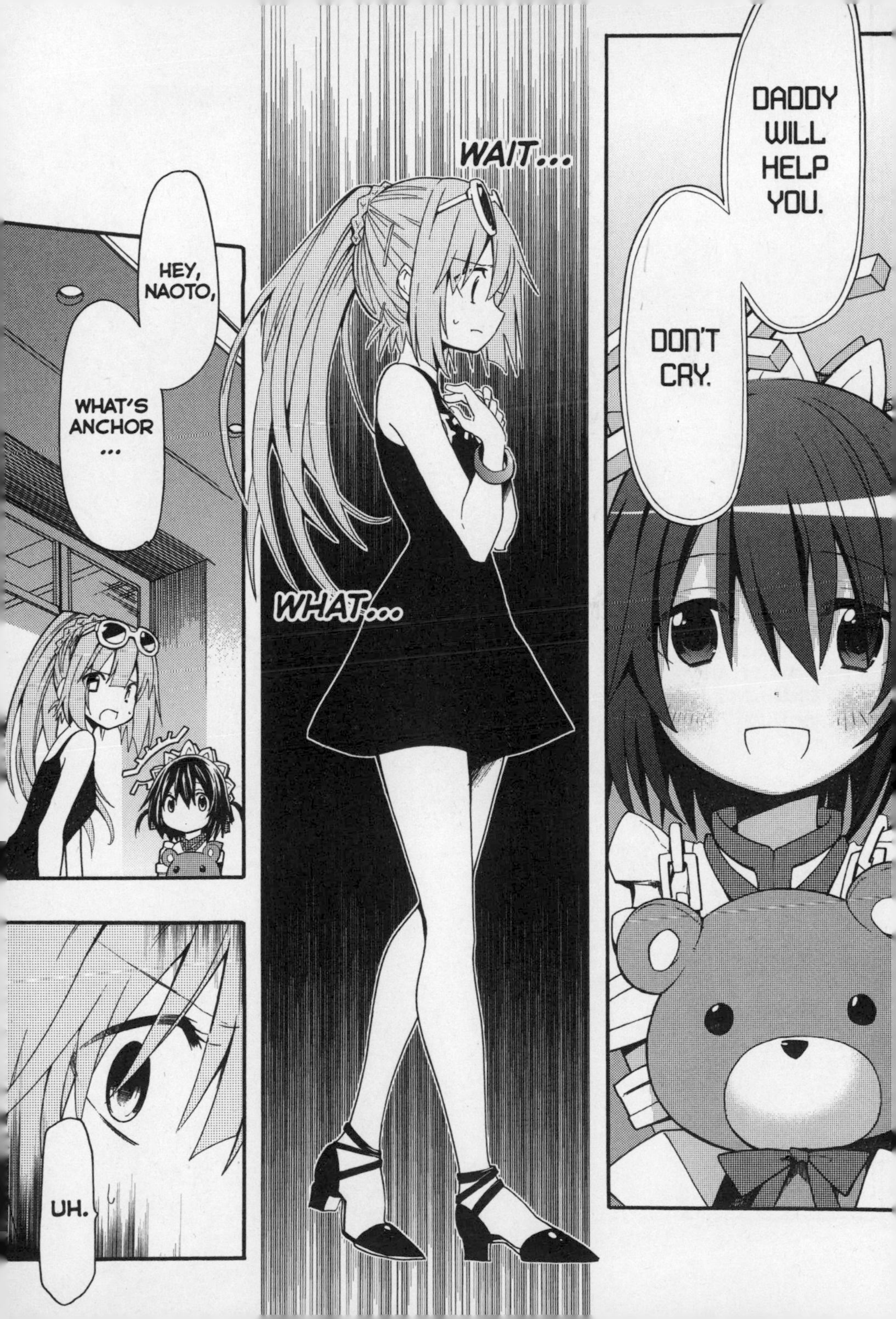
DADDY WILL HELP YOU.
DON'T CRY.
WAIT...
WHAT...
HEY, NAOTO,
WHAT'S ANCHOR ...
UH.

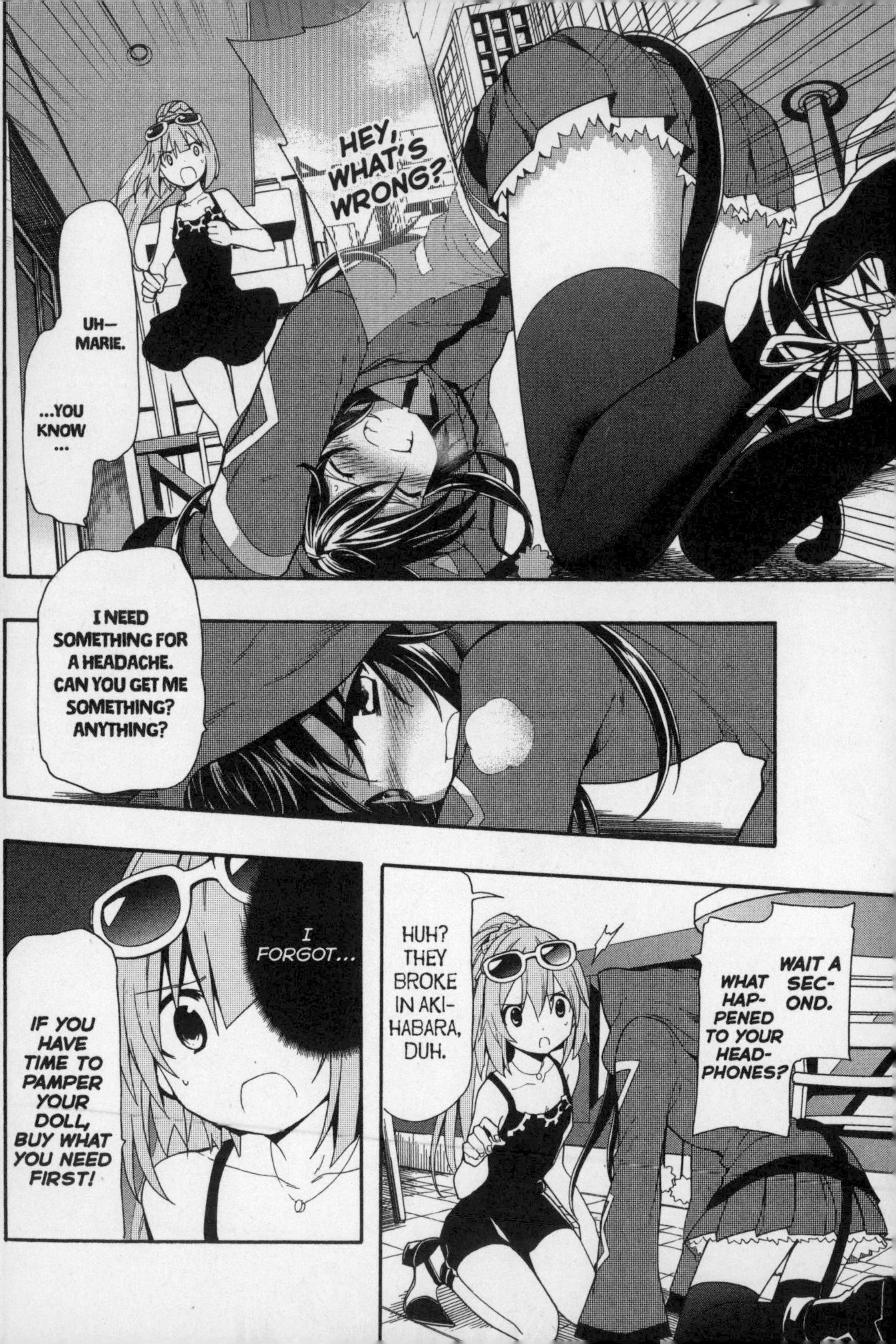
HEY, WHAT'S WRONG?
UH— MARIE. ...YOU KNOW ...
I NEED SOMETHING FOR A HEADACHE. CAN YOU GET ME SOMETHING? ANYTHING?
WAIT A SEC-OND. WHAT HAP-PENED TO YOUR HEAD-PHONES?
HUH? THEY BROKE IN AKI-HABARA, DUH.
I FORGOT...
IF YOU HAVE TIME TO PAMPER YOUR DOLL, BUY WHAT YOU NEED FIRST!

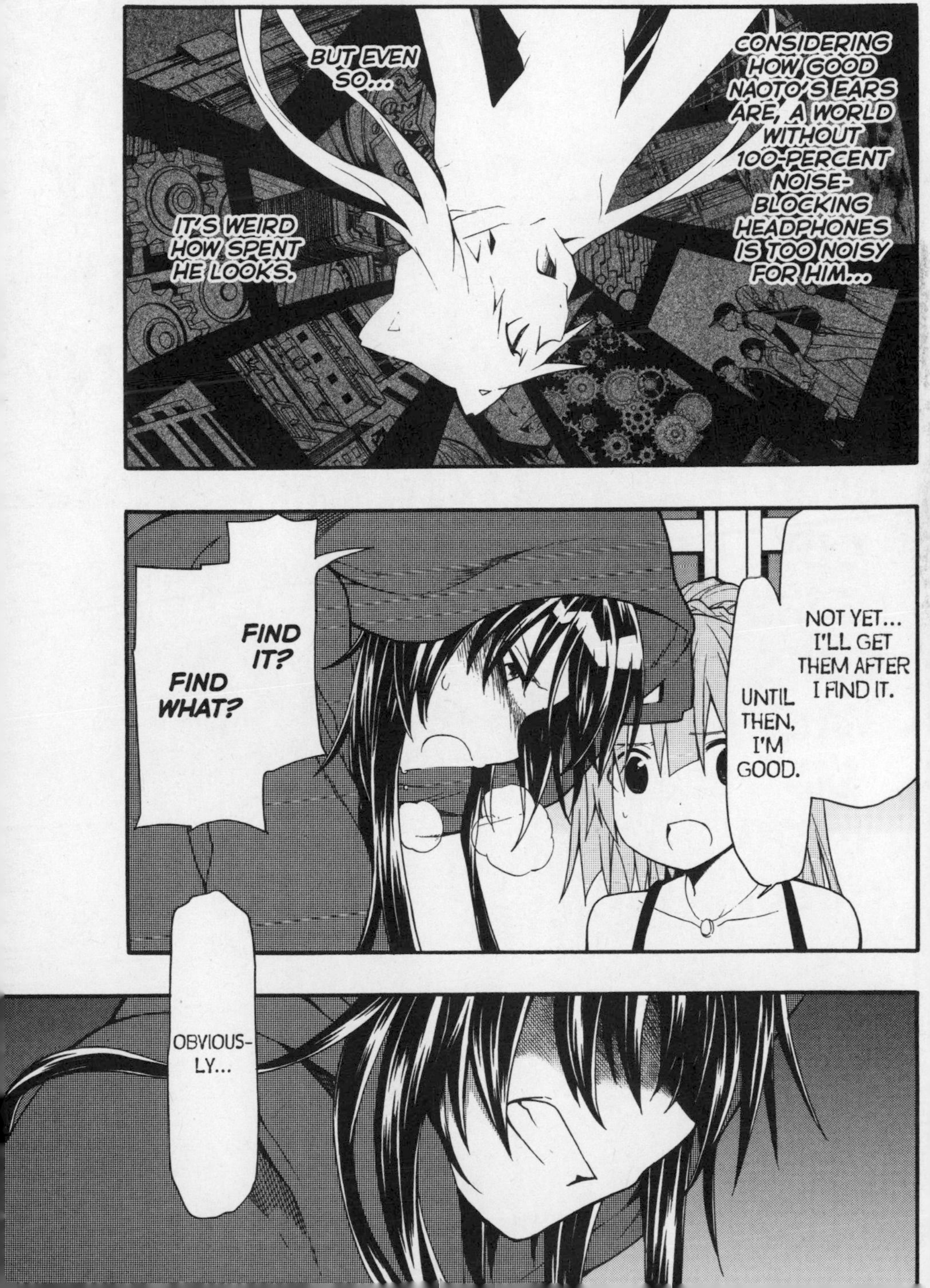
CONSIDERING HOW GOOD NAOTO'S EARS ARE, A WORLD WITHOUT 100-PERCENT NOISE-BLOCKING HEADPHONES IS TOO NOISY FOR HIM...
BUT EVEN SO...
IT'S WEIRD HOW SPENT HE LOOKS.
NOT YET... I'LL GET THEM AFTER I FIND IT.
UNTIL THEN, I'M GOOD.
FIND IT? FIND WHAT?
OBVIOUS-LY...

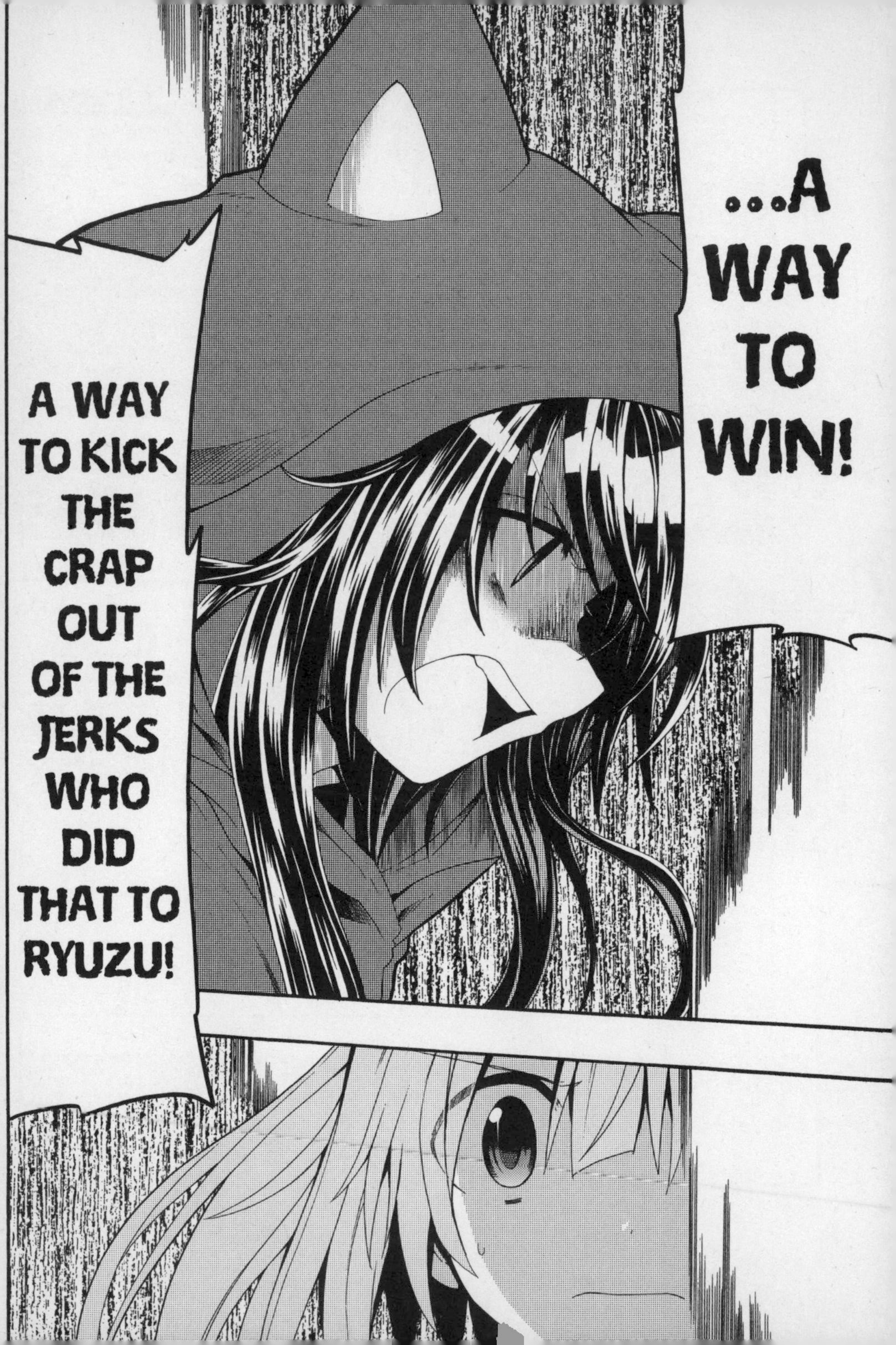
...A WAY TO WIN!
A WAY TO KICK THE CRAP OUT OF THE JERKS WHO DID THAT TO RYUZU!

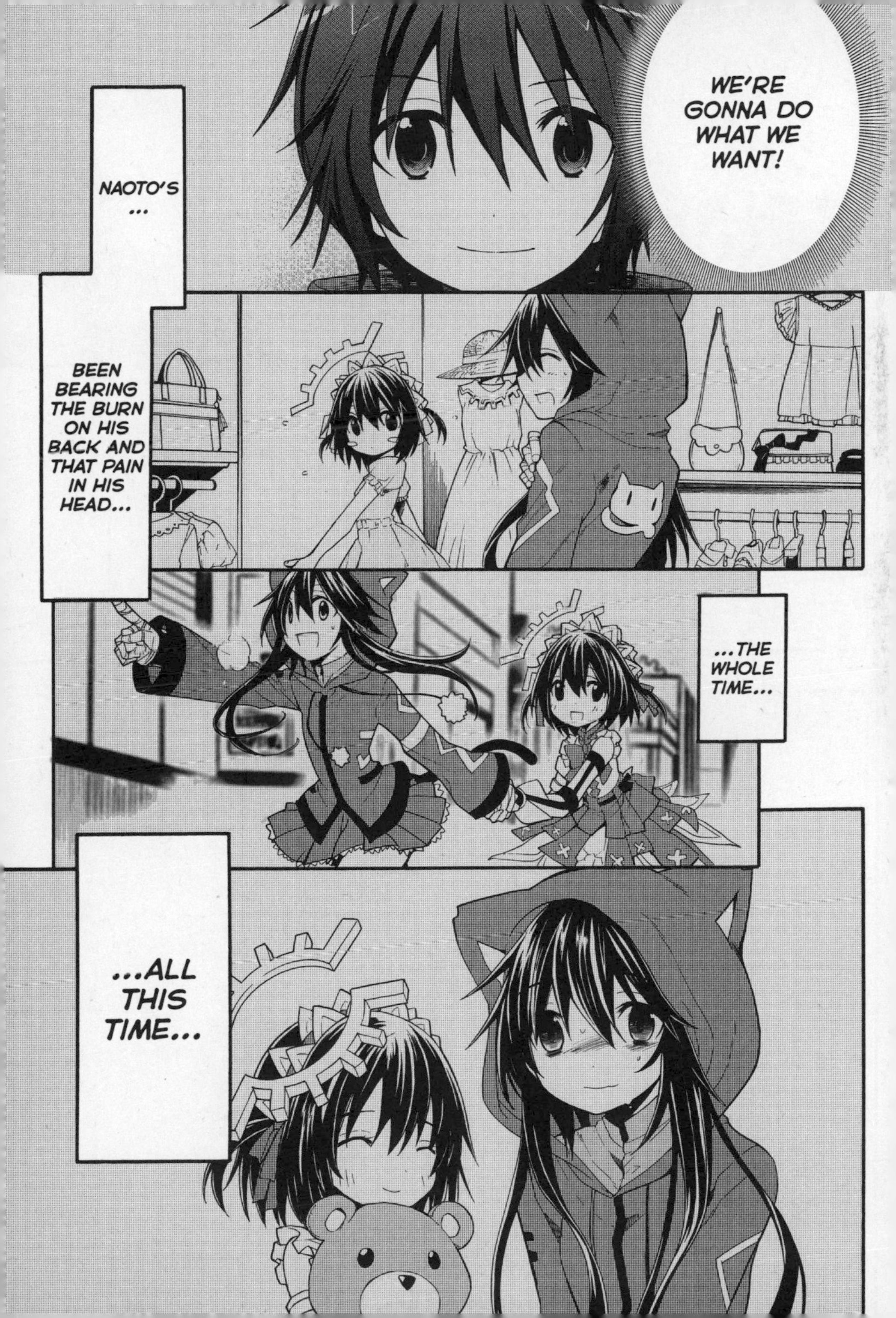
WE'RE GONNA DO WHAT WE WANT!
NAOTO'S ...
BEEN BEARING THE BURN ON HIS BACK AND THAT PAIN IN HIS HEAD...
...THE WHOLE TIME...
...ALL THIS TIME...

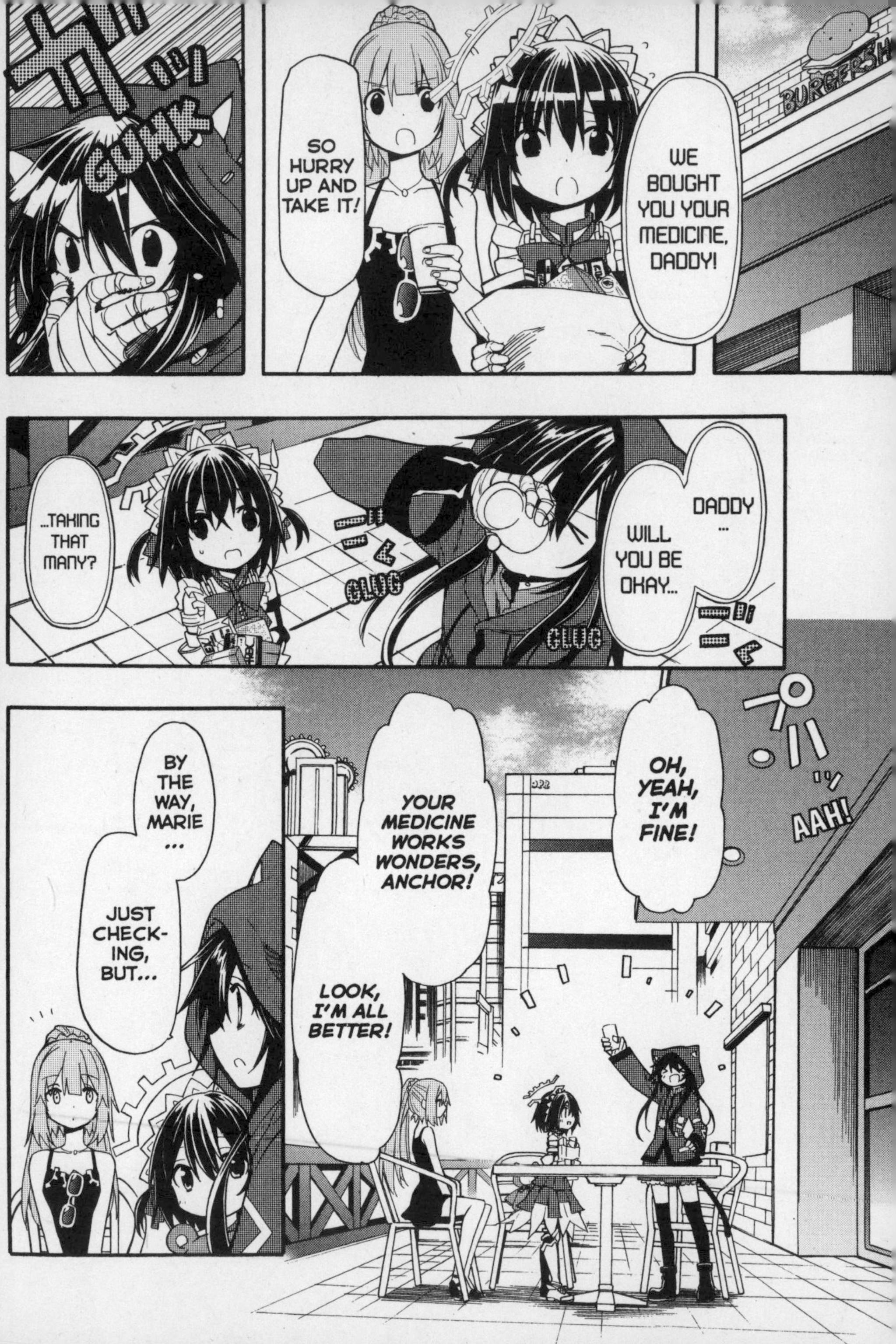
BURGERSH
WE BOUGHT YOU YOUR MEDICINE, DADDY!
SO HURRY UP AND TAKE IT!
GUHK
DADDY ...
WILL YOU BE OKAY...
GLUG
GLUG
...TAKING THAT MANY?
AAH!
OH, YEAH, I'M FINE!
YOUR MEDICINE WORKS WONDERS, ANCHOR!
LOOK, I'M ALL BETTER!
BY THE WAY, MARIE ...
JUST CHECKING, BUT...

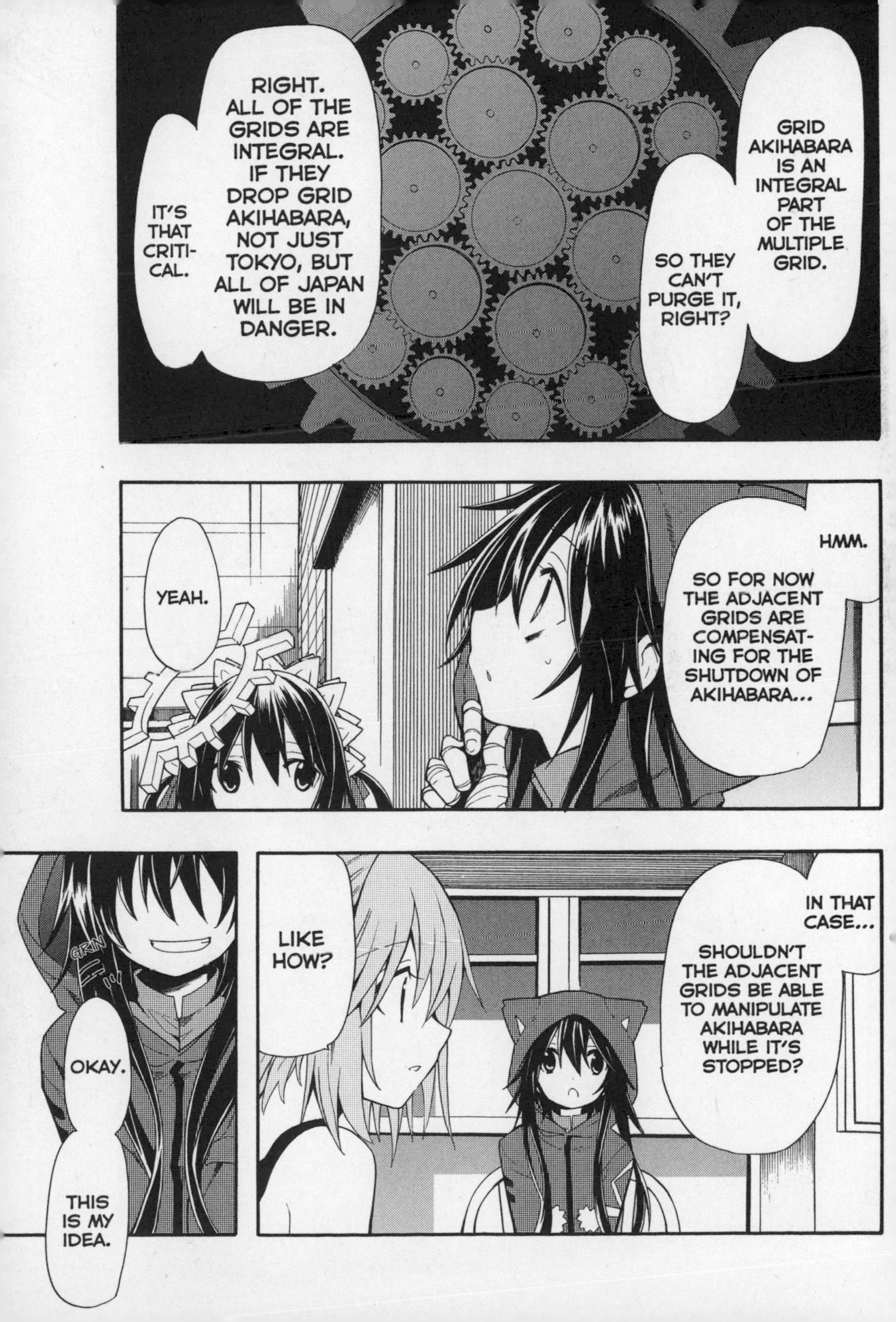
GRID AKIHABARA IS AN INTEGRAL PART OF THE MULTIPLE GRID.
SO THEY CAN'T PURGE IT, RIGHT?
RIGHT. ALL OF THE GRIDS ARE INTEGRAL. IF THEY DROP GRID AKIHABARA, NOT JUST TOKYO, BUT ALL OF JAPAN WILL BE IN DANGER.
IT'S THAT CRITI-CAL.
HMM.
SO FOR NOW THE ADJACENT GRIDS ARE COMPENSAT-ING FOR THE SHUTDOWN OF AKIHABARA...
YEAH.
IN THAT CASE...
SHOULDN'T THE ADJACENT GRIDS BE ABLE TO MANIPULATE AKIHABARA WHILE IT'S STOPPED?
LIKE HOW?
GRIN
OKAY.
THIS IS MY IDEA.

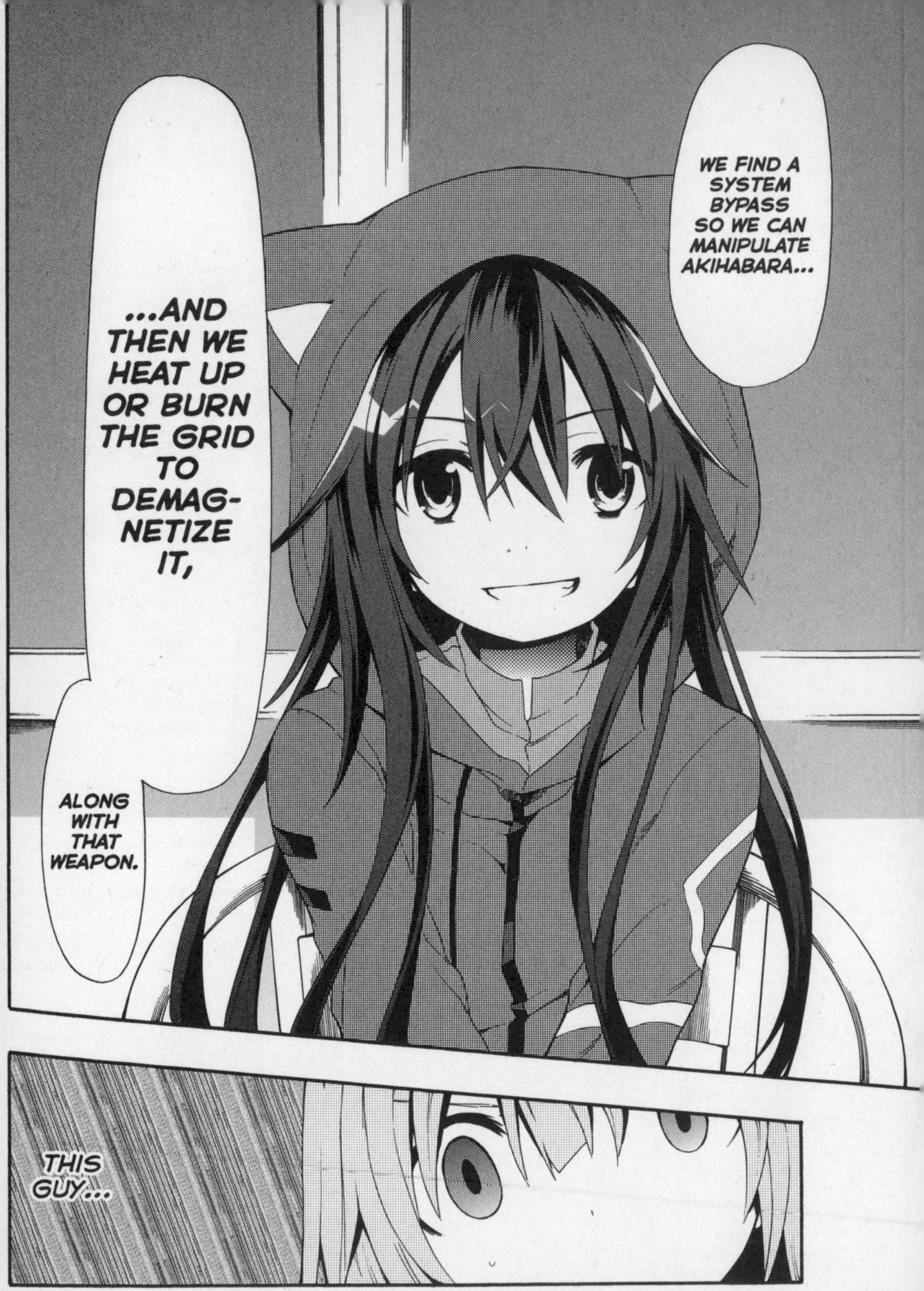
WE FIND A SYSTEM BYPASS SO WE CAN MANIPULATE AKIHABARA...
...AND THEN WE HEAT UP OR BURN THE GRID TO DEMAG- NETIZE IT,
ALONG WITH THAT WEAPON.
THIS GUY...

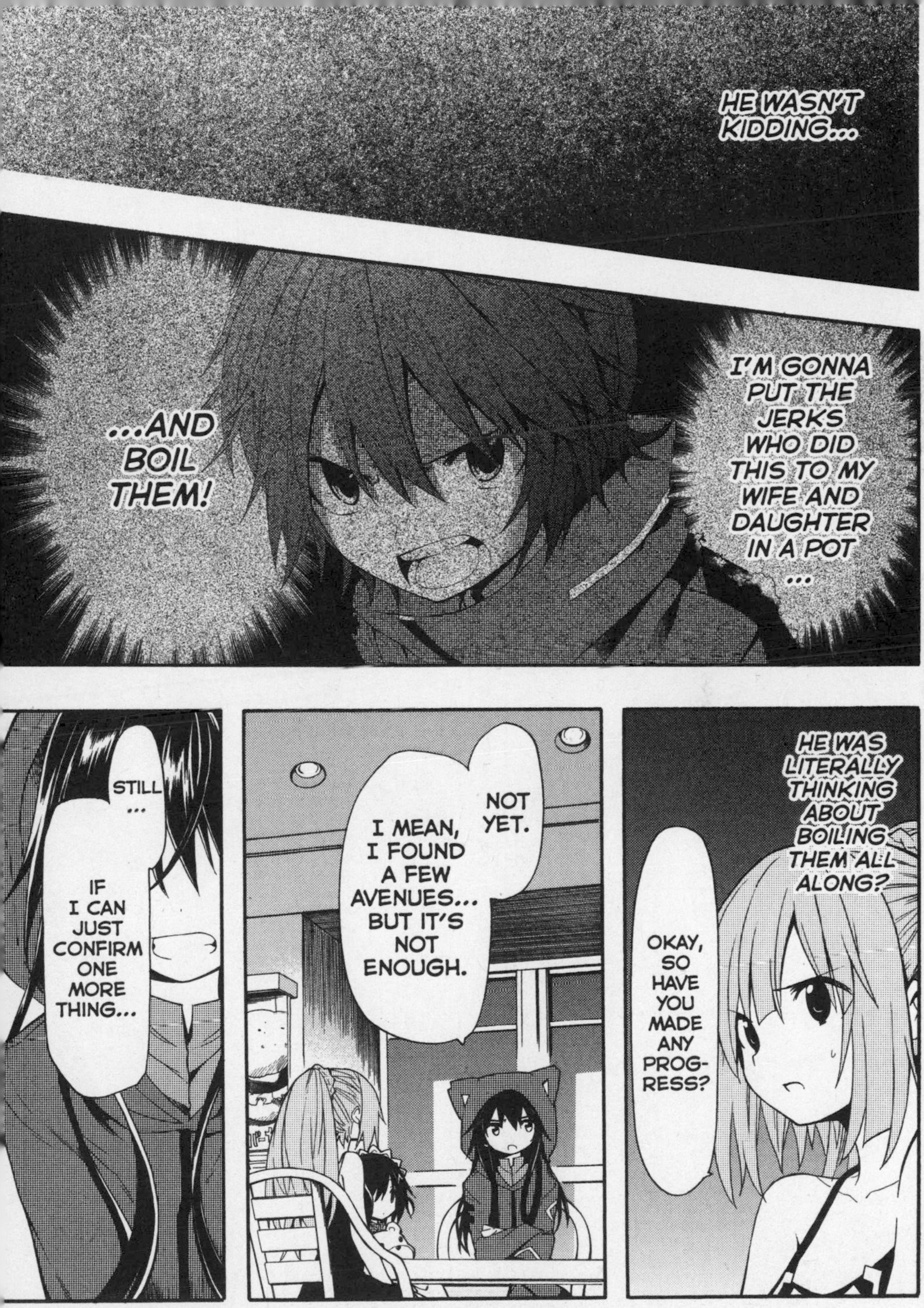
HE WASN'T KIDDING...
I'M GONNA PUT THE JERKS WHO DID THIS TO MY WIFE AND DAUGHTER IN A POT ...
...AND BOIL THEM!
HE WAS LITERALLY THINKING ABOUT BOILING THEM ALL ALONG?
OKAY, SO HAVE YOU MADE ANY PROG-RESS?
NOT YET.
I MEAN, I FOUND A FEW AVENUES... BUT IT'S NOT ENOUGH.
STILL ...
IF I CAN JUST CONFIRM ONE MORE THING...

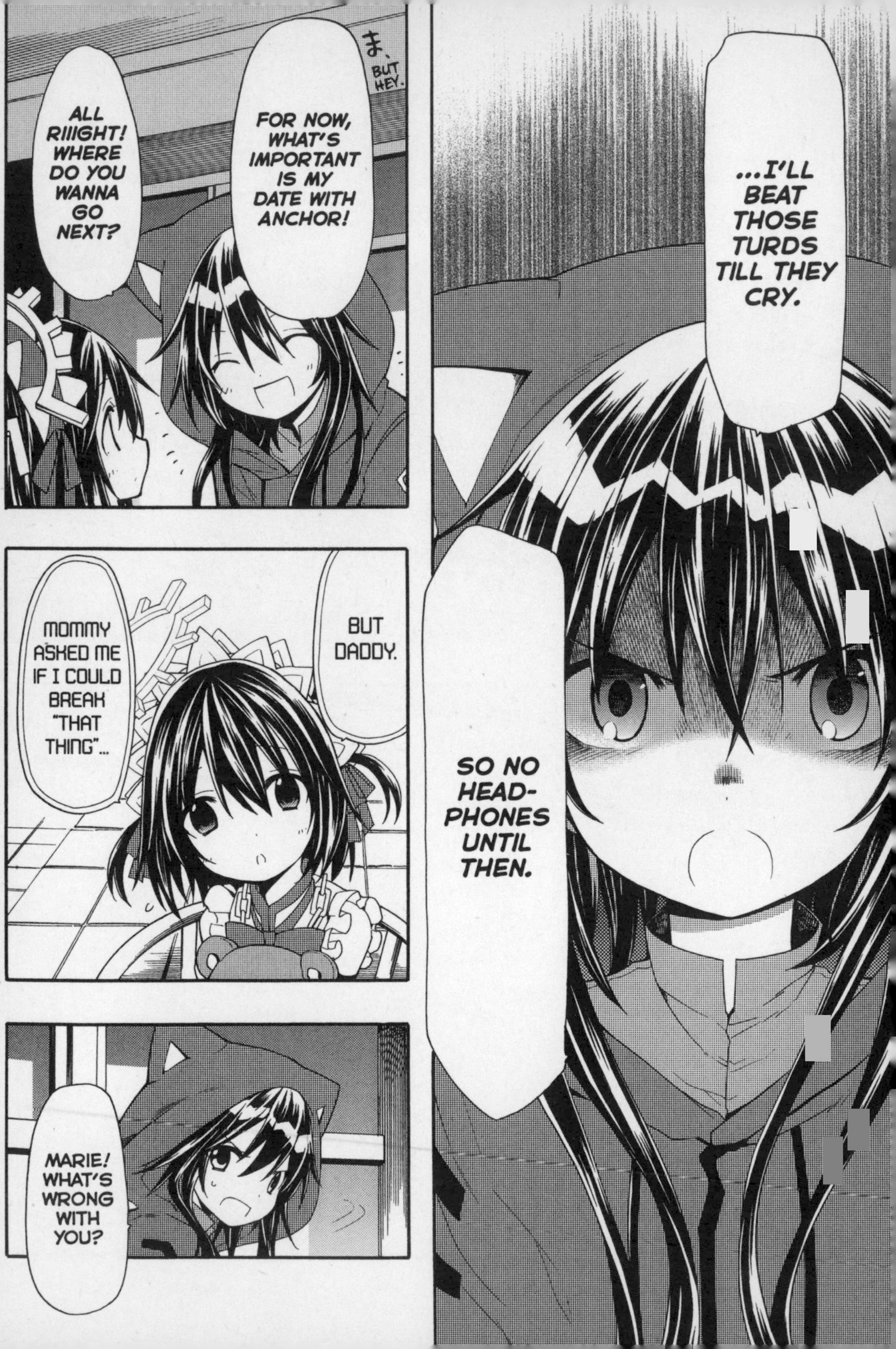
...I'LL BEAT THOSE TURDS TILL THEY CRY.
SO NO HEAD-PHONES UNTIL THEN.
ま、BUT HEY.
FOR NOW, WHAT'S IMPORTANT IS MY DATE WITH ANCHOR!
ALL RIIIGHT! WHERE DO YOU WANNA GO NEXT?
BUT DADDY.
MOMMY ASKED ME IF I COULD BREAK "THAT THING"...
MARIE! WHAT'S WRONG WITH YOU?

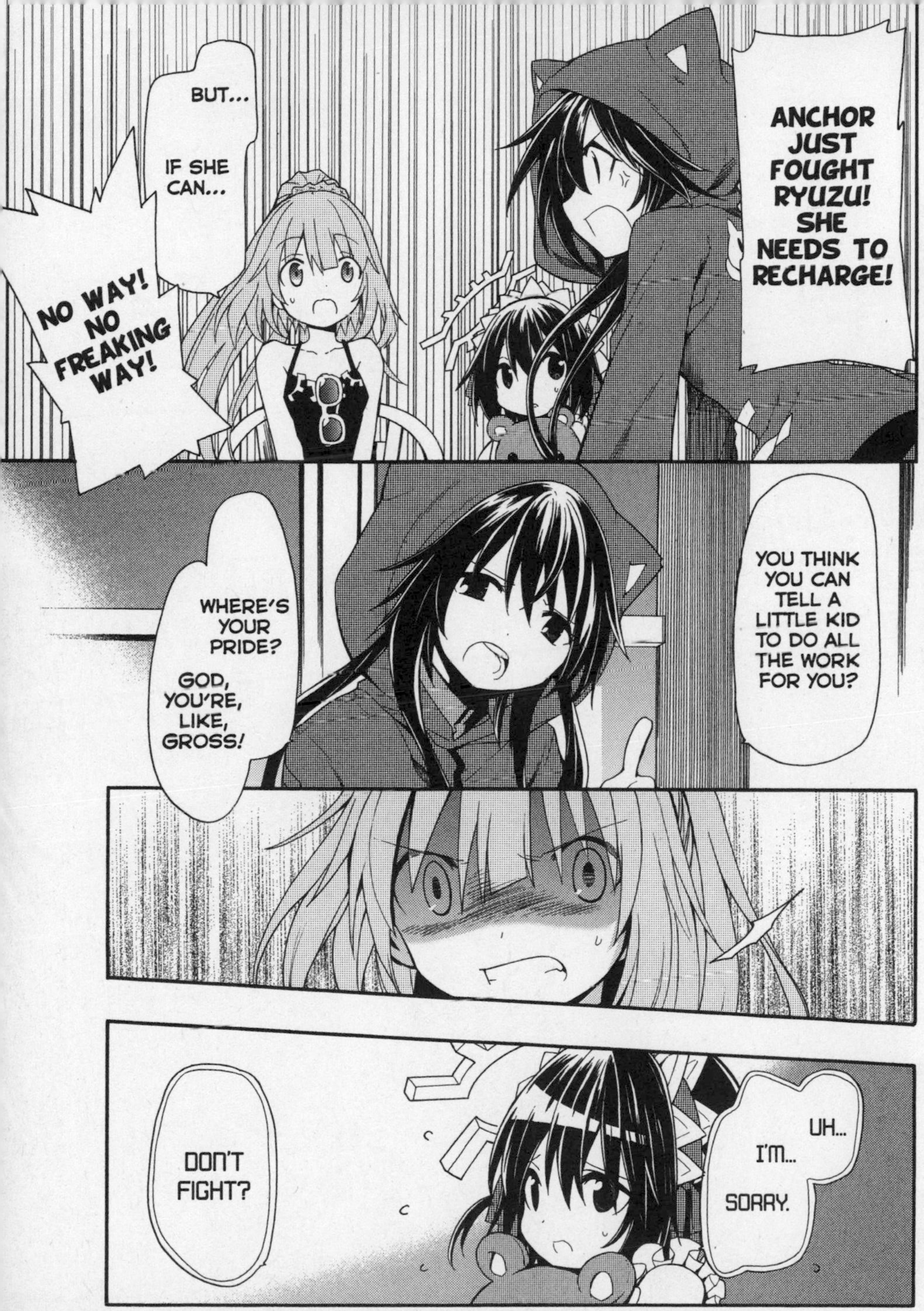
ANCHOR JUST FOUGHT RYUZU! SHE NEEDS TO RECHARGE!
BUT...
IF SHE CAN...
NO WAY! NO FREAKING WAY!
YOU THINK YOU CAN TELL A LITTLE KID TO DO ALL THE WORK FOR YOU?
WHERE'S YOUR PRIDE?
GOD, YOU'RE, LIKE, GROSS!
UH... I'M... SORRY.
DON'T FIGHT?

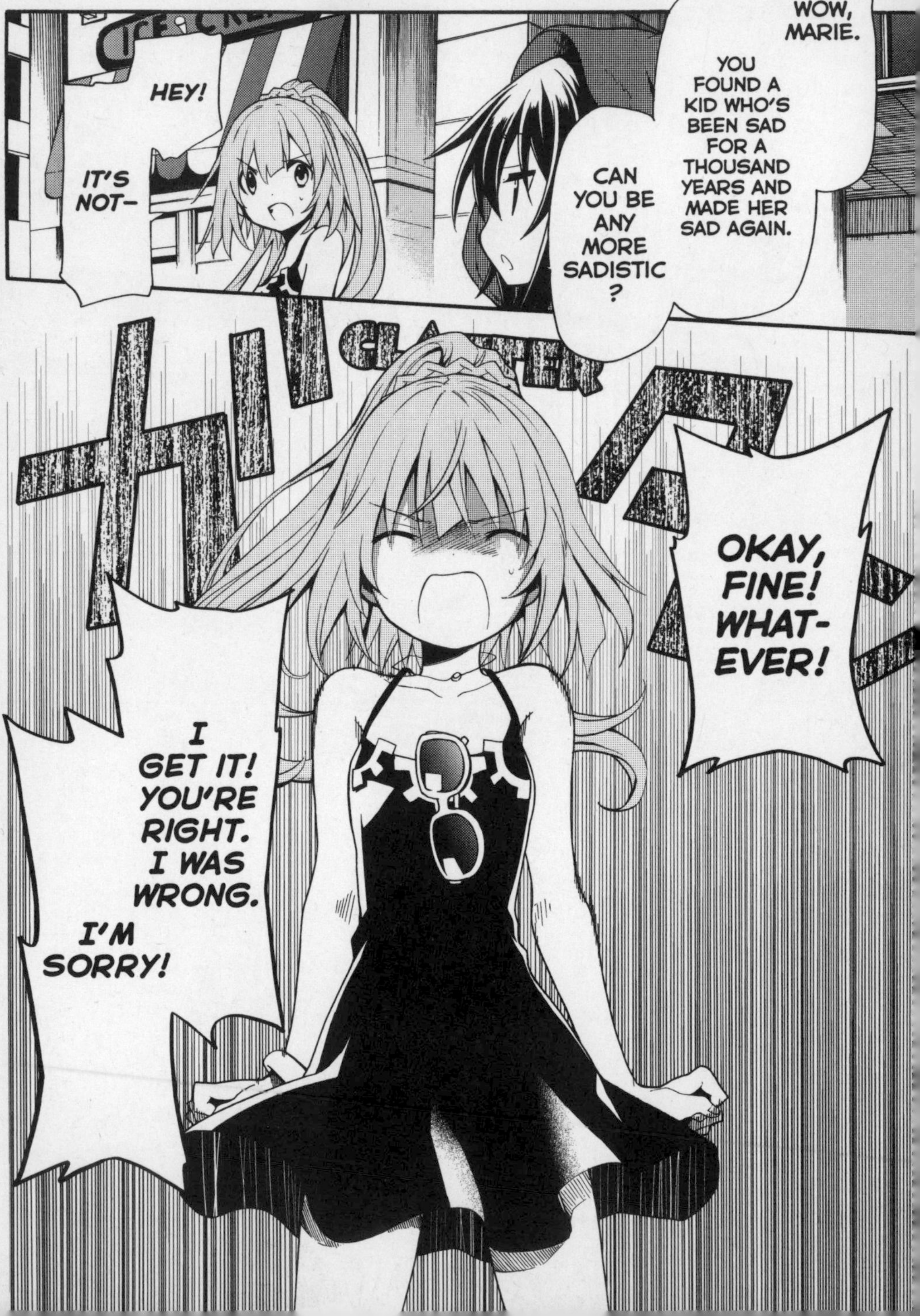
WOW, MARIE.
YOU FOUND A KID WHO'S BEEN SAD FOR A THOUSAND YEARS AND MADE HER SAD AGAIN.
CAN YOU BE ANY MORE SADISTIC?
HEY!
IT'S NOT–
CLATTER
OKAY, FINE! WHAT-EVER!
I GET IT! YOU'RE RIGHT. I WAS WRONG.
I'M SORRY!

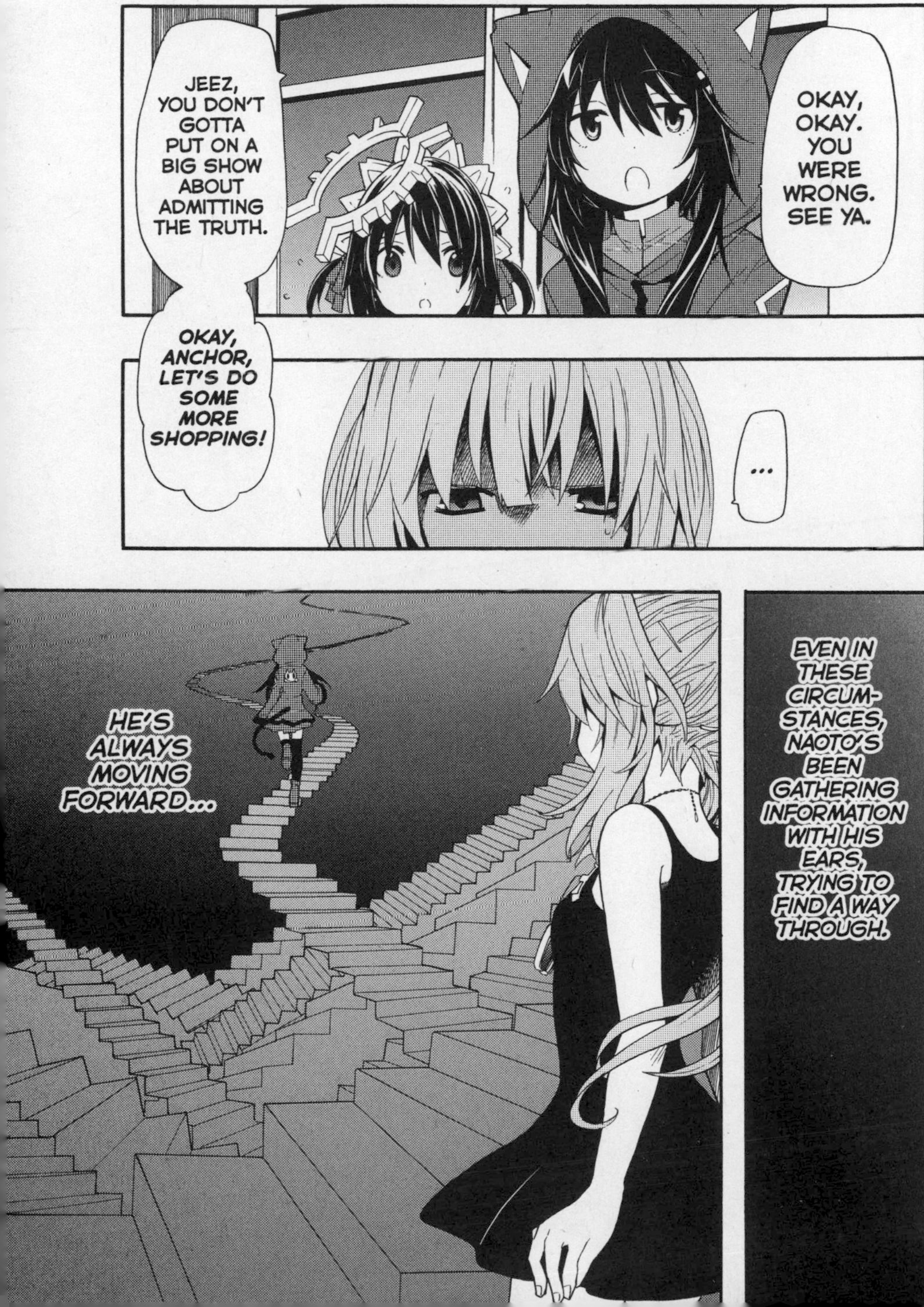
OKAY, OKAY. YOU WERE WRONG. SEE YA.
JEEZ, YOU DON'T GOTTA PUT ON A BIG SHOW ABOUT ADMITTING THE TRUTH.
OKAY, ANCHOR, LET'S DO SOME MORE SHOPPING!
...
EVEN IN THESE CIRCUM-STANCES, NAOTO'S BEEN GATHERING INFORMATION WITH HIS EARS, TRYING TO FIND A WAY THROUGH.
HE'S ALWAYS MOVING FORWARD...

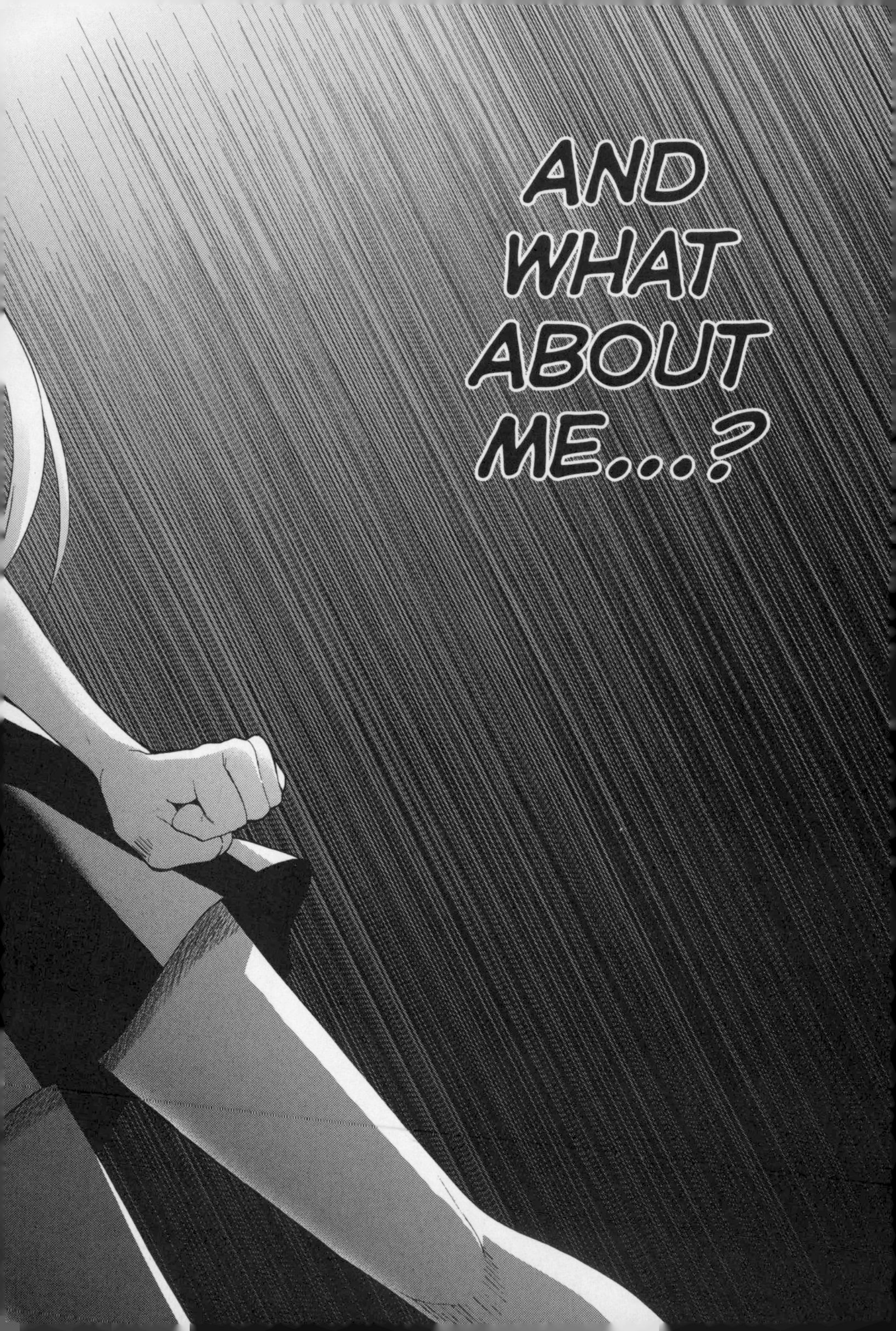
AND WHAT ABOUT ME...?

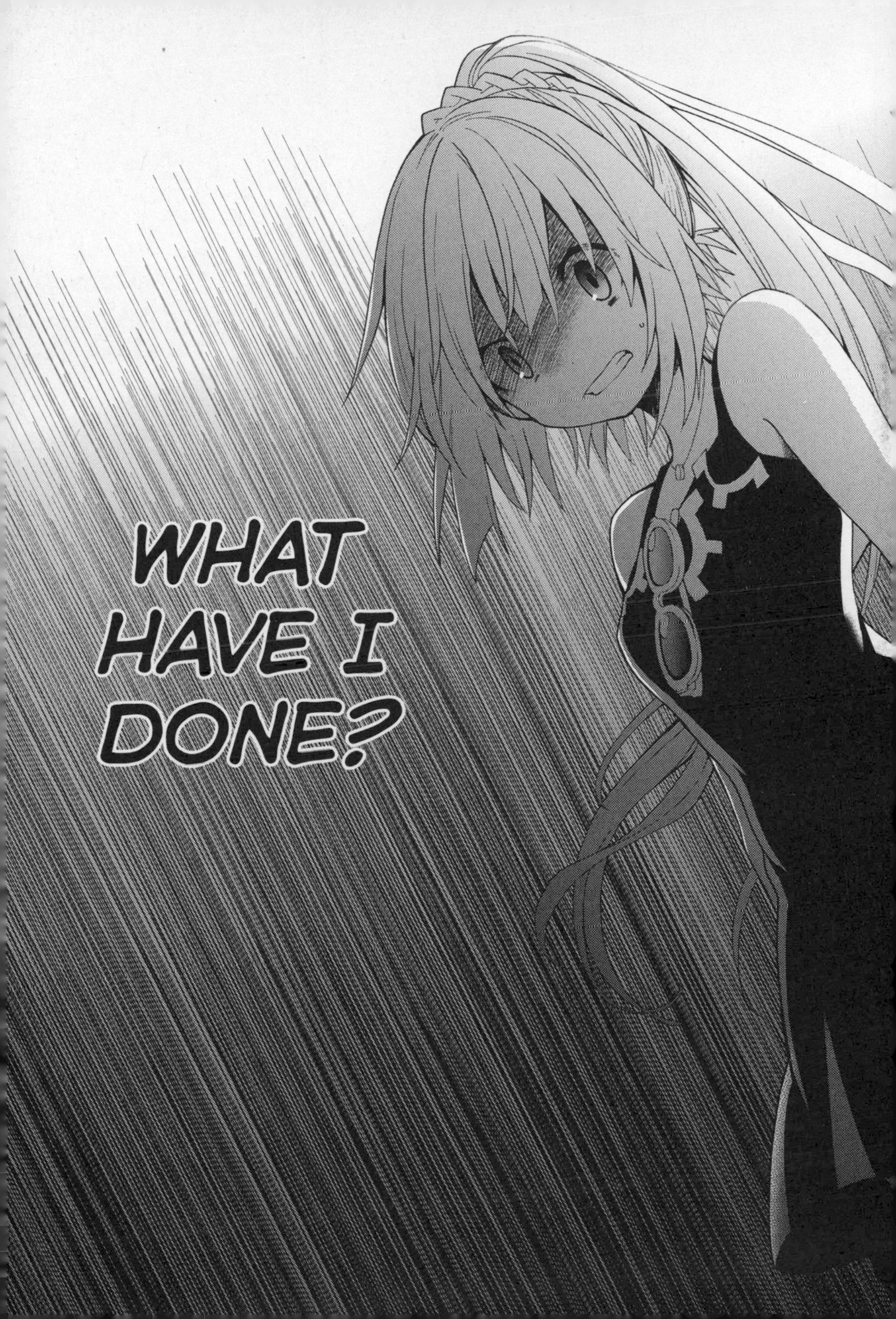
WHAT
HAVE I
DONE?

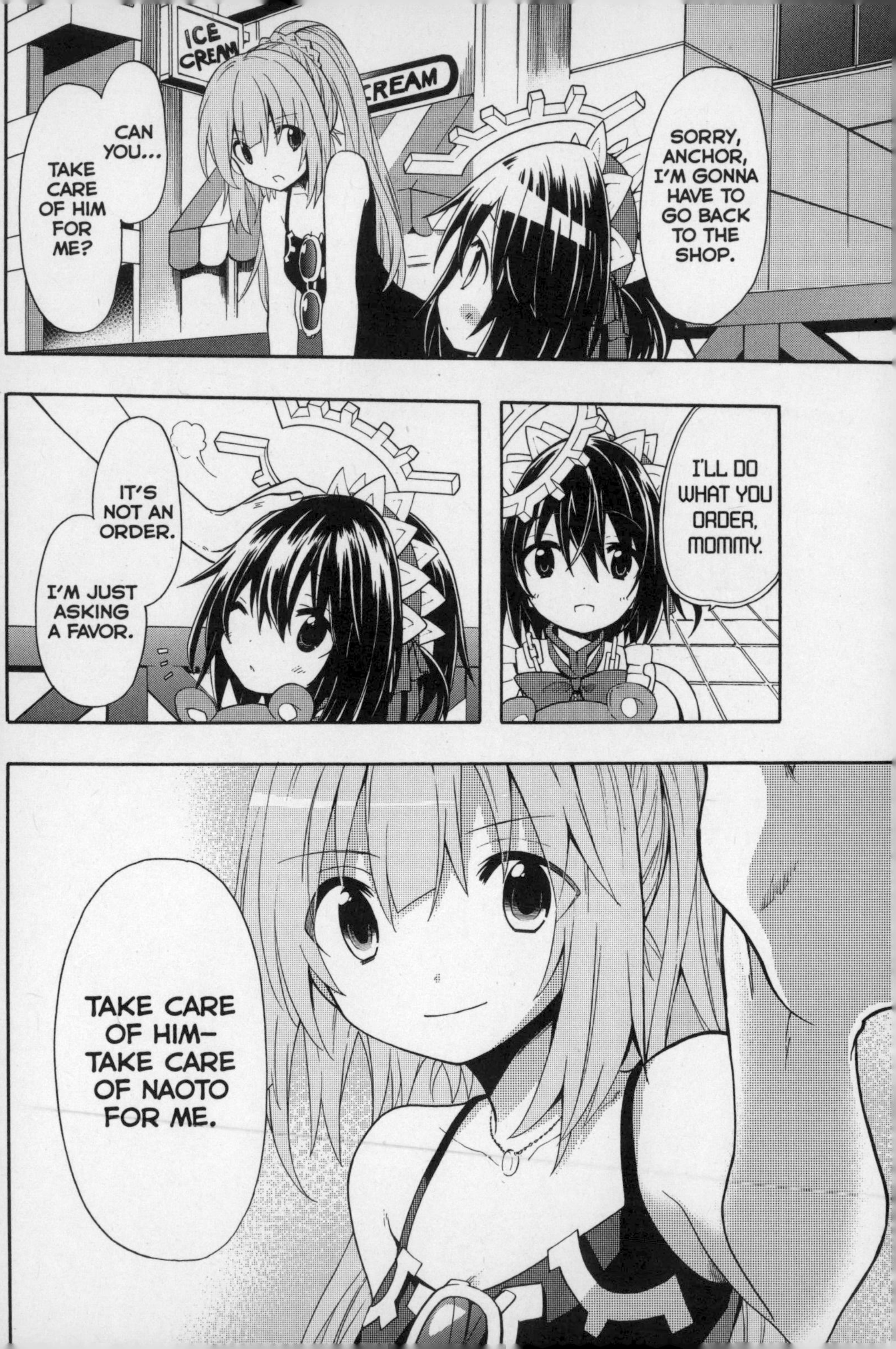
ICE CREAM
CREAM
SORRY, ANCHOR, I'M GONNA HAVE TO GO BACK TO THE SHOP.
CAN YOU...
TAKE CARE OF HIM FOR ME?
I'LL DO WHAT YOU ORDER, MOMMY.
IT'S NOT AN ORDER.
I'M JUST ASKING A FAVOR.
TAKE CARE OF HIM—TAKE CARE OF NAOTO FOR ME.

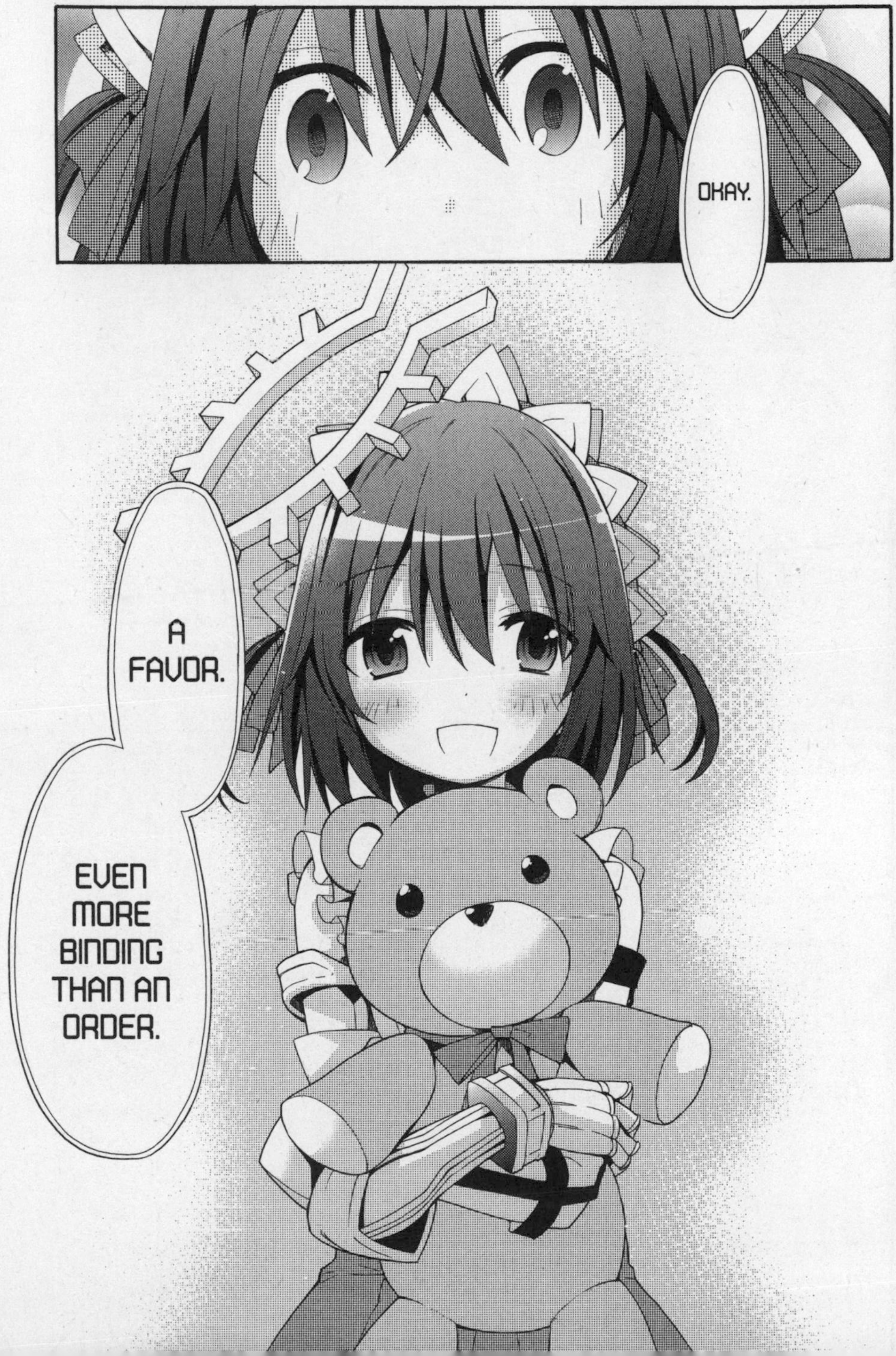
OKAY.
A FAVOR.
EVEN MORE BINDING THAN AN ORDER.

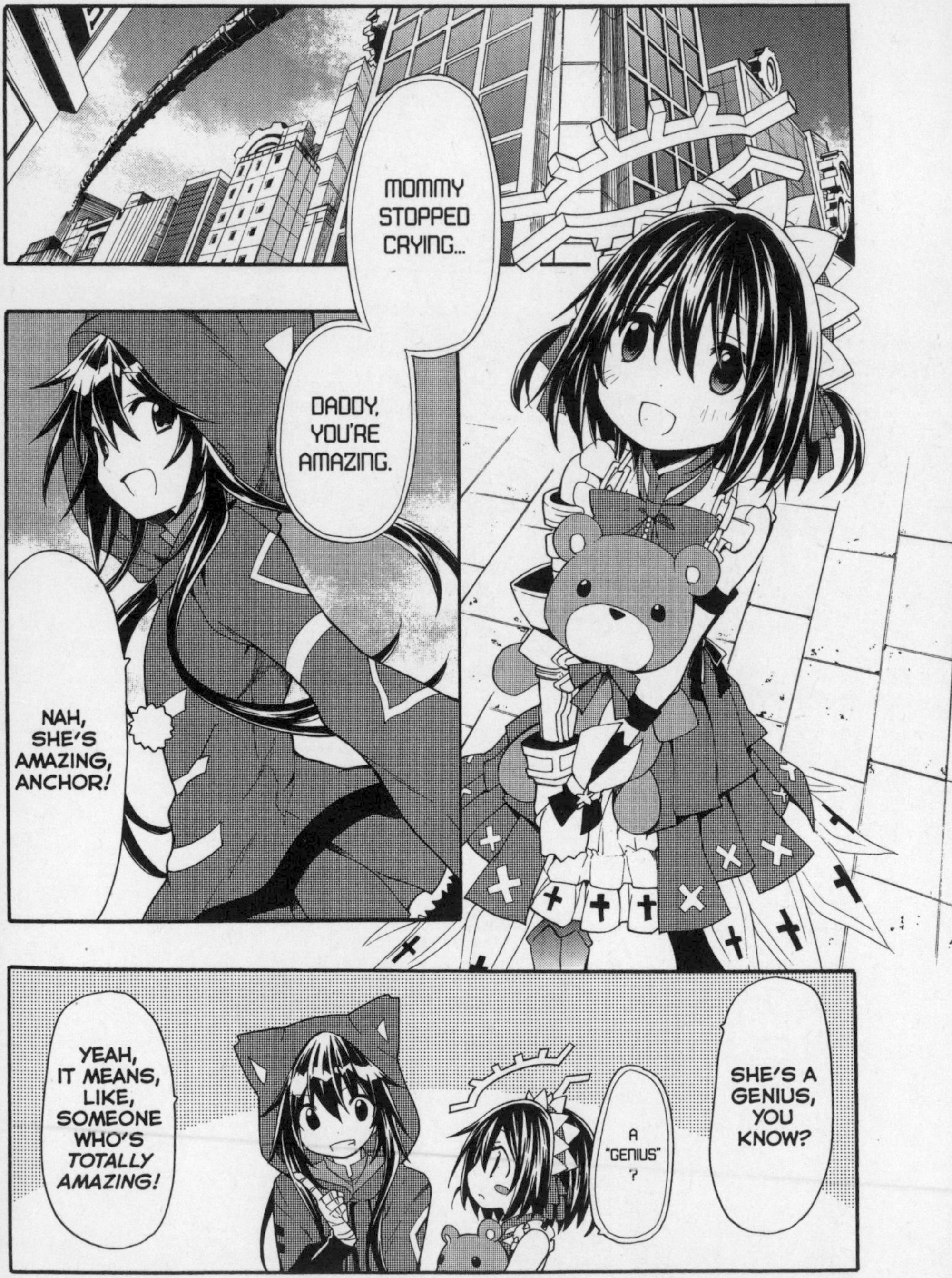
MOMMY STOPPED CRYING...
DADDY, YOU'RE AMAZING.
NAH, SHE'S AMAZING, ANCHOR!
SHE'S A GENIUS, YOU KNOW?
A "GENIUS"?
YEAH, IT MEANS, LIKE, SOMEONE WHO'S *TOTALLY AMAZING!*

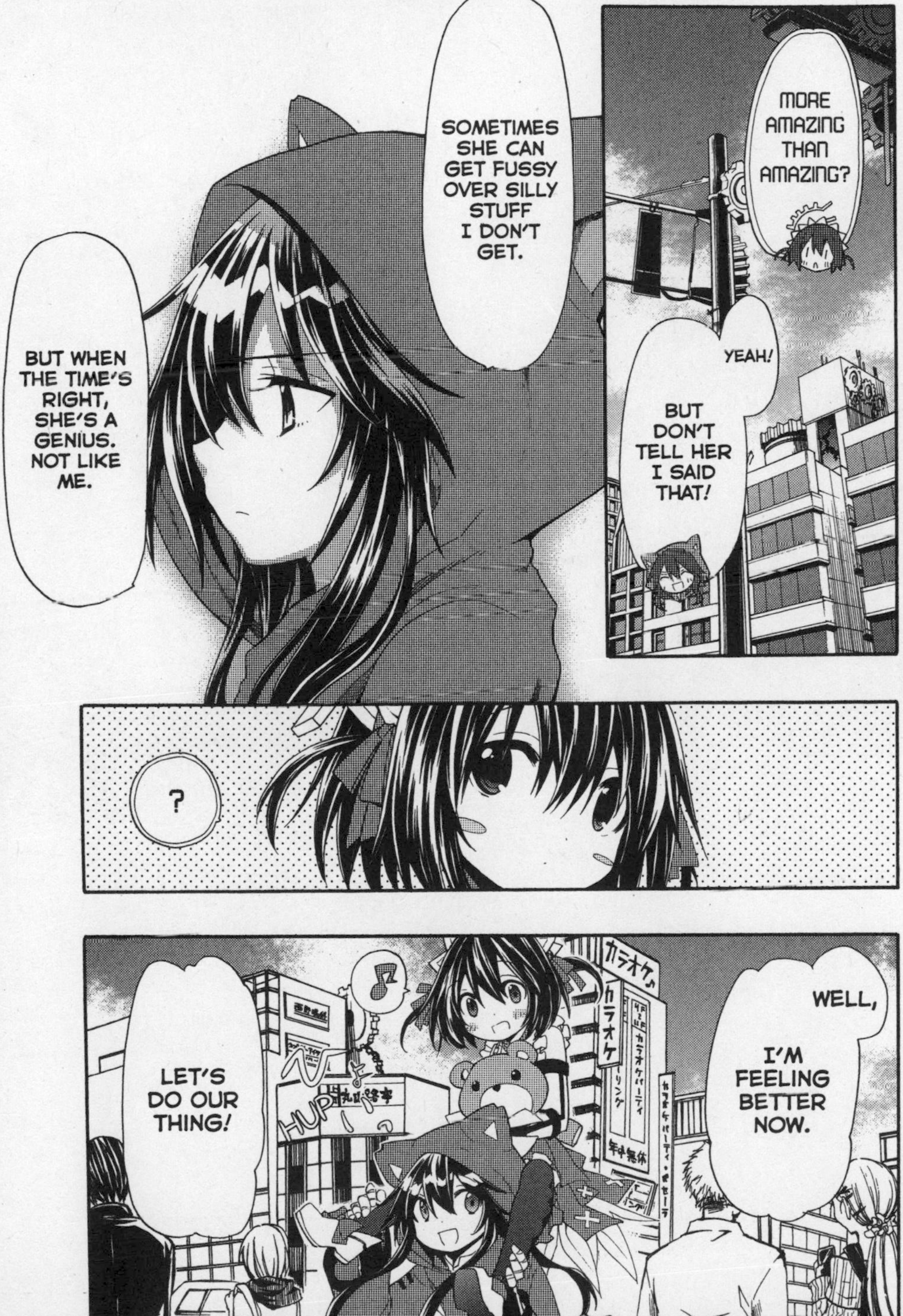
MORE AMAZING THAN AMAZING?
YEAH!
BUT DON'T TELL HER I SAID THAT!
SOMETIMES SHE CAN GET FUSSY OVER SILLY STUFF I DON'T GET.
BUT WHEN THE TIME'S RIGHT, SHE'S A GENIUS. NOT LIKE ME.
?
WELL,
I'M FEELING BETTER NOW.
LET'S DO OUR THING!
HUP
カラオケ

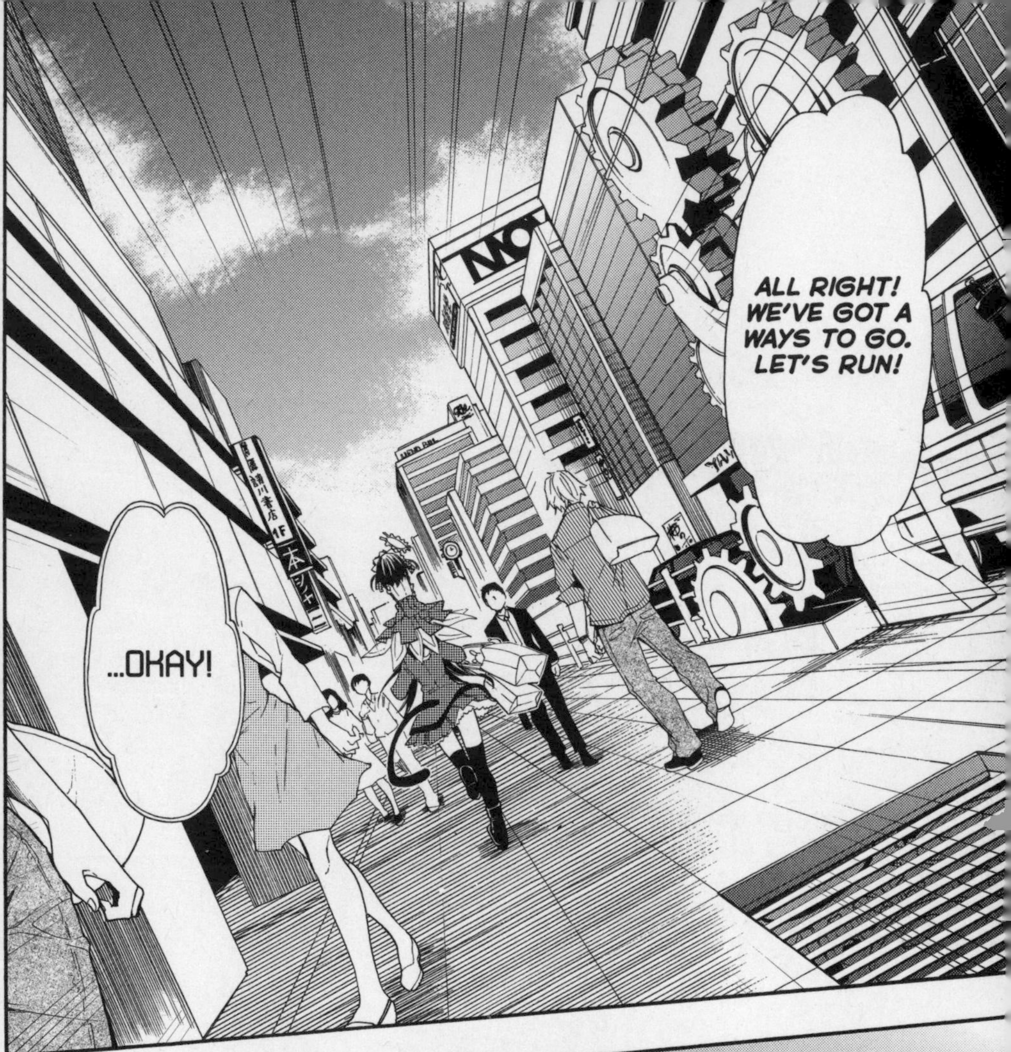
ALL RIGHT! WE'VE GOT A WAYS TO GO. LET'S RUN!
...OKAY!

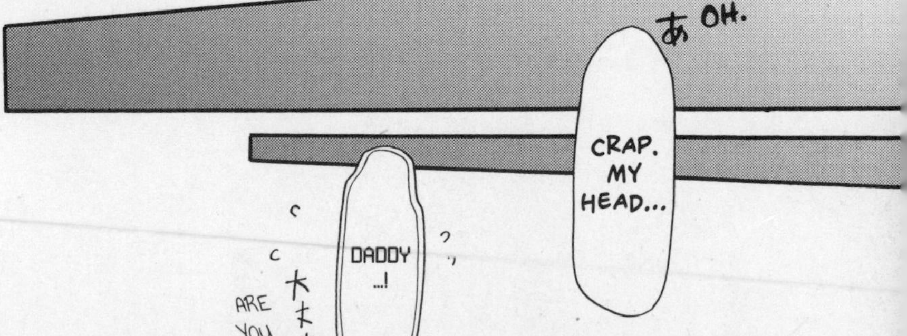
あ OH.
CRAP. MY HEAD...
DADDY ...!
大丈夫？
ARE YOU OKAY?

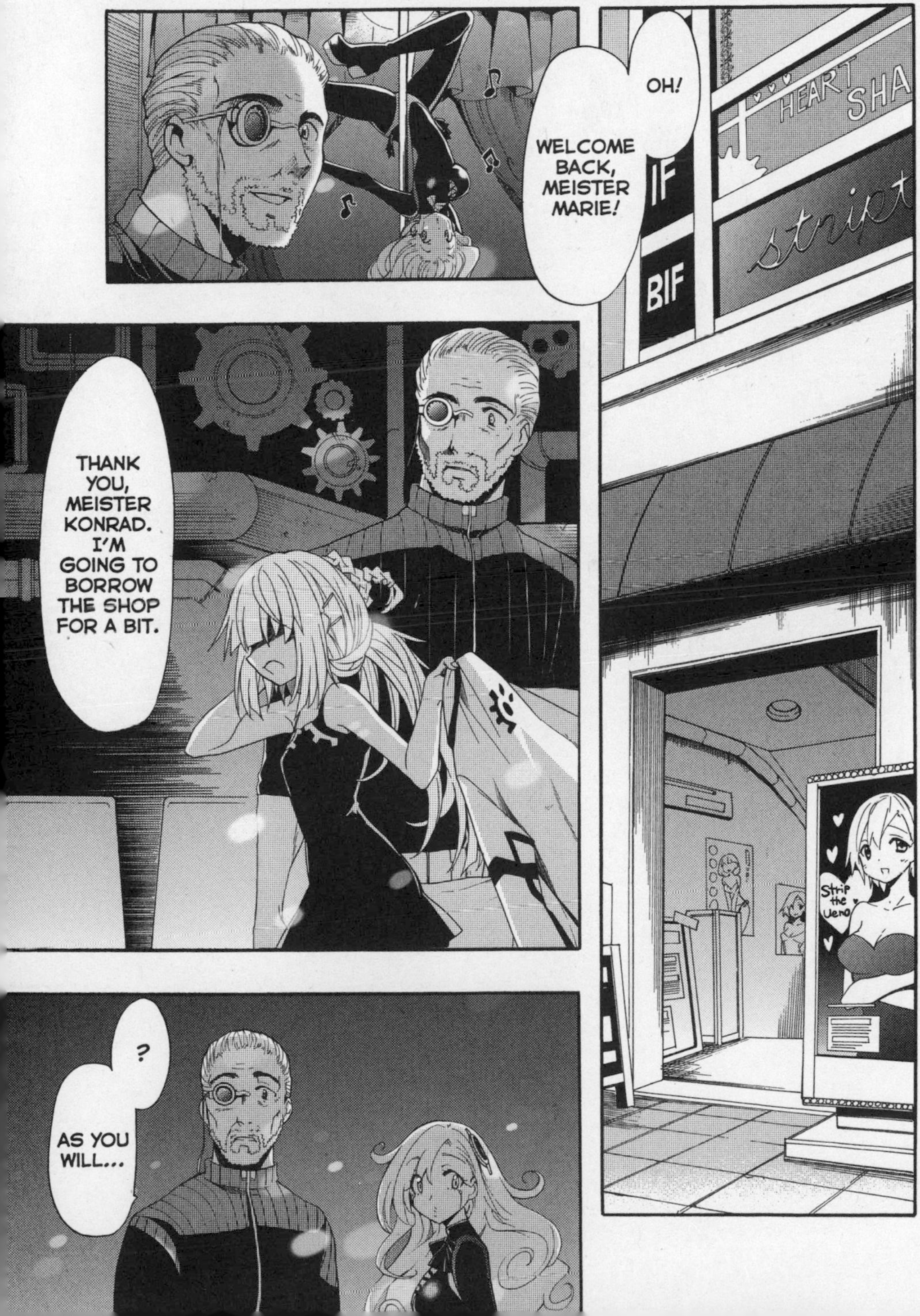
OH!
WELCOME BACK, MEISTER MARIE!
Strip the Ueno
THANK YOU, MEISTER KONRAD. I'M GOING TO BORROW THE SHOP FOR A BIT.
?
AS YOU WILL...

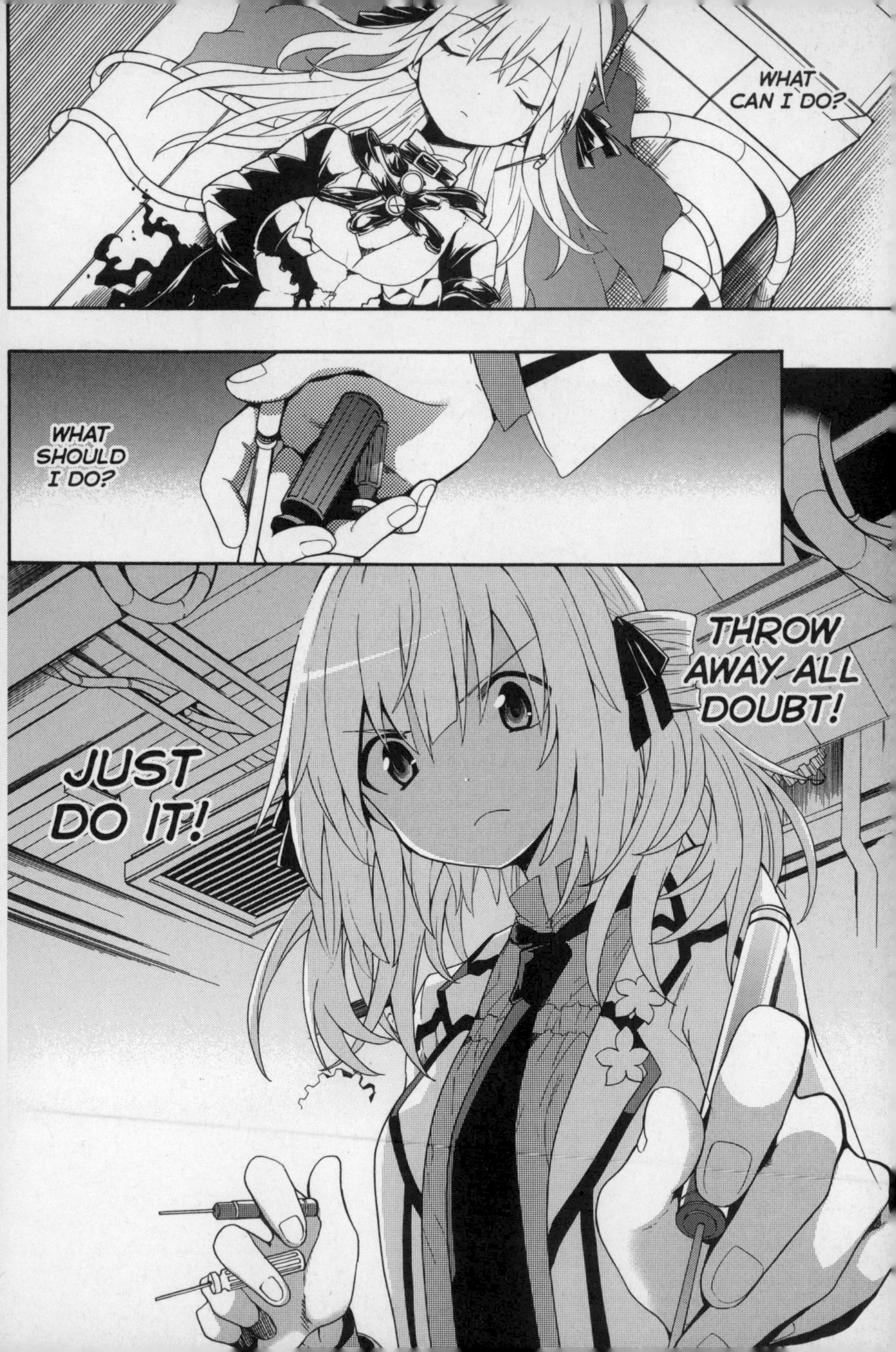
WHAT CAN I DO?
WHAT SHOULD I DO?
THROW AWAY ALL DOUBT!
JUST DO IT!

Clockwork Planet

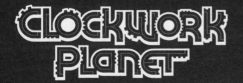

CLOCKWORK
PLANET

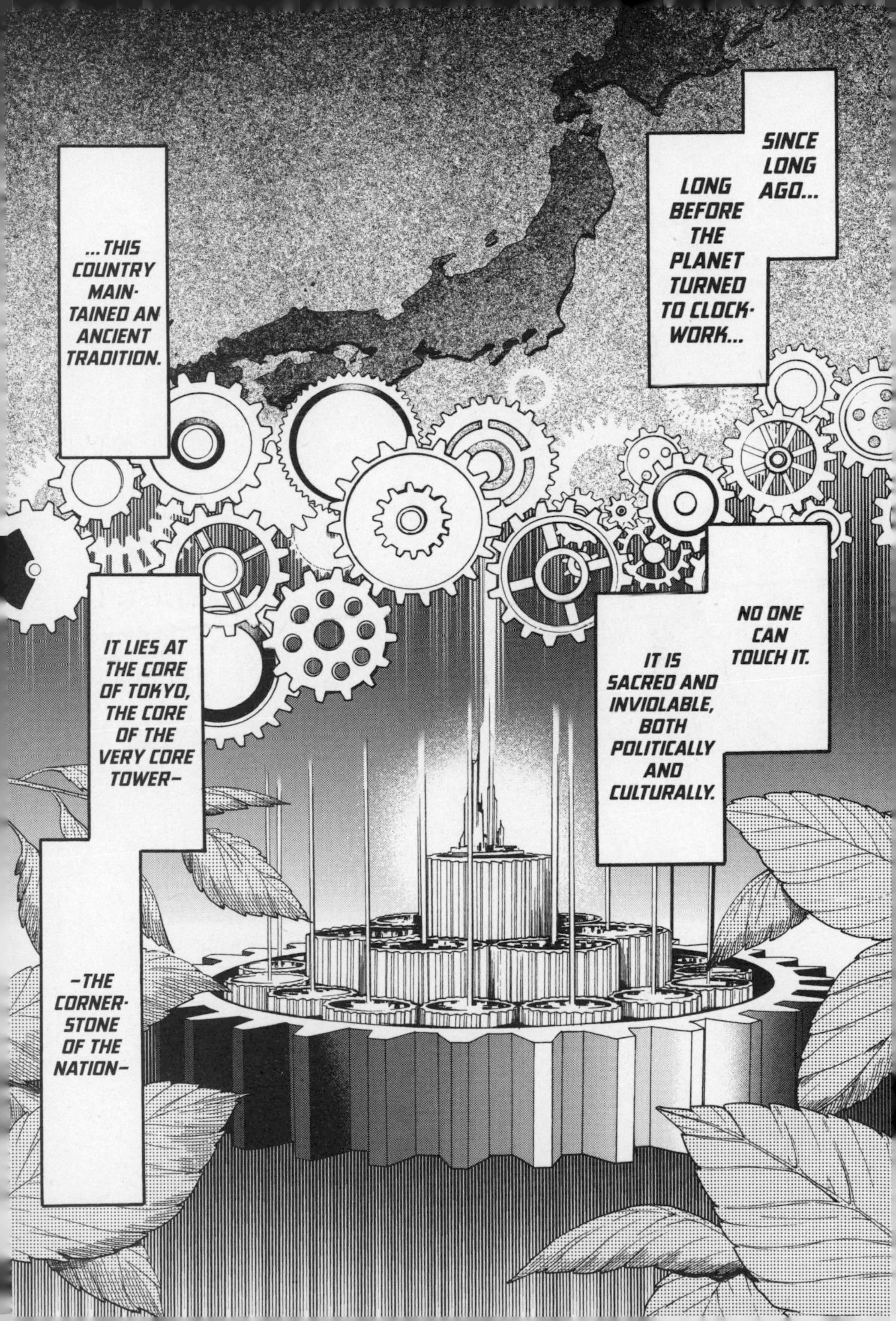
SINCE LONG AGO...
LONG BEFORE THE PLANET TURNED TO CLOCK-WORK...
...THIS COUNTRY MAIN-TAINED AN ANCIENT TRADITION.
NO ONE CAN TOUCH IT.
IT IS SACRED AND INVIOLABLE, BOTH POLITICALLY AND CULTURALLY.
IT LIES AT THE CORE OF TOKYO, THE CORE OF THE VERY CORE TOWER—
—THE CORNER-STONE OF THE NATION—

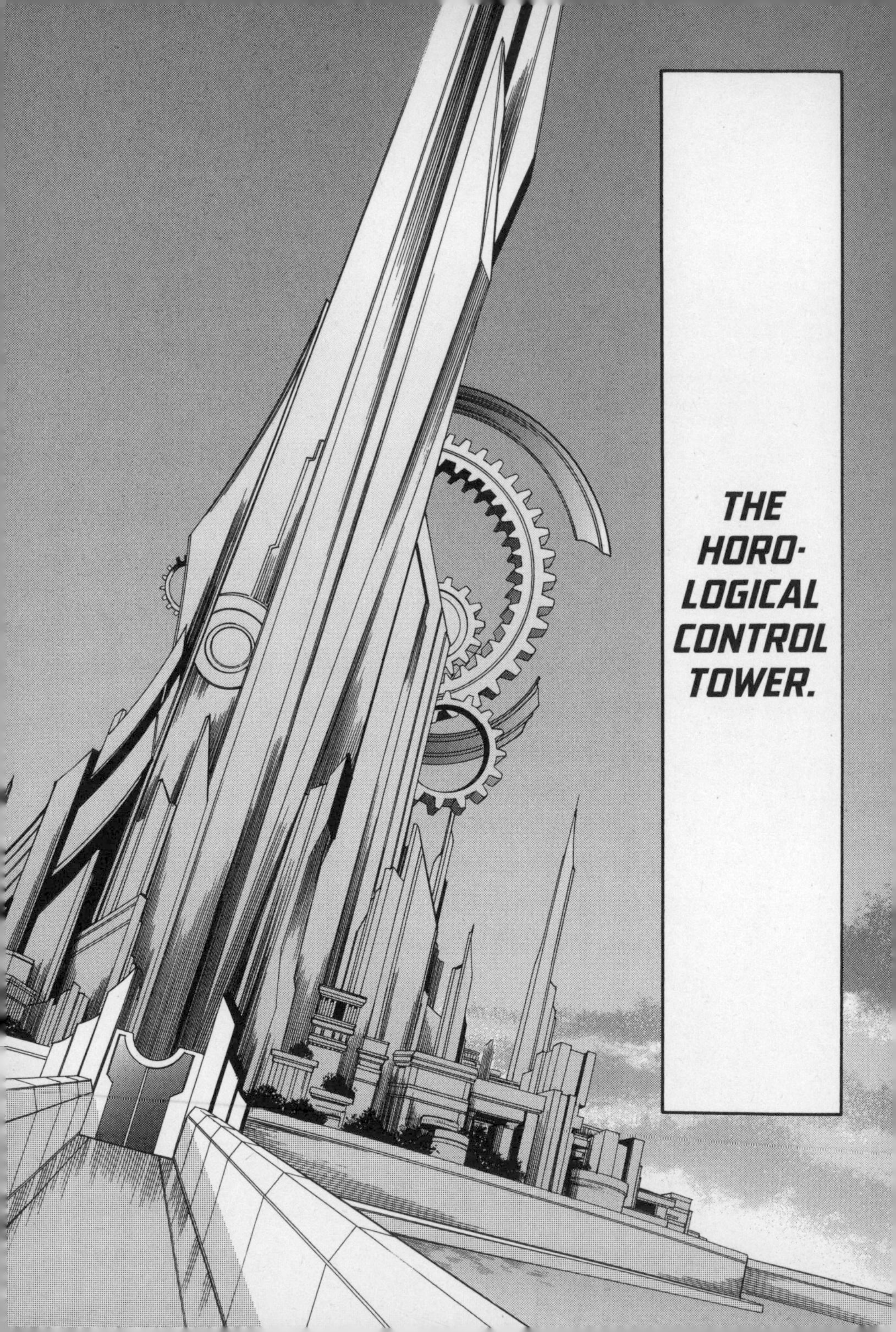
THE HORO-LOGICAL CONTROL TOWER.

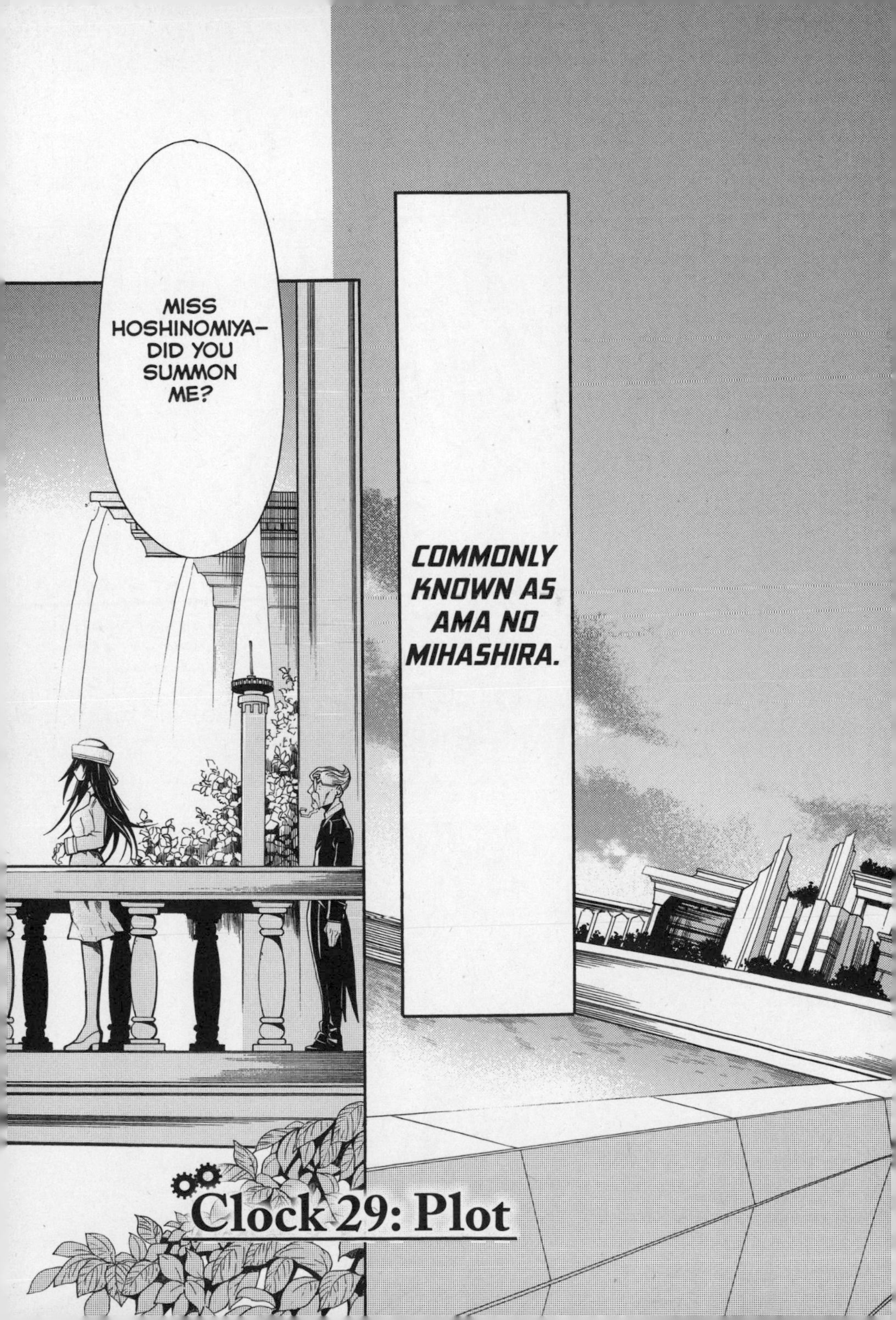
COMMONLY KNOWN AS AMA NO MIHASHIRA.
MISS HOSHINOMIYA–DID YOU SUMMON ME?
Clock 29: Plot

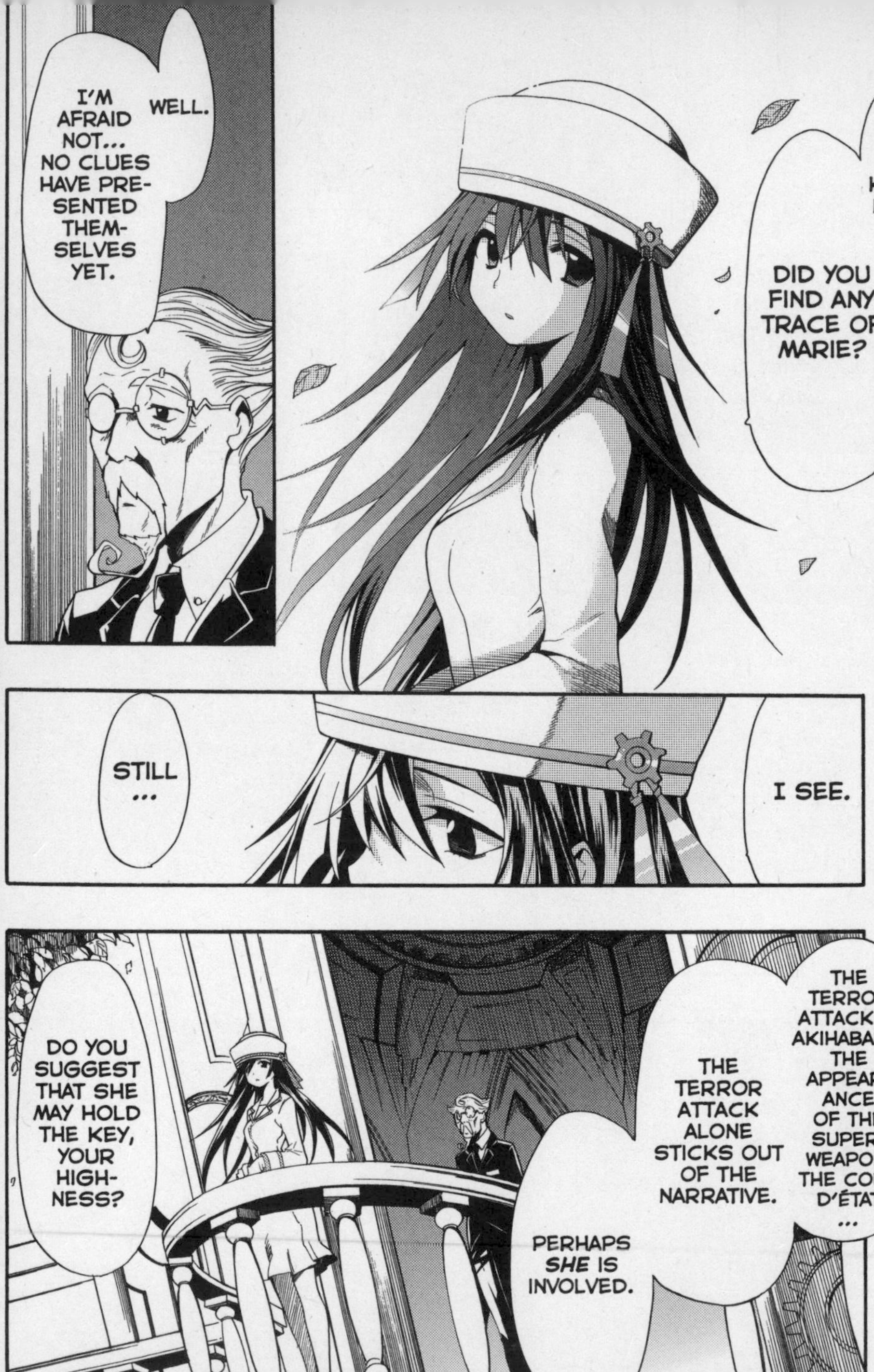
MR. KUSUNOKI.
DID YOU FIND ANY TRACE OF MARIE?
WELL.
I'M AFRAID NOT... NO CLUES HAVE PRESENTED THEMSELVES YET.
I SEE.
STILL...
THE TERROR ATTACK IN AKIHABARA, THE APPEARANCE OF THE SUPERWEAPON, THE COUP D'ÉTAT...
THE TERROR ATTACK ALONE STICKS OUT OF THE NARRATIVE.
PERHAPS *SHE* IS INVOLVED.
DO YOU SUGGEST THAT SHE MAY HOLD THE KEY, YOUR HIGHNESS?

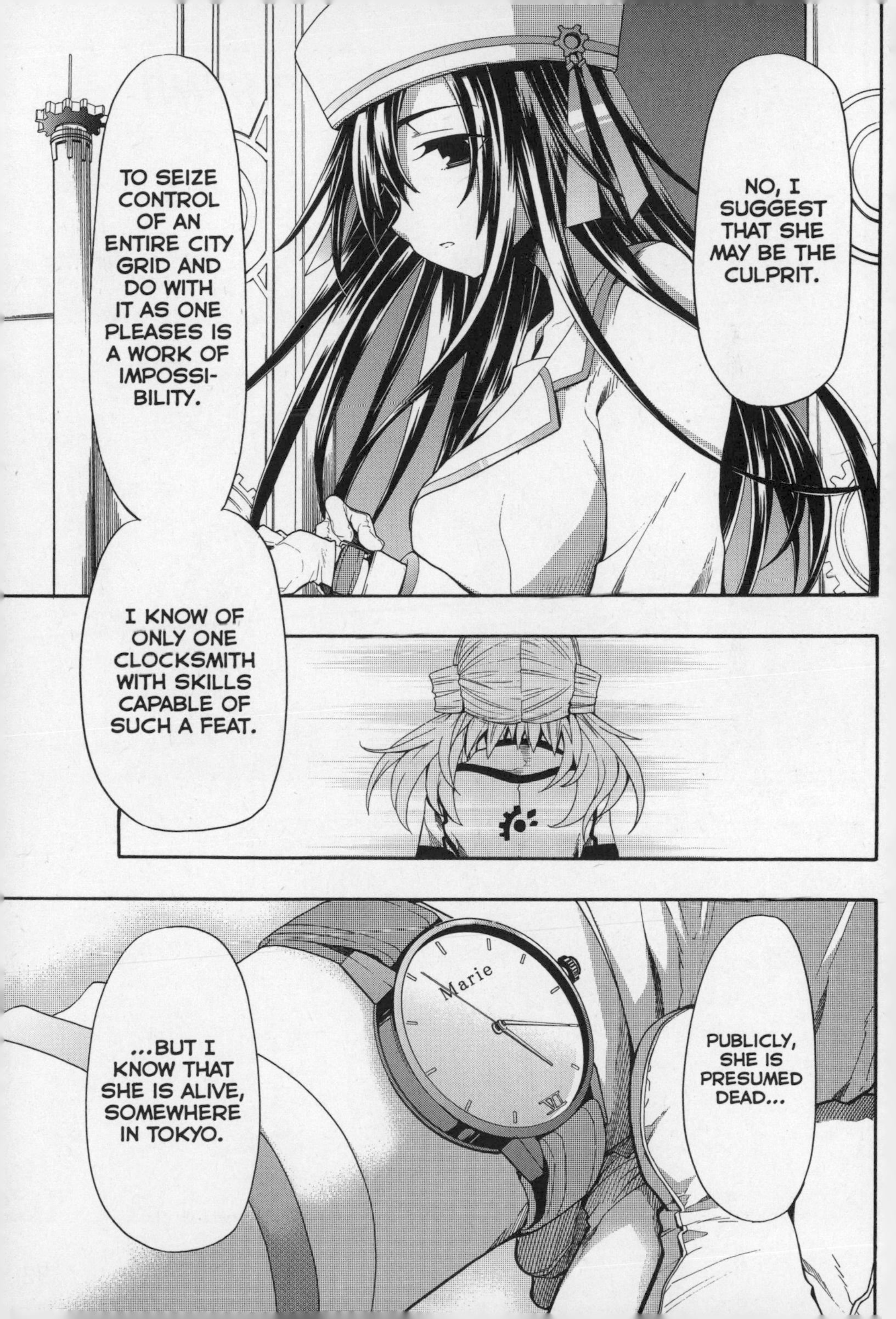
NO, I SUGGEST THAT SHE MAY BE THE CULPRIT.
TO SEIZE CONTROL OF AN ENTIRE CITY GRID AND DO WITH IT AS ONE PLEASES IS A WORK OF IMPOSSI-BILITY.
I KNOW OF ONLY ONE CLOCKSMITH WITH SKILLS CAPABLE OF SUCH A FEAT.
PUBLICLY, SHE IS PRESUMED DEAD...
Marie
...BUT I KNOW THAT SHE IS ALIVE, SOMEWHERE IN TOKYO.

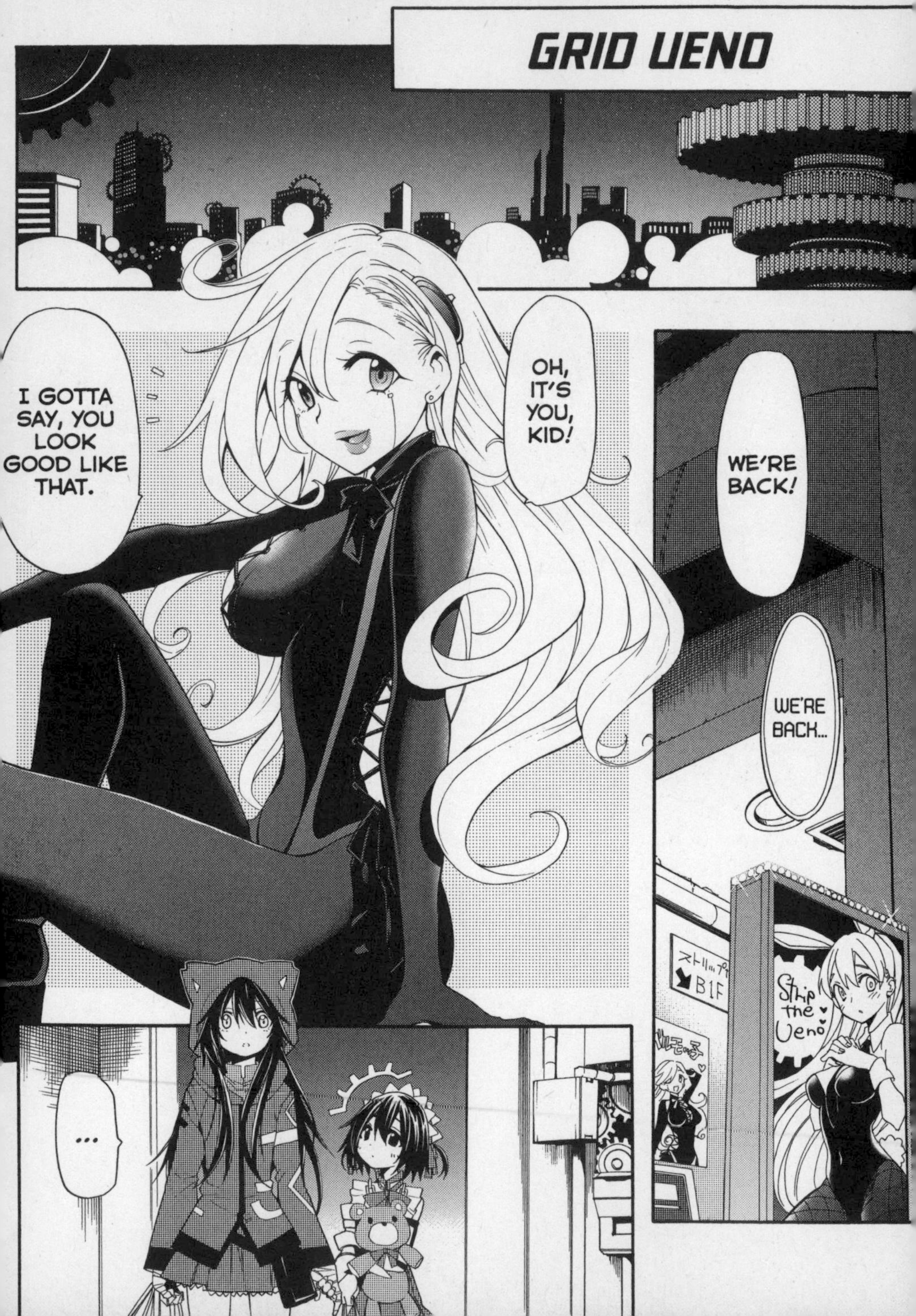
GRID UENO
WE'RE BACK!
WE'RE BACK...
ストリップ
B1F
Strip the Ueno
OH, IT'S YOU, KID!
I GOTTA SAY, YOU LOOK GOOD LIKE THAT.
...

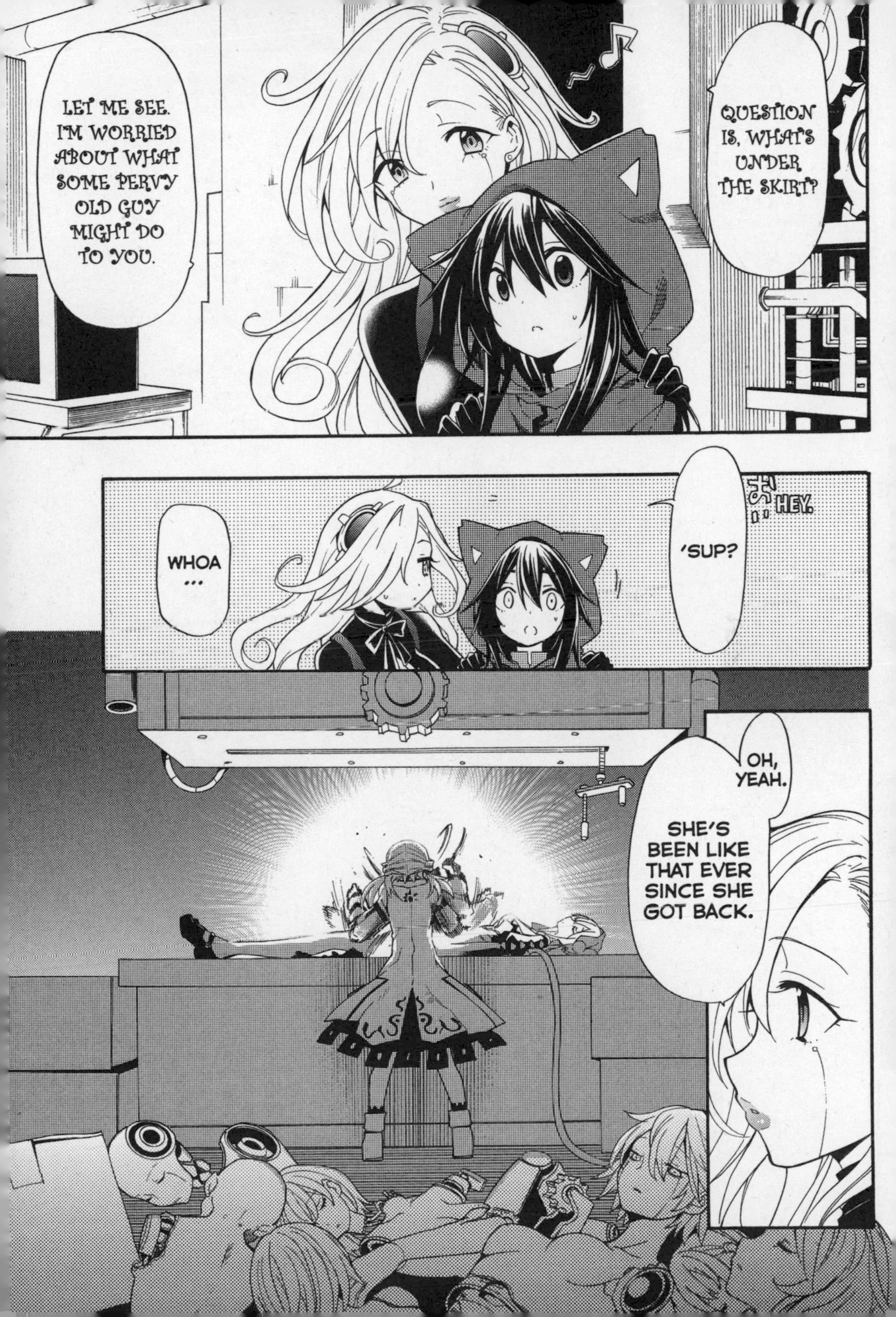
QUESTION IS, WHAT'S UNDER THE SKIRT?
LET ME SEE. I'M WORRIED ABOUT WHAT SOME PERVY OLD GUY MIGHT DO TO YOU.
HEY.
'SUP?
WHOA ...
OH, YEAH.
SHE'S BEEN LIKE THAT EVER SINCE SHE GOT BACK.

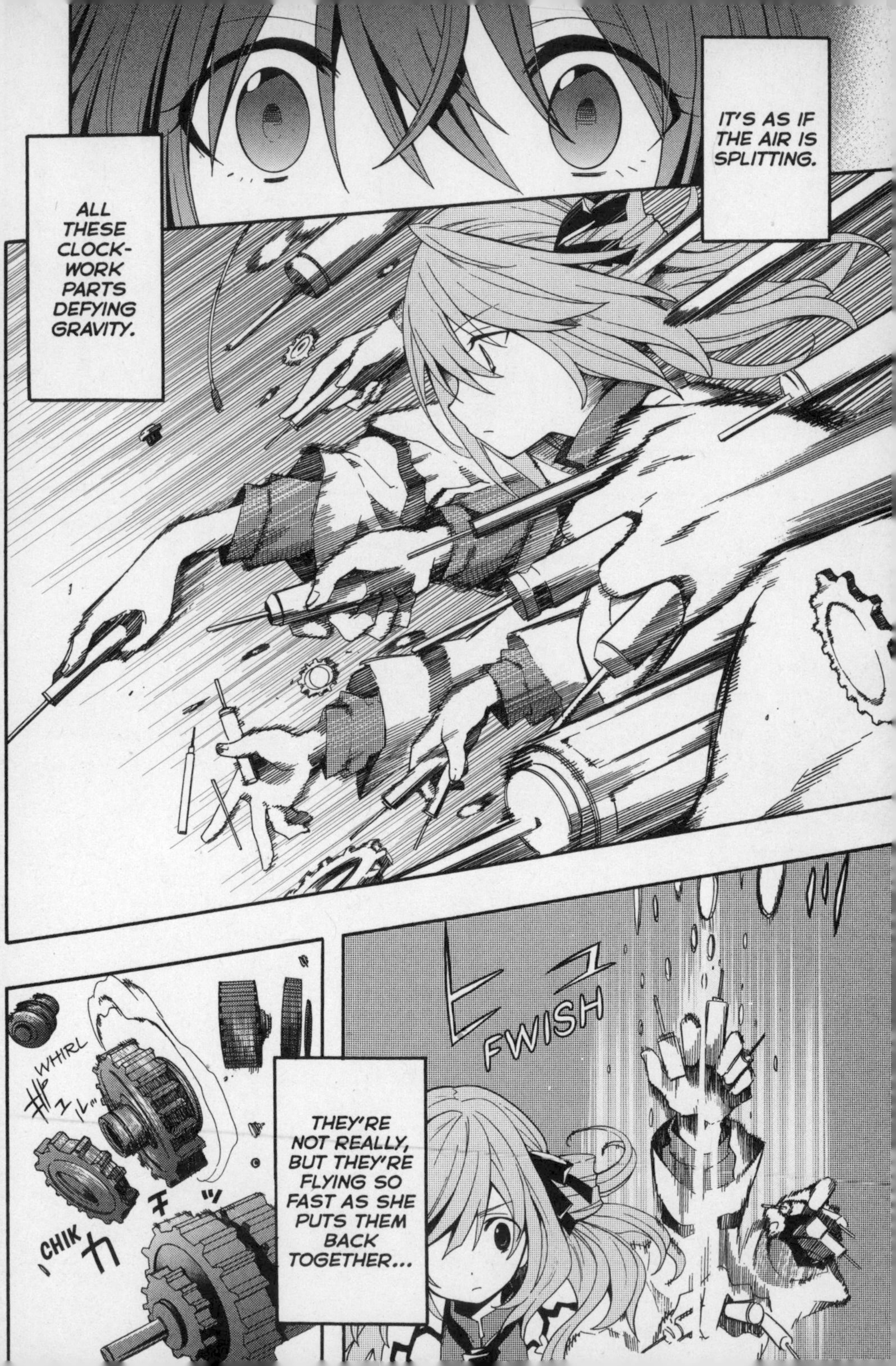
IT'S AS IF THE AIR IS SPLITTING.
ALL THESE CLOCK-WORK PARTS DEFYING GRAVITY.
FWISH
THEY'RE NOT REALLY, BUT THEY'RE FLYING SO FAST AS SHE PUTS THEM BACK TOGETHER...
WHIRL
CHIK

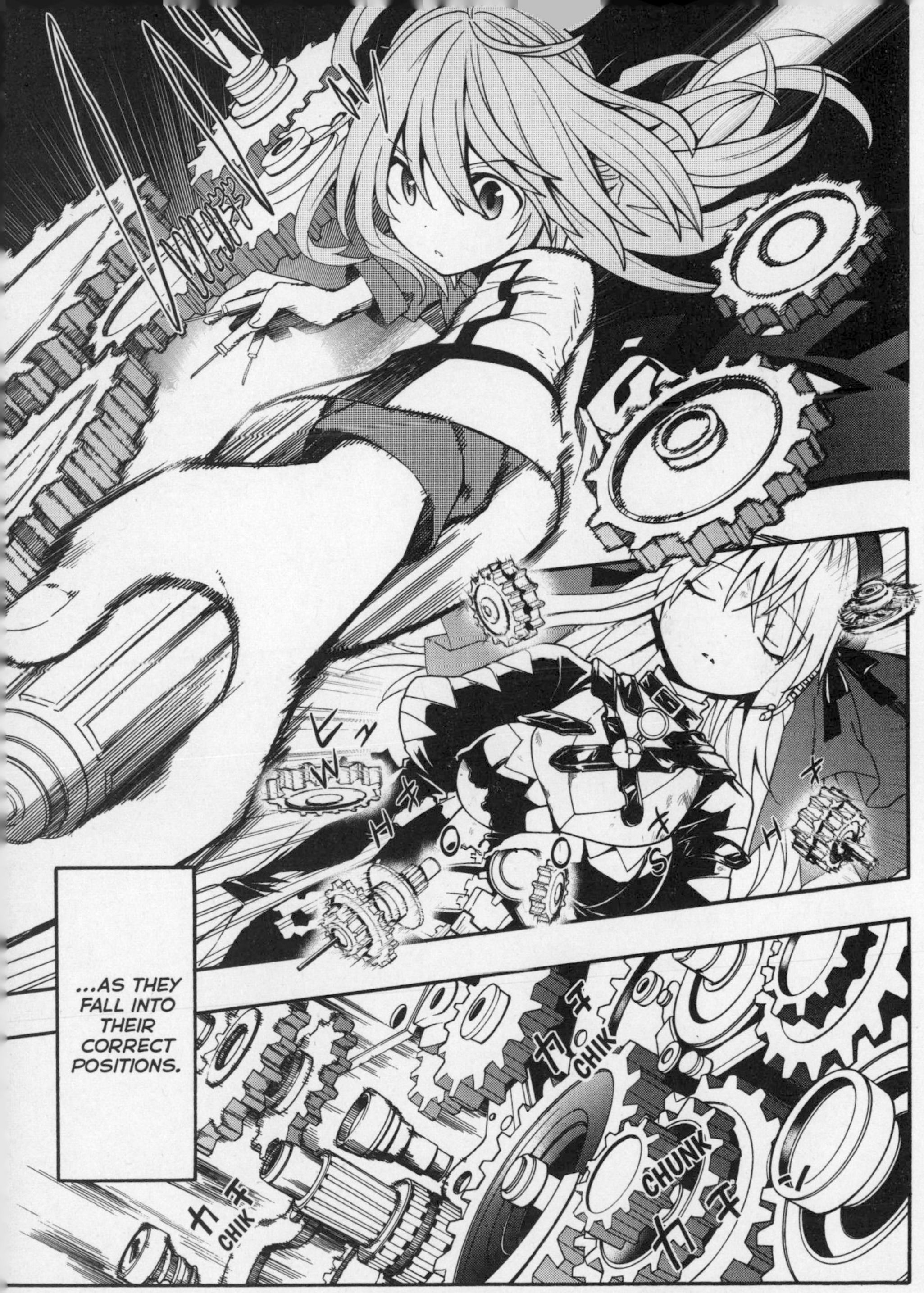
CHIK
CHUNK
...AS THEY FALL INTO THEIR CORRECT POSITIONS.
CHIK

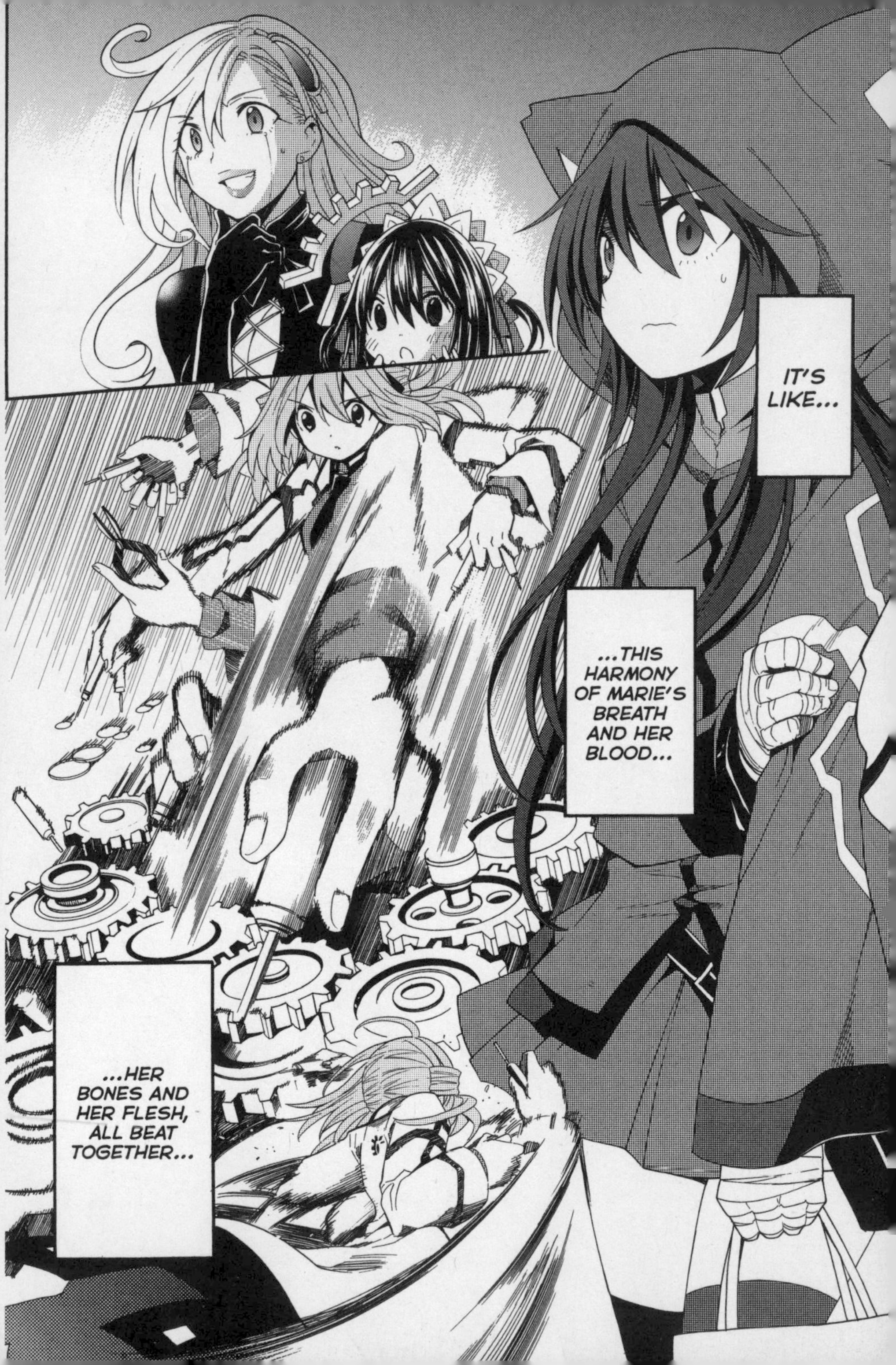
IT'S LIKE...
...THIS HARMONY OF MARIE'S BREATH AND HER BLOOD...
...HER BONES AND HER FLESH, ALL BEAT TOGETHER...

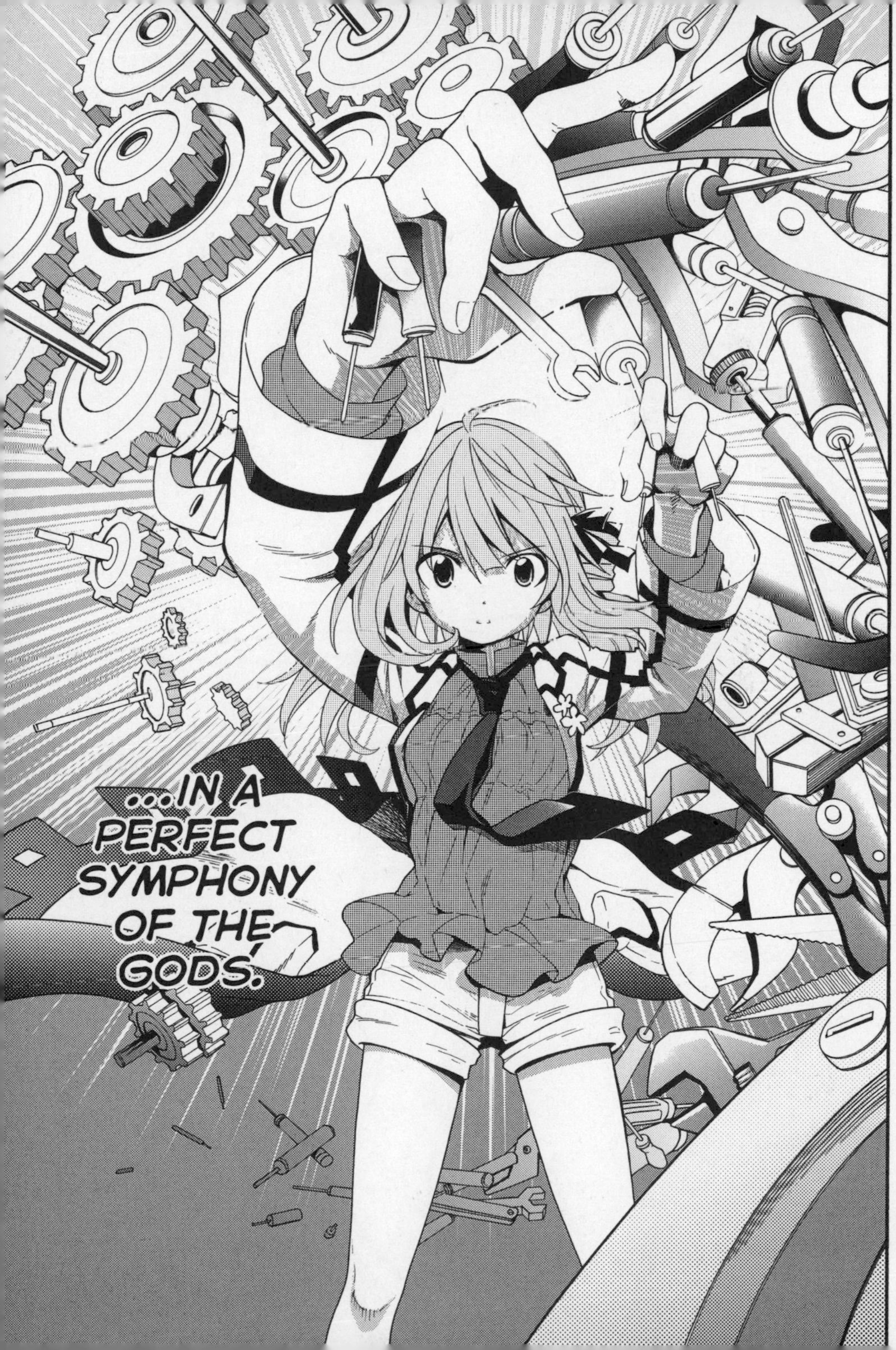
...IN A PERFECT SYMPHONY OF THE GODS.

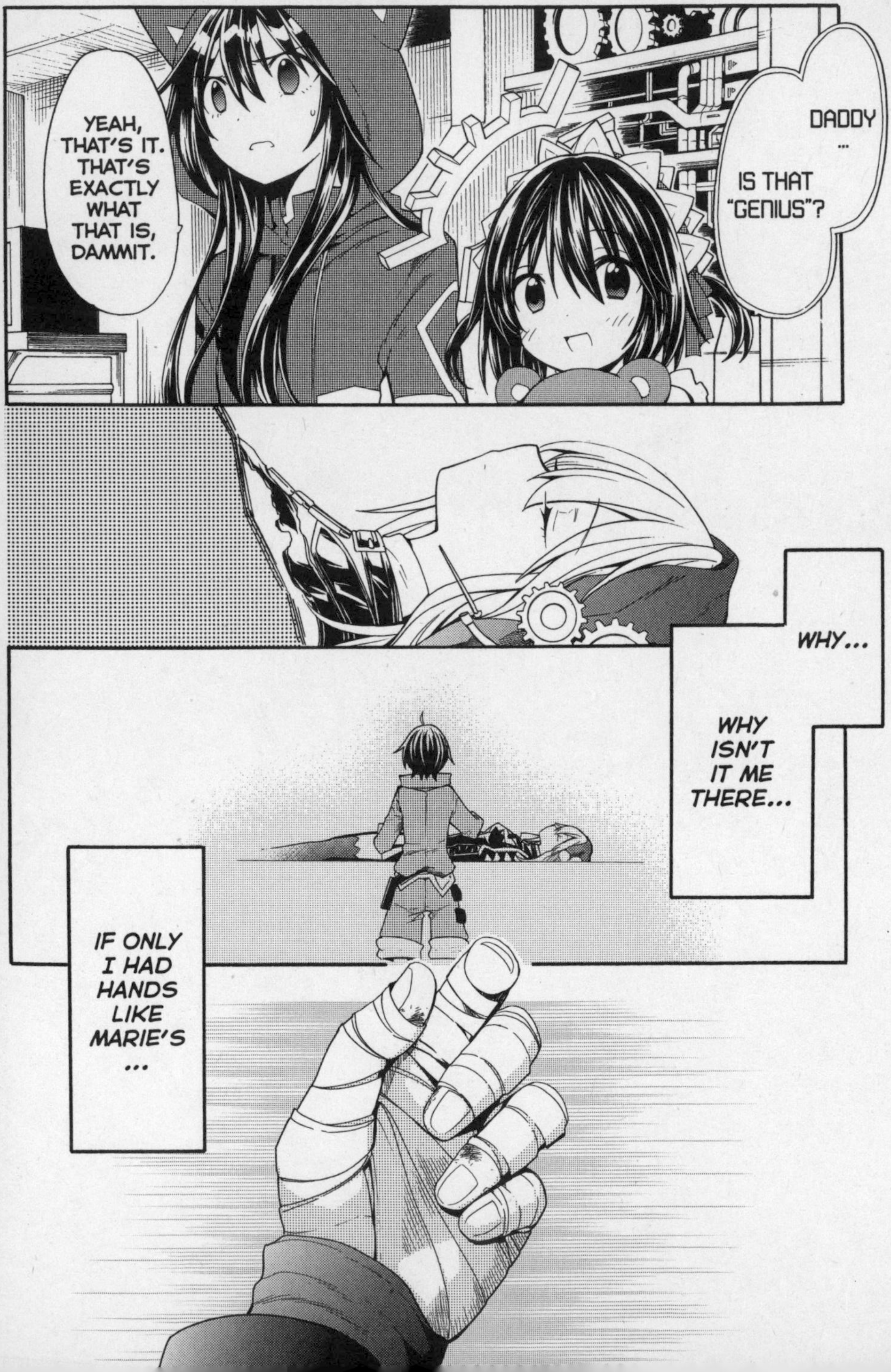
DADDY ... IS THAT "GENIUS"?
YEAH, THAT'S IT. THAT'S EXACTLY WHAT THAT IS, DAMMIT.
WHY...
WHY ISN'T IT ME THERE...
IF ONLY I HAD HANDS LIKE MARIE'S ...

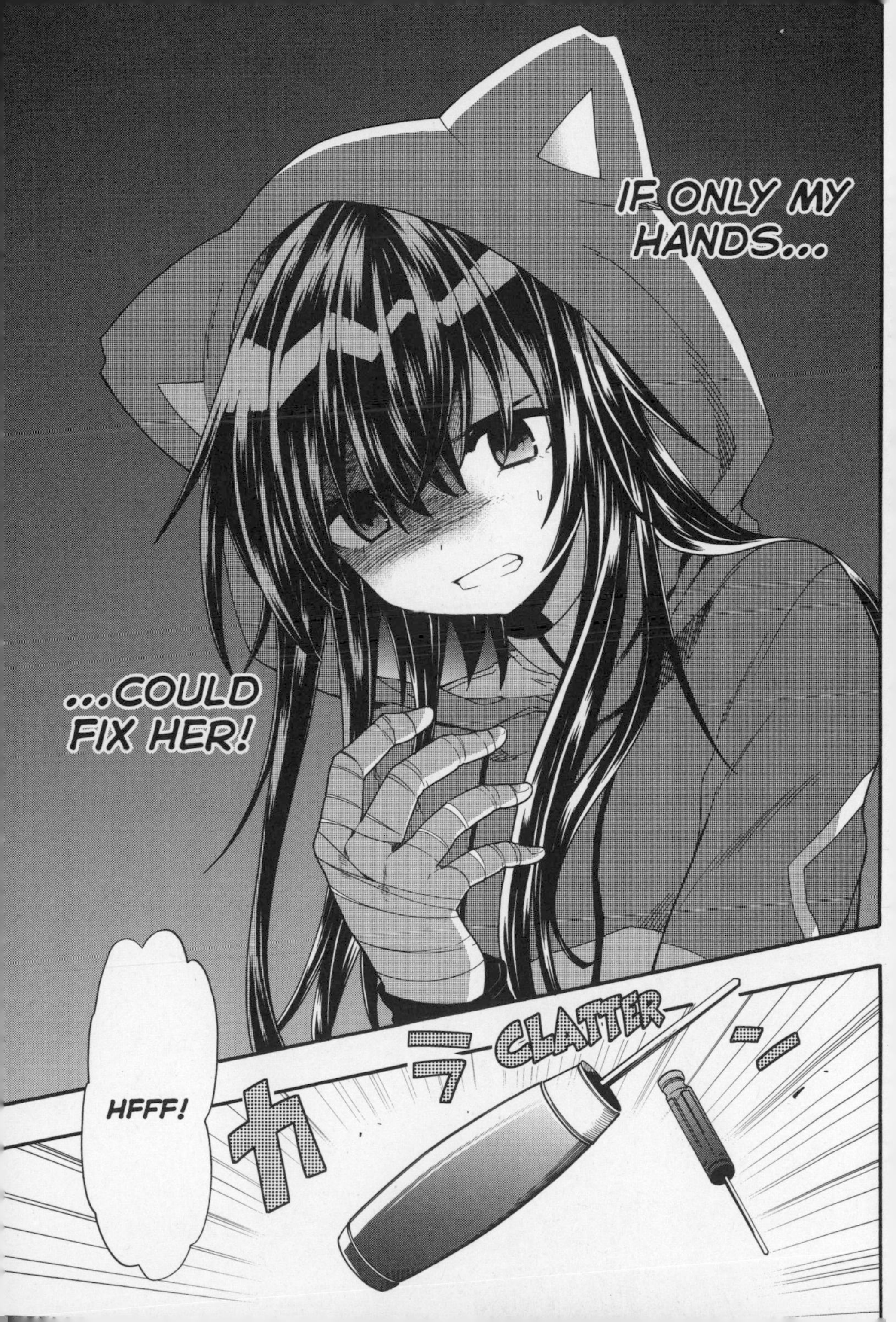
IF ONLY MY HANDS...
...COULD FIX HER!
CLATTER
カラ
HFFF!

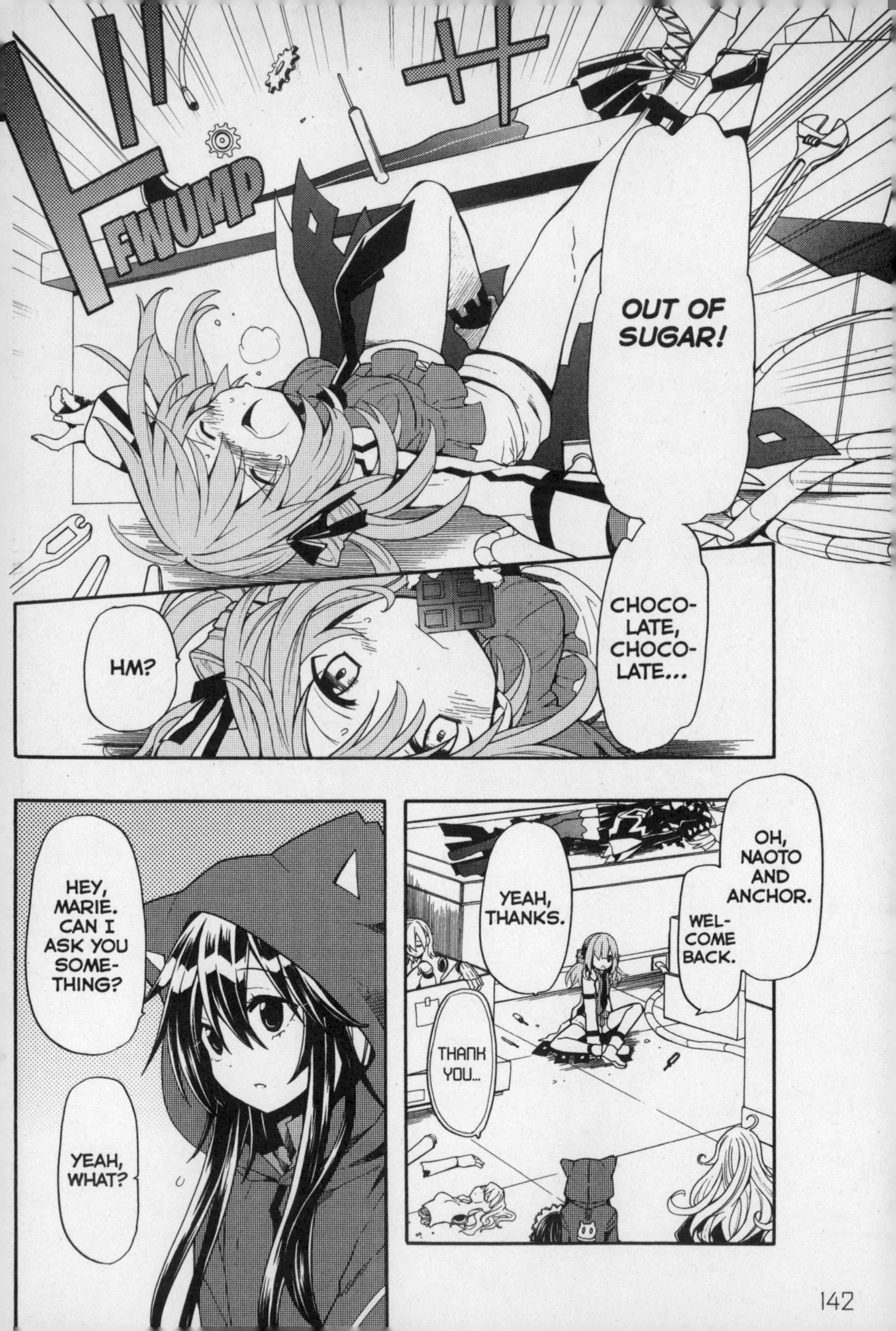
FWUMP
OUT OF SUGAR!
CHOCOLATE, CHOCOLATE...
HM?
OH, NAOTO AND ANCHOR.
WELCOME BACK.
YEAH, THANKS.
THANK YOU...
HEY, MARIE. CAN I ASK YOU SOMETHING?
YEAH, WHAT?

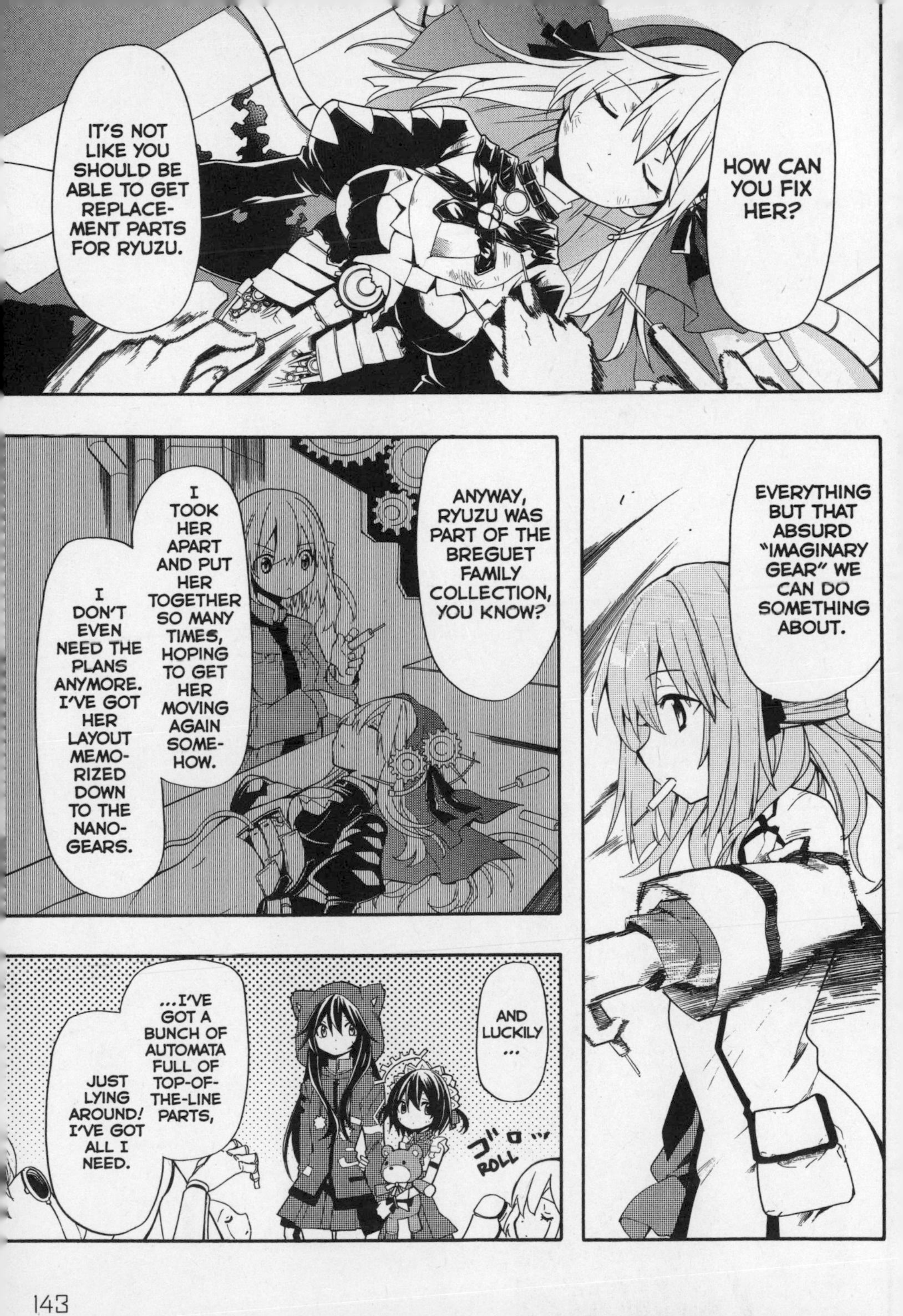
HOW CAN YOU FIX HER?
IT'S NOT LIKE YOU SHOULD BE ABLE TO GET REPLACEMENT PARTS FOR RYUZU.
EVERYTHING BUT THAT ABSURD "IMAGINARY GEAR" WE CAN DO SOMETHING ABOUT.
ANYWAY, RYUZU WAS PART OF THE BREGUET FAMILY COLLECTION, YOU KNOW?
I TOOK HER APART AND PUT HER TOGETHER SO MANY TIMES, HOPING TO GET HER MOVING AGAIN SOMEHOW.
I DON'T EVEN NEED THE PLANS ANYMORE. I'VE GOT HER LAYOUT MEMORIZED DOWN TO THE NANO-GEARS.
AND LUCKILY...
...I'VE GOT A BUNCH OF AUTOMATA FULL OF TOP-OF-THE-LINE PARTS,
JUST LYING AROUND! I'VE GOT ALL I NEED.
ゴロッ ROLL

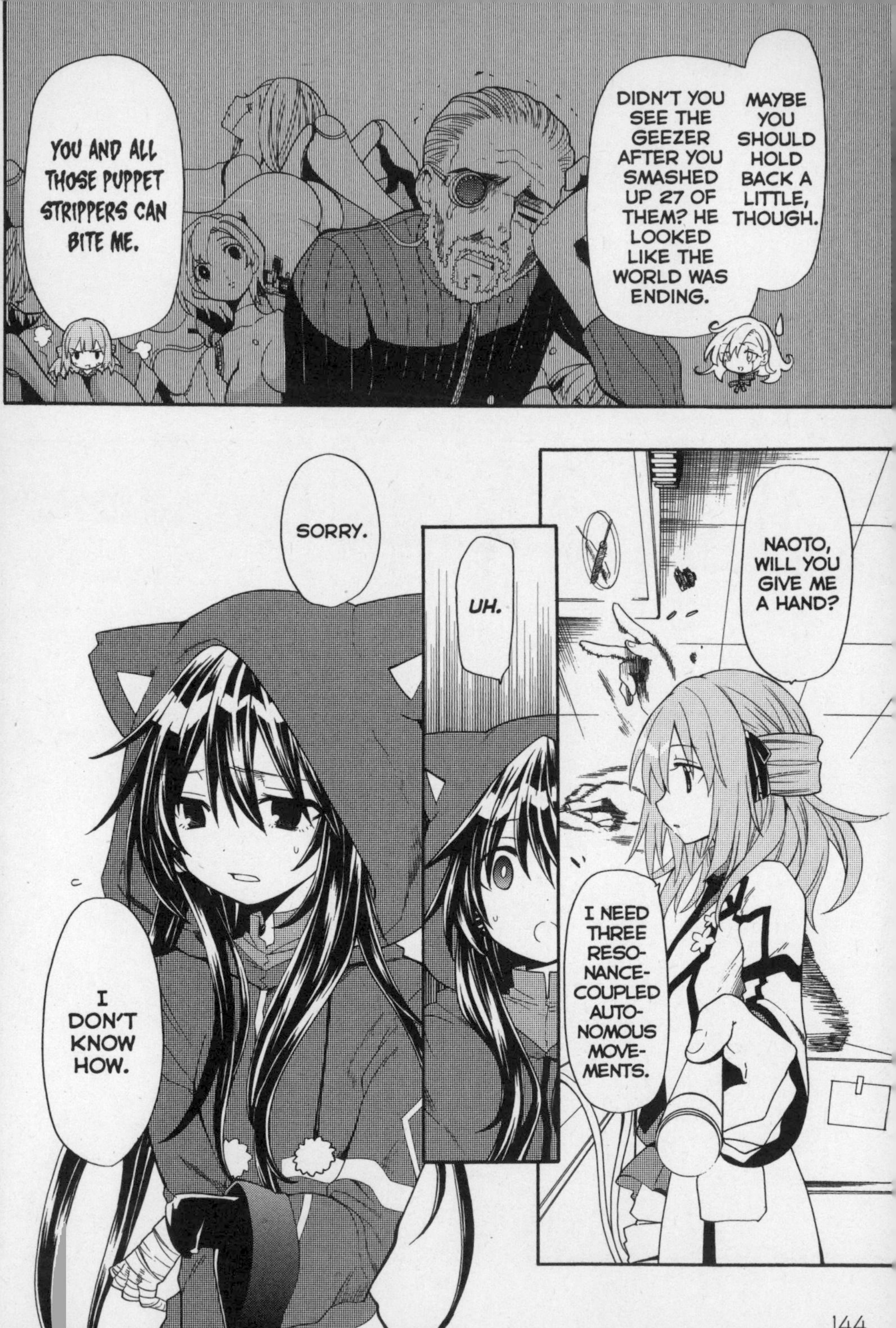
MAYBE YOU SHOULD HOLD BACK A LITTLE, THOUGH.
DIDN'T YOU SEE THE GEEZER AFTER YOU SMASHED UP 27 OF THEM? HE LOOKED LIKE THE WORLD WAS ENDING.
YOU AND ALL THOSE PUPPET STRIPPERS CAN BITE ME.
NAOTO, WILL YOU GIVE ME A HAND?
I NEED THREE RESONANCE-COUPLED AUTONOMOUS MOVEMENTS.
UH.
SORRY.
I DON'T KNOW HOW.

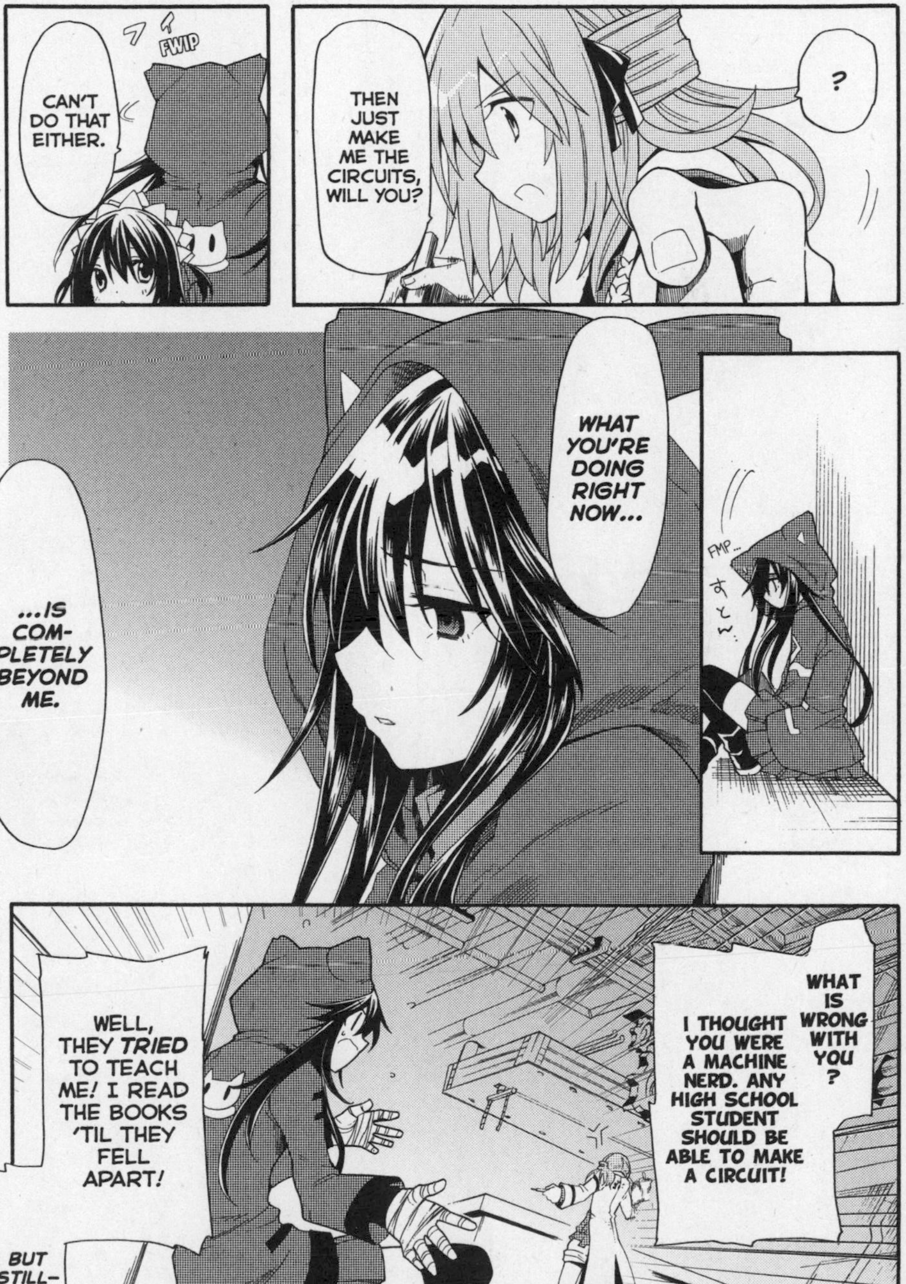
?
THEN JUST MAKE ME THE CIRCUITS, WILL YOU?
FWIP
CAN'T DO THAT EITHER.
FMP...
WHAT YOU'RE DOING RIGHT NOW...
...IS COM-PLETELY BEYOND ME.
WHAT IS WRONG WITH YOU?
I THOUGHT YOU WERE A MACHINE NERD. ANY HIGH SCHOOL STUDENT SHOULD BE ABLE TO MAKE A CIRCUIT!
WELL, THEY *TRIED* TO TEACH ME! I READ THE BOOKS 'TIL THEY FELL APART!
BUT STILL-

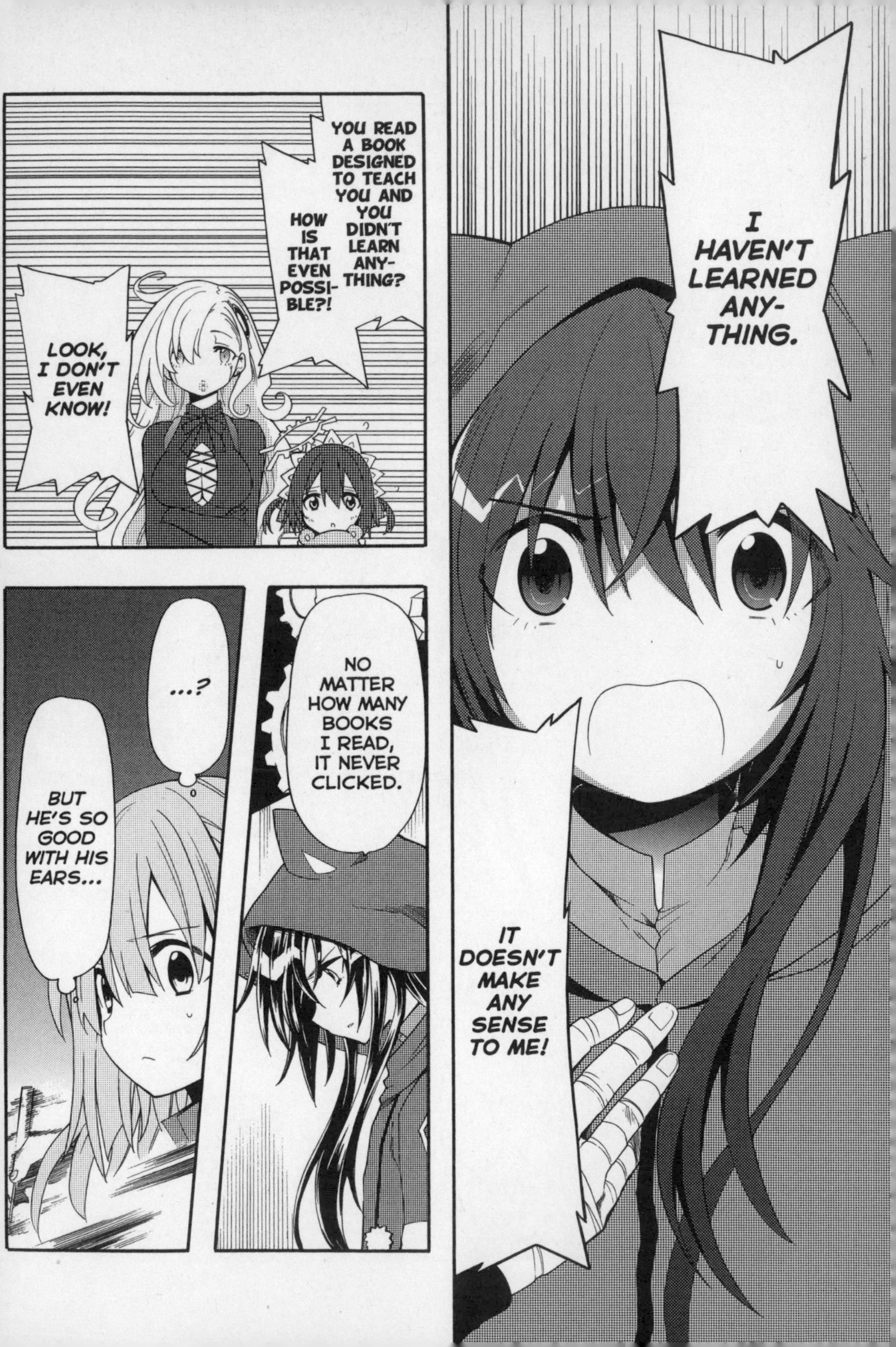
I HAVEN'T LEARNED ANY-THING.
IT DOESN'T MAKE ANY SENSE TO ME!
YOU READ A BOOK DESIGNED TO TEACH YOU AND YOU DIDN'T LEARN ANY-THING?
HOW IS THAT EVEN POSSI-BLE?!
LOOK, I DON'T EVEN KNOW!
NO MATTER HOW MANY BOOKS I READ, IT NEVER CLICKED.
...?
BUT HE'S SO GOOD WITH HIS EARS...

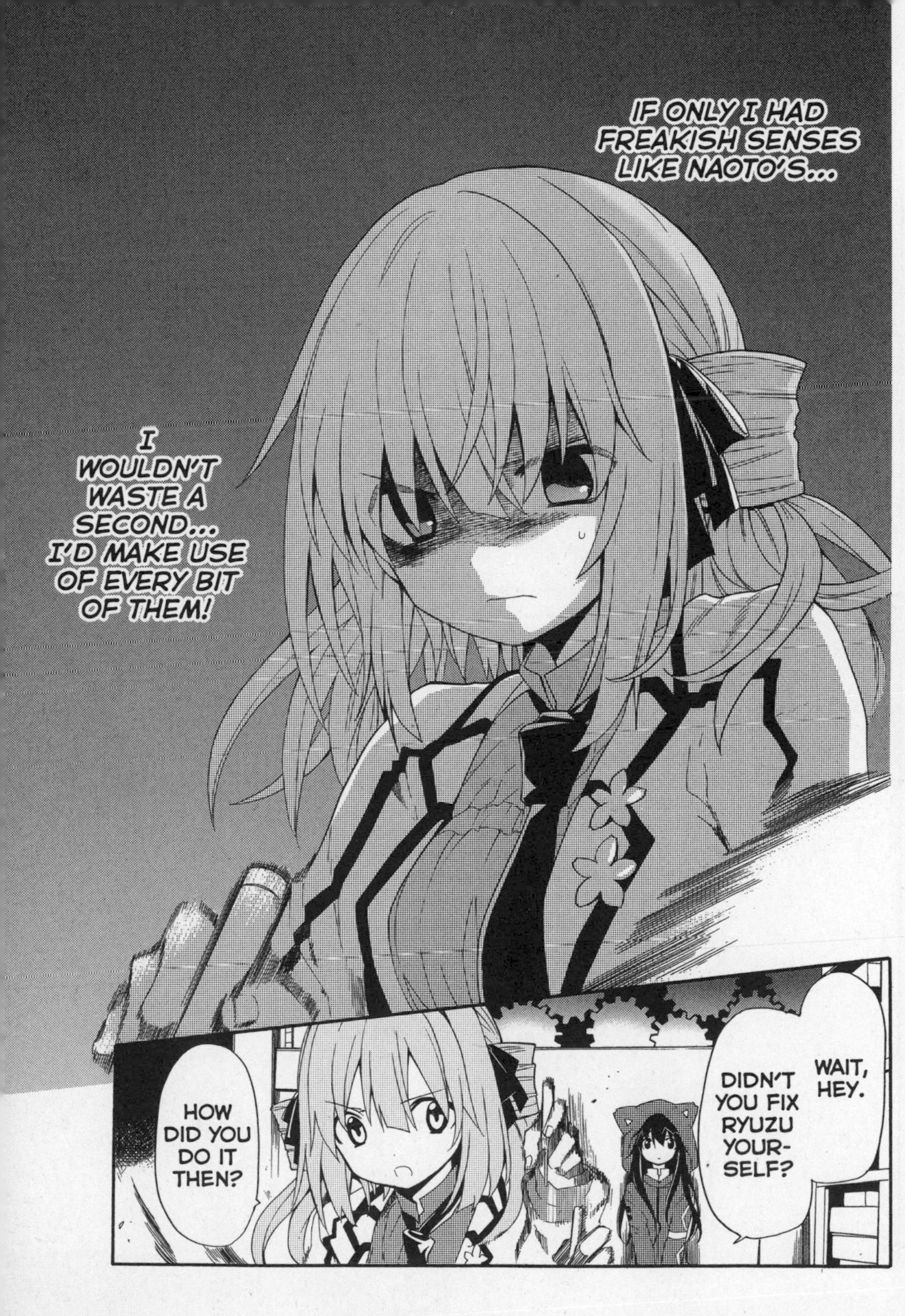
IF ONLY I HAD FREAKISH SENSES LIKE NAOTO'S...
I WOULDN'T WASTE A SECOND... I'D MAKE USE OF EVERY BIT OF THEM!
WAIT, HEY.
DIDN'T YOU FIX RYUZU YOUR-SELF?
HOW DID YOU DO IT THEN?

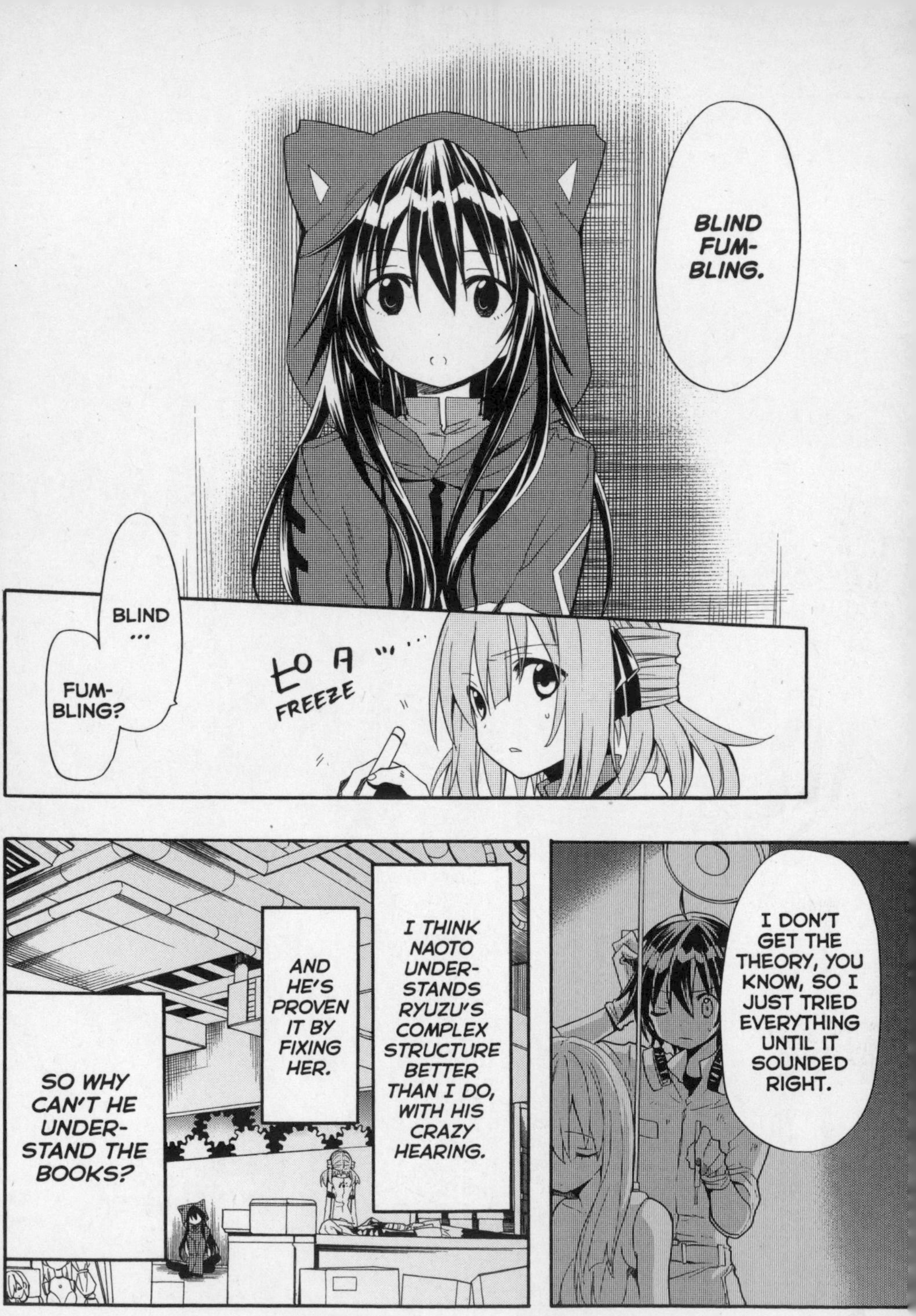
BLIND FUM-BLING.
BLIND ... FUM-BLING?
FREEZE
I DON'T GET THE THEORY, YOU KNOW, SO I JUST TRIED EVERYTHING UNTIL IT SOUNDED RIGHT.
I THINK NAOTO UNDER-STANDS RYUZU'S COMPLEX STRUCTURE BETTER THAN I DO, WITH HIS CRAZY HEARING.
AND HE'S PROVEN IT BY FIXING HER.
SO WHY CAN'T HE UNDER-STAND THE BOOKS?

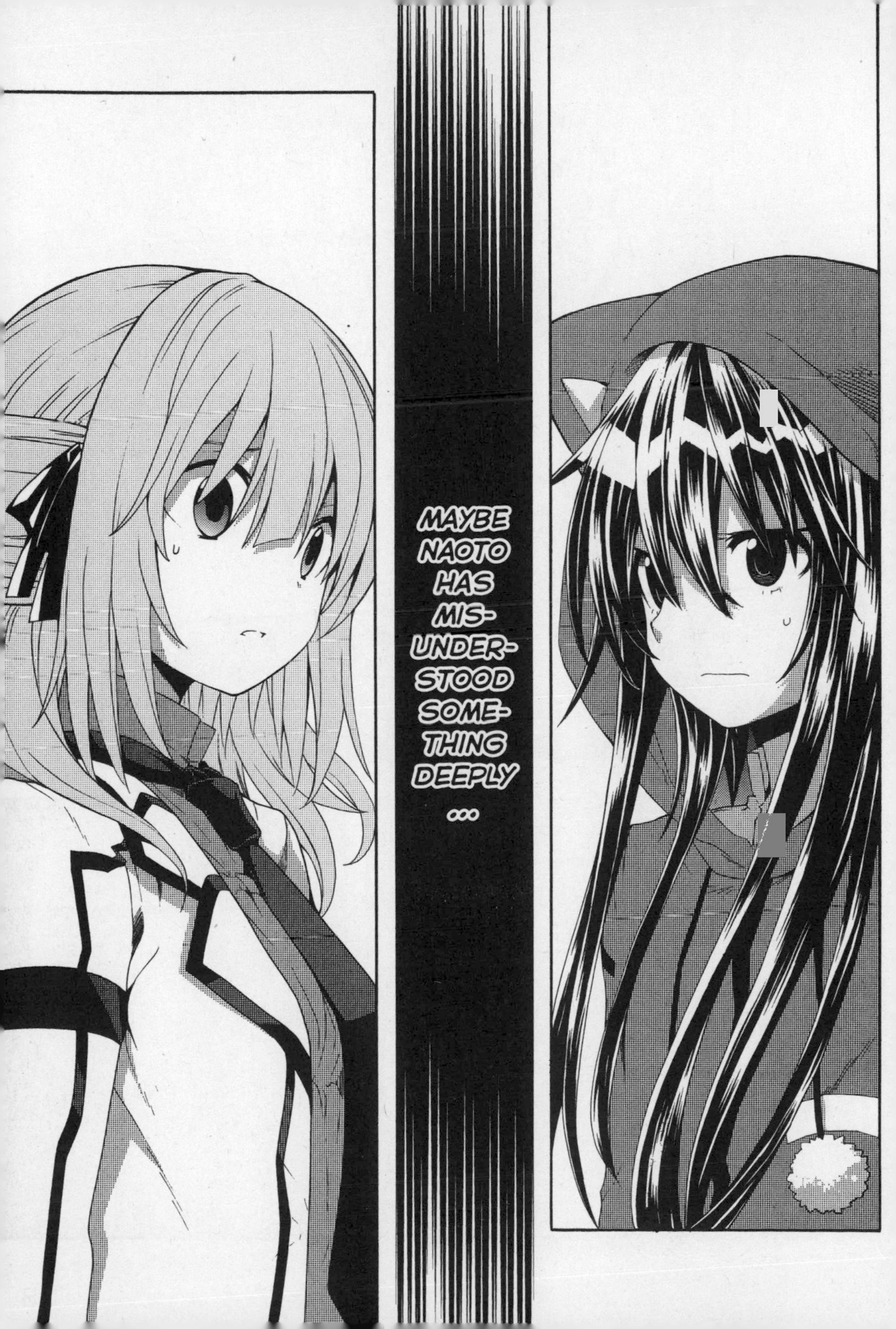
MAYBE NAOTO HAS MIS-UNDER-STOOD SOME-THING DEEPLY...

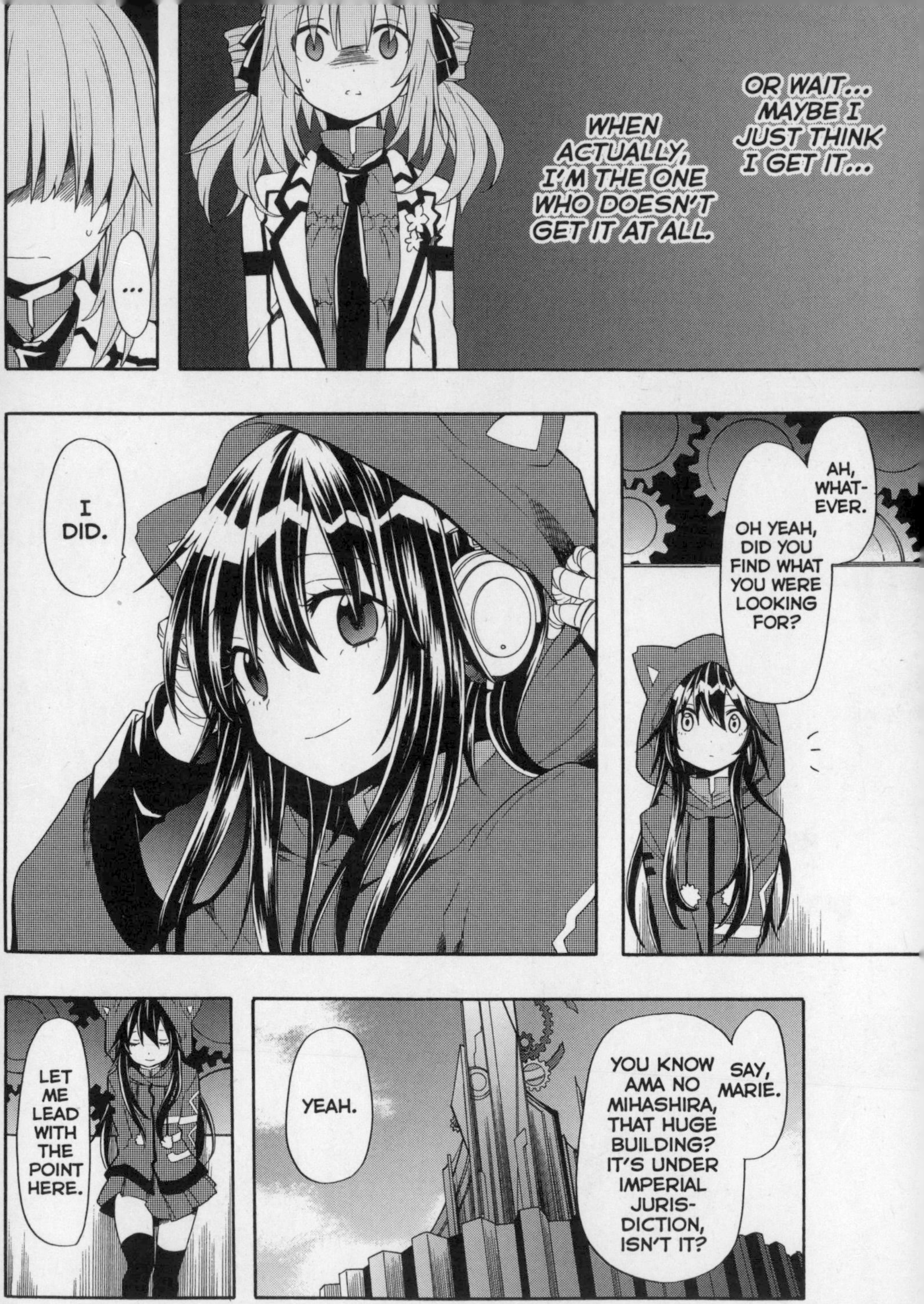
OR WAIT... MAYBE I JUST THINK I GET IT...
WHEN ACTUALLY, I'M THE ONE WHO DOESN'T GET IT AT ALL.
...
AH, WHATEVER.
OH YEAH, DID YOU FIND WHAT YOU WERE LOOKING FOR?
I DID.
SAY, MARIE.
YOU KNOW AMA NO MIHASHIRA, THAT HUGE BUILDING? IT'S UNDER IMPERIAL JURIS-DICTION, ISN'T IT?
YEAH.
LET ME LEAD WITH THE POINT HERE.

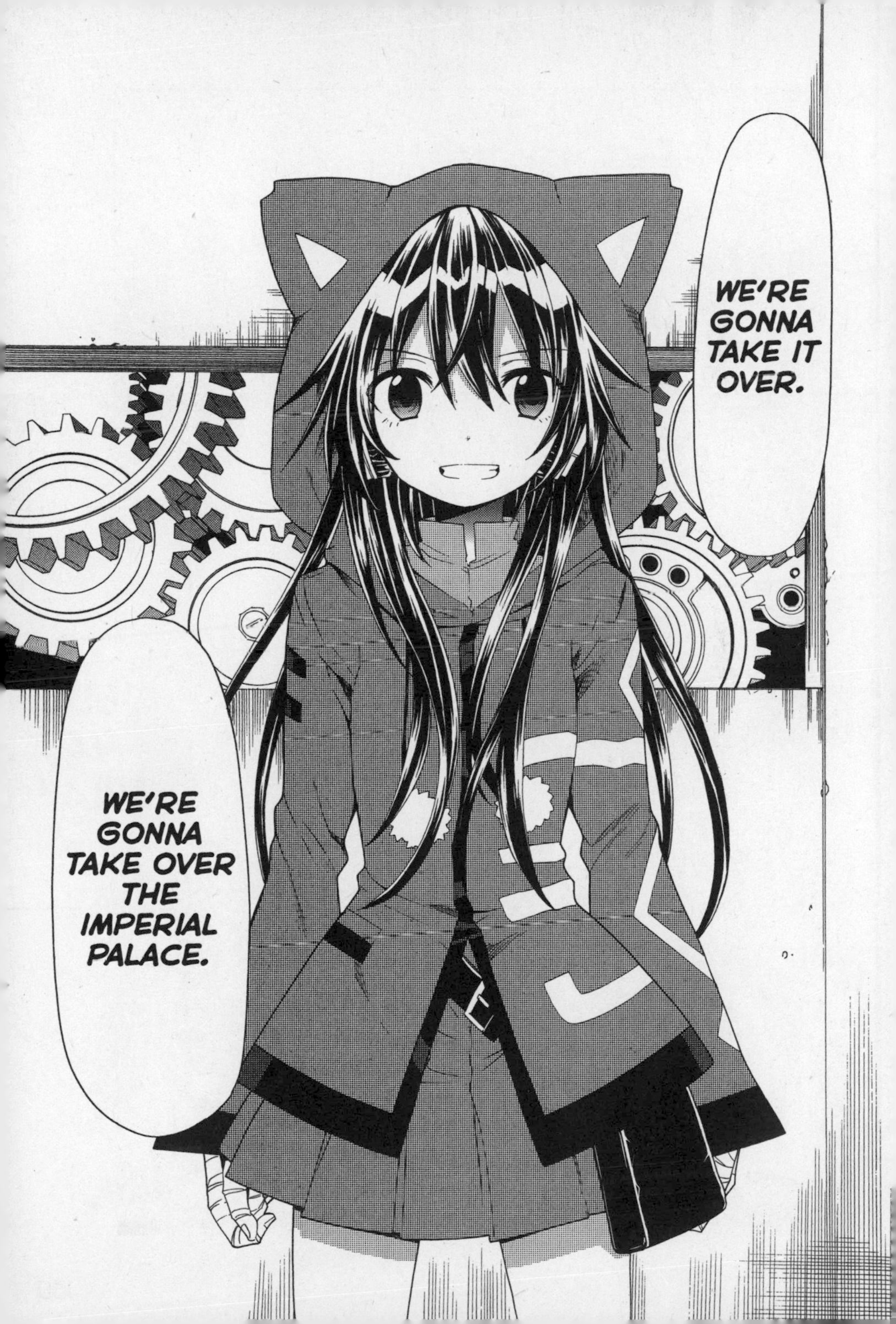
WE'RE GONNA TAKE IT OVER.
WE'RE GONNA TAKE OVER THE IMPERIAL PALACE.

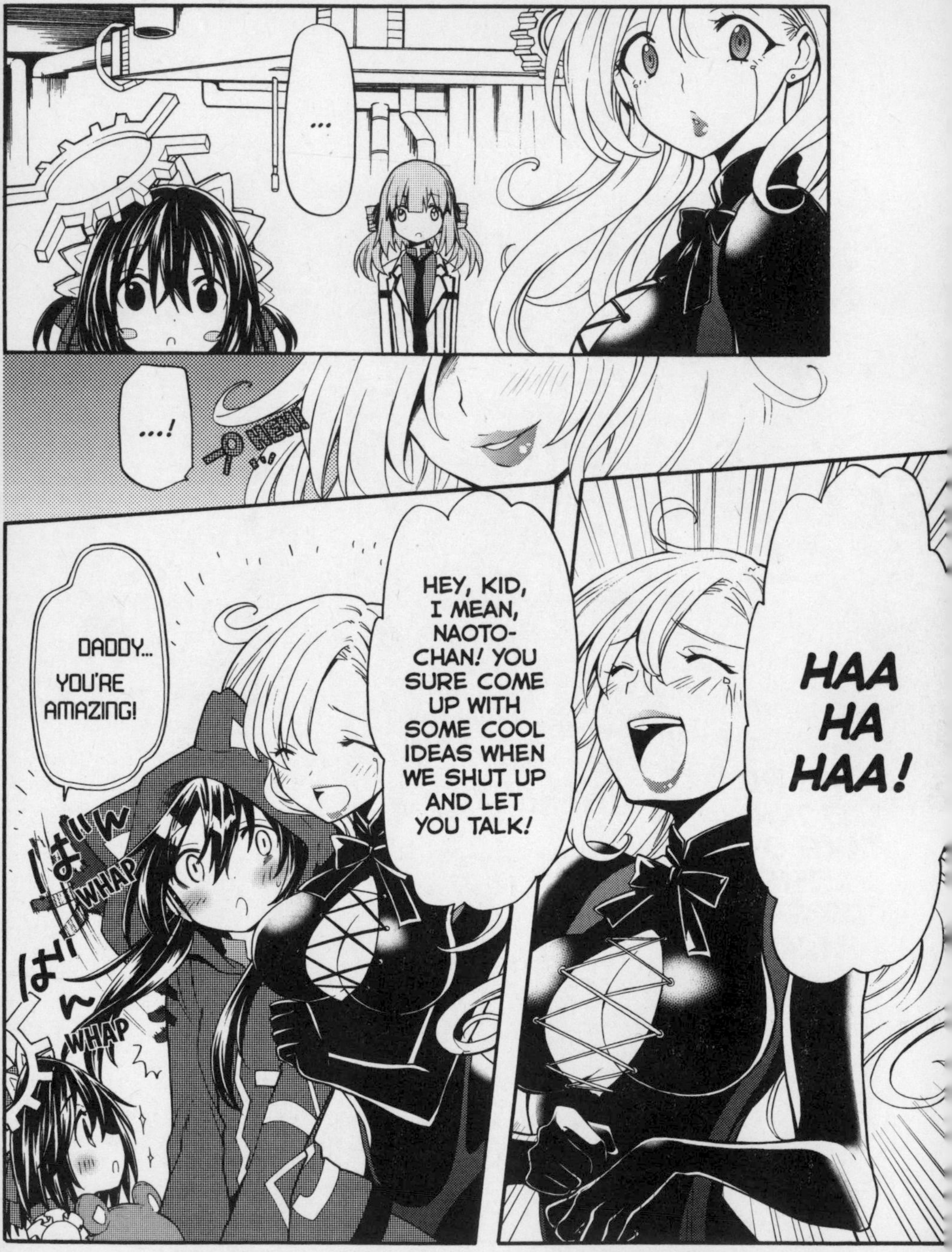
...
...!
HEH!
HAA HA HAA!
HEY, KID, I MEAN, NAOTO-CHAN! YOU SURE COME UP WITH SOME COOL IDEAS WHEN WE SHUT UP AND LET YOU TALK!
DADDY... YOU'RE AMAZING!
WHAP
WHAP

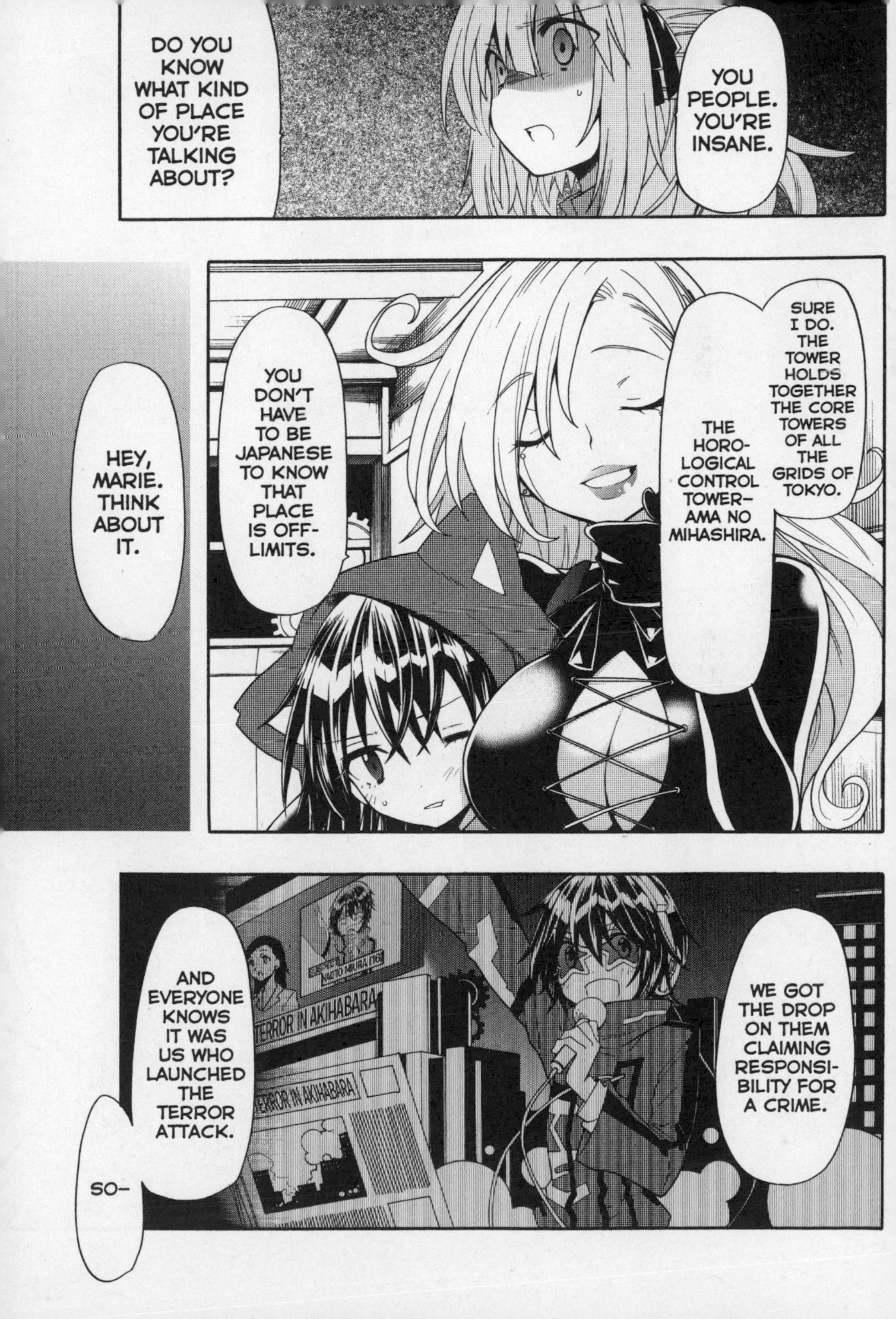
YOU PEOPLE. YOU'RE INSANE.
DO YOU KNOW WHAT KIND OF PLACE YOU'RE TALKING ABOUT?
SURE I DO. THE TOWER HOLDS TOGETHER THE CORE TOWERS OF ALL THE GRIDS OF TOKYO.
THE HOROLOGICAL CONTROL TOWER–AMA NO MIHASHIRA.
YOU DON'T HAVE TO BE JAPANESE TO KNOW THAT PLACE IS OFF-LIMITS.
HEY, MARIE. THINK ABOUT IT.
WE GOT THE DROP ON THEM CLAIMING RESPONSIBILITY FOR A CRIME.
TERROR IN AKIHABARA
TERROR IN AKIHABARA
AND EVERYONE KNOWS IT WAS US WHO LAUNCHED THE TERROR ATTACK.
SO–

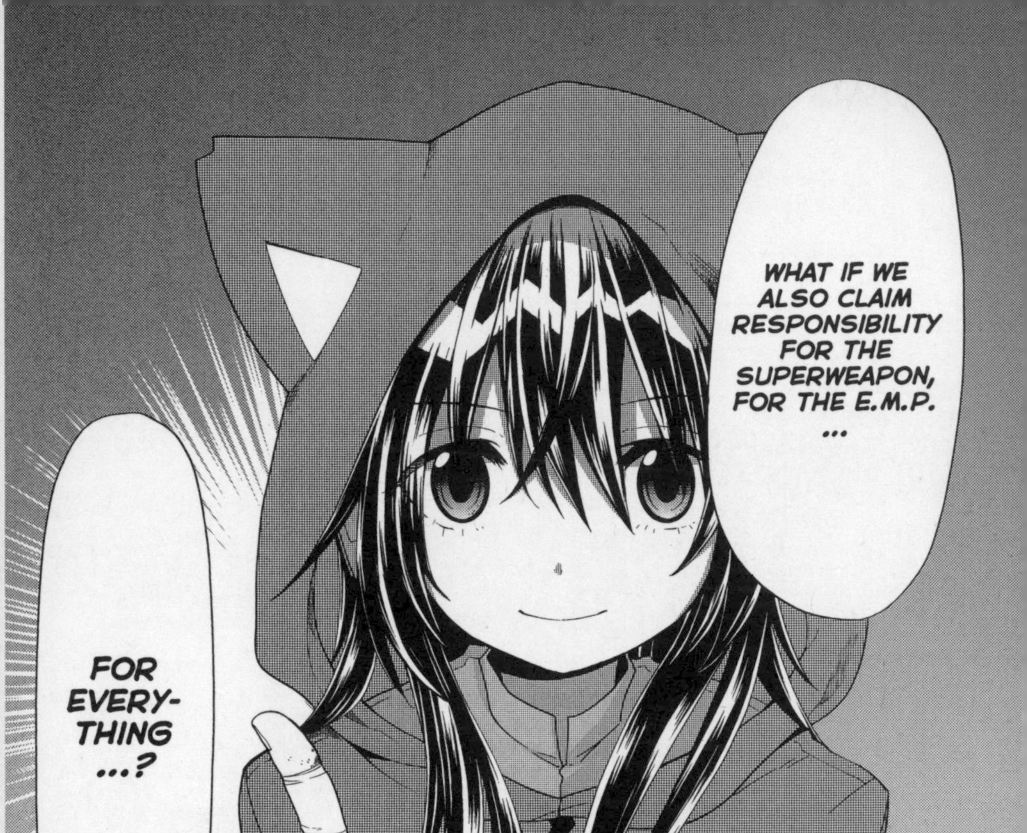
WHAT IF WE ALSO CLAIM RESPONSIBILITY FOR THE SUPERWEAPON, FOR THE E.M.P. ...
FOR EVERY-THING ...?
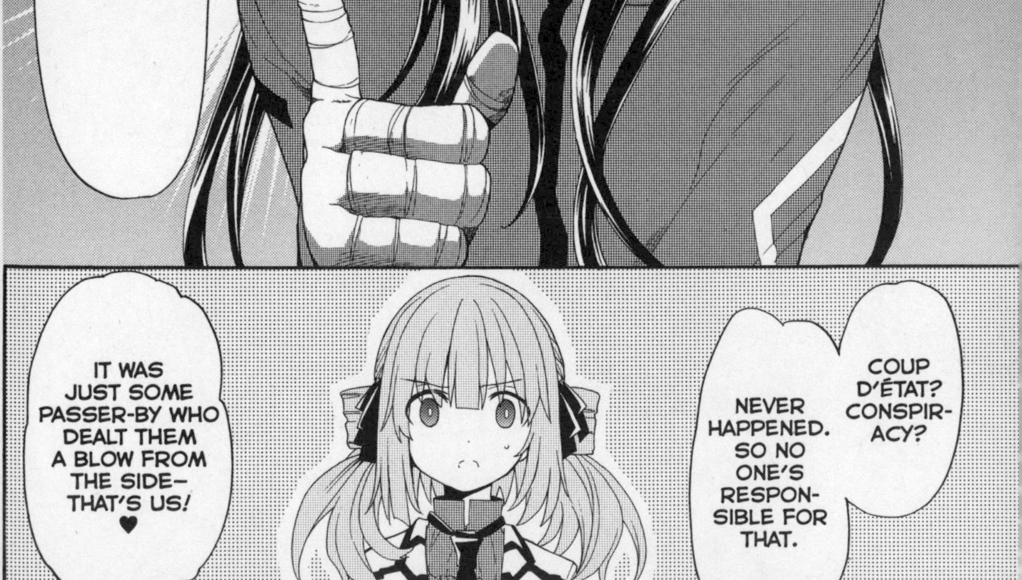
COUP D'ÉTAT? CONSPIR-ACY? NEVER HAPPENED. SO NO ONE'S RESPON-SIBLE FOR THAT.
IT WAS JUST SOME PASSER-BY WHO DEALT THEM A BLOW FROM THE SIDE— THAT'S US! ♥

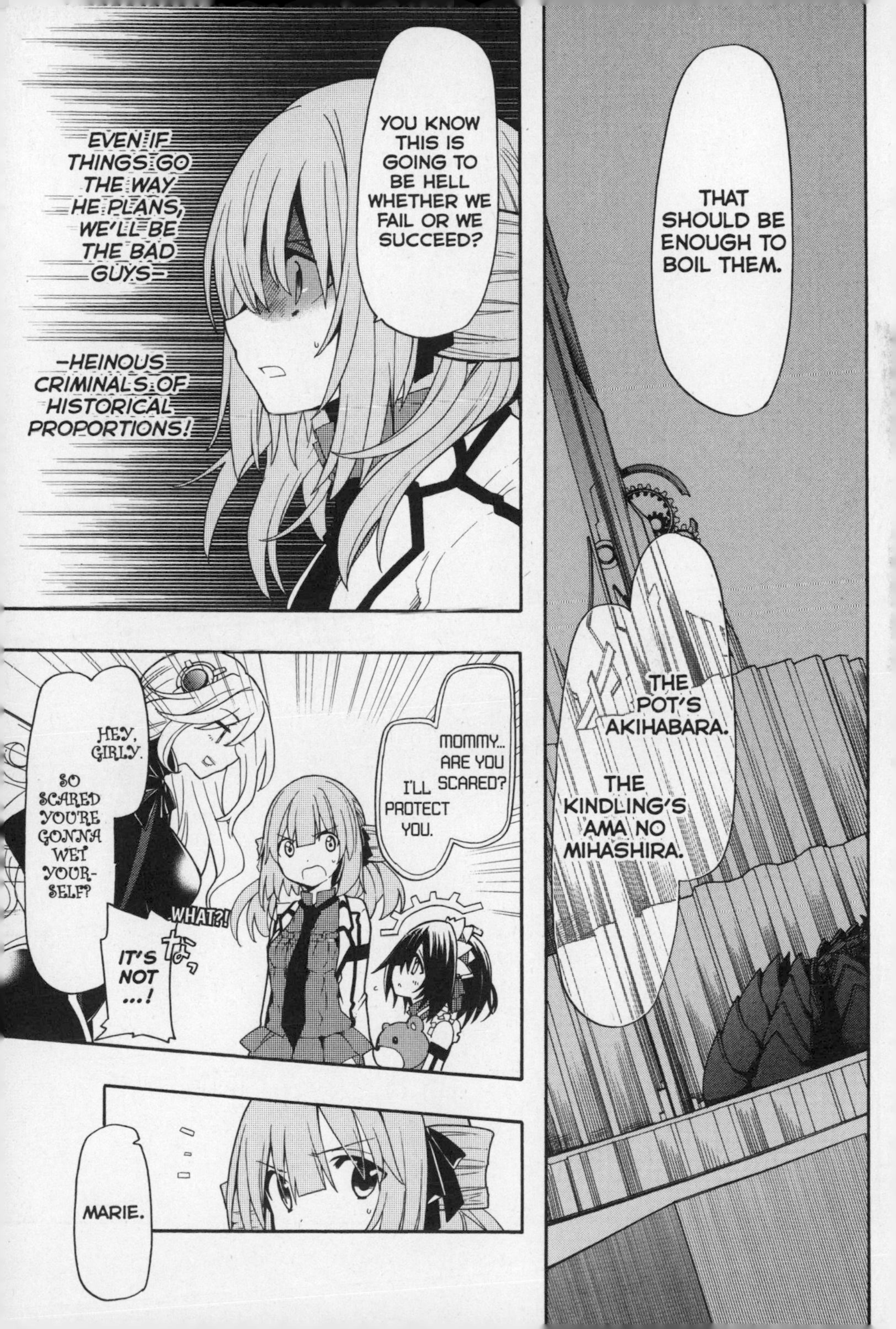
THAT SHOULD BE ENOUGH TO BOIL THEM.
THE POT'S AKIHABARA.
THE KINDLING'S AMA NO MIHASHIRA.
YOU KNOW THIS IS GOING TO BE HELL WHETHER WE FAIL OR WE SUCCEED?
EVEN IF THINGS GO THE WAY HE PLANS, WE'LL BE THE BAD GUYS—
—HEINOUS CRIMINALS OF HISTORICAL PROPORTIONS!
MOMMY... ARE YOU SCARED? I'LL PROTECT YOU.
HEY, GIRLY. SO SCARED YOU'RE GONNA WET YOURSELF?
WHAT?!
IT'S NOT ...!
...
MARIE.

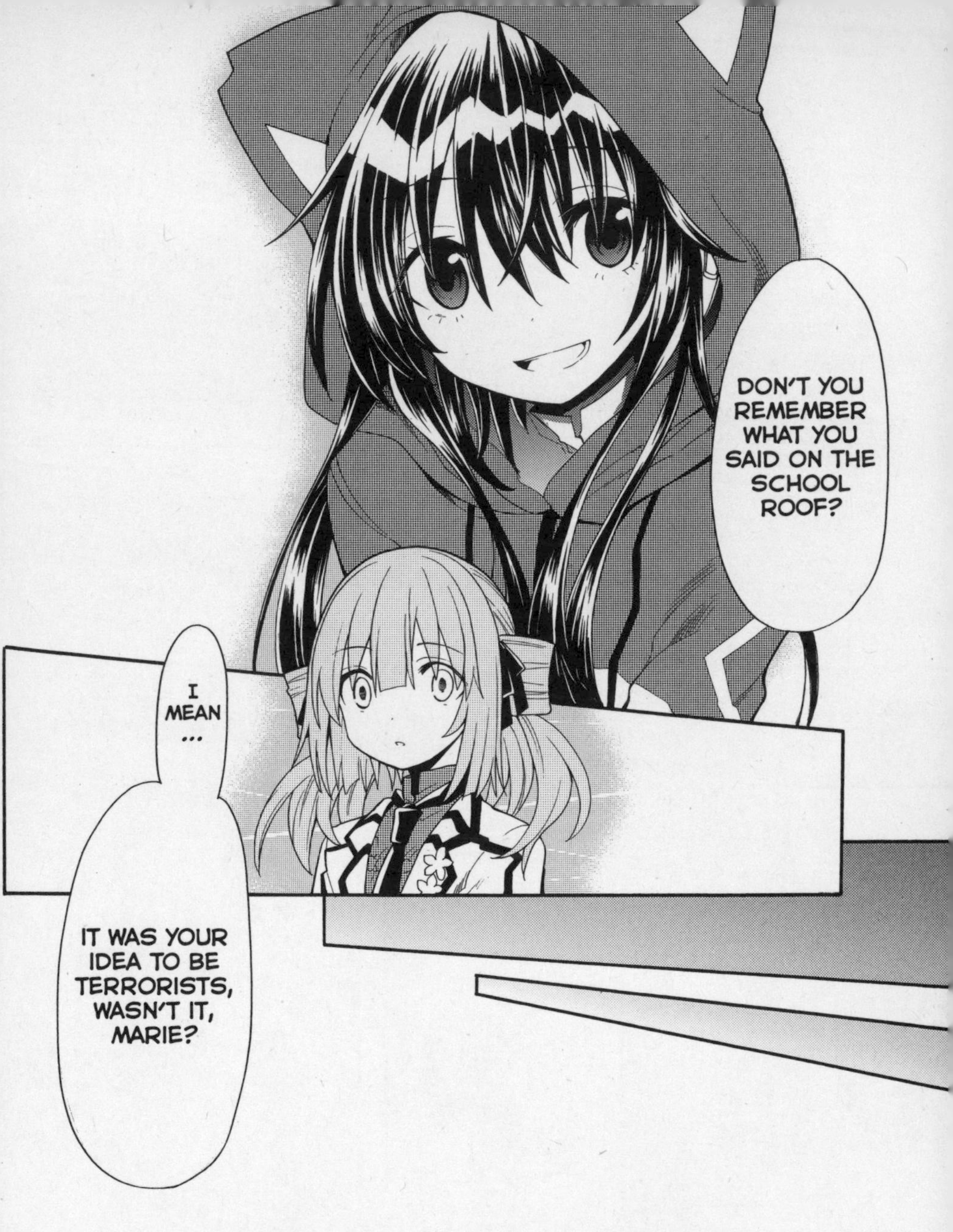
DON'T YOU REMEMBER WHAT YOU SAID ON THE SCHOOL ROOF?
I MEAN ...
IT WAS YOUR IDEA TO BE TERRORISTS, WASN'T IT, MARIE?

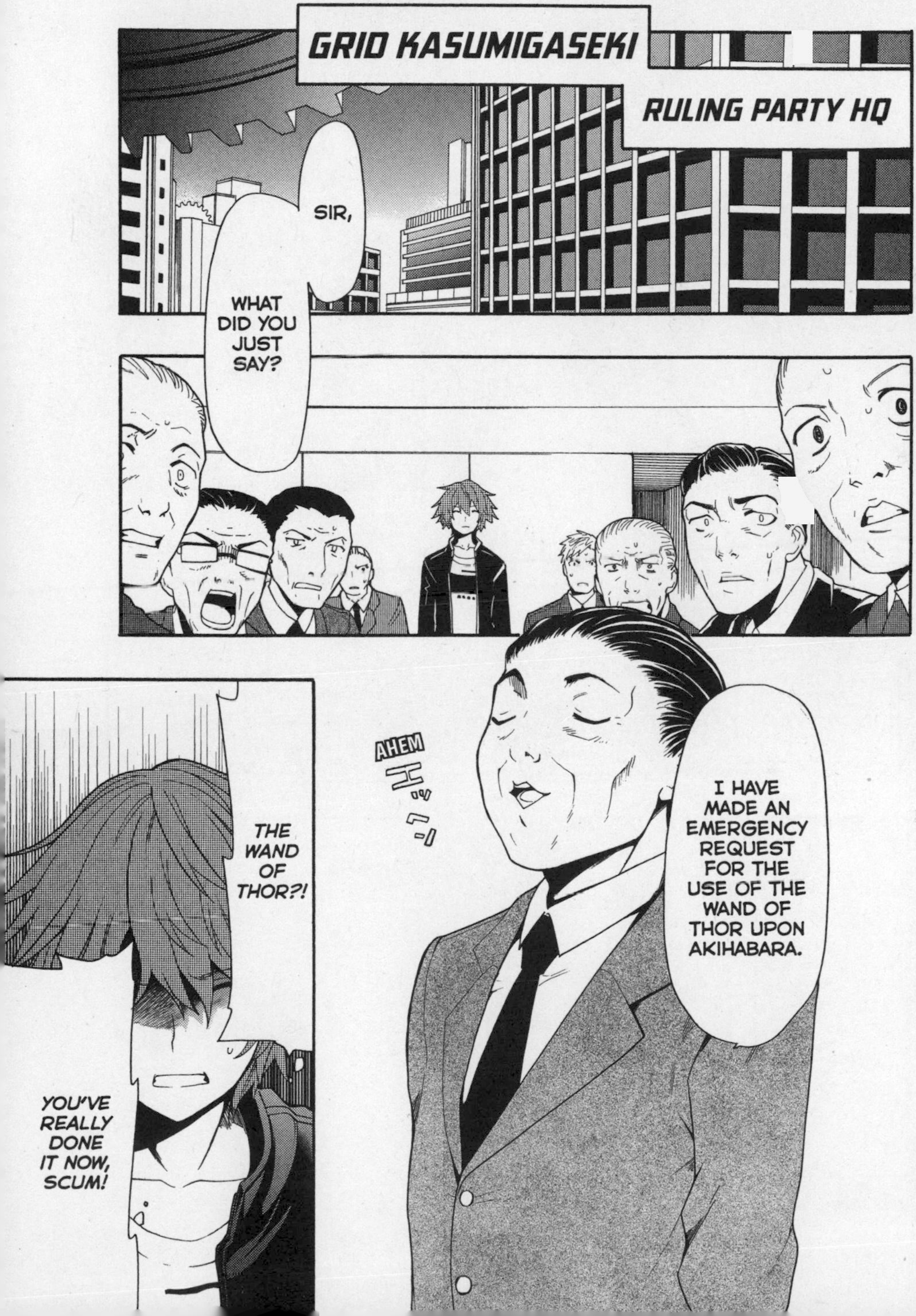
GRID KASUMIGASEKI
RULING PARTY HQ
SIR, WHAT DID YOU JUST SAY?
AHEM
I HAVE MADE AN EMERGENCY REQUEST FOR THE USE OF THE WAND OF THOR UPON AKIHABARA.
THE WAND OF THOR?!
YOU'VE REALLY DONE IT NOW, SCUM!

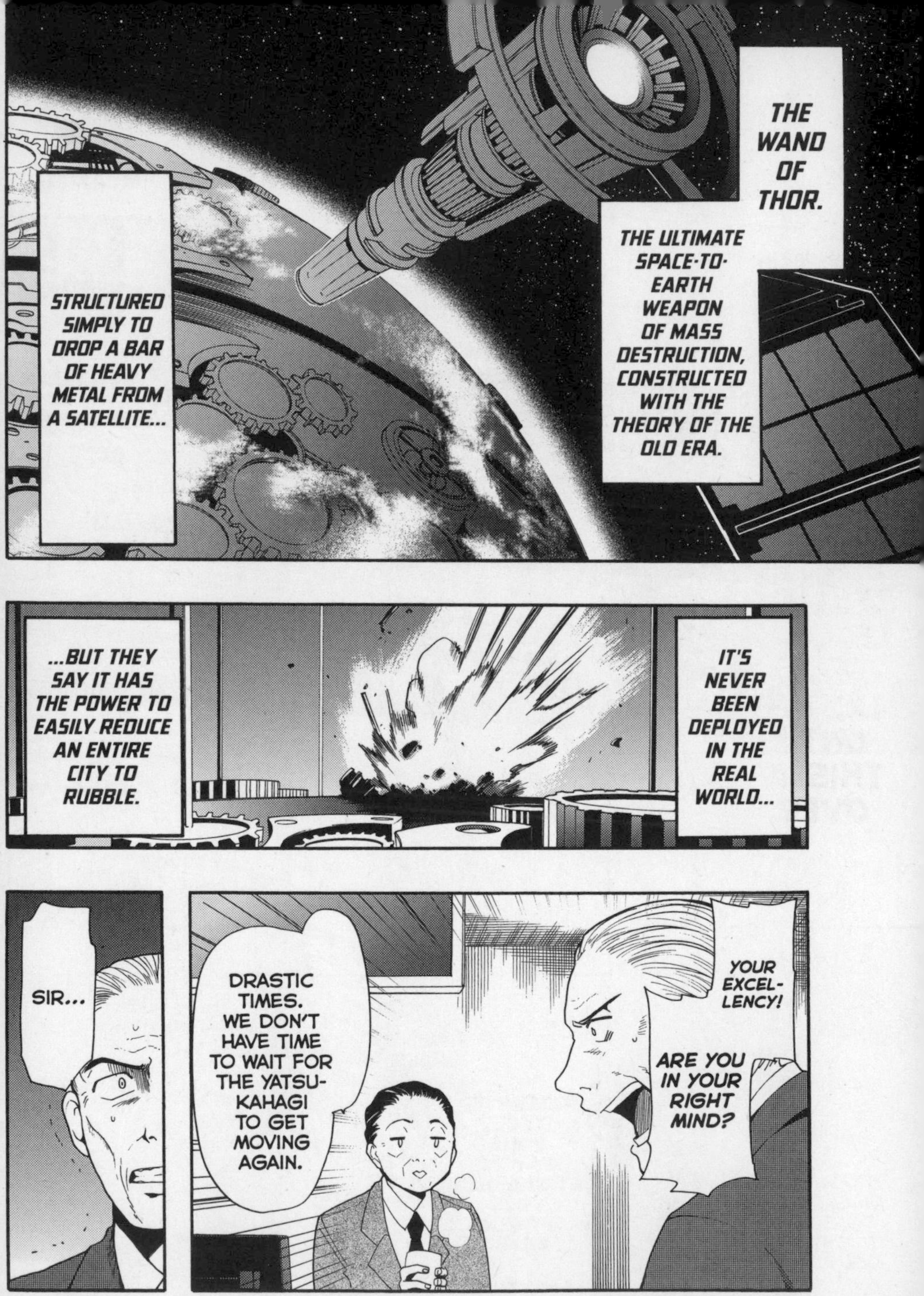
THE WAND OF THOR.
THE ULTIMATE SPACE-TO-EARTH WEAPON OF MASS DESTRUCTION, CONSTRUCTED WITH THE THEORY OF THE OLD ERA.
STRUCTURED SIMPLY TO DROP A BAR OF HEAVY METAL FROM A SATELLITE...
IT'S NEVER BEEN DEPLOYED IN THE REAL WORLD...
...BUT THEY SAY IT HAS THE POWER TO EASILY REDUCE AN ENTIRE CITY TO RUBBLE.
YOUR EXCEL-LENCY!
ARE YOU IN YOUR RIGHT MIND?
DRASTIC TIMES. WE DON'T HAVE TIME TO WAIT FOR THE YATSU-KAHAGI TO GET MOVING AGAIN.
SIR...

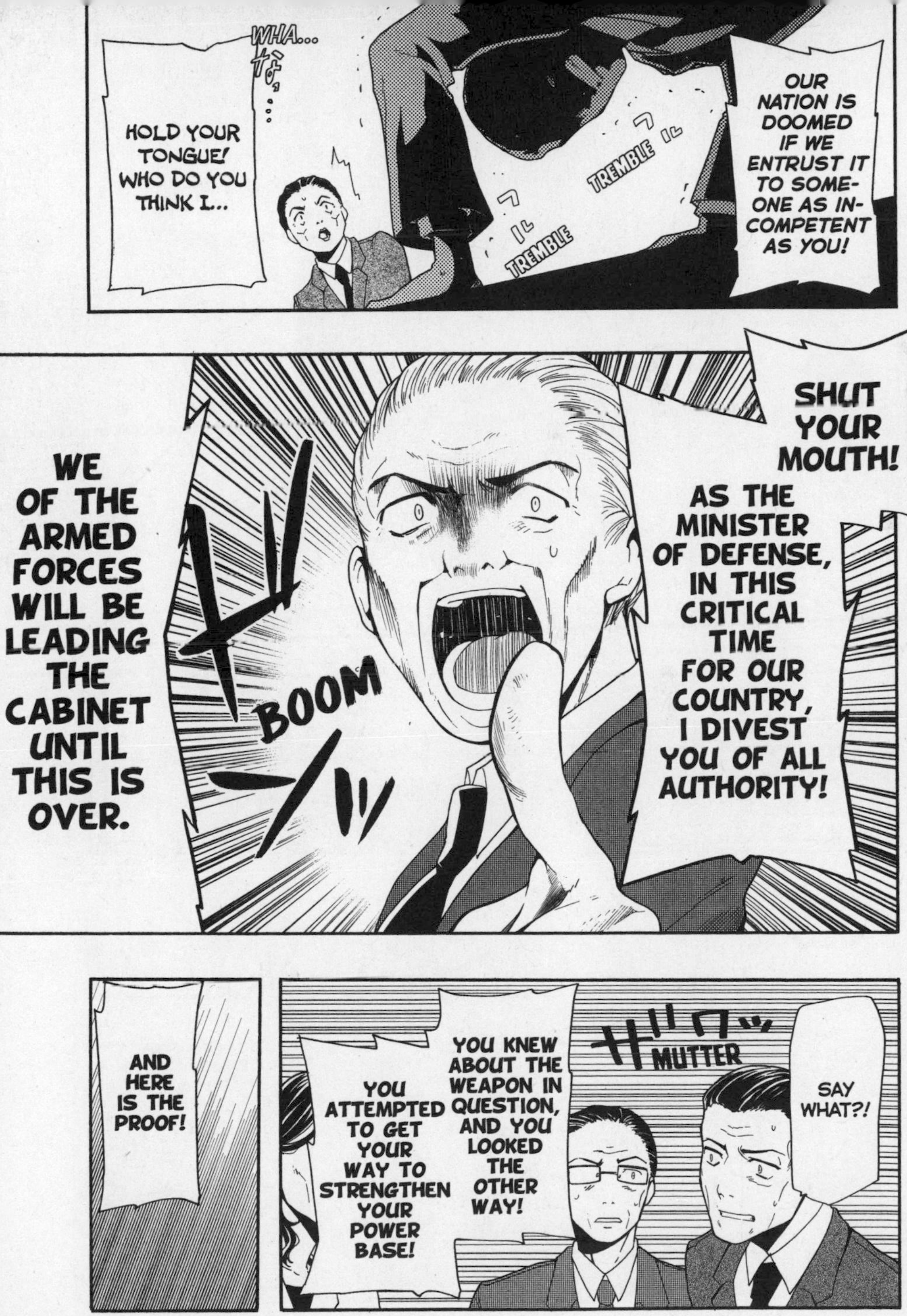
OUR NATION IS DOOMED IF WE ENTRUST IT TO SOME-ONE AS IN-COMPETENT AS YOU!
WHA...
TREMBLE TREMBLE
HOLD YOUR TONGUE! WHO DO YOU THINK I...
SHUT YOUR MOUTH!
AS THE MINISTER OF DEFENSE, IN THIS CRITICAL TIME FOR OUR COUNTRY, I DIVEST YOU OF ALL AUTHORITY!
BOOM
WE OF THE ARMED FORCES WILL BE LEADING THE CABINET UNTIL THIS IS OVER.
SAY WHAT?!
MUTTER
YOU KNEW ABOUT THE WEAPON IN QUESTION, AND YOU LOOKED THE OTHER WAY!
YOU ATTEMPTED TO GET YOUR WAY TO STRENGTHEN YOUR POWER BASE!
AND HERE IS THE PROOF!

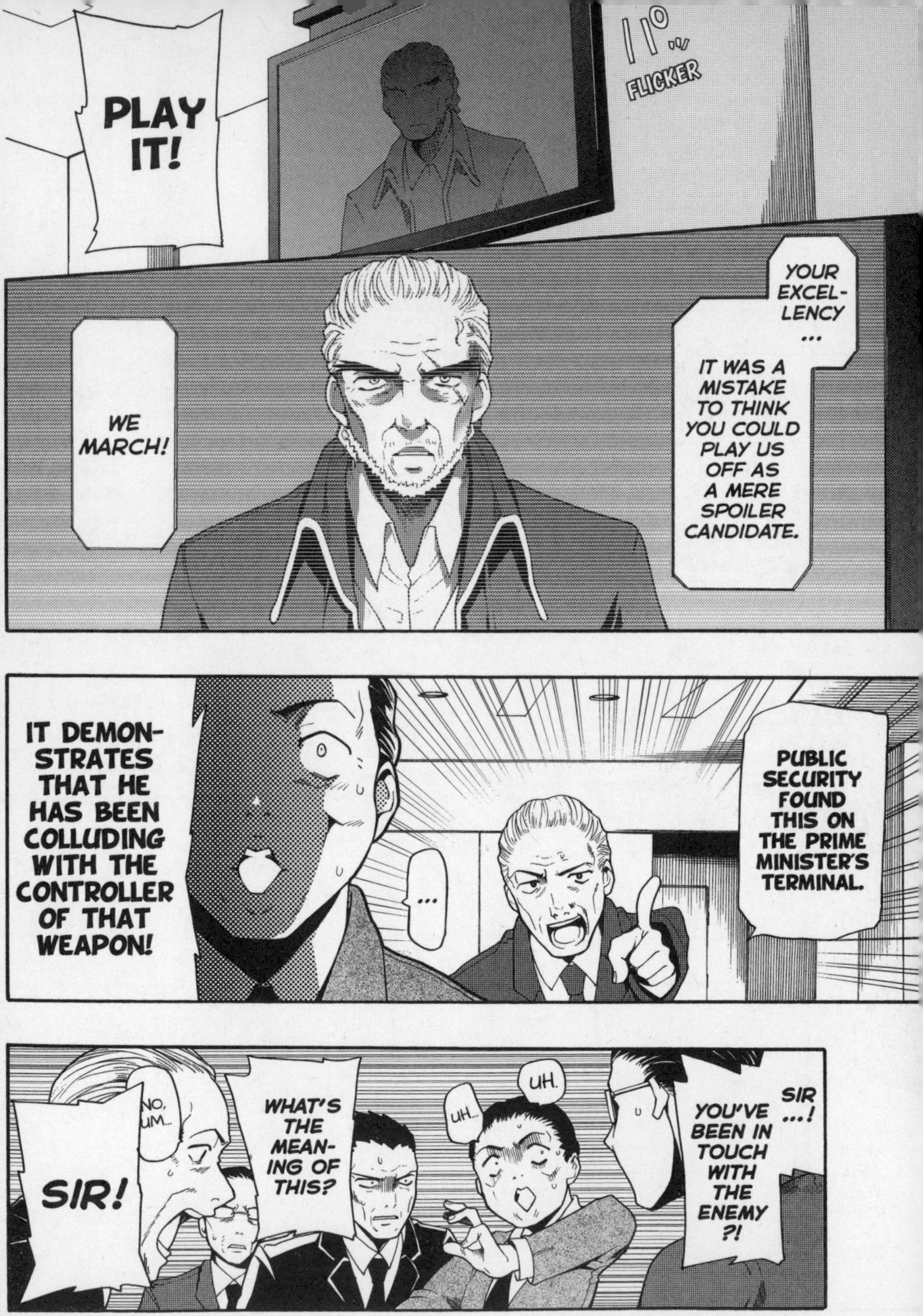
FLICKER
PLAY IT!
YOUR EXCEL-LENCY ...
IT WAS A MISTAKE TO THINK YOU COULD PLAY US OFF AS A MERE SPOILER CANDIDATE.
WE MARCH!
PUBLIC SECURITY FOUND THIS ON THE PRIME MINISTER'S TERMINAL.
...
IT DEMON-STRATES THAT HE HAS BEEN COLLUDING WITH THE CONTROLLER OF THAT WEAPON!
SIR ...!
YOU'VE BEEN IN TOUCH WITH THE ENEMY ?!
UH.
UH...
WHAT'S THE MEAN-ING OF THIS?
NO, UM...
SIR!

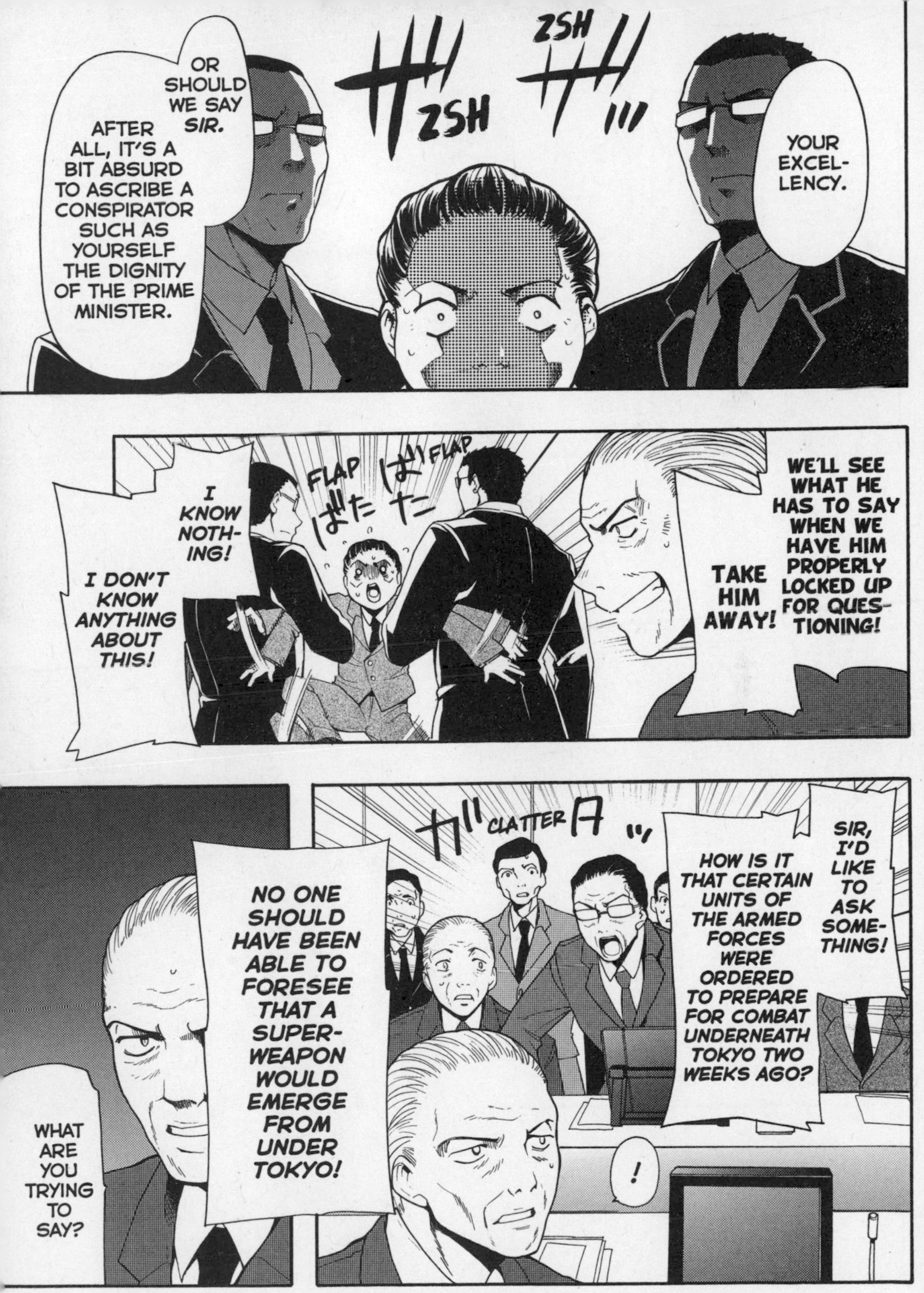
YOUR EXCELLENCY.
ZSH
ZSH
OR SHOULD WE SAY SIR.
AFTER ALL, IT'S A BIT ABSURD TO ASCRIBE A CONSPIRATOR SUCH AS YOURSELF THE DIGNITY OF THE PRIME MINISTER.
WE'LL SEE WHAT HE HAS TO SAY WHEN WE HAVE HIM PROPERLY LOCKED UP FOR QUESTIONING!
TAKE HIM AWAY!
FLAP
FLAP
I KNOW NOTHING!
I DON'T KNOW ANYTHING ABOUT THIS!
SIR, I'D LIKE TO ASK SOMETHING!
HOW IS IT THAT CERTAIN UNITS OF THE ARMED FORCES WERE ORDERED TO PREPARE FOR COMBAT UNDERNEATH TOKYO TWO WEEKS AGO?
CLATTER
!
NO ONE SHOULD HAVE BEEN ABLE TO FORESEE THAT A SUPER-WEAPON WOULD EMERGE FROM UNDER TOKYO!
WHAT ARE YOU TRYING TO SAY?

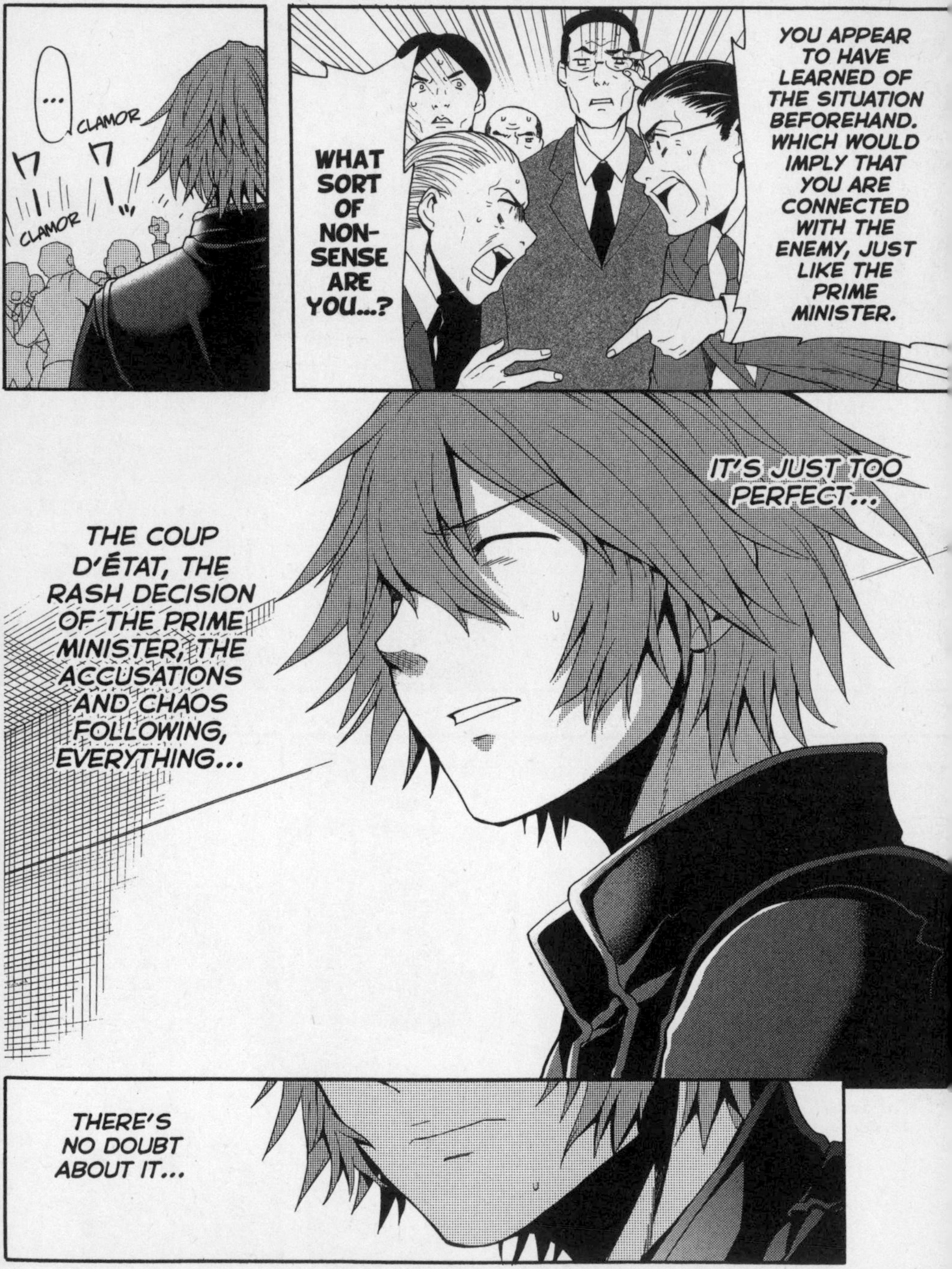
YOU APPEAR TO HAVE LEARNED OF THE SITUATION BEFOREHAND. WHICH WOULD IMPLY THAT YOU ARE CONNECTED WITH THE ENEMY, JUST LIKE THE PRIME MINISTER.
WHAT SORT OF NON-SENSE ARE YOU...?
...
CLAMOR
CLAMOR
IT'S JUST TOO PERFECT...
THE COUP D'ÉTAT, THE RASH DECISION OF THE PRIME MINISTER, THE ACCUSATIONS AND CHAOS FOLLOWING, EVERYTHING...
THERE'S NO DOUBT ABOUT IT...

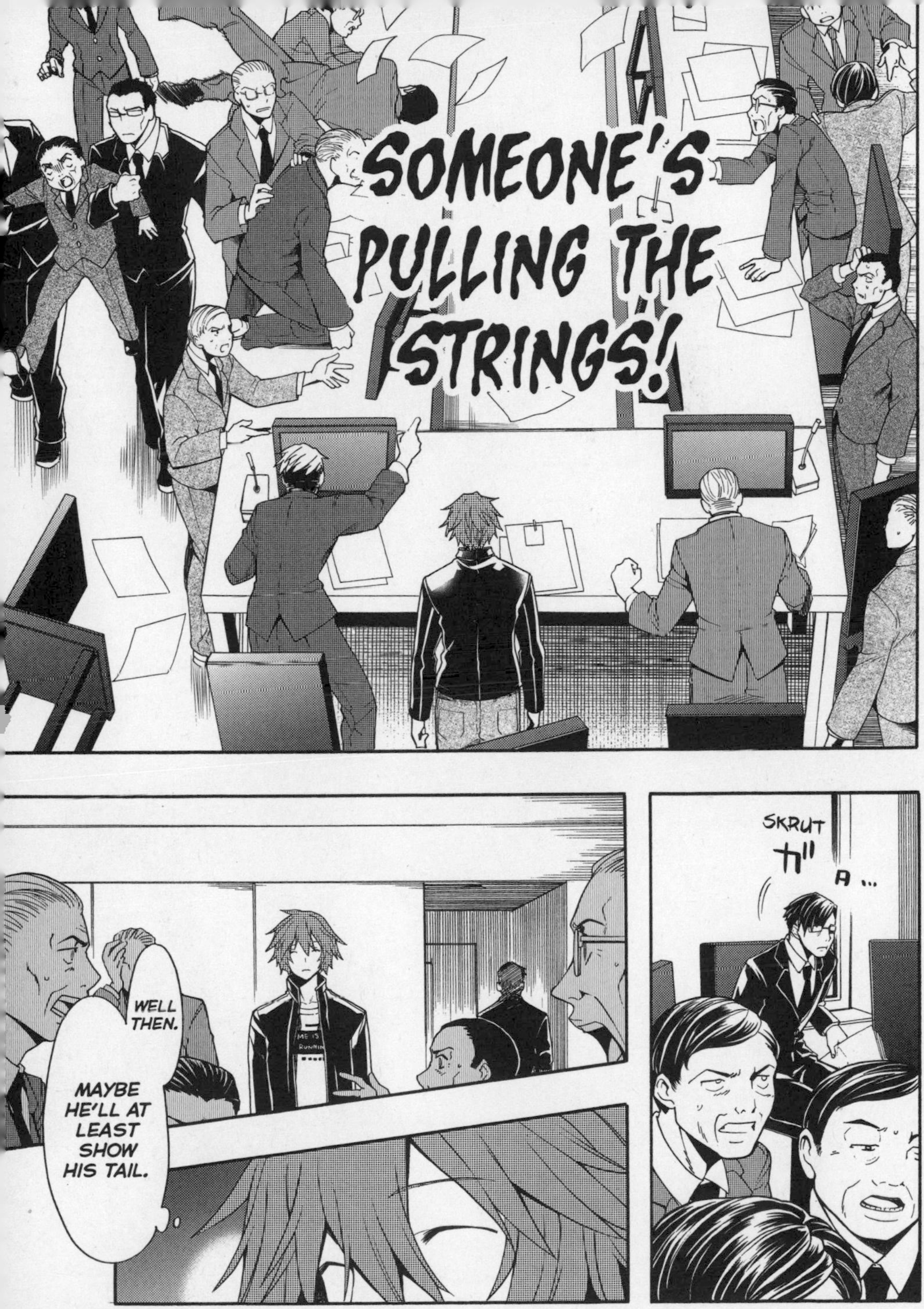
SOMEONE'S PULLING THE STRINGS!
SKRUT
ガ
A...
WELL THEN.
MAYBE HE'LL AT LEAST SHOW HIS TAIL.

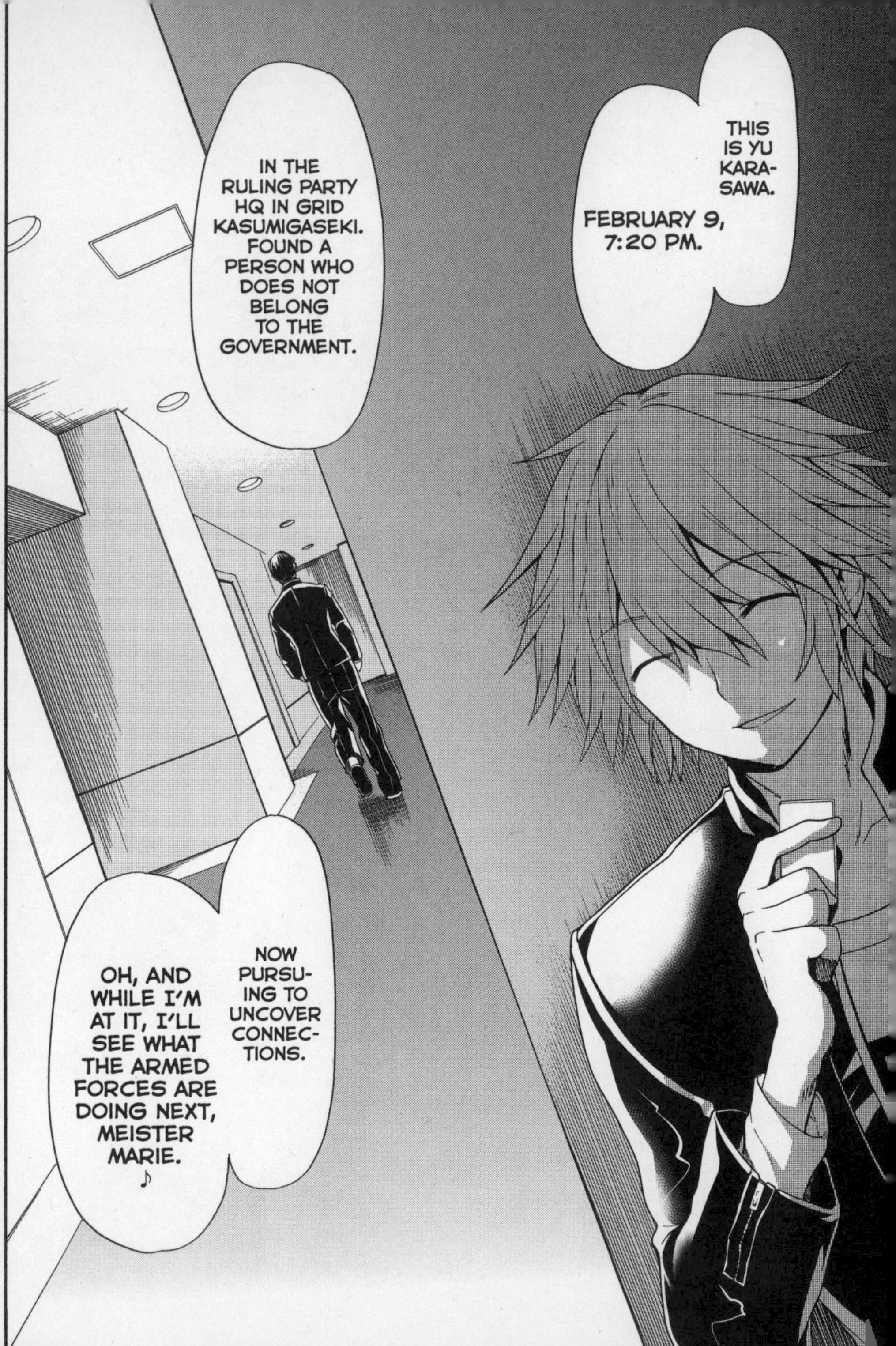
THIS IS YU KARA-SAWA.
FEBRUARY 9, 7:20 PM.
IN THE RULING PARTY HQ IN GRID KASUMIGASEKI. FOUND A PERSON WHO DOES NOT BELONG TO THE GOVERNMENT.
NOW PURSU-ING TO UNCOVER CONNEC-TIONS.
OH, AND WHILE I'M AT IT, I'LL SEE WHAT THE ARMED FORCES ARE DOING NEXT, MEISTER MARIE. ♪

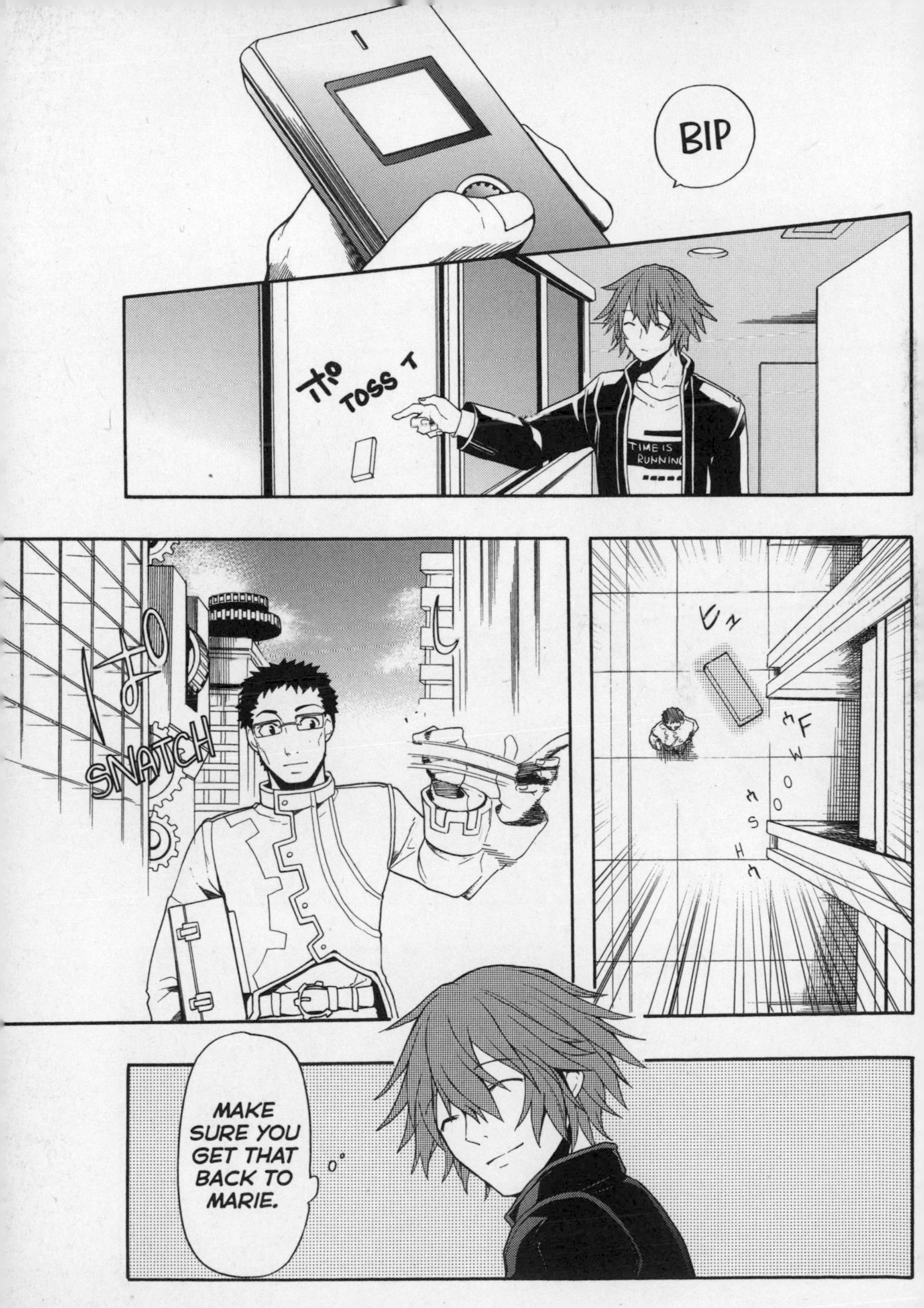
BIP
TOSS
FWOOSH
SNATCH
MAKE SURE YOU GET THAT BACK TO MARIE.

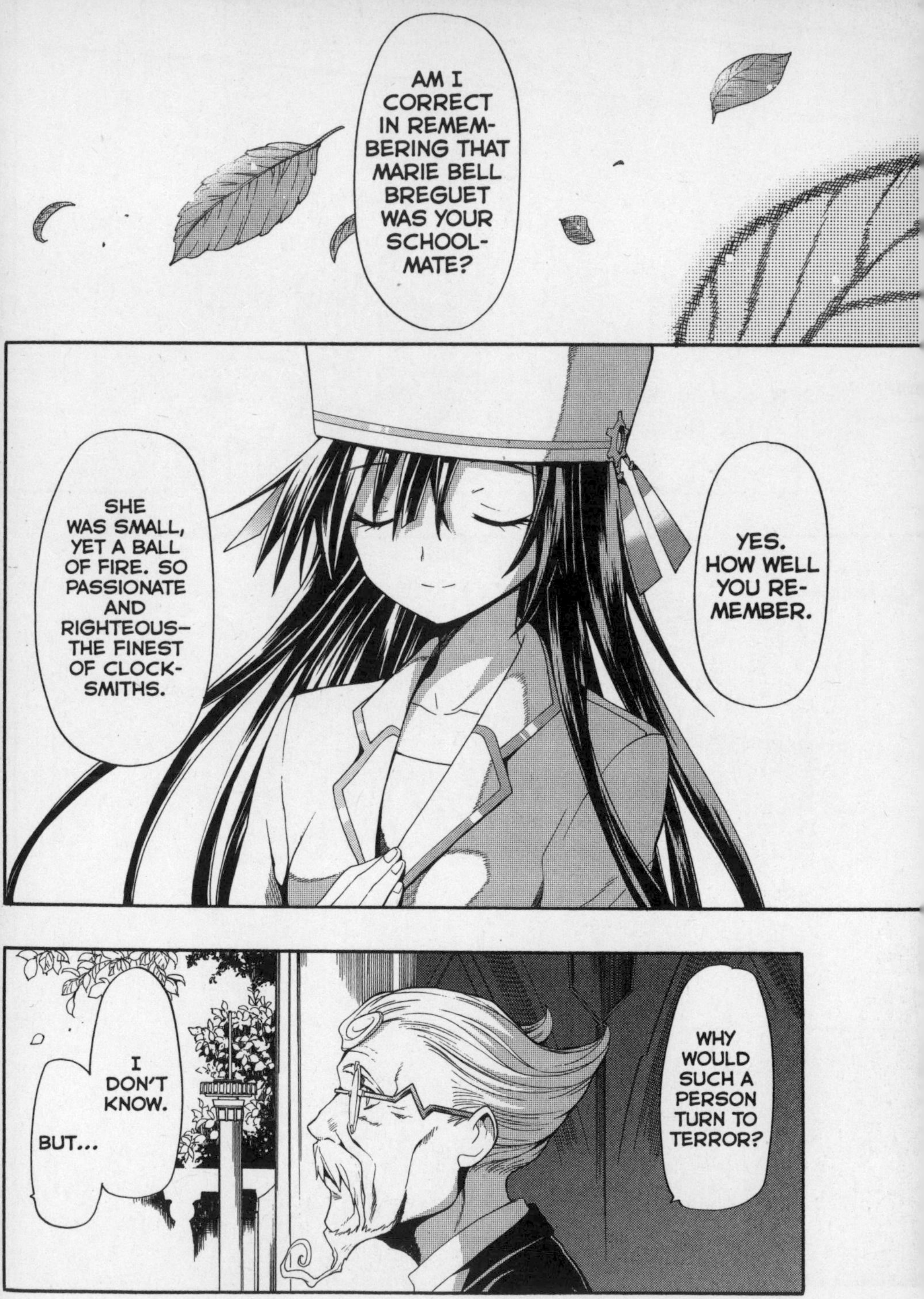
AM I CORRECT IN REMEMBERING THAT MARIE BELL BREGUET WAS YOUR SCHOOLMATE?
YES. HOW WELL YOU REMEMBER.
SHE WAS SMALL, YET A BALL OF FIRE. SO PASSIONATE AND RIGHTEOUS– THE FINEST OF CLOCKSMITHS.
WHY WOULD SUCH A PERSON TURN TO TERROR?
I DON'T KNOW.
BUT...

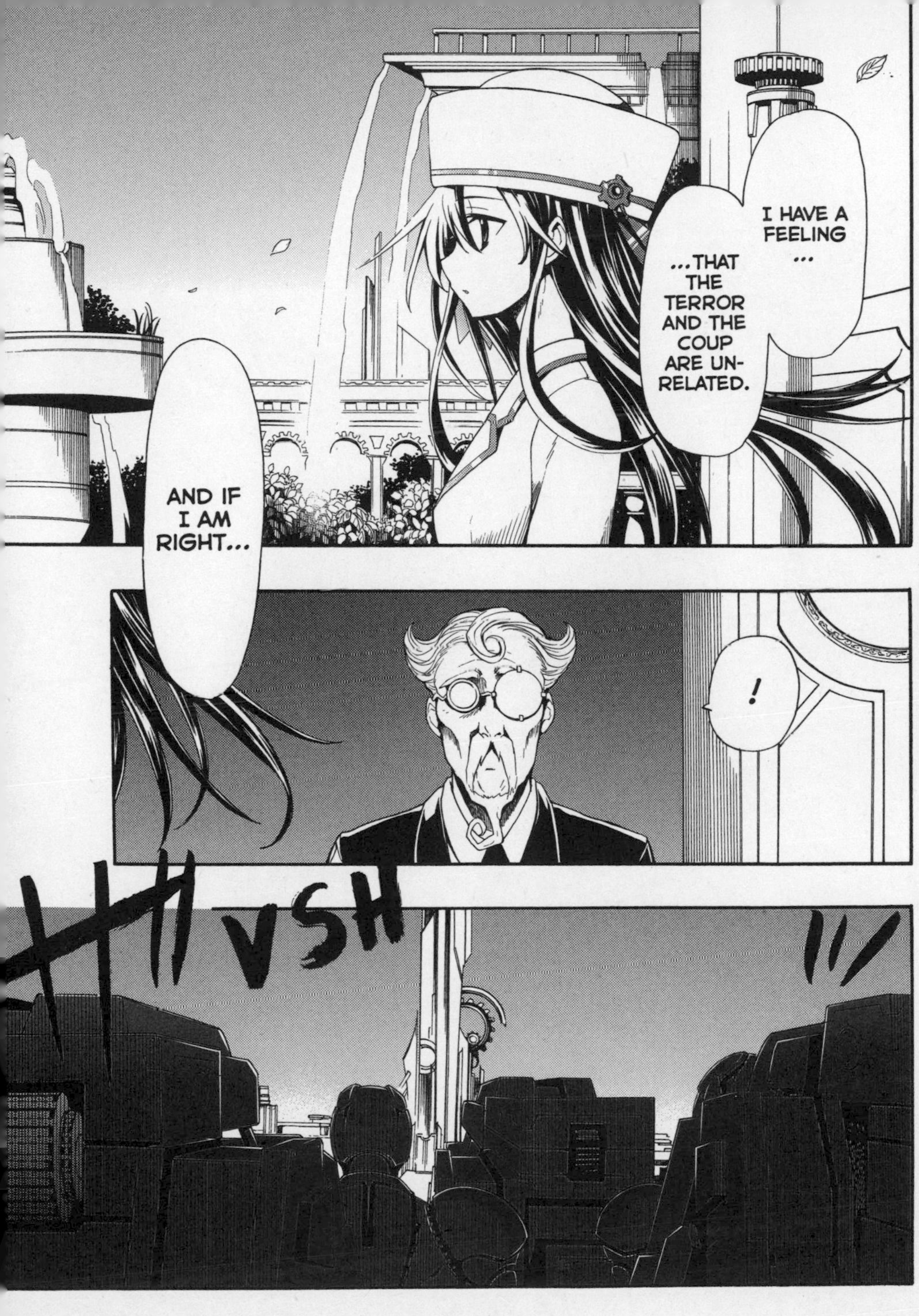
I HAVE A FEELING ...
...THAT THE TERROR AND THE COUP ARE UN-RELATED.
AND IF I AM RIGHT...
!

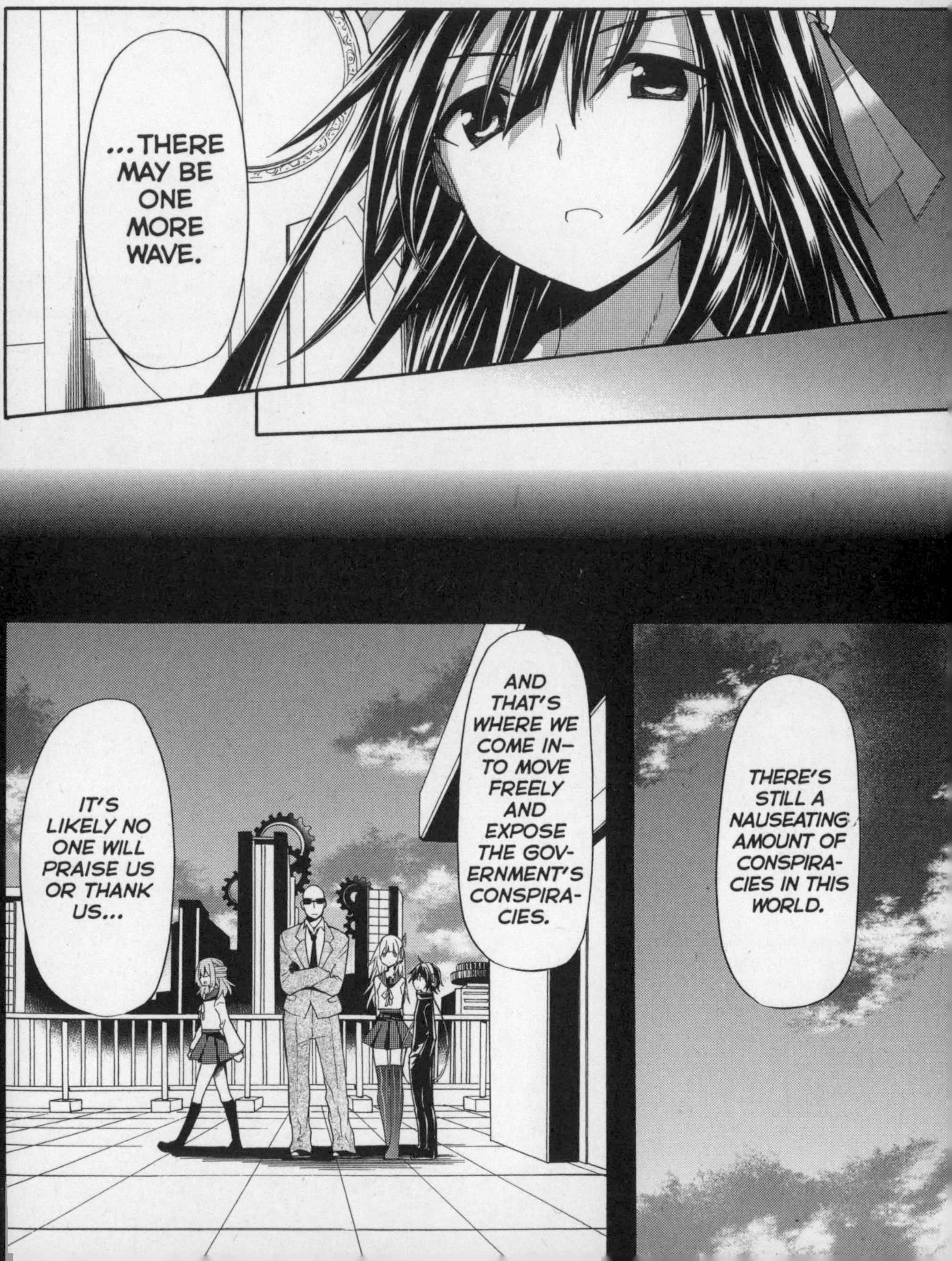
...THERE MAY BE ONE MORE WAVE.
THERE'S STILL A NAUSEATING AMOUNT OF CONSPIRACIES IN THIS WORLD.
AND THAT'S WHERE WE COME IN—TO MOVE FREELY AND EXPOSE THE GOVERNMENT'S CONSPIRACIES.
IT'S LIKELY NO ONE WILL PRAISE US OR THANK US...

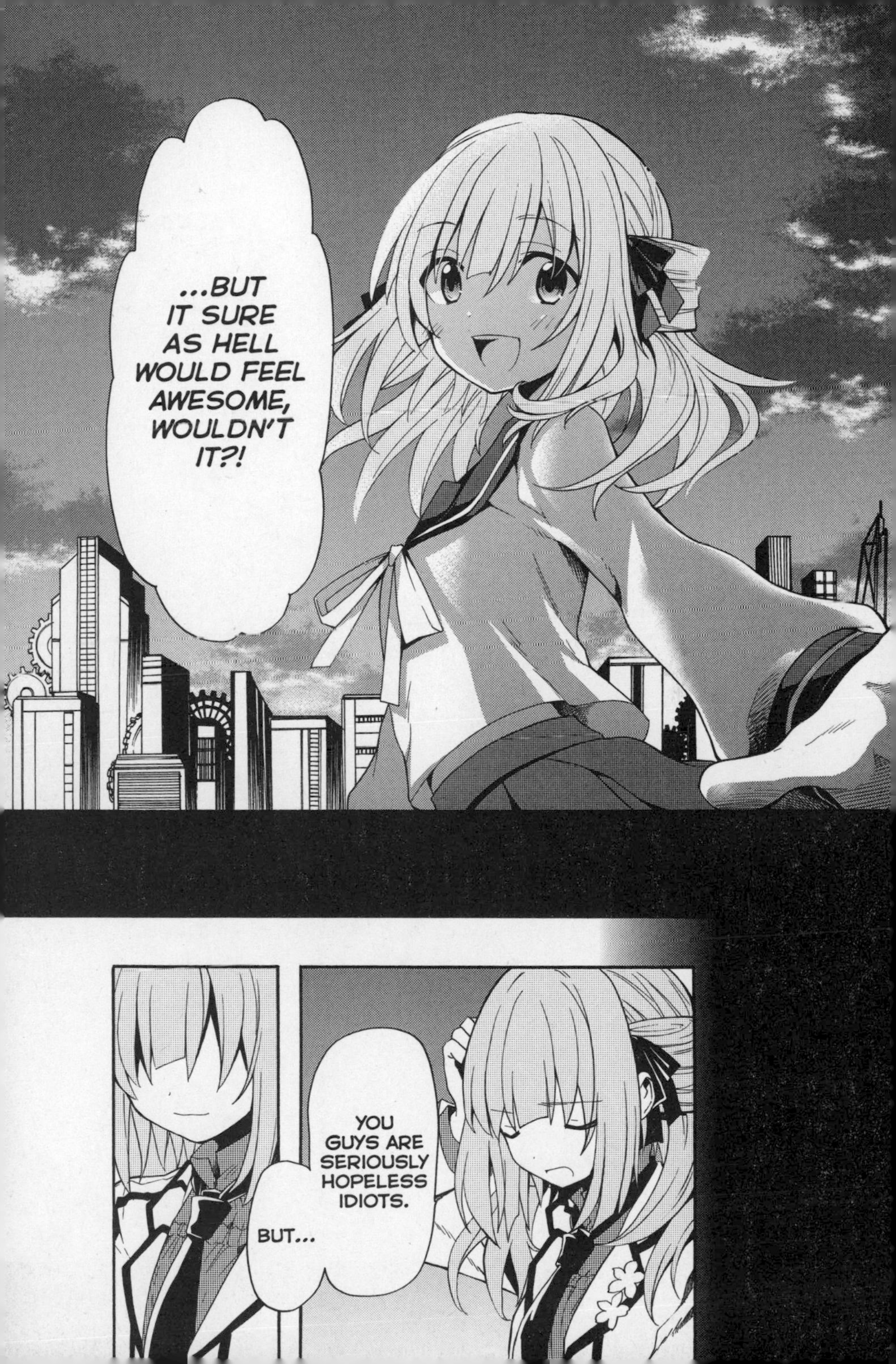
...BUT IT SURE AS HELL WOULD FEEL AWESOME, WOULDN'T IT?!
YOU GUYS ARE SERIOUSLY HOPELESS IDIOTS.
BUT...

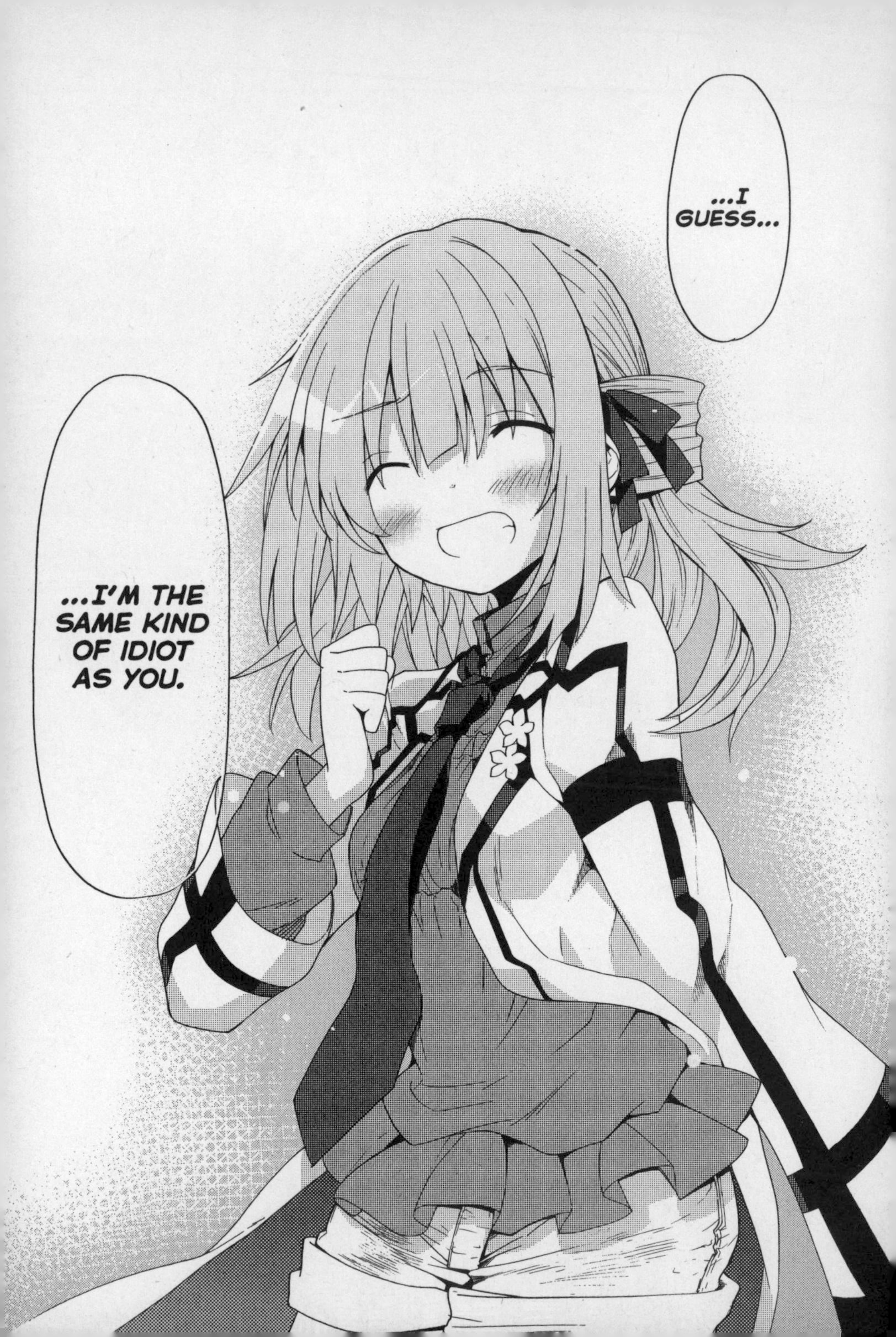
...I GUESS...
...I'M THE SAME KIND OF IDIOT AS YOU.

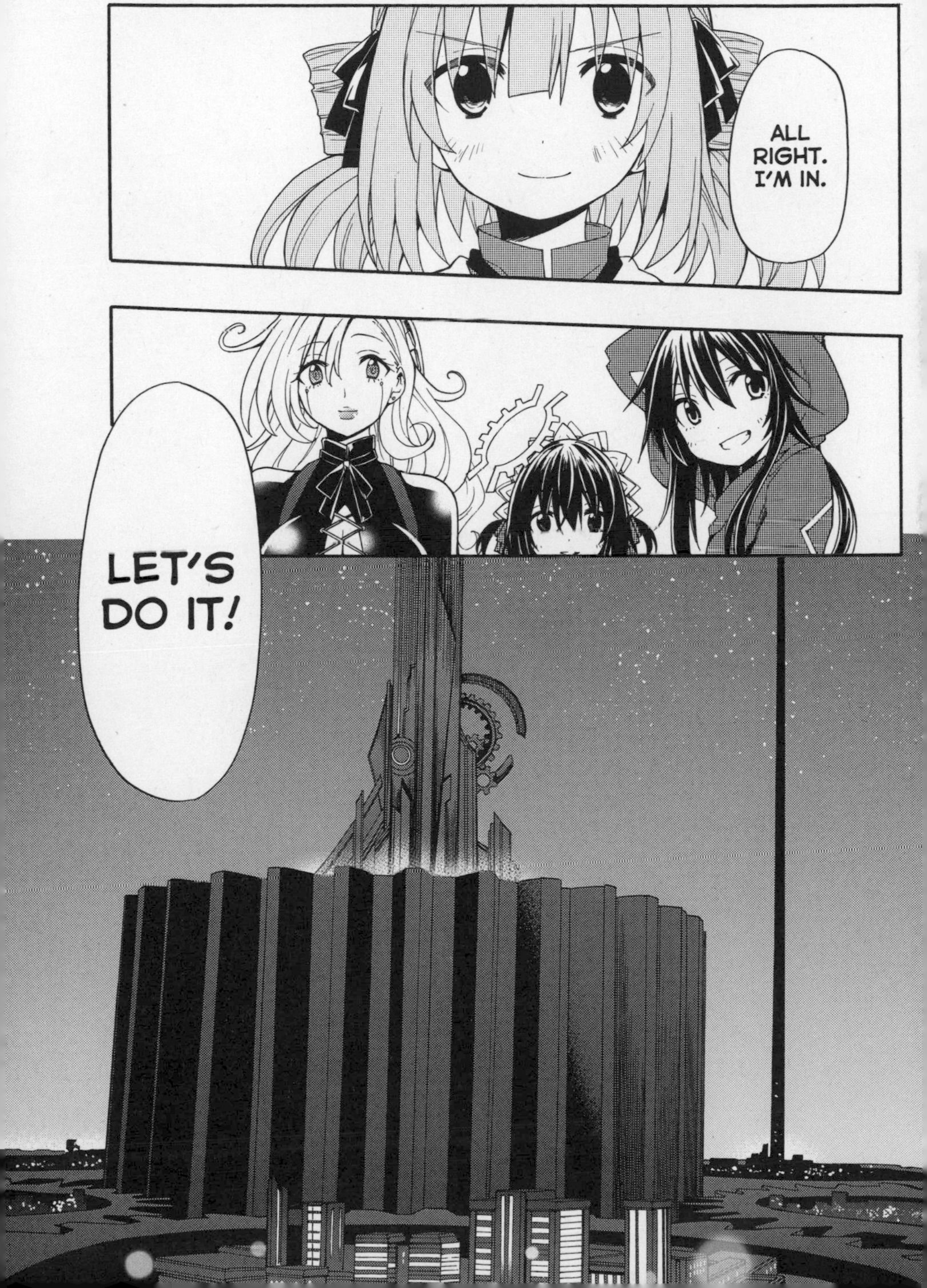
ALL RIGHT. I'M IN.
LET'S DO IT!

Clockwork Planet

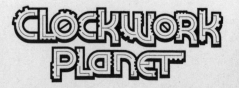

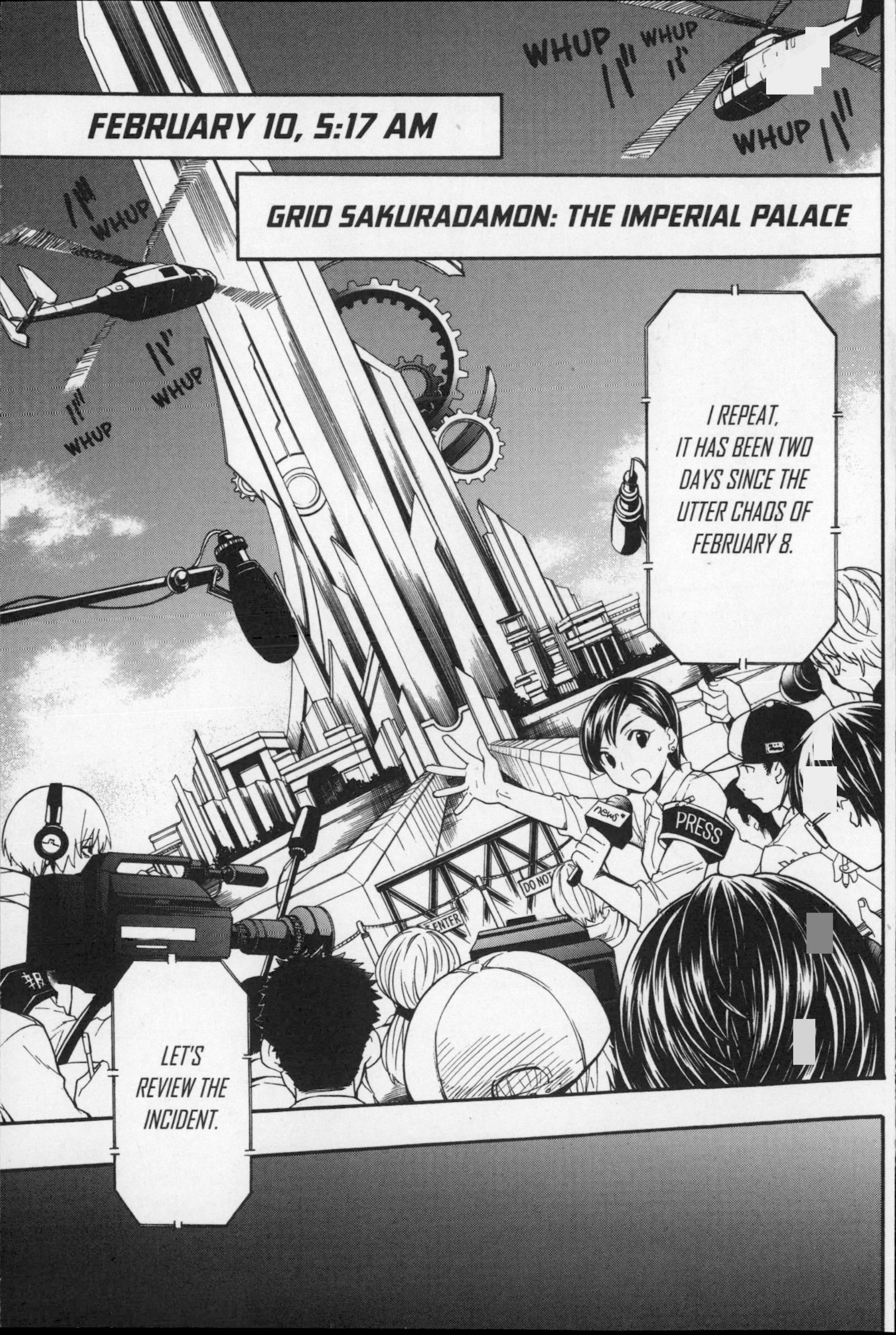
WHUP WHUP
WHUP
FEBRUARY 10, 5:17 AM
WHUP
GRID SAKURADAMON: THE IMPERIAL PALACE
WHUP
WHUP
I REPEAT, IT HAS BEEN TWO DAYS SINCE THE UTTER CHAOS OF FEBRUARY 8.
PRESS
LET'S REVIEW THE INCIDENT.

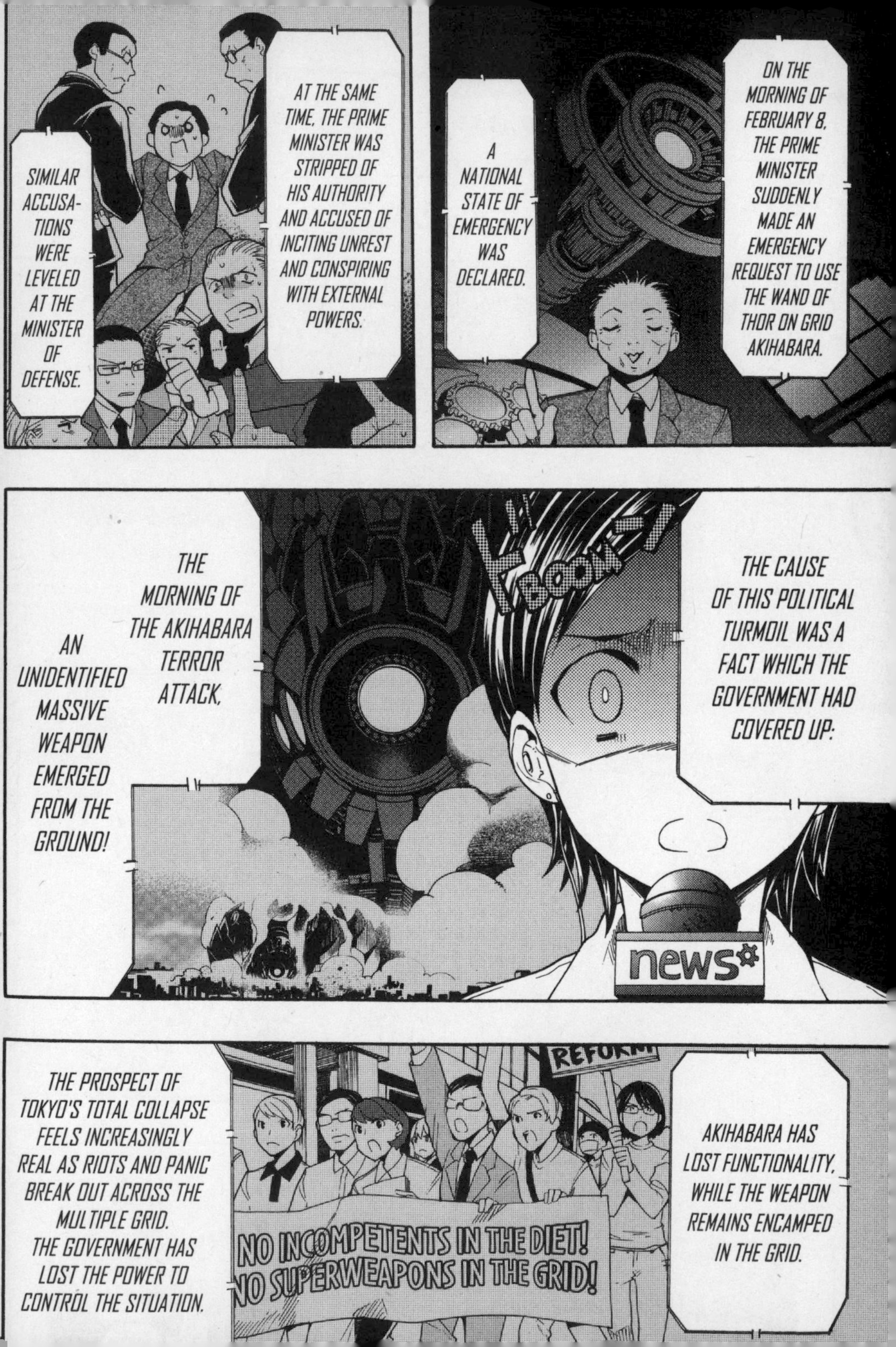
ON THE MORNING OF FEBRUARY 8, THE PRIME MINISTER SUDDENLY MADE AN EMERGENCY REQUEST TO USE THE WAND OF THOR ON GRID AKIHABARA.
A NATIONAL STATE OF EMERGENCY WAS DECLARED.
AT THE SAME TIME, THE PRIME MINISTER WAS STRIPPED OF HIS AUTHORITY AND ACCUSED OF INCITING UNREST AND CONSPIRING WITH EXTERNAL POWERS.
SIMILAR ACCUSA-TIONS WERE LEVELED AT THE MINISTER OF DEFENSE.
THE CAUSE OF THIS POLITICAL TURMOIL WAS A FACT WHICH THE GOVERNMENT HAD COVERED UP:
BOOM
THE MORNING OF THE AKIHABARA TERROR ATTACK,
AN UNIDENTIFIED MASSIVE WEAPON EMERGED FROM THE GROUND!
news
AKIHABARA HAS LOST FUNCTIONALITY, WHILE THE WEAPON REMAINS ENCAMPED IN THE GRID.
REFORM
NO INCOMPETENTS IN THE DIET! NO SUPERWEAPONS IN THE GRID!
THE PROSPECT OF TOKYO'S TOTAL COLLAPSE FEELS INCREASINGLY REAL AS RIOTS AND PANIC BREAK OUT ACROSS THE MULTIPLE GRID. THE GOVERNMENT HAS LOST THE POWER TO CONTROL THE SITUATION.

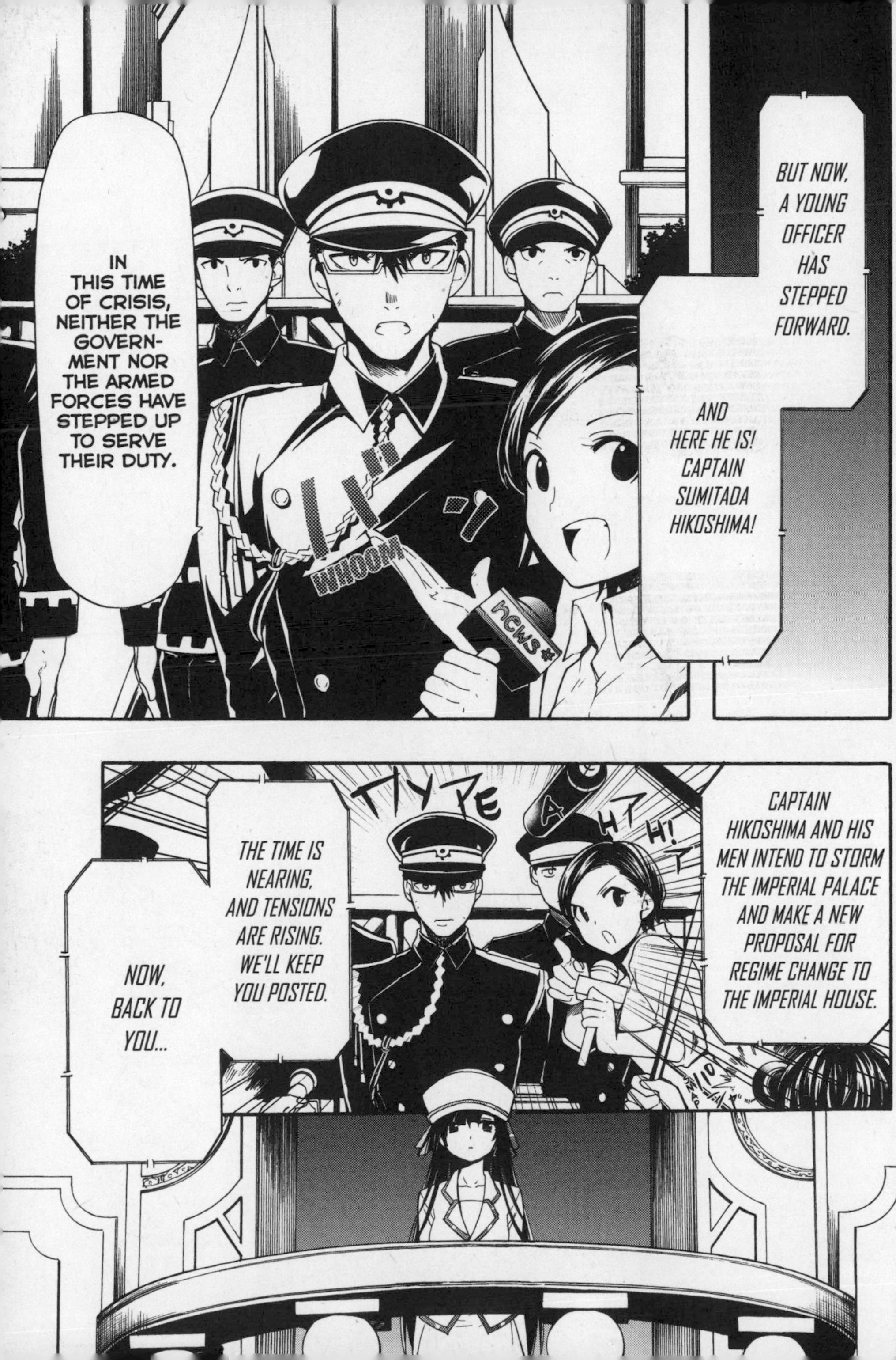
BUT NOW, A YOUNG OFFICER HAS STEPPED FORWARD.
AND HERE HE IS! CAPTAIN SUMITADA HIKOSHIMA!
WHOOM
IN THIS TIME OF CRISIS, NEITHER THE GOVERNMENT NOR THE ARMED FORCES HAVE STEPPED UP TO SERVE THEIR DUTY.
CAPTAIN HIKOSHIMA AND HIS MEN INTEND TO STORM THE IMPERIAL PALACE AND MAKE A NEW PROPOSAL FOR REGIME CHANGE TO THE IMPERIAL HOUSE.
THE TIME IS NEARING, AND TENSIONS ARE RISING. WE'LL KEEP YOU POSTED.
NOW, BACK TO YOU...

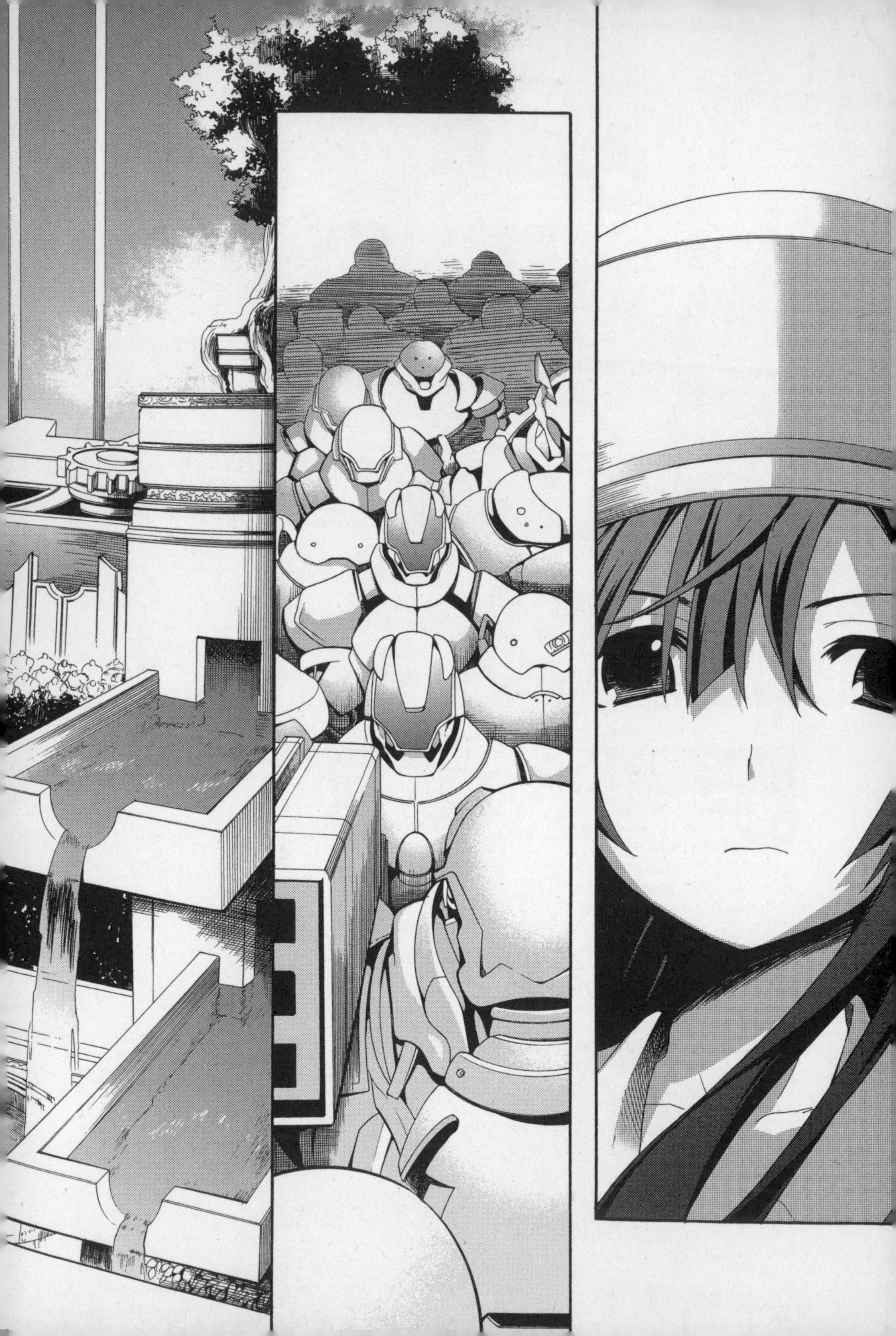

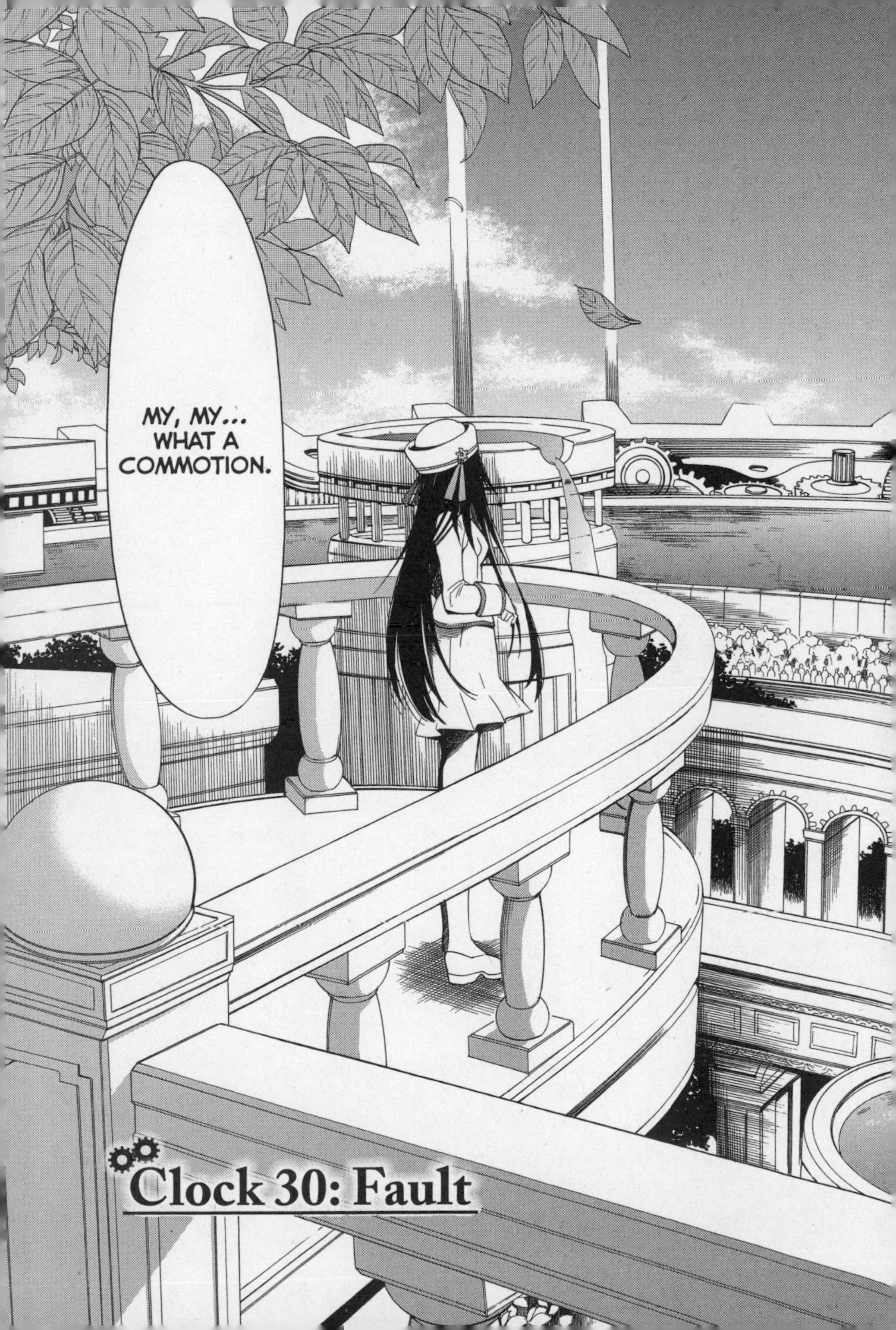
MY, MY...
WHAT A
COMMOTION.
Clock 30: Fault

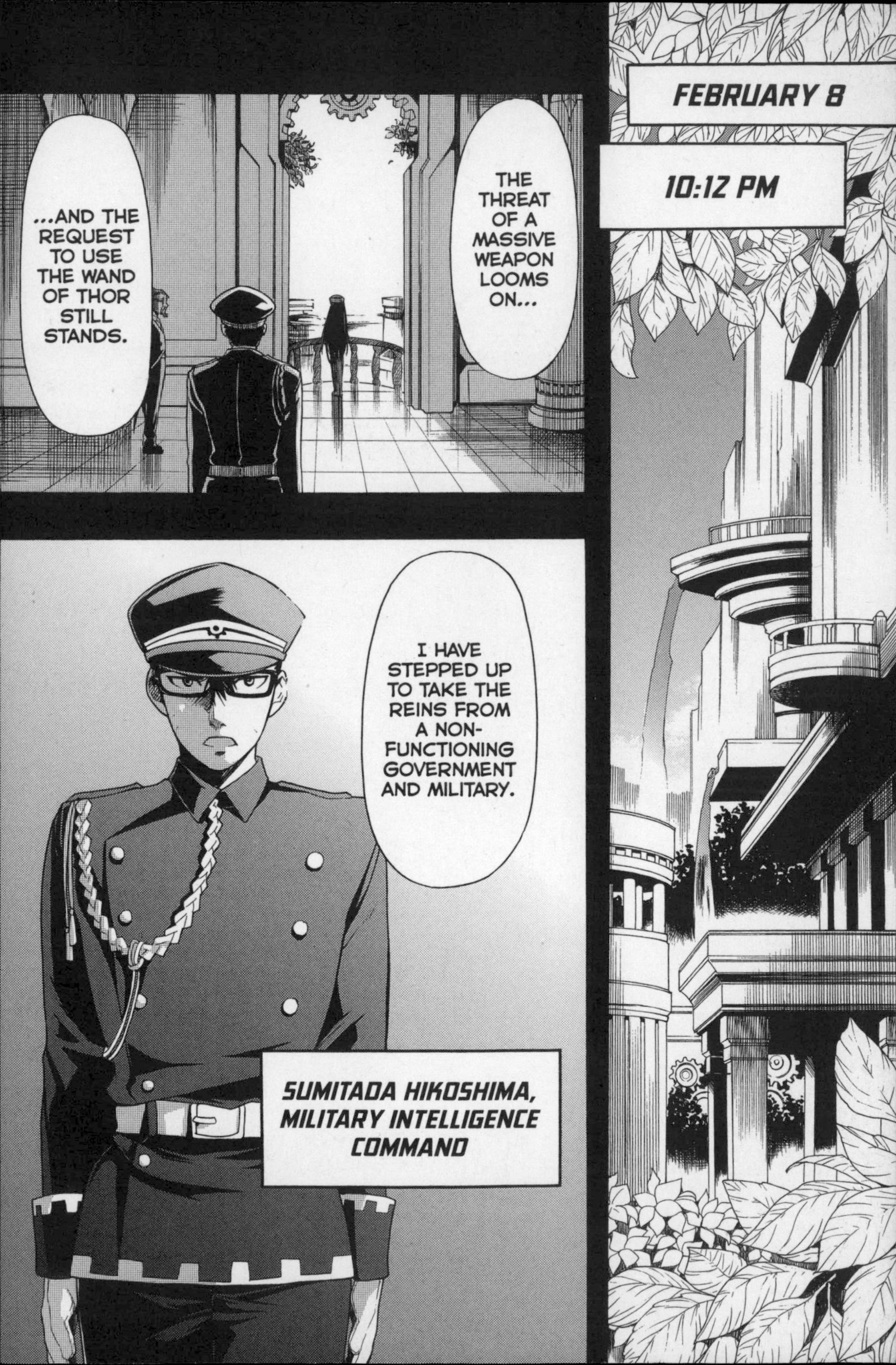
FEBRUARY 8
10:12 PM
THE THREAT OF A MASSIVE WEAPON LOOMS ON...
...AND THE REQUEST TO USE THE WAND OF THOR STILL STANDS.
I HAVE STEPPED UP TO TAKE THE REINS FROM A NON-FUNCTIONING GOVERNMENT AND MILITARY.
SUMITADA HIKOSHIMA, MILITARY INTELLIGENCE COMMAND

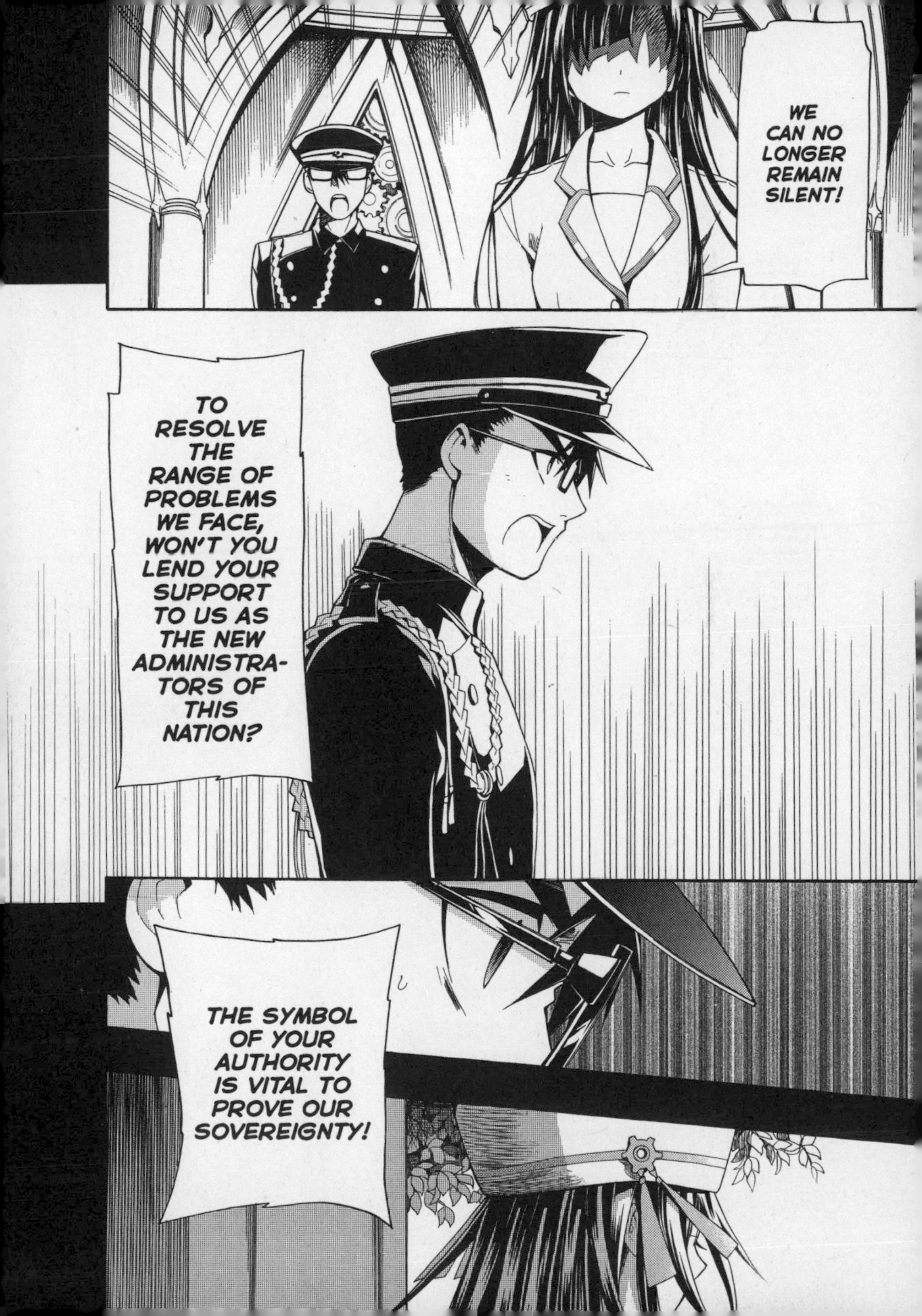
WE CAN NO LONGER REMAIN SILENT!
TO RESOLVE THE RANGE OF PROBLEMS WE FACE, WON'T YOU LEND YOUR SUPPORT TO US AS THE NEW ADMINISTRATORS OF THIS NATION?
THE SYMBOL OF YOUR AUTHORITY IS VITAL TO PROVE OUR SOVEREIGNTY!

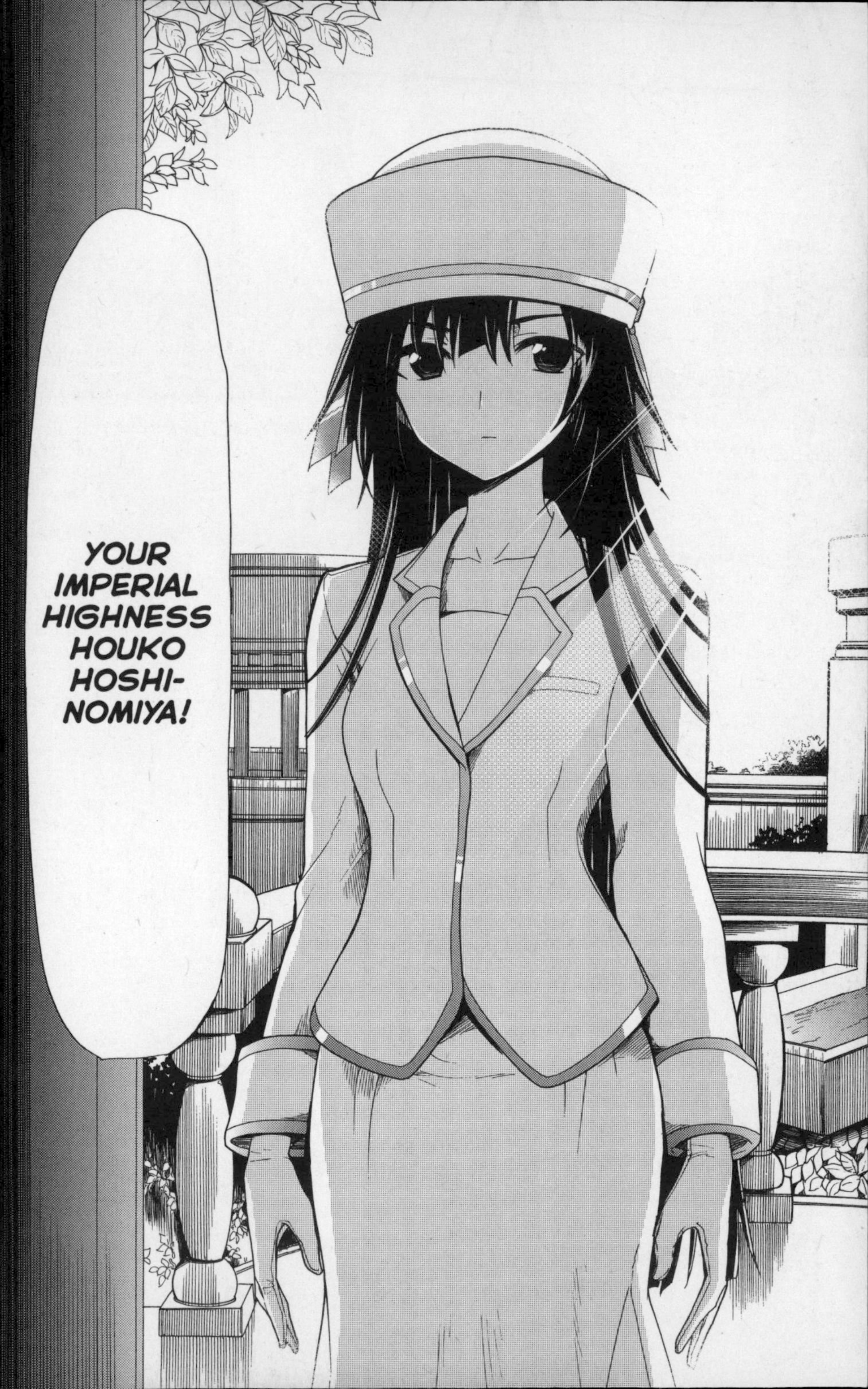
YOUR IMPERIAL HIGHNESS HOUKO HOSHI-NOMIYA!

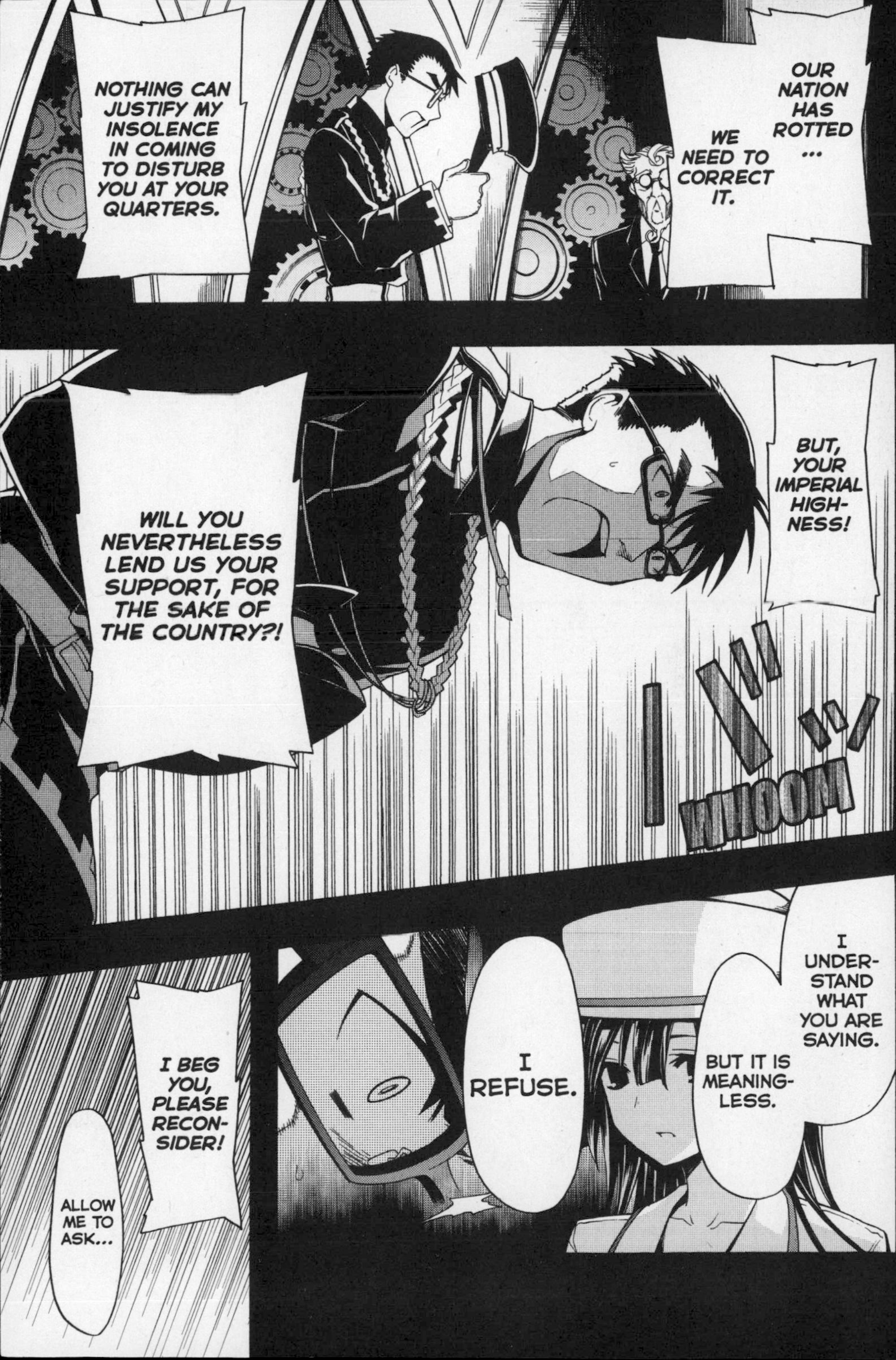
OUR NATION HAS ROTTED...
WE NEED TO CORRECT IT.
NOTHING CAN JUSTIFY MY INSOLENCE IN COMING TO DISTURB YOU AT YOUR QUARTERS.
BUT, YOUR IMPERIAL HIGH-NESS!
WILL YOU NEVERTHELESS LEND US YOUR SUPPORT, FOR THE SAKE OF THE COUNTRY?!
WHOOM
I UNDER-STAND WHAT YOU ARE SAYING.
BUT IT IS MEANING-LESS.
I REFUSE.
I BEG YOU, PLEASE RECON-SIDER!
ALLOW ME TO ASK...

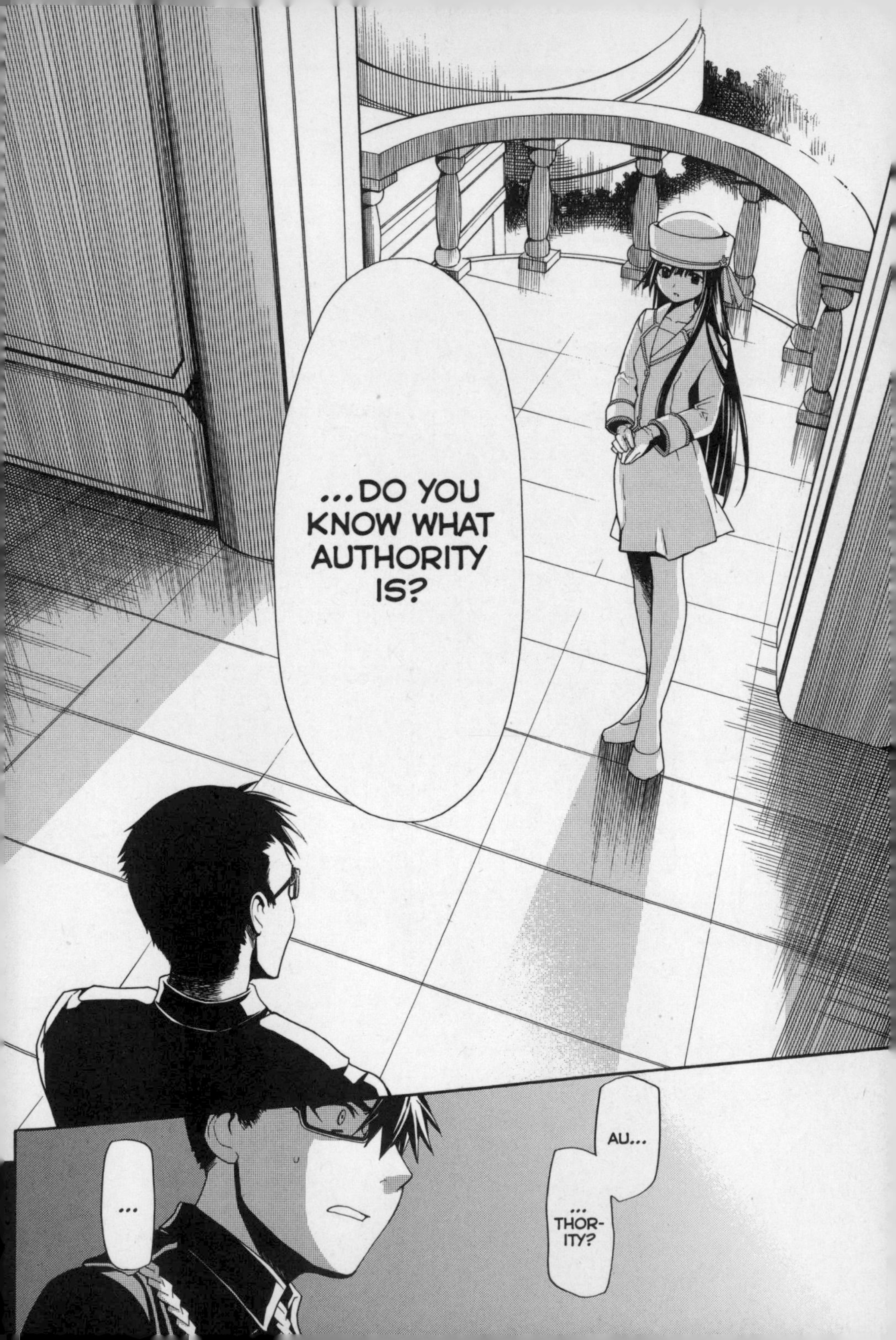
...DO YOU KNOW WHAT AUTHORITY IS?
AU... ...THOR-ITY?
...

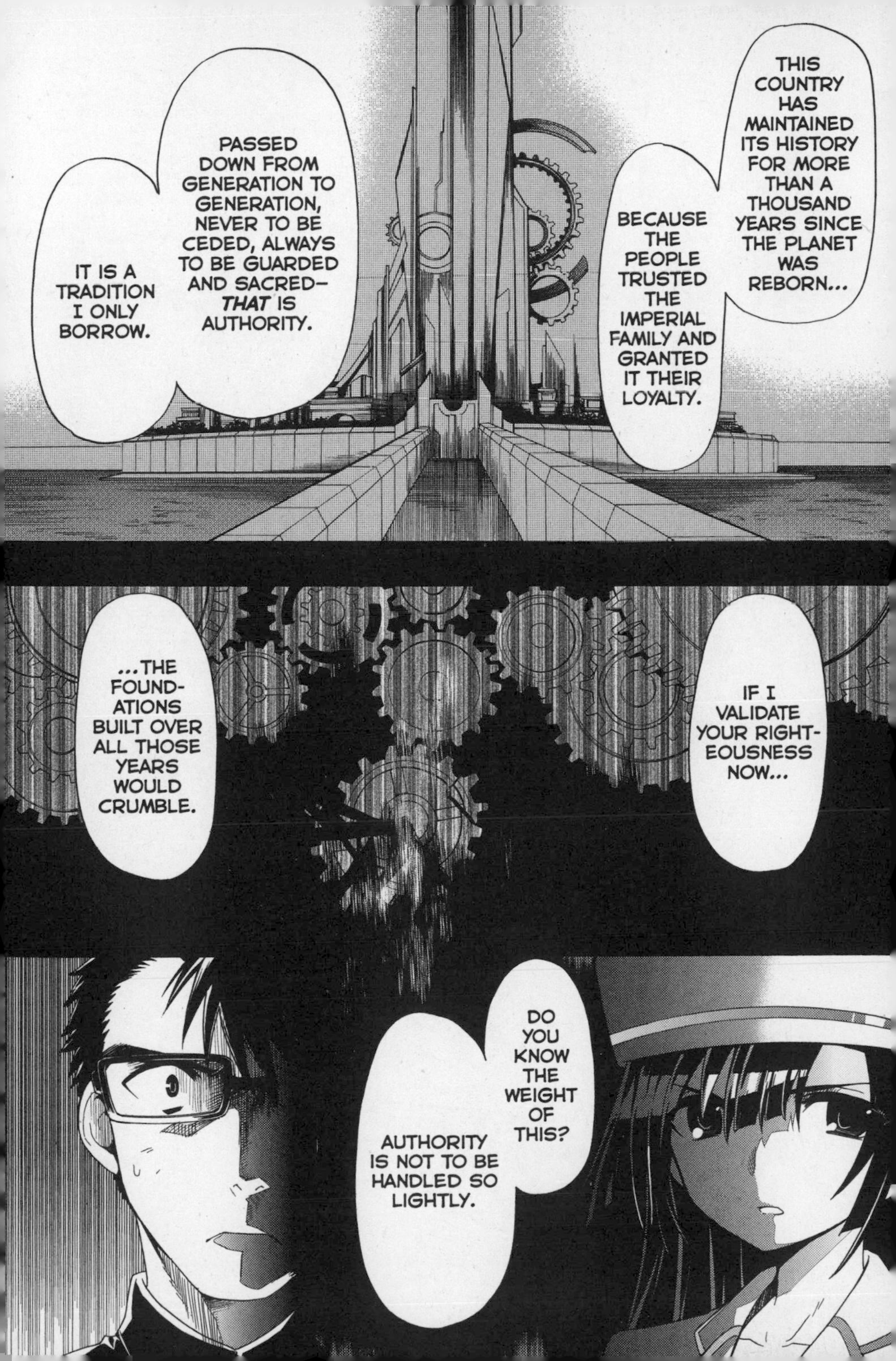
THIS COUNTRY HAS MAINTAINED ITS HISTORY FOR MORE THAN A THOUSAND YEARS SINCE THE PLANET WAS REBORN...
BECAUSE THE PEOPLE TRUSTED THE IMPERIAL FAMILY AND GRANTED IT THEIR LOYALTY.
PASSED DOWN FROM GENERATION TO GENERATION, NEVER TO BE CEDED, ALWAYS TO BE GUARDED AND SACRED—*THAT* IS AUTHORITY.
IT IS A TRADITION I ONLY BORROW.
IF I VALIDATE YOUR RIGHT-EOUSNESS NOW...
...THE FOUND-ATIONS BUILT OVER ALL THOSE YEARS WOULD CRUMBLE.
DO YOU KNOW THE WEIGHT OF THIS?
AUTHORITY IS NOT TO BE HANDLED SO LIGHTLY.

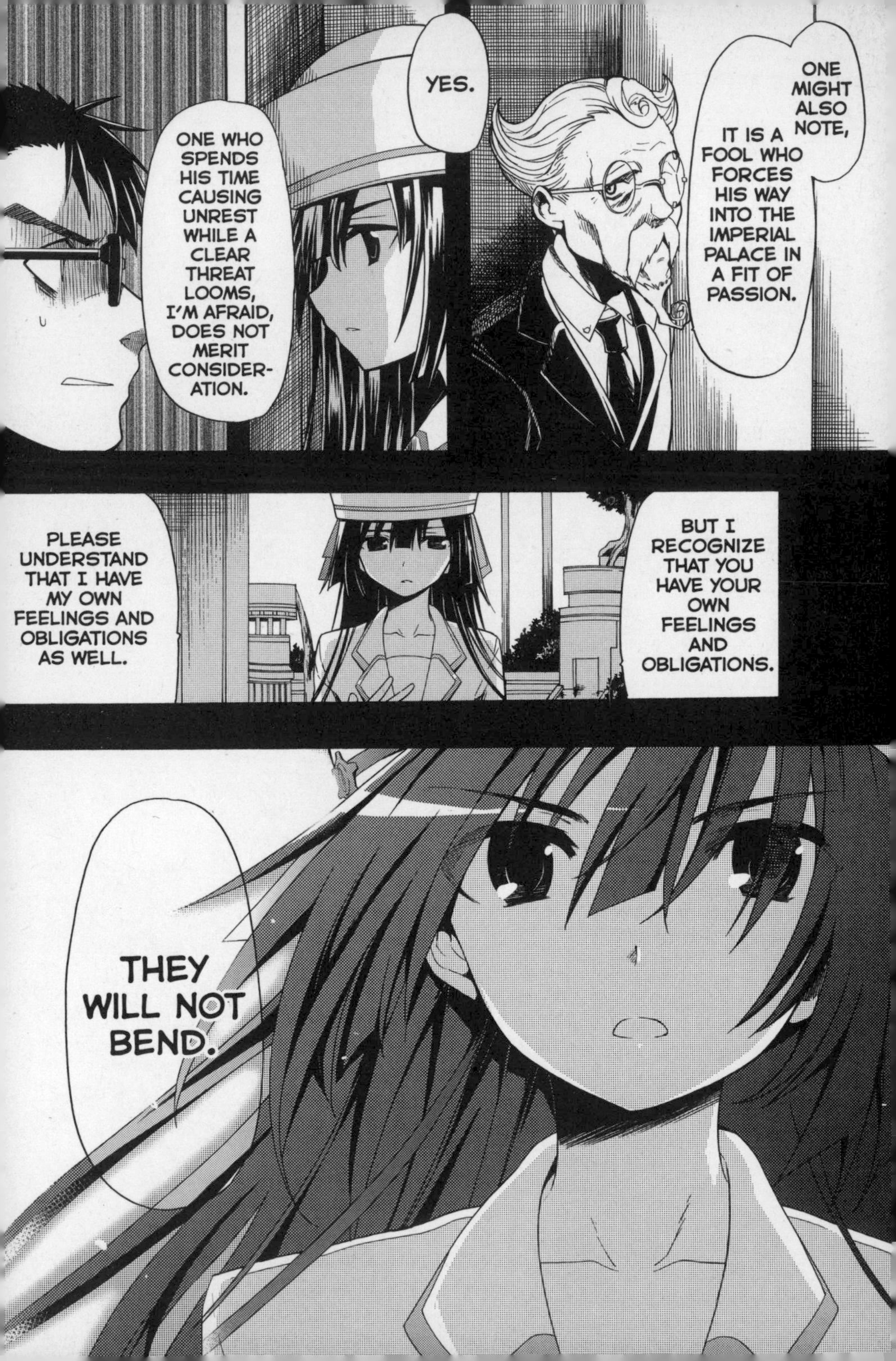

ONE MIGHT ALSO NOTE,
IT IS A FOOL WHO FORCES HIS WAY INTO THE IMPERIAL PALACE IN A FIT OF PASSION.
YES.
ONE WHO SPENDS HIS TIME CAUSING UNREST WHILE A CLEAR THREAT LOOMS, I'M AFRAID, DOES NOT MERIT CONSIDER-ATION.
BUT I RECOGNIZE THAT YOU HAVE YOUR OWN FEELINGS AND OBLIGATIONS.
PLEASE UNDERSTAND THAT I HAVE MY OWN FEELINGS AND OBLIGATIONS AS WELL.
THEY WILL NOT BEND.

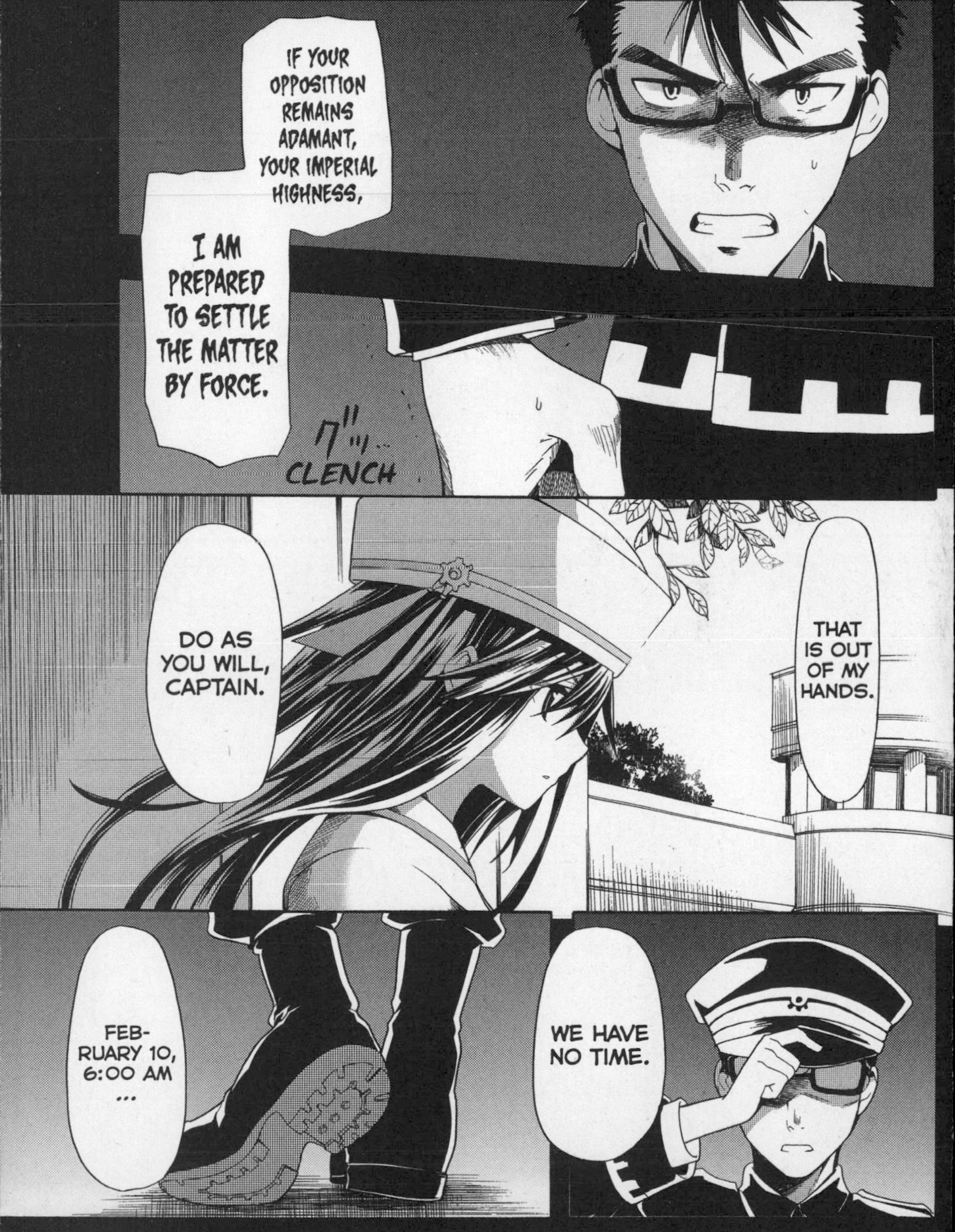
IF YOUR OPPOSITION REMAINS ADAMANT, YOUR IMPERIAL HIGHNESS,
I AM PREPARED TO SETTLE THE MATTER BY FORCE.
グッ…
CLENCH
THAT IS OUT OF MY HANDS.
DO AS YOU WILL, CAPTAIN.
WE HAVE NO TIME.
FEB-RUARY 10, 6:00 AM ...

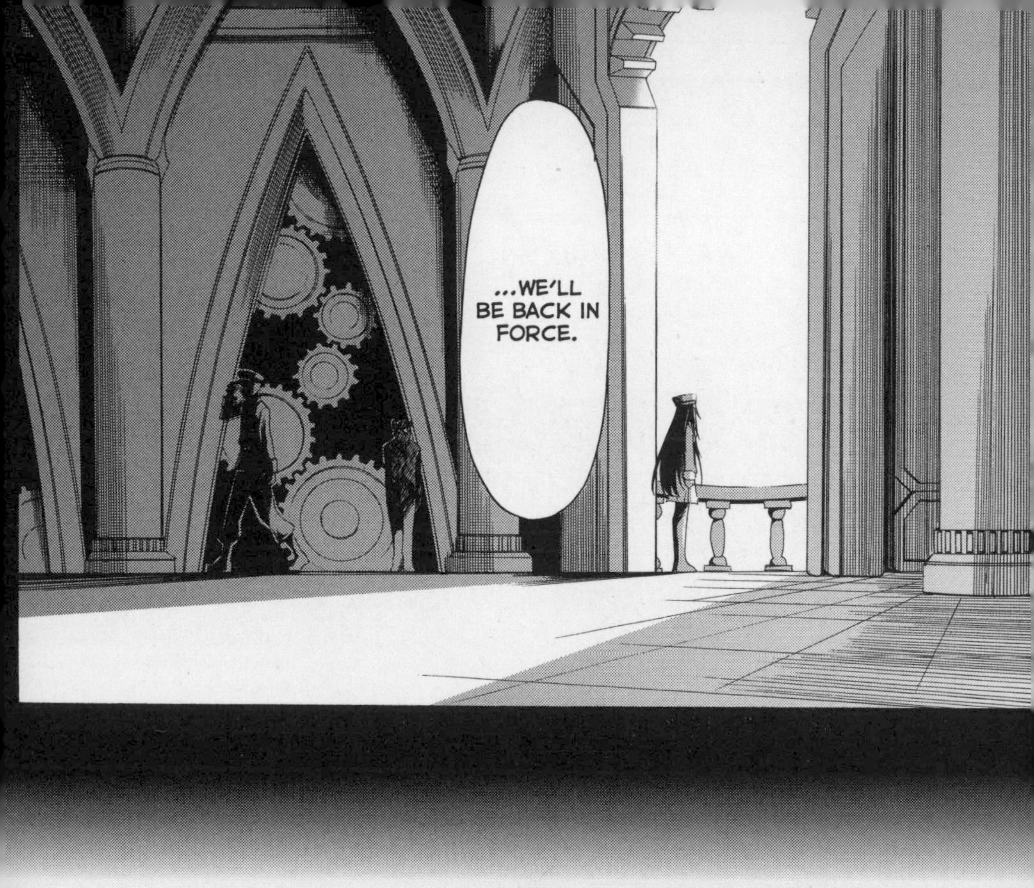
...WE'LL BE BACK IN FORCE.
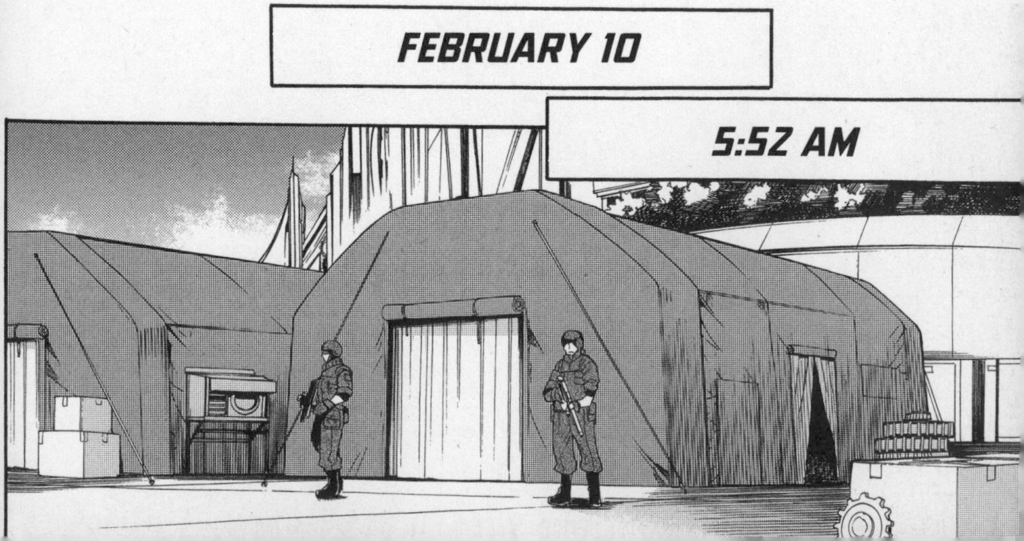
FEBRUARY 10
5:52 AM

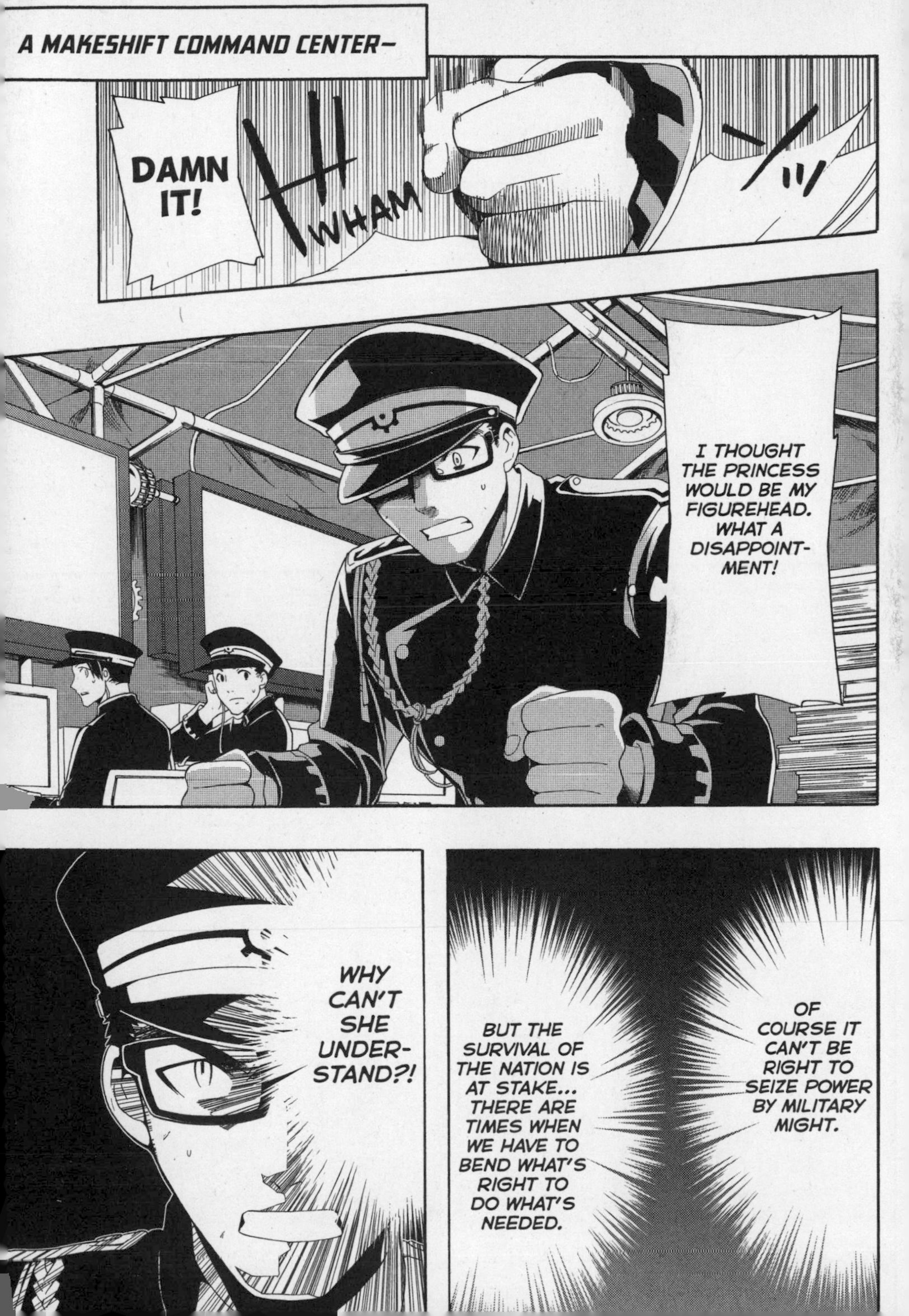
A MAKESHIFT COMMAND CENTER—
WHAM
DAMN IT!
I THOUGHT THE PRINCESS WOULD BE MY FIGUREHEAD. WHAT A DISAPPOINTMENT!
OF COURSE IT CAN'T BE RIGHT TO SEIZE POWER BY MILITARY MIGHT.
BUT THE SURVIVAL OF THE NATION IS AT STAKE... THERE ARE TIMES WHEN WE HAVE TO BEND WHAT'S RIGHT TO DO WHAT'S NEEDED.
WHY CAN'T SHE UNDERSTAND?!

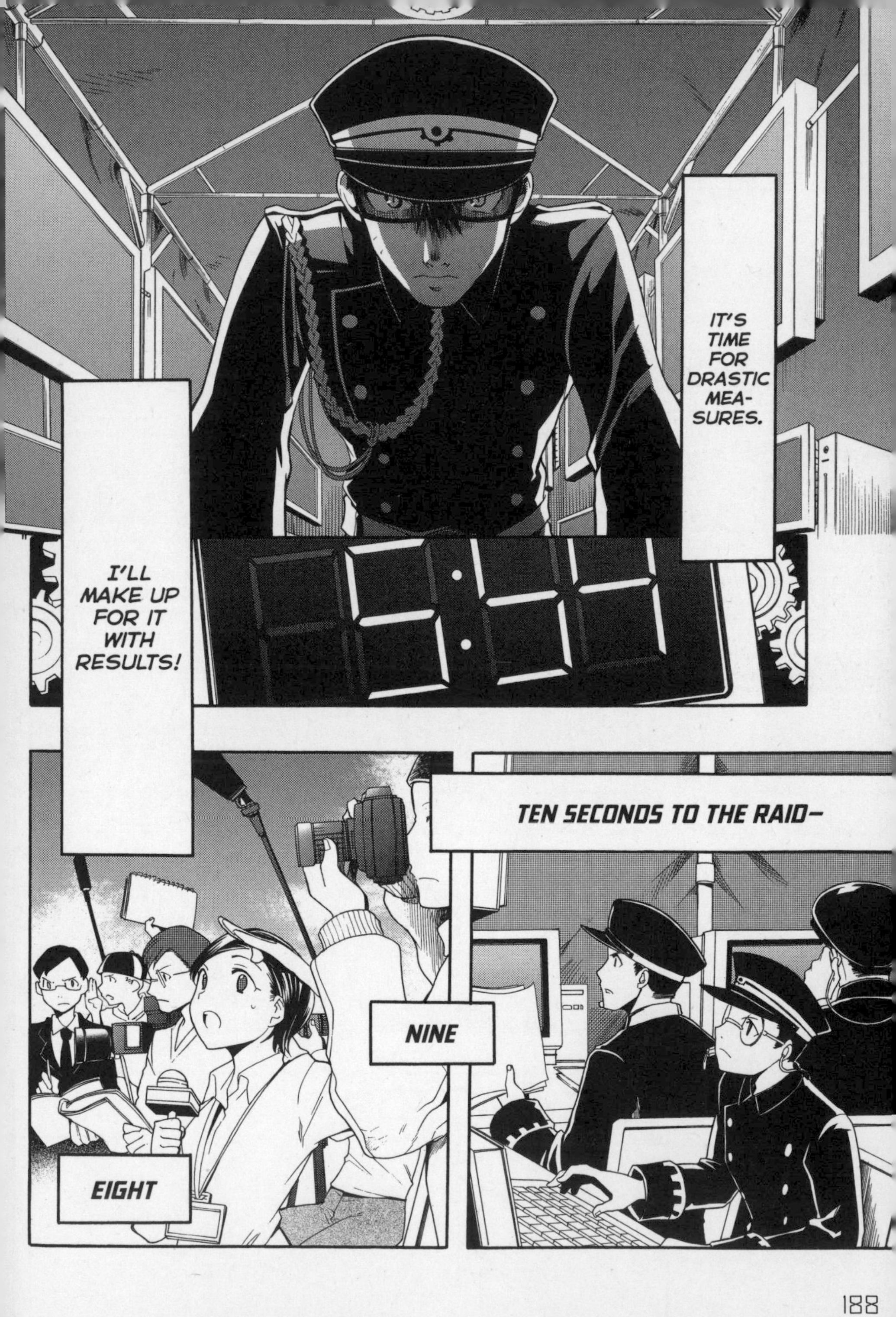
IT'S TIME FOR DRASTIC MEA-SURES.
I'LL MAKE UP FOR IT WITH RESULTS!
TEN SECONDS TO THE RAID—
NINE
EIGHT

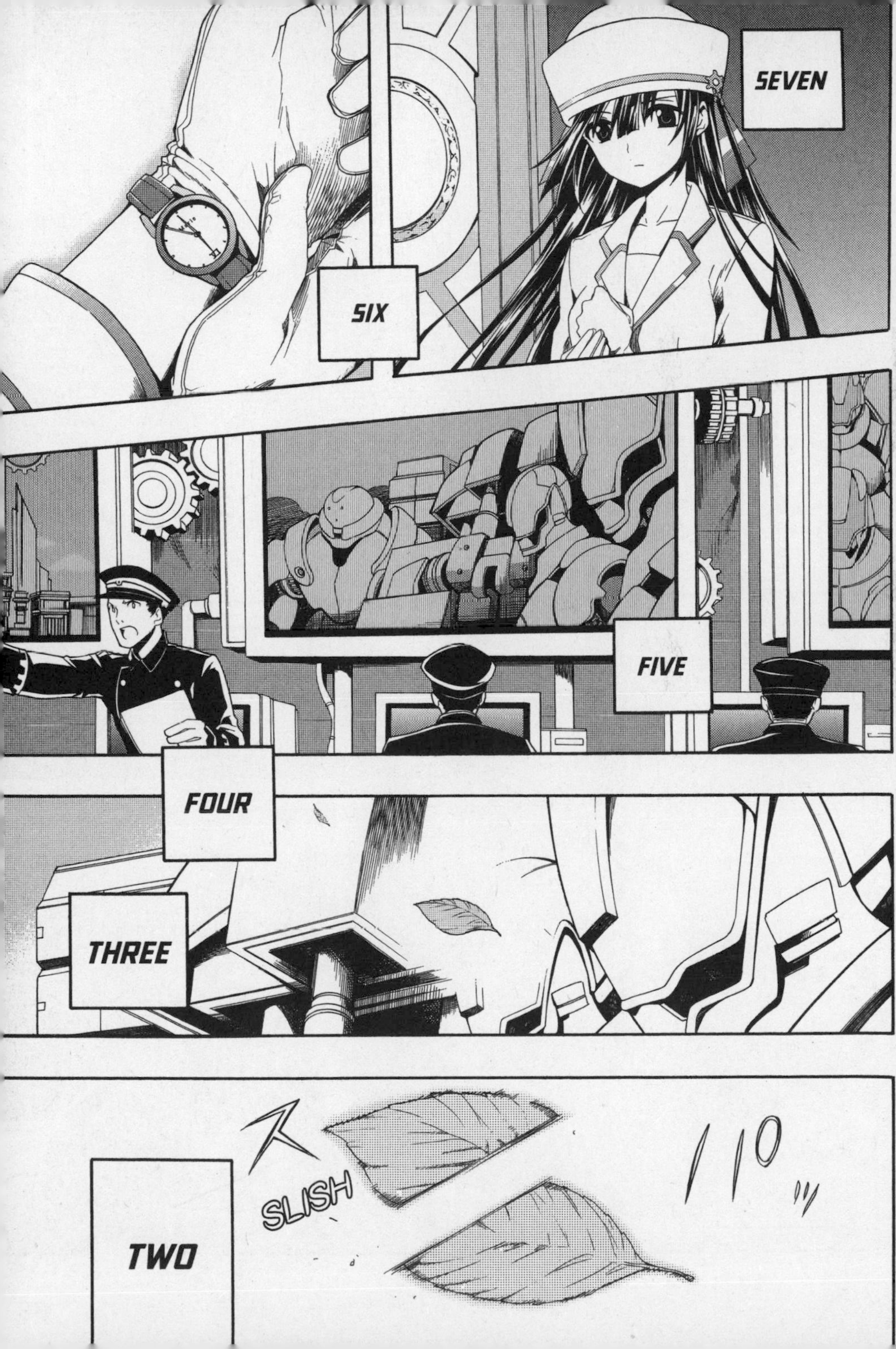
SEVEN
SIX
FIVE
FOUR
THREE
SLISH
TWO

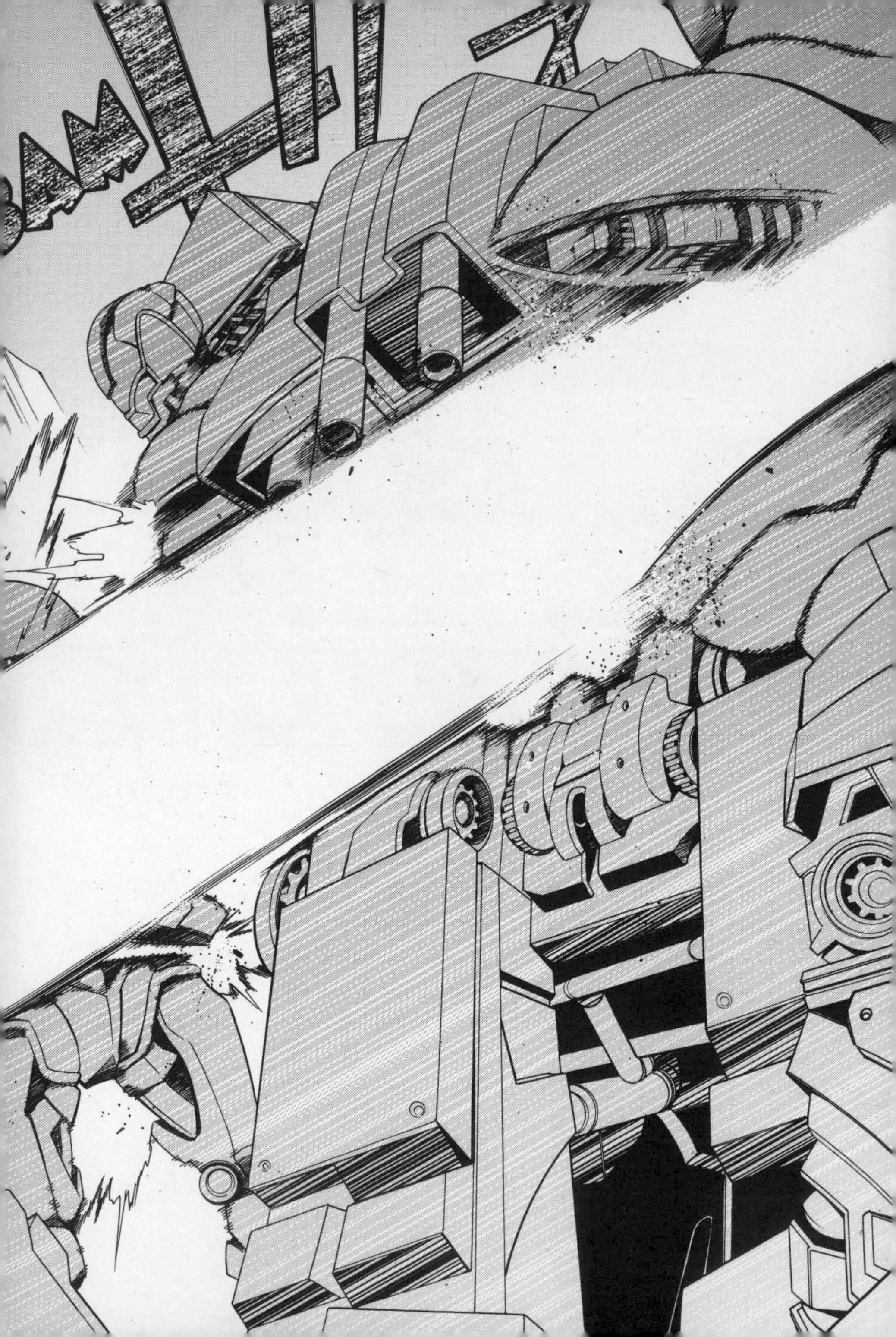
BAM

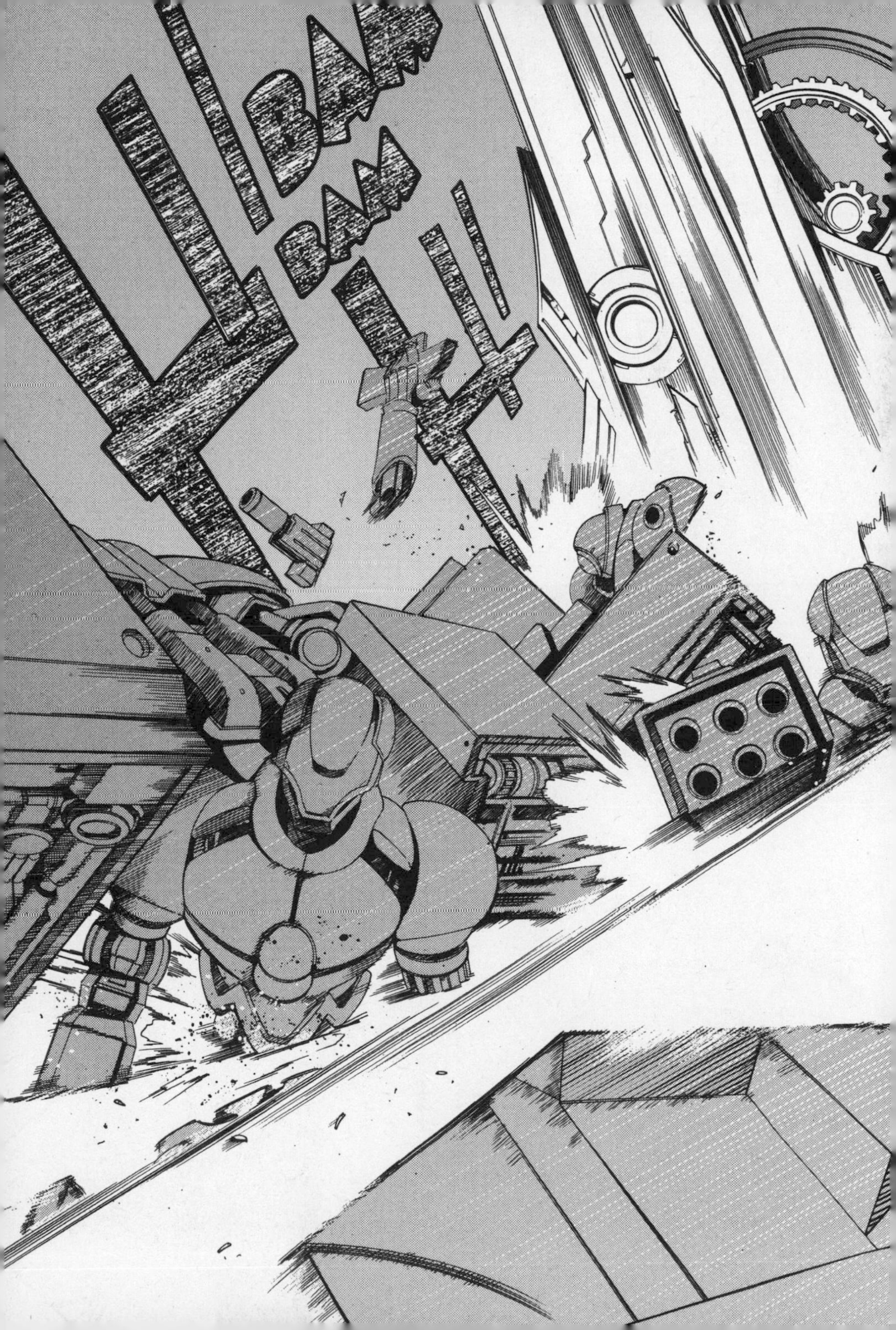
BAM BAM!!!

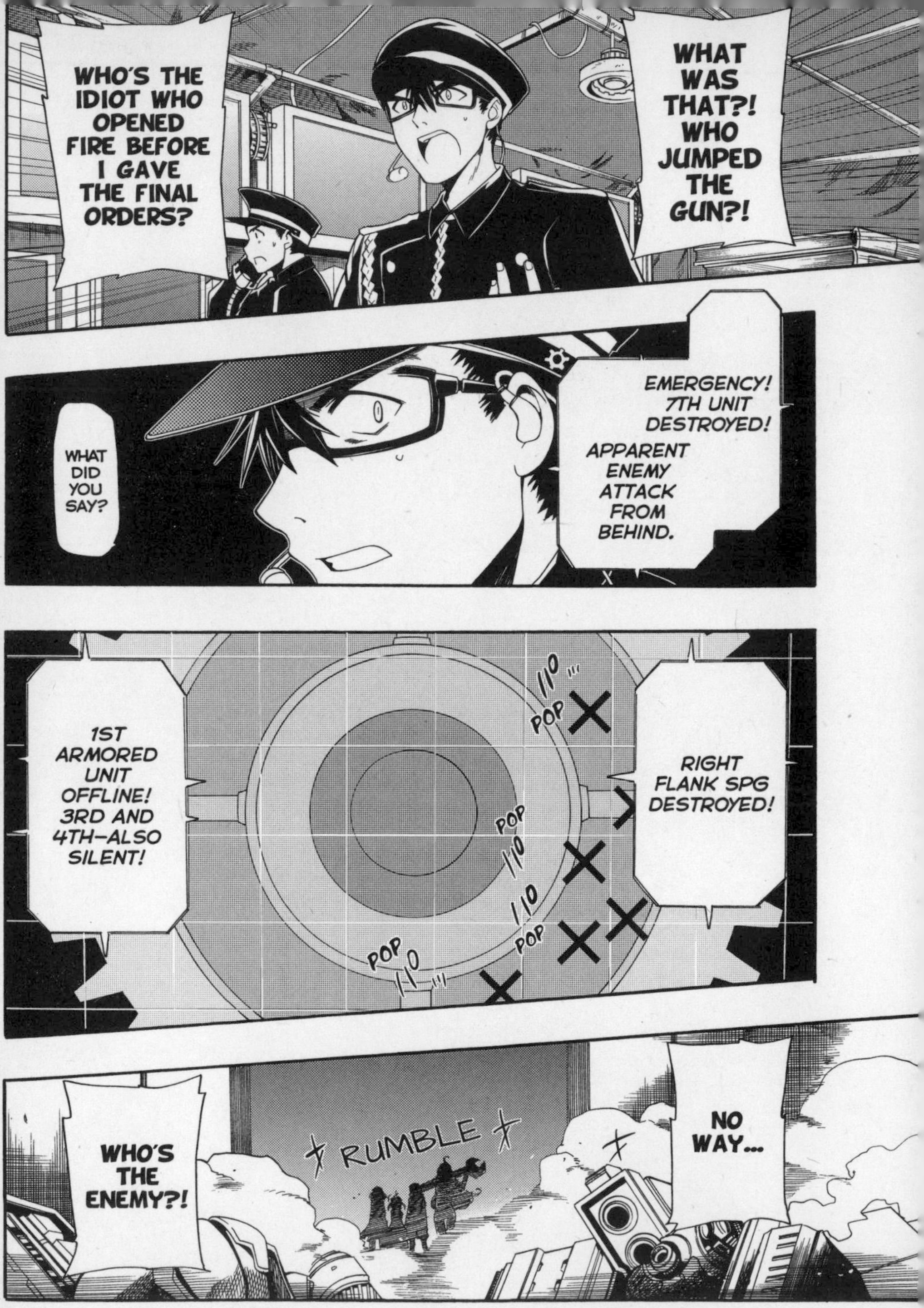
WHAT WAS THAT?! WHO JUMPED THE GUN?!
WHO'S THE IDIOT WHO OPENED FIRE BEFORE I GAVE THE FINAL ORDERS?
EMERGENCY! 7TH UNIT DESTROYED!
APPARENT ENEMY ATTACK FROM BEHIND.
WHAT DID YOU SAY?
RIGHT FLANK SPG DESTROYED!
POP
POP
POP
POP
1ST ARMORED UNIT OFFLINE! 3RD AND 4TH—ALSO SILENT!
NO WAY...
RUMBLE
WHO'S THE ENEMY?!

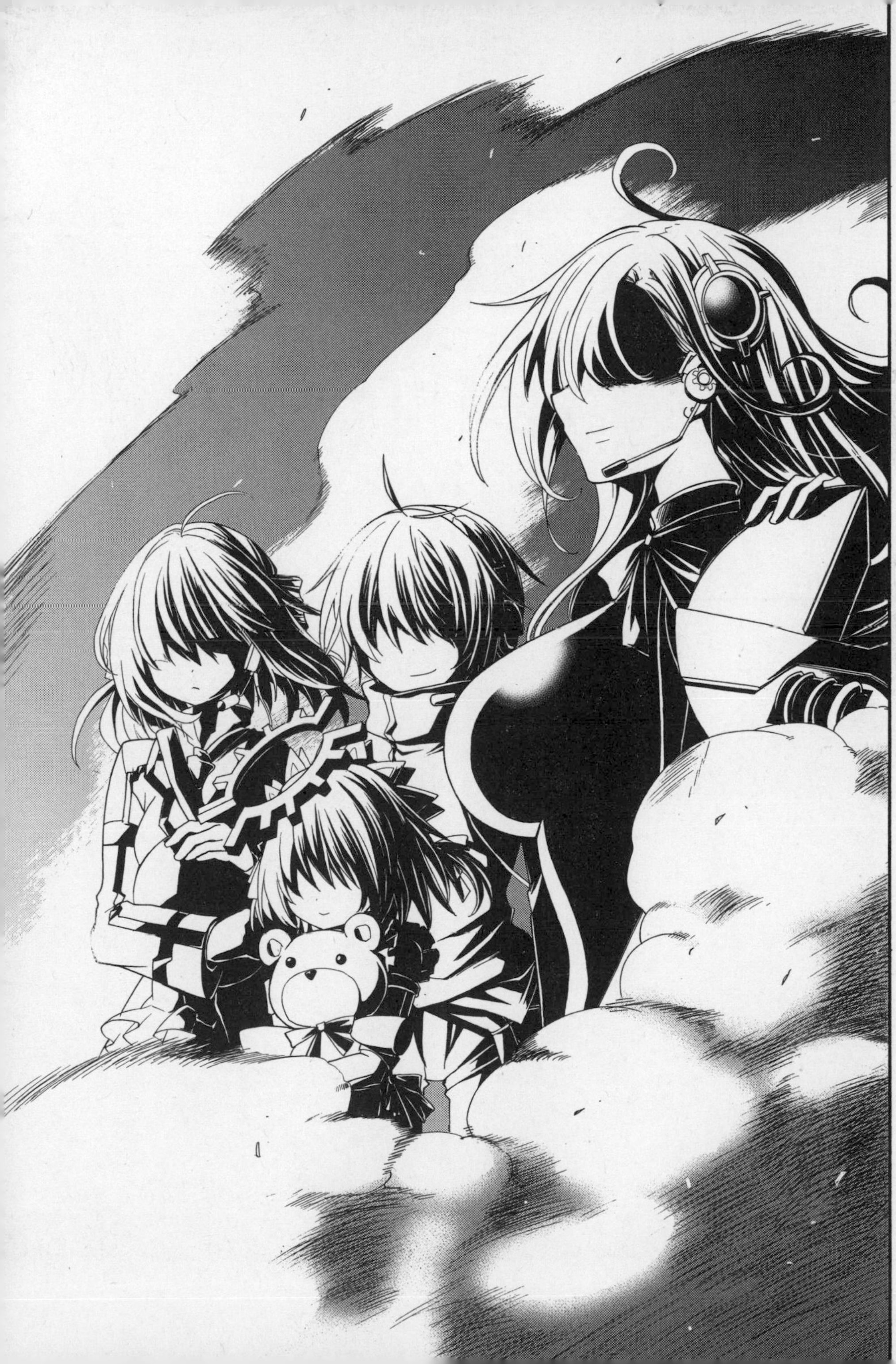

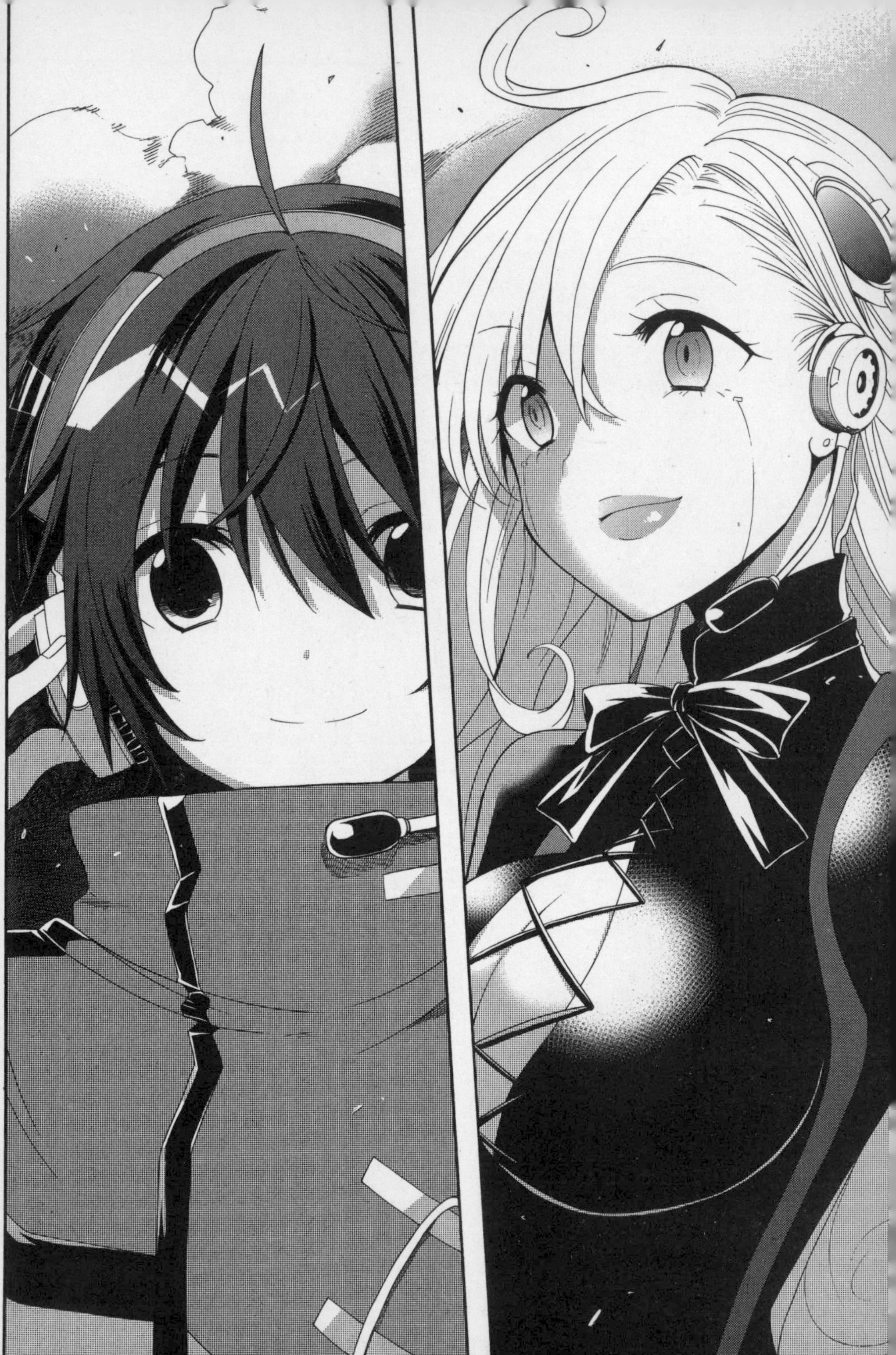

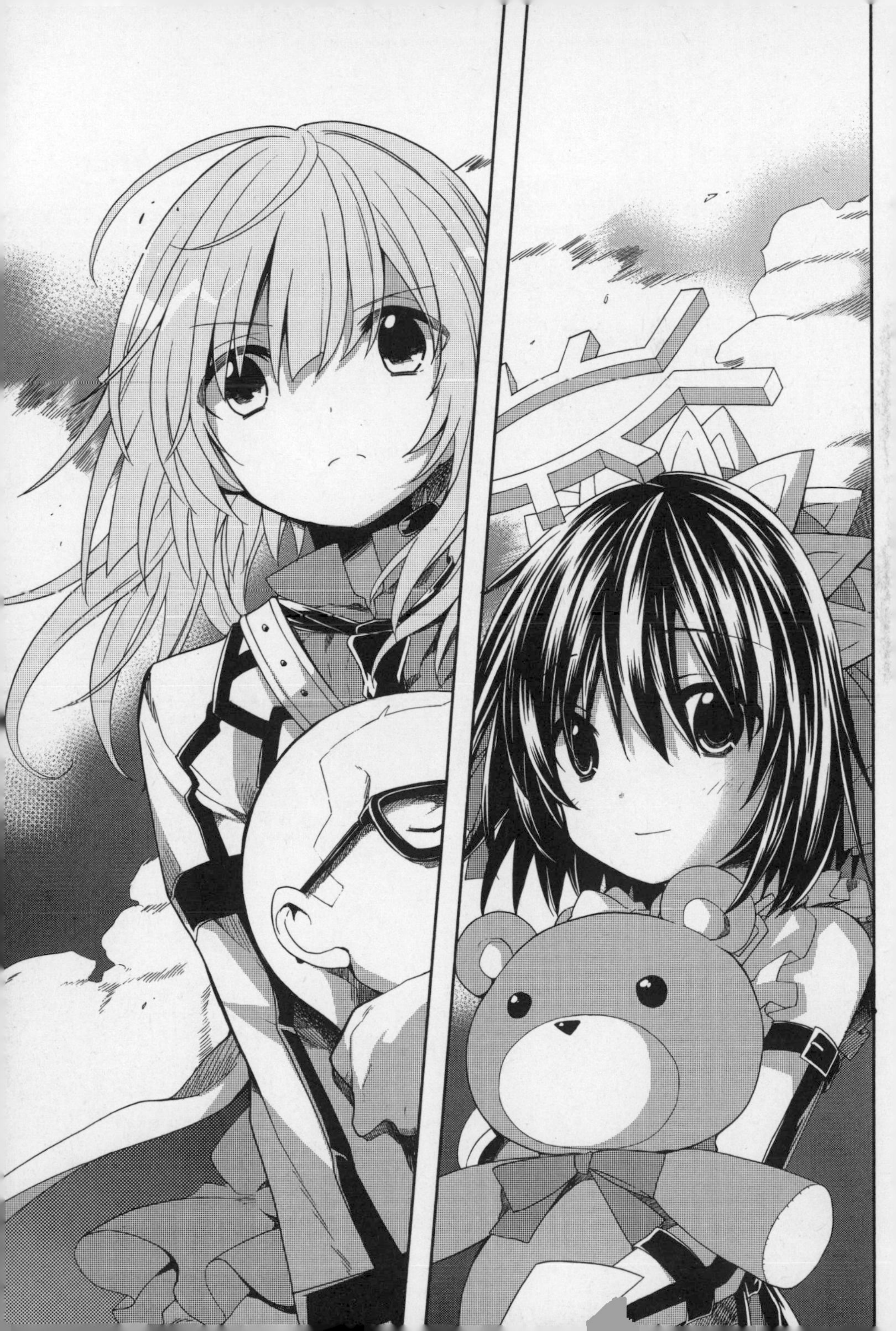

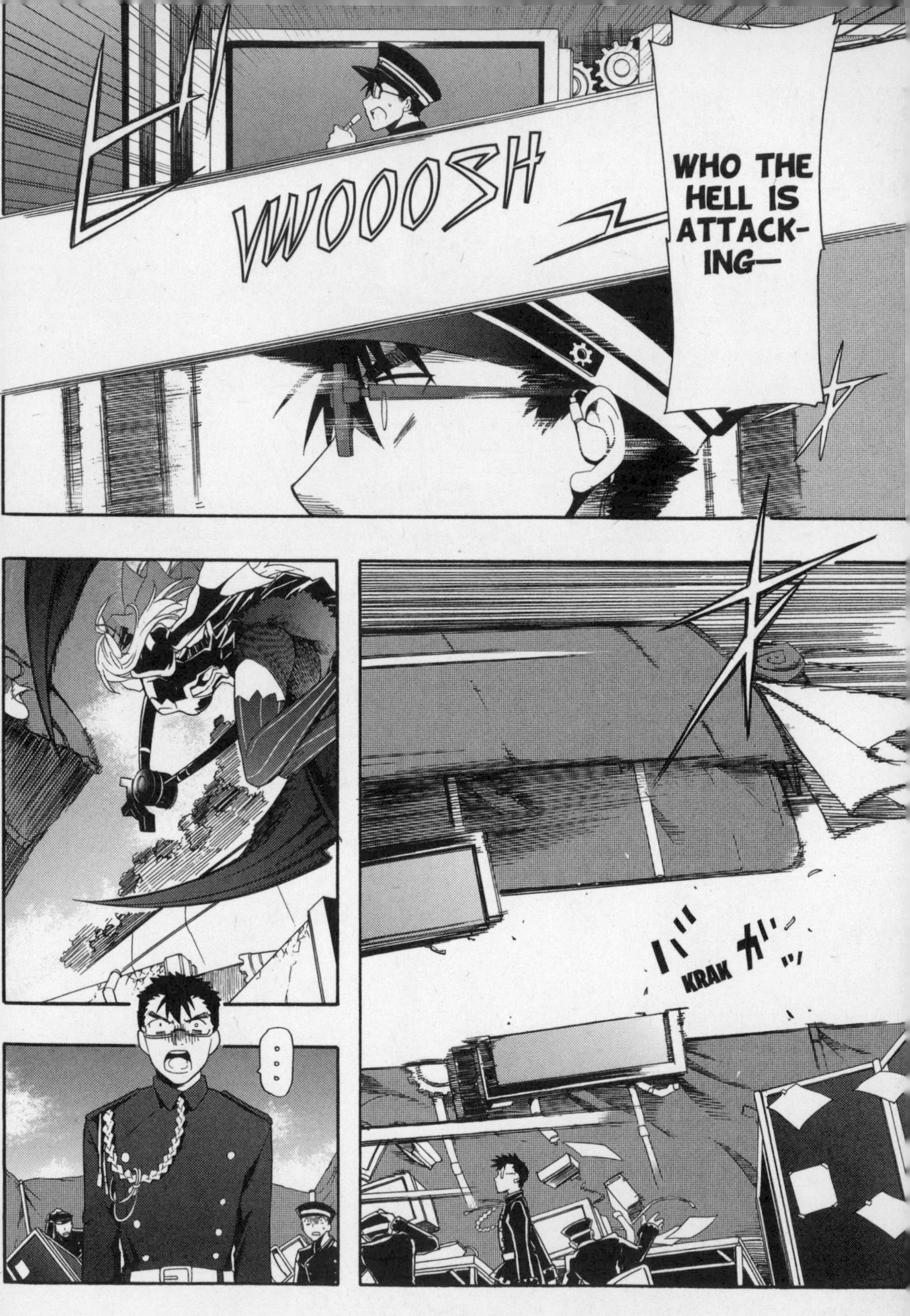
WHO THE HELL IS ATTACK-ING—
VWOOOSH
バガッ
KRAK
...

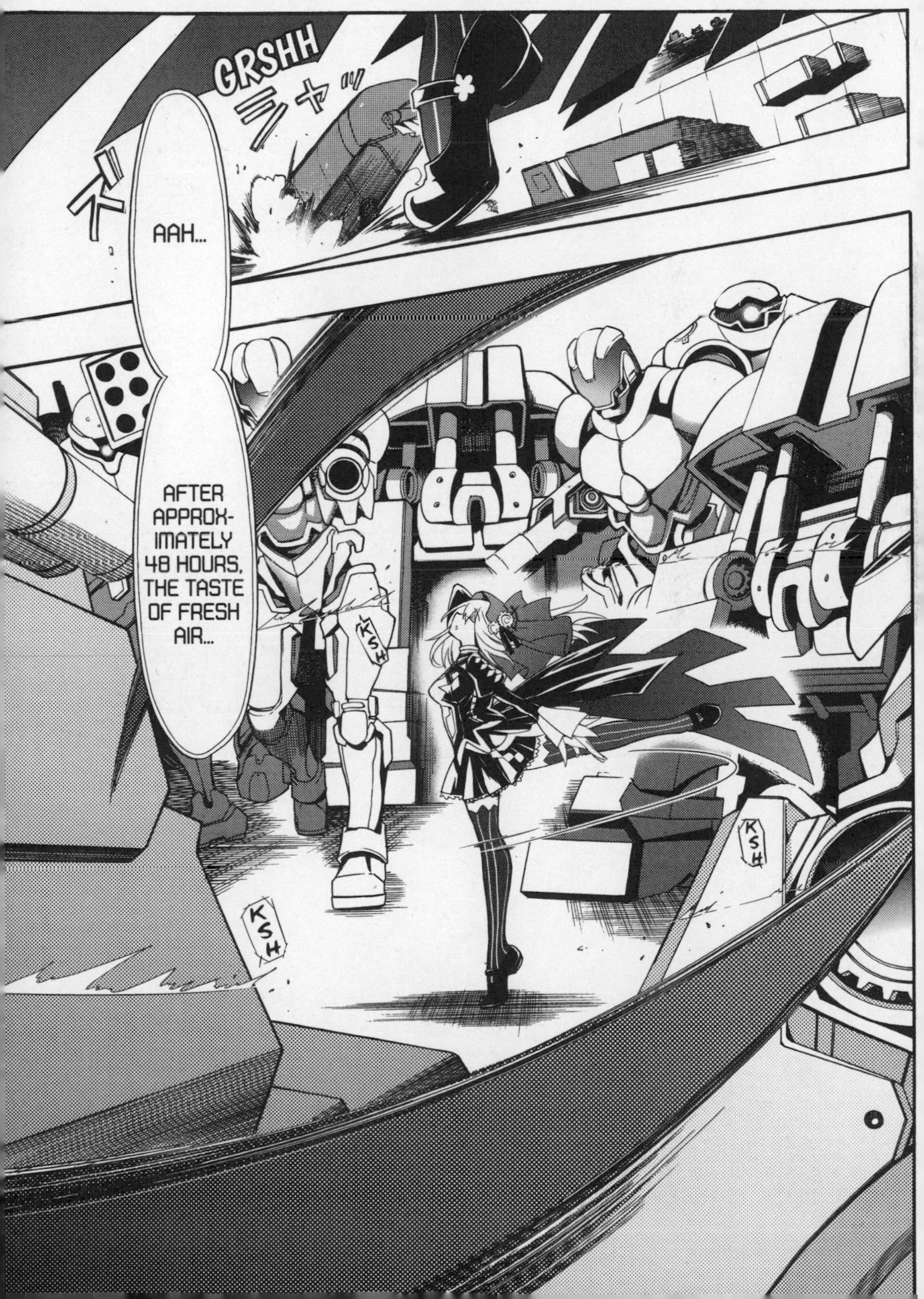
GRSHH
ズ
シャッ
AAH...
AFTER APPROX-IMATELY 48 HOURS, THE TASTE OF FRESH AIR...
KSH
KSH
KSH

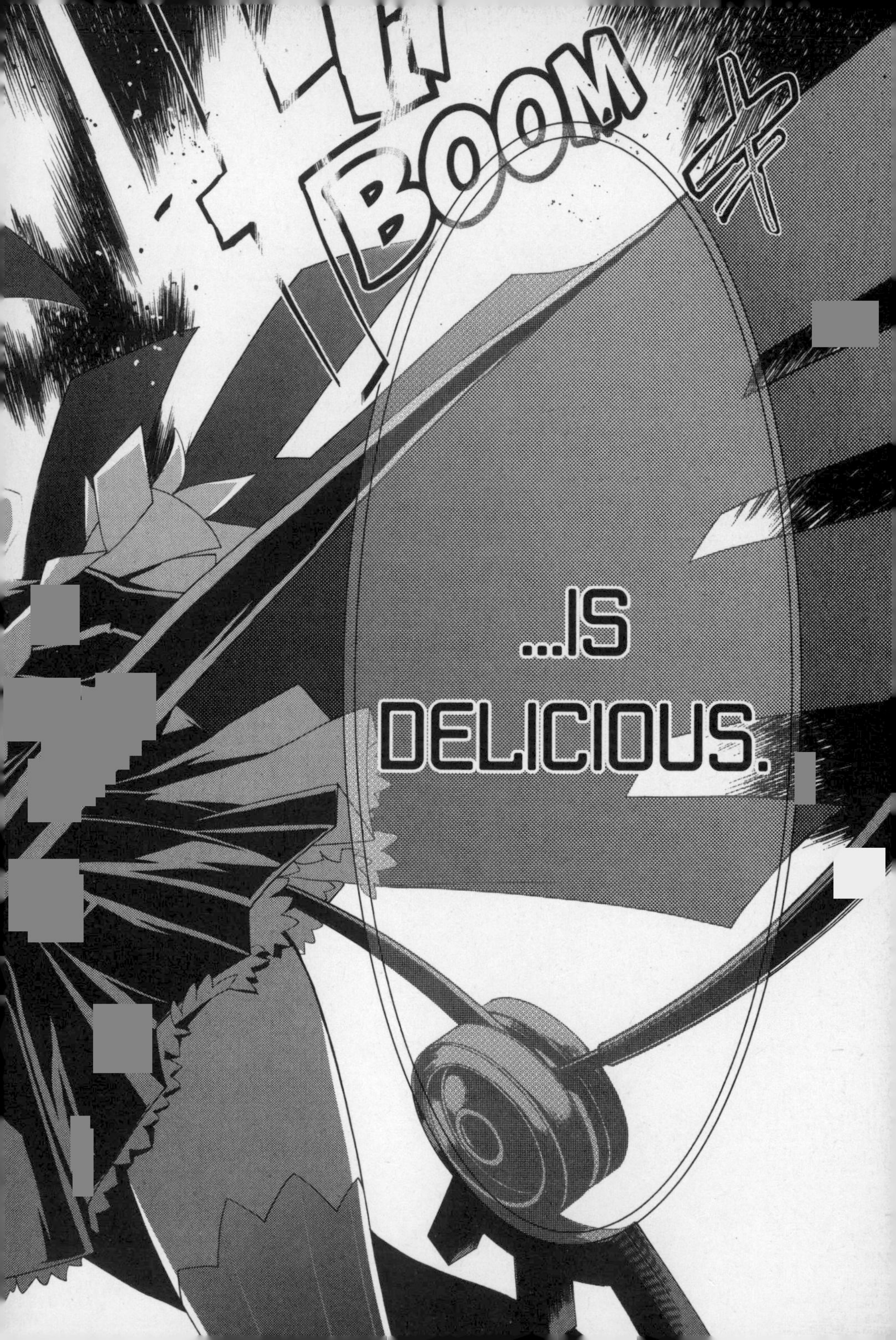
BOOM
...IS DELICIOUS.

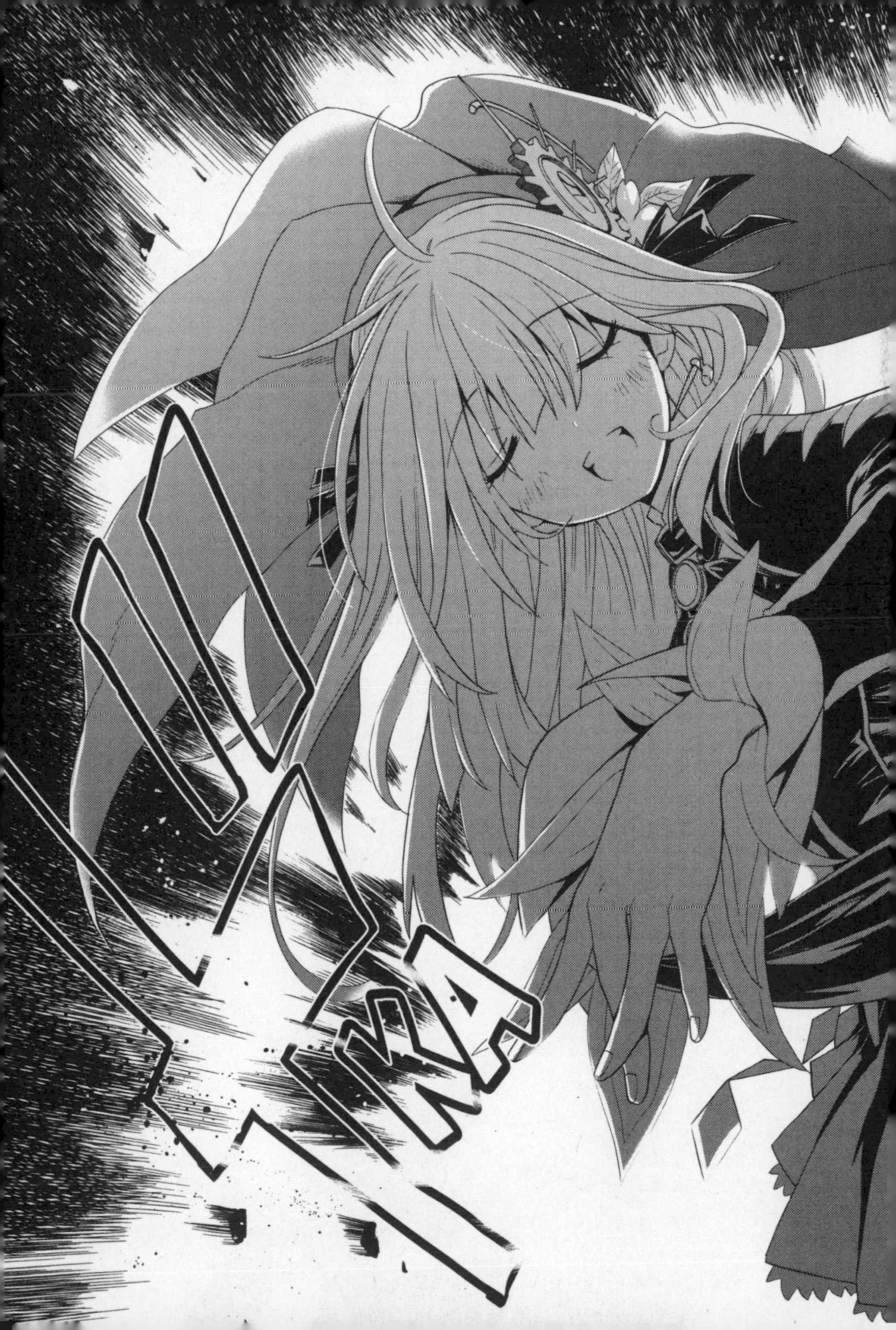

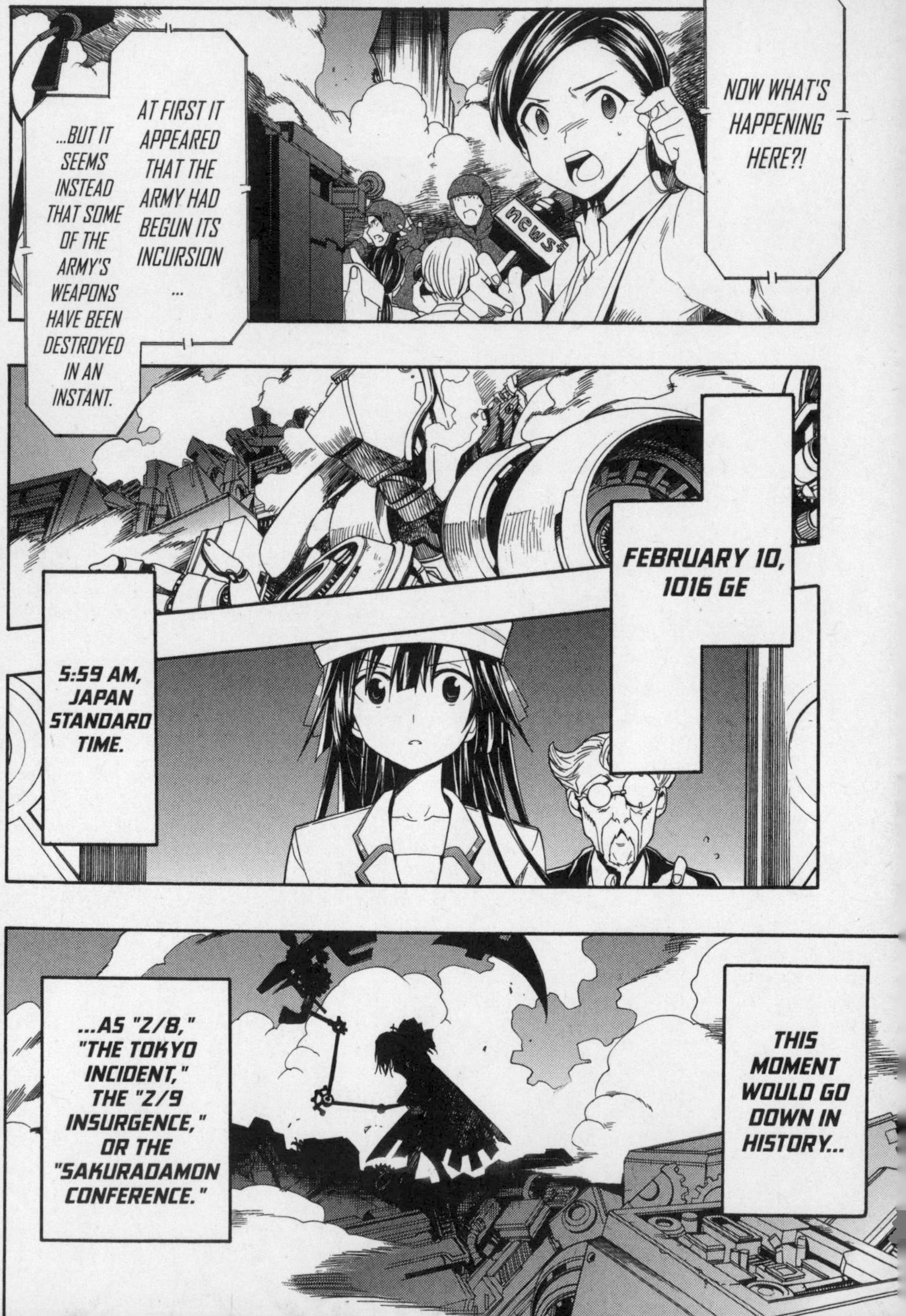
NOW WHAT'S HAPPENING HERE?!
AT FIRST IT APPEARED THAT THE ARMY HAD BEGUN ITS INCURSION ...
...BUT IT SEEMS INSTEAD THAT SOME OF THE ARMY'S WEAPONS HAVE BEEN DESTROYED IN AN INSTANT.
news+
FEBRUARY 10, 1016 GE
5:59 AM, JAPAN STANDARD TIME.
THIS MOMENT WOULD GO DOWN IN HISTORY...
...AS "2/8," "THE TOKYO INCIDENT," THE "2/9 INSURGENCE," OR THE "SAKURADAMON CONFERENCE."

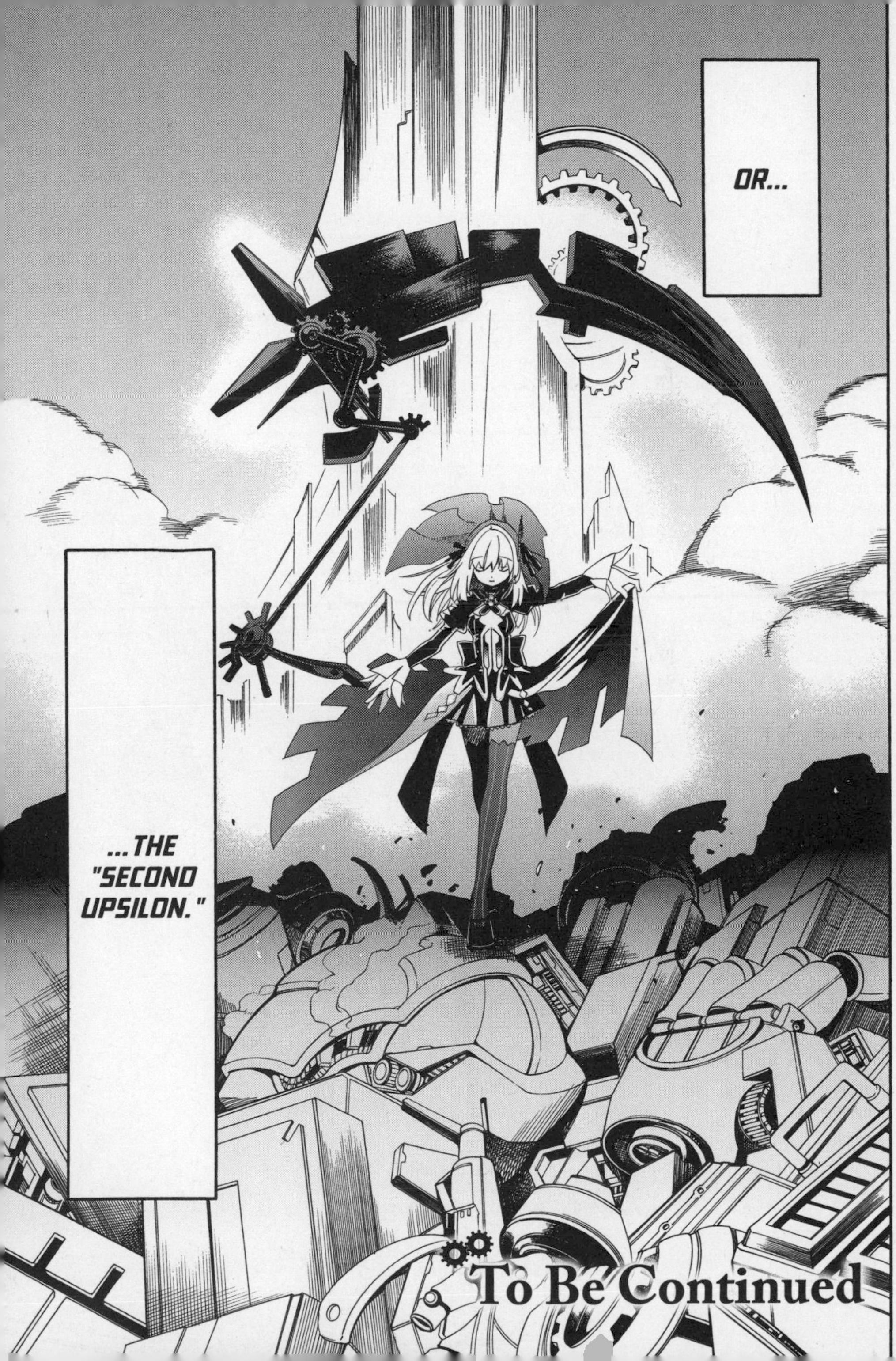
OR...
...THE "SECOND UPSILON."
To Be Continued

K: *(looking like a boxer in the tenth round)* Sorry I look like this, but here I am, Yuu Kamiya!
H: *(looking like a boxer who's been knocked out)* We just finished assigning blame for the delay in the novels with our fists! I'm Tsubaki Himana!
K: So, it's "Say something funny" again—you got something?
H: Huh? You know the only time I went out this year was for the anime meetings. Why ask me?
...

K: Hmm. If hermitage on a mountaintop far from the vulgar world is enough to lead one to an understanding of all things, perhaps we, by secluding ourselves in our homes, may see the light... You seen anything?
H: Oh. Uh. Actually, I think I have, maybe. For instance—

H: I mean, this is more your bailiwick—but you know the event horizon?
K: ...Sorry. I don't really feel like hitting you so hard that your consciousness goes beyond the observable uni—
H: No, I mean, we just skyped the novel editor saying, "We really don't have anything funny," and was like, "Okay, then, shall we skip it?" You could hear the "lol."
K: Yeah. And we contemplated how much we've suffered for this section and entertained idle fantasies of killing this person?
H: So that's my point. My heart was swayed not in the least. *(Smiles like a Buddha.)*
K: ...
H: I only pondered the mysteries of the universe...specifically, what lies beyond that hat our editor always wears—indeed, beyond the event horizon.
K: Curiosity...it is a form of attachment. It may resemble enlightenment and yet differ fundamentally—however! Is it not the case that, 2,500 years ago, Gautama crossed his legs in meditation in search of the truth of this world? Then to behold before us a clear mystery and then to not engage with is not enlightenment, but sloth! A fatass who has lost the will to endeavor is nothing more than a fatass! Or rather, indeed, a farm animal! I feel that my scale is calling out to me as the number of kilograms it displays breaks into three digits. What shall we make of it?!
H: ...Oh *(gets it)*. Frankly I was considering how to run away, but now I see what you mean.

K: Yes, we see that to tear that hat from his head, take a photograph, and release it upon the great sea of electrons [the Internet] cannot be construed as retaliation or mere displacement of frustration! For it is to do just as Gautama taught us—to contribute to human efforts to build a tower of wisdom! And this, therefore, shall justify our actions without the trace of a doubt!
H: How true! "The Truth that ends all pain, the Truth that is forever True"!

> To tear off his hat might be no mean task.
> In the nearly five years we have known him, he has never removed it.
> Even in the office, none have once observed the cosmic mystery within.
> But all the more! A human must endeavor.

H: By the way, what do you think lies within the hat?
K: In descending order of odds: Baldness. Another hat. A supersymmetric universe. Pandora's last hope.
H: I'm going with Schrödinger's cat, the primordial sea, a cockpit—or if you want to bet on the dark horse, a zipper.
K: That's dark. *(Gulp.)*
H: It's dark. *(Gulp.)*

K: Uh, so! Now that we've reinvigorated our resolve! By the time this goes on sale, we'll be hard at work on the new novel, and the anime will be in production! We're really hoping you're looking forward to it!
H: So if we make it back alive, let's meet again!
—

K: Oh, and, Kuro! Nice job on female Vermouth!
H: We've got away from that, but now I'm racking my brain trying to figure out how we can bring her back!

Yuu
Kamiya
&
Tsubaki
Himana

1

Afterword

202

AFTERWORD

SINCE I FIGURED THE MANGA READERS OUGHT TO ENJOY THE DRAWINGS AS MUCH AS POSSIBLE, I FIXED UP VERMOUTH A LITTLE EARLY.
THERE'S VERMOUTH WORKING FOR THE CLUB LIKE IT'S NOTHING. → WHAT SPRIT. AND NEXT VOLUME YOU'LL GET TO SEE MORE OF HER (?) SPIRIT, SO I HOPE YOU'LL PICK IT UP. WITH THAT, SEE YOU IN VOLUME 7.

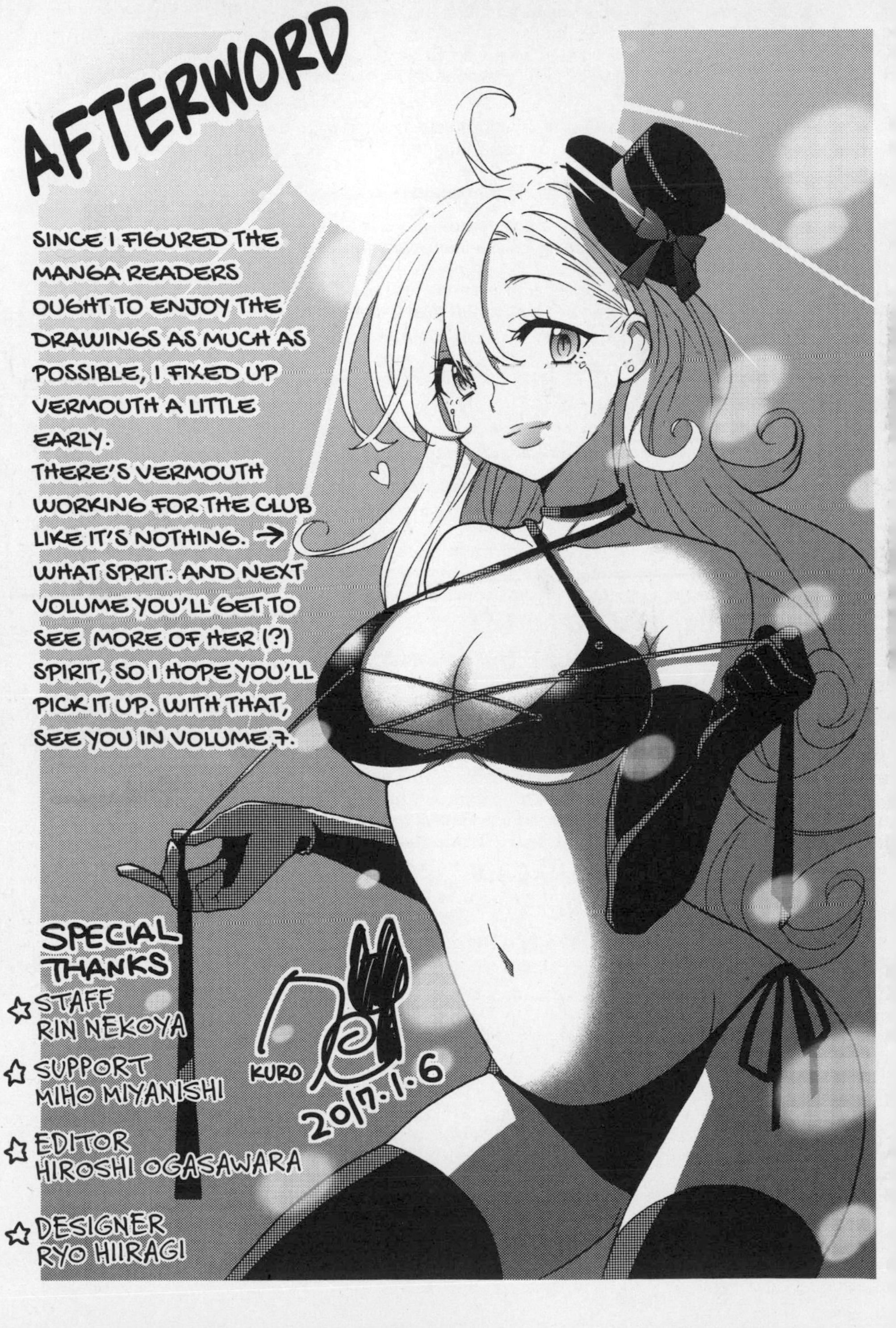

SPECIAL THANKS

☆ STAFF
RIN NEKOYA

☆ SUPPORT
MIHO MIYANISHI

☆ EDITOR
HIROSHI OGASAWARA

☆ DESIGNER
RYO HIIRAGI

KURO
2017.1.6

Translation Notes

Your Excellency, page 6
A number of countries, including Japan, expect government ministers to be addressed as "Your Excellency."

Someone's got to take responsibility, page 11
In Japan, it's conventional for officials to resign after something goes drastically wrong.

Ama no Mihashira, page 131
Ama no Mihashira ("the Pillar of Heaven") is a pillar built by the early gods Izanagi and Izanami on the mythical first island of Japan, Onogoro. They circled the pillar on opposite sides, met, and became one, whereupon they bore the various islands of Japan.

"The truth that ends all pain," page 202
A famous quote from the Heart Sutra. Dwight Goddard's 1932 translation is used here for the English version.

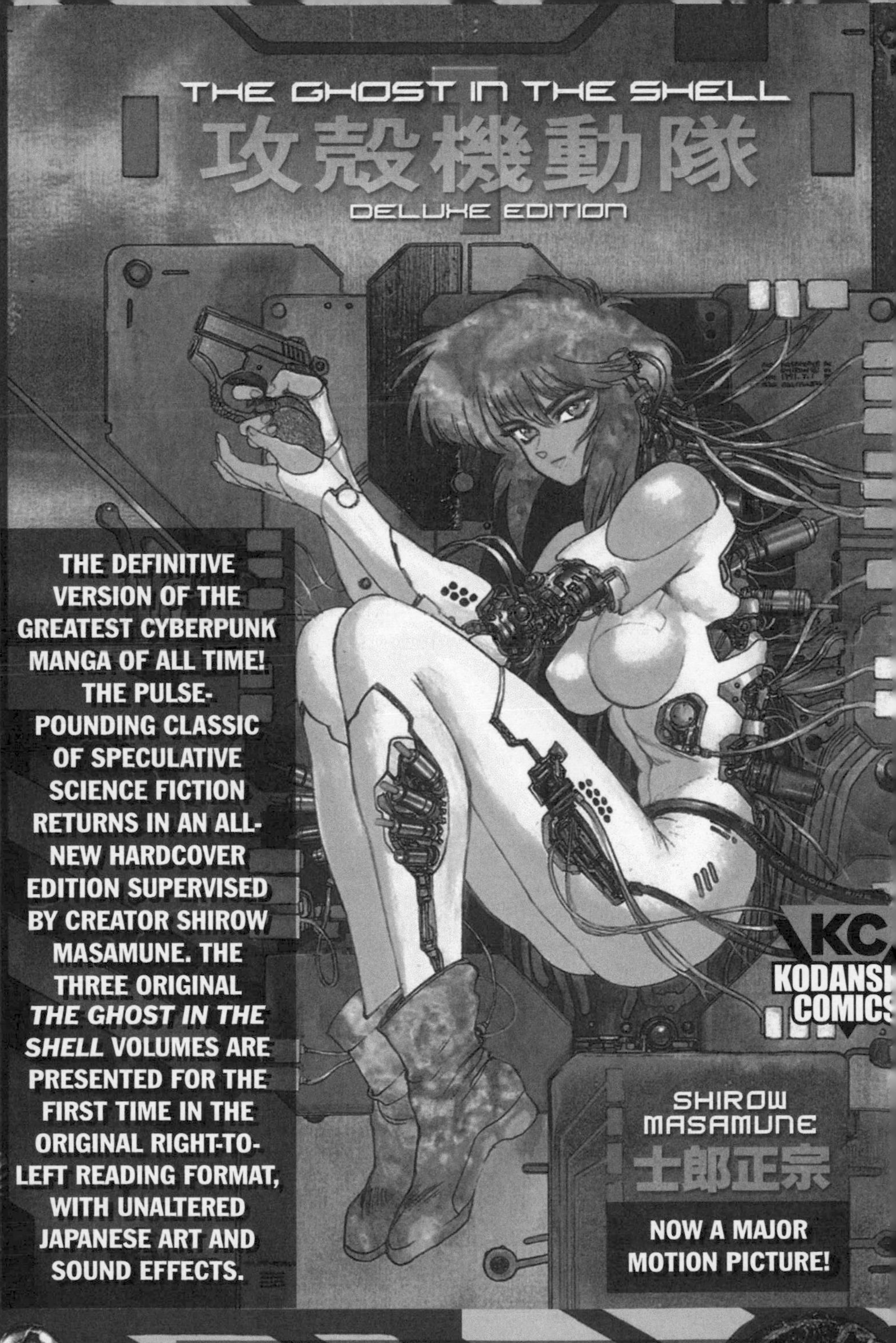
THE GHOST IN THE SHELL
攻殻機動隊
DELUXE EDITION
THE DEFINITIVE VERSION OF THE GREATEST CYBERPUNK MANGA OF ALL TIME! THE PULSE-POUNDING CLASSIC OF SPECULATIVE SCIENCE FICTION RETURNS IN AN ALL-NEW HARDCOVER EDITION SUPERVISED BY CREATOR SHIROW MASAMUNE. THE THREE ORIGINAL *THE GHOST IN THE SHELL* VOLUMES ARE PRESENTED FOR THE FIRST TIME IN THE ORIGINAL RIGHT-TO-LEFT READING FORMAT, WITH UNALTERED JAPANESE ART AND SOUND EFFECTS.
KC
KODANSHA COMICS
SHIROW MASAMUNE
士郎正宗
NOW A MAJOR MOTION PICTURE!

OTOMO
大友克洋

A GLOBAL TRIBUTE TO THE MIND BEHIND AKIRA

A celebration of manga legend Katsuhiro Otomo from more than 80
world-renowned fine artists and comics legends
With contributions from:
- Stan Sakai
- Tomer and Asaf Hanuka
- Sara Pichelli
- Range Murata
- Aleksi Briclot
And more!
168 pages of stunning, full-color art

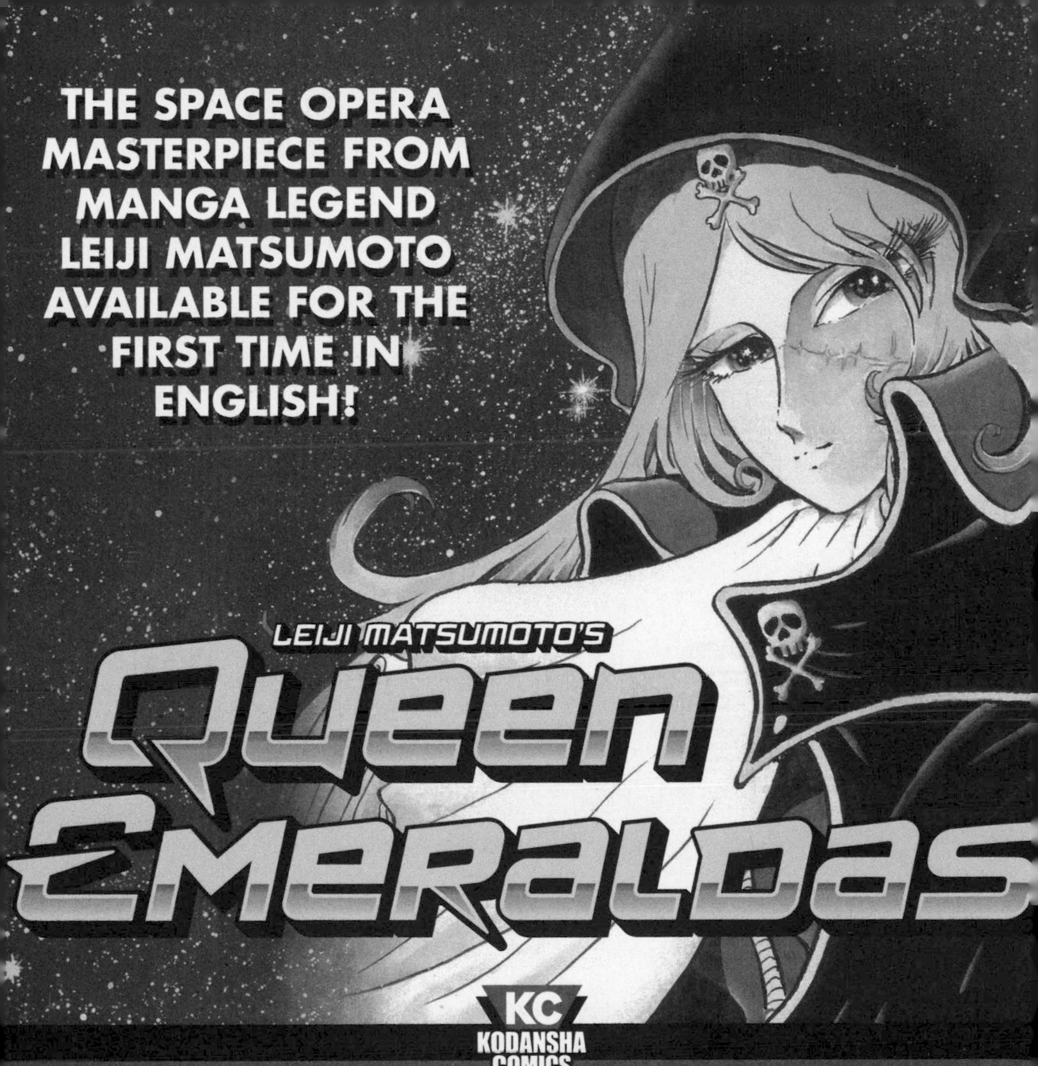
THE SPACE OPERA MASTERPIECE FROM MANGA LEGEND LEIJI MATSUMOTO AVAILABLE FOR THE FIRST TIME IN ENGLISH!
LEIJI MATSUMOTO'S
Queen Emeraldas
KC
KODANSHA COMICS

"If you like space cowboys and pirates or simply want to get lost in a strange dreamlike story, Kodansha's beautiful hardcover is worth checking out."
- *Anime News Network*

"It's not so much a manga as it is a song. But you'll want to listen to it again and again."
- *A Case for Suitable Treatment*

A Kodansha Comics Trade Paperback Original
Clockwork Planet volume 6 copyright © 2017 Yuu Kamiya/Tsubaki Himana/Sino/Kuro
English translation copyright © 2017 Yuu Kamiya/Tsubaki Himana/Sino/Kuro
All rights reserved.

Published in the United States by Kodansha Comics, an imprint of Kodansha USA Publishing, LLC, New York.

Publication rights for this English edition arranged through Kodansha Ltd, Tokyo.

First published in Japan in 2017 by Kodansha Ltd., Tokyo

ISBN 978-1-63236-467-8

Printed in the United States of America.

www.kodanshacomics.com

9 8 7 6 5 4 3 2 1
Translation: Daniel Komen
Lettering: David Yoo
Editing: Haruko Hashimoto
Kodansha Comics edition cover design by Phil Balsman